Last Words

Last Words

A Dictionary of Deathbed Quotations

by
C. BERNARD RUFFIN

McFarland & Company, Inc., Publishers
Jefferson, North Carolina, and London

British Library Cataloguing-in-Publication data are available

Library of Congress Cataloguing-in-Publication Data

Ruffin, C. Bernard, 1947–
   Last words : a dictionary of deathbed quotations / by C.
Bernard Ruffin.
     p.   cm.
   Includes index.
   ISBN 0-7864-0043-9 (lib. bdg. : 50# alk. paper) ∞
   1. Quotations — Dictionaries.   2. Death — Quotations,
maxims, etc. — Dictionaries. I. Title.
PN6081.R84   1995
082 — dc20   95-3196
                                                CIP

Manufactured in the United States of America

McFarland & Company, Inc., Publishers
  Box 611, Jefferson, North Carolina 28640

To the students, faculty, and administration
of South Lakes High School, Reston, Virginia,
especially the Class of 1995

Table of Contents

Introduction

What is so important about "last words"? Why are the words of the dying of any special significance? While many would dismiss an interest in deathbed utterances as morbid and perverse, the more than two dozen collections of "last words" in the Library of Congress (including volumes in French, Spanish, German, Hebrew, Swedish, Arabic, and Japanese) attest to the intense interest in the subject. In fact, from earliest antiquity the dying expressions of celebrated men and women have commanded attention, as in the Bible, which records not only the last words of Jesus, but of Moses, Joshua, Elijah, David, Stephen, and others. Even a casual study of the literature of Western civilization makes it clear that, throughout the centuries, deathbed words have provoked considerable fascination.

The reasons for this are many. Shakespeare (for whom, incidentally, no last words are recorded) eloquently expresses one reason, through the dying words of John of Gaunt in *Richard II*, Act II, Scene I, who declares:

> O! but they say the tongues of dying men
> Enforce attention like deep harmony:
> When words are scarce, they are seldom spent in vain,
> For they breathe truth that breathe their words in pain.
> He that no more must say is listened more
> Than they whom youth and ease have taught to glose;
> More are men's ends marked than their lives before;
> The setting sun and music at the close
> As the last taste of sweets, is sweetest last,
> Writ in remembrance more than things long past.

In other words, final remarks are remembered because they are *the last*. When people realize that a familiar and admired voice will soon be silenced forever, they pay attention and cherish the last words as "the taste of sweets."

It has sometimes been held that a dying person somehow recapitulates, in a few phrases, the meaning of his entire life. Lance Morrow, in an essay in *Time* (January 16, 1984), wrote, "There was a time when the deathbed was a kind of proscenium, from which the personage could issue one last dramatic utterance, full of the compacted significance of his life."

It was common, from antiquity until well into the nineteenth century,

1

for dying men and women to assemble their family and friends and deliver a last counsel or exhortation, which had obviously been carefully prepared. We see this, for example, in the Biblical patriarchs Jacob and Joseph, in Moses and Joshua, in many mediæval and Renaissance kings and queens, and even former U.S. president Andrew Jackson and first lady Sarah Childress Polk. Such deathbed scenes were not confined to the great and powerful. Abraham Lincoln's mother, an obscure pioneer farm-wife, likewise summoned her family to her bedside for some last pious instructions. In cases of this sort, we are often able to perceive "the compacted significance" of the life of the person who is dying.

Davis W. Clark, a Victorian minister who compiled *Deathbed Scenes* in 1851, gave another reason for interest in last words, namely, that "departing spirits, especially those of good men, receive supernatural manifestations" at the time of death. There are recorded instances in which the dying seem to see into the world beyond. Often this concerns men and women of deep spirituality, such as Clare of Assisi, Anthony of Padua, John Donne, William Blake, Dwight Lyman Moody, and Charles Haddon Spurgeon. Persons not particularly noted for their piety, however, such as the agnostic Thomas Alva Edison (at least if one chooses to interpret his last words in a certain way) and the acerbic journalist Maury Paul, seem to have had intimations of the other world. But perhaps the experience of gunfighter Morgan Earp is more the norm. Dying of gunshot wounds, he responded to a promise made earlier in life to report any visions of the next world when he was on the point of death. He told his brother Wyatt: "I can't see a damned thing."

Another reason why the last words, at least of famous people, are of interest is that, even if they are spontaneous and not in the form of a formal farewell, they tell something about the character of the person who is passing from the world. How a man or woman faces the last hours on earth reveals a great deal about the character of the individual. Sometimes the recorded expressions are very much in keeping with the popular stereotype of the historical personage. The cold, dispassionate instructions of George Washington are an example of this. Thomas Jefferson was very much in character when he kept asking, the day before he died, "Is this the Fourth [of July]?" So was John Adams the next day when he insisted, "Thomas Jefferson still survives." Cold War Secretary of State John Foster Dulles was also in character when, a few days before he died, he told a friend, "If the United States is willing to go to war over Berlin, there won't be a war over Berlin." On the other hand, the reported dying words of certain individuals present a picture quite at variance with the popular reputation. The mediaeval Asian conqueror Tamerlane was renowned for his cruelty, but his last words to his heirs bid them govern with justice and beneficence. The final pious expressions attributed to baseball star Babe Ruth and blues singer Bessie Smith defy their racy and irreverent public images.

Yet another reason for interest in last words is the fact that many people feel that the experiences of others in the face of death give them an idea of what to expect when the inevitable moment presents itself. Various individuals (such as Charles Lindbergh, the wife of Mohandas Gandhi, U.S. Surgeon General William Crawford Gorgas, and German-American political leader Carl Schurz) commented on the process of dying. Individuals who died bravely or piously have always served as role models or as inspiration.

But what exactly is meant by the term "last words"? In some collections, an attempt has been made to record only the very last thing the subject said. The very last utterances of most people are, however, often trivial, monosyllabic, or incomprehensible. Although in the movies and in television dying people talk right up to the very last instant, this scenario is not common in actual experience (and apparently never was, even in the days when most people died unsedated at home), in which hours, or even days (and in a few instances, months) of unconsciousness or delirium often pass between the last attempt at speech and death itself.

What are reported as "last words" are often the last *recorded* words. In the days when witnesses at deathbeds were asked for the last words of the Great Man or Great Woman, they often recounted the last *interesting* or *meaningful* remarks made by the invalid. Often accounts describing the last hours of some noted individual imply or even flatly state that the speaker did in fact say something after the recorded remarks, but that these words were neither memorable nor interesting. For instance, after former President Andrew Johnson forbade his family to call a doctor after he suffered a stroke, all accounts of his death note that he talked "imperfectly" for the next 24 hours, yet, when family members present at his deathbed were asked by reporters just a few days later to recall some "particulars" of what he said, they were unable. After Einstein spoke to his son for the last time, a nurse heard him murmur something, evidently in German, which she could not understand, prompting one newspaper to lament that the last words of the world's greatest mind had been forever lost, owing to a nurse who did not understand German.

Sometimes last words are interpretations by friends or family members of the efforts to speak of individuals whose tongues were thickened by illness, weakness, medication, or, in the case of British poet Tennyson, by the fact of "having no teeth in." The wife of comedian Oliver Hardy *thought* that the actor, who had been incapacitated by strokes, was *trying* to say, "I love you." Some at the deathbed of newspaperman and political leader Horace Greeley thought him to say, "I know that my Redeemer liveth!" Others thought he asked his daughter to raise his head. Still others thought he was cursing!

There often exists more than one version of the last words of notable persons. Unless there is recording equipment present or a stenographer taking notes in shorthand (as at the deathbeds of mobster Dutch Schultz and movie idol Rudolph Valentino), if there is more than one witness, accounts will, at best, vary slightly. For instance, when President Kennedy was shot in Dallas, one witness heard him cry, "My God, I've been hit!" Another attributed those words to Governor John Connally, who was also hit by the rifle fire. Other witnesses heard nothing at all. There are several versions of how Martin

Luther King worded his request, just before he was shot, to have his favorite hymn played at the dinner he was planning to attend. Such discrepancy is not limited to victims of assassination. Some understood former president John Quincy Adams to say, "This is the last of earth. I am content." Others heard, "This is the end of earth, but I am composed."

The existence of completely different versions of the last words of a given individual might be attributed to the presence of different witnesses, who visited the invalid at different times. For instance, a hypothetical Great Man may have been visited, shortly before his death, by his pastor, who heard him murmur, "Our Father..."; by his daughter, who heard the words, "Farewell, dear child"; and by his doctor, whom he begged, "Let me go." It is conceivable that our Great Man said all three things, at different times, to different people. It is unlikely, given the existence of three sets of recollections, that one could determine the actual sequence.

It is difficult to check the authenticity of last words. The ones of which the researcher can be most confident are those based on letters and diaries of witnesses. The last words of George Washington, for instance, were written down within days of his passing by his secretary, Tobias Lear. Even here, the two accounts he compiled at roughly the same time recall the same substance of the General's dying words with a slightly different wording. Some last words were reported by newspapers. Late nineteenth and early twentieth century papers frequently printed extensive accounts of the last hours of celebrities and sometimes rendered the last words in bold type. Sometimes one wonders if some biographers invent last words for their subjects, especially when earlier accounts mention nothing. Least reliable of all, of course, are accounts in modern-day supermarket tabloids, which routinely report the details of the "tragic last days" of various celebrities. The compiler found three different tabloids reporting three different versions of the last words of entertainer Sammy Davis, Jr., and included the most picturesque. Quotations which have their origins in tabloids are duly noted.

Thomas Bedell, writing in *Reader's Digest*, noted, "The living may supplant truth, eager to maintain the reputation that might be tarnished if the *real* last words got out." Some years ago the compiler was told an interesting story. A prominent politician had died in a small Maine town and the local newspaper announced that his last words were: "I know that my Redeemer liveth!" A professor from a nearby college approached the physician who had attended the deceased and asked whether the acerbic old man had *really* said, "I know that my Redeemer liveth!" The crusty doctor snorted, "Hell, no! He actually said, 'Bring me a bedpan, quick!' but, well . . . you couldn't put *that* in the paper."

Three eyewitness accounts of the death of Thomas Jefferson recount that, the night before he died, he asked repeatedly, "Is this the Fourth?" (or, "This is the Fourth" or "Is it the Fourth?"). However, a grandson recalled that *later* the statesman called the servants, "perfectly conscious of his wants." Why did the grandson fail to report exactly what Jefferson said? What exactly *did* the Great Man say to the servants? What, specifically, were his "wants"? Inasmuch as the cause of Jefferson's death was officially listed as "diarrhea," it is quite possible that his "wants" were of an unprintably biological nature.

For many years it was reported that King George V of Great Britain finished his days praying the Our Father and piously clutching the hand of the Archbishop of Canterbury. Years later, when the notes of his physician became public, they revealed not only that the King had been euthanized, but that he had died cursing.

Although we can be reasonably certain of the drift of most last words, we can never be exactly sure of the precise wording. Because the substance is all that of which we can be reasonably certain, several quotations here are reconstructed from indirect quotations. In many instances, this is what the eyewitnesses seem to have done, and this would explain the slight variation in different eyewitness accounts of well-attested quotations, as we have mentioned before.

There are certain categories of people who are better represented than others. The dying words, however innocuous, of European monarchs and American presidents were once routinely recorded. There is a disproportionately large number of last words of Christian clergy. Although the recording of last words has been important in many cultures, Christians, because of their belief in the Resurrection perhaps, seem to have been, at least in the past, particularly interested in the phenomenon. Some of the most enthusiastic collectors of last words in the eighteenth and nineteenth centuries were Christian clergymen (of all persuasions). The dying words of Roman Catholic saints are almost always noted in the documents relative to their process for beatification. There simply does not exist as extensive a reservoir—at least in English—of the last words of religious leaders of other faiths. While the dying words of *hundreds* of priests, ministers, and other Christian religious appear in this collection, there appear the dying utterances of only four rabbis! The imbalance reflects the availability of material.

Again, for some reason, the last words of dozens of former baseball players have been recorded, as opposed to only a handful of representatives from other sports. Writers, artists, and musicians tend to be well represented.

The last words in this collection cover a wide range of emotions and reactions. Some, like Martha Washington, Andrew Jackson, Sarah Polk, Sir Walter Scott, Edmund Burke, and Ernestine Schumann-Heink, died with blessings on their lips. Others, like George V, actor Laurence Olivier, playwright Eugene O'Neill, and entertainers Ethel Merman and W.C. Fields, died cursing. Singer John McCormack, authors A.E. Housman and James Whitcomb Riley, and (appropriately) comedians Stan Laurel and Chico Marx, joked on their deathbeds. Others, such as Francis Marion, the Revolutionary general, Noah Webster, the lexicographer, and former president Grover Cleveland, seemed to want to justify their lives. Poet Goethe, storyteller O. Henry, and actor Rudolph Valentino expressed a desire for light. Theodore Roosevelt and Italian physician and theologian Agostino Gemelli requested their attendants to put the lights out. Scientists Einstein and Carver and musicians Caruso and Weber spoke of a desire for sleep. Monarchs Henry VII of England and Philip III of Spain bargained with God. Many, such as Jane Austen, the English writer, Moshe Dayan, the Israeli general, Dorothea Dix, the reformer, and statesmen Benjamin Franklin, George Washington, and William Henry Harrison, expressed a desire to die or ordered physicians to allow them to go in peace. Many pious people, including Columbus, Catherine of Aragon, Pope John XXIII, St. John of the Cross, and actor Henry Irving died with some version on their lips of the final prayer of Christ ("Into Thy hands, O Lord, I commend my spirit").

Former vice president John Nance Garner, baseball manager John Mc-Graw, football coach Vince Lombardi, philosopher Jean-Paul Sartre, author Harriet Beecher Stowe, and actors John Wayne and Oliver Hardy died pronouncing (or trying to pronounce) the words, "I love you."

An interesting phenomenon is the number of people who died singing. Many of these were professional singers, such as Jean De Reszke, Nellie Melba, Jenny Lind, Ira Sankey, and Philip Phillips. But a number of non-musicians, such as clergyman Henry Melchior Muhlenberg, military leader J.E.B. Stuart, abolitionist Harriet Tubman, and religious lecturer Corrie ten Boom, also ended their lives in song.

It is interesting to note the instances of very different people who said almost the same thing. For instance, British prime minister Winston Churchill said, "I am bored of it all," and American author James Baldwin declared, "I'm bored." Assassinated civil rights leader Medgar Evers directed, "Lift me up! Turn me loose!" while assassinated Russian premier Peter Stolypin cried, "Lift me! Light up!" (On the other hand, assassinated U.S. Senator Robert Kennedy said, "Do not lift me.") Abolitionist Frederick Douglass, dying suddenly of a stroke in 1895, asked his wife, "What's that?"; author Robert Louis Stevenson, also dying suddenly of a stroke in 1894, asked his wife, "What's that? Do I look strange?" King Humbert I of Italy, Henry IV of France, and Archduke Franz Ferdinand of Austria-Hungary, all victims of assassins and all attacked in cars or carriages, all insisted, "It is nothing." Mahatma Gandhi and Mormon leader Joseph Smith, also assassinated, both cried, "Oh, God!" American colonial religious leader Cotton Mather confided, "My will is now entirely resigned to the will of God," while twentieth century Pope Pius X affirmed, "I give myself entirely to God's holy will." The most interesting parallel concerns the wife of president-elect Andrew Jackson and twentieth century U.S. senator Alban Barkley. The latter, in the midst of a speech, remarked, "I would rather be a servant in the House of the Lord than sit in the seat of the mighty," and dropped dead. Rachel Jackson, speaking to a friend of her reluctance to live in the White House, said, "I'd rather be a doorkeeper in the House of God than live in that palace!" Shortly afterwards, she had a heart attack and died.

It is interesting that *recorded* expressions of doubt or unbelief, as well as of fear and mental anguish, are rare and outnumbered more than tenfold by expressions of acceptance, serenity, peace, and joy. Whether this is due to a tendency for family, friends, and biographers to omit information that might prove disturbing or depressing is not clear. While there are on record the last words of many Christian monarchs, the dying words of very few communist leaders have been recorded. Does a belief in the Resurrection make the dying more communicative? Do happy (or at least accepting) people tend to talk more?

The cumulative effect of reading through the dying words of the individuals here represented is not one of depression or dismay, but of hope and serenity. Dr. Elisabeth Kübler-Ross, in her famous book *On Death and Dying*, describes several phases through which the dying typically react to their predicament. The last of these stages is that of acceptance. That this is generally true is borne out by the overwhelming majority of the voices that speak from the threshold of eternity.

The Dictionary

1 ABD AR-RAHMAN III, Caliph of Cordoba (891–961) The first and greatest ruler of the Moslem Umayyad Dynasty in Spain declared on his deathbed: "O man, place not thy confidence in this present world!"

2 ABELARD, Pierre (1079–1142) The French scholastic theologian, perhaps best remembered for his tragic romance with Heloise, said: "I don't know. I don't know."

3 ABIMELECH (12th century B.C.) The brutal king of the Israelite state of Shechem, trying to quell a revolt in the town of Thebez, advanced close enough to one of the towers in the wall for a woman who had taken refuge there to heave a millstone onto his head. His skull crushed, Abimelech ordered his armor-bearer: "Draw your sword and kill me, so that they can't say, 'A woman killed him.'"

4 ADAMS, Abigail Smith (1744–1818) The wife of America's second president and the first mistress of the White House was a prolific writer of letters, in some of which she argued for the rights of women. Dying of a fever at her home in Quincy, Massachusetts, she insisted: "If I cannot be useful, I do not wish to live."

5 ADAMS, Henry (1838–1918) The great-grandson of Abigail and John Adams was a prominent historian, who died in his sleep, after bidding his housekeeper: "Goodnight, my dear."

6 ADAMS, John (1735–1826) America's second president died on the fiftieth anniversary of the signing of the Declaration of Independence, a document he helped to prepare. Emerging from a coma around noon, he spoke of one of the two remaining signers (who, unbeknownst to him, was also close to death and would actually expire a few hours before Adams): "Thomas Jefferson still survives." Six hours later, the statesman died, in the words of a grandson, "as calmly as an infant sleeps."

7 ADAMS, John Quincy (1767–1848) Son of John Adams and sixth president of the United States, he was serving as a congressman from Massachusetts when he suffered a stroke on the floor of the House. Carried into the Speaker's office, he whispered: "Thank the officers of the House." A few minutes later he said: "This is the last of earth. I am content." He lost the power of speech and died two days later.

8 ADDAMS, Jane (1860–1935) The American settlement founder, social reformer, and peace worker remarked to her doctor, after cancer surgery: "When I was a child, I had an old doctor friend who told me that the hardest thing in the world to kill was an old woman. He seems to have been right." Later, when asked if she wanted water, she spoke for the last time: "Always. Always water for me."

9 ADDISON, Joseph (1672–1719) The English journalist, essayist, and poet told his valet: "My boy, see in what peace a Christian can die."

10 ADENAUER, Konrad (1876–1967) The founder of the Christian Democrat Party in West Germany and the first chancellor of that nation, he exhorted his family: "Stick together. See as much as possible of one another."

11 AGASSIZ, Louis (1807–1873) The Swiss-born zoologist, who taught at Harvard for many years, declared in his native French: "All is finished. The game is finished."

12 AGATHA (d. 249) A wealthy Sicilian Christian girl who had taken a private vow of celibacy, Agatha was arrested and imprisoned so that she might have time to consider renouncing her faith. When the governor asked her if she had changed her mind, she replied: "The service of Jesus Christ is the highest nobility and the truest freedom!" The governor thereupon ordered her broken on the rack. When again invited to reject Christ, she shook her head. After her breasts were ripped off with hot combs, she fainted and was thrown, unconscious, back into her prison cell, where she died four days later.

13 AGNES (c.292–304) A wealthy Roman girl betrothed by her pagan family to a prosperous unbeliever, she refused to marry him and, in doing so, revealed that she was a Christian, which was a capital offense at the time. Given a chance to save her life by renouncing her faith, Agnes refused, declaring: "Destroy the body that draws the admiration of those eyes from which I shrink!"

14 AGRIPPINA the Younger (16–60) Sister of the sinister Roman emperor Caligula, she married her uncle Claudius. A few years later she poisoned him and made her teen-aged son (by a previous marriage) emperor. Six years later she was assassinated on orders of her son Nero. Pointing to her abdomen, she shouted at the soldiers dispatched to end her life: "Strike here, for this bore Nero!"

15 AGUSTÍN I, Emperor of Mexico (1783–1824) Born Agustín Iturbide, the military leader made himself emperor and ruled for just a year before he was overthrown. Afterwards he returned to Mexico, only to be arrested and executed as a traitor. He cried: "I am no traitor! Such a stain will never attach to my children or to their descendants!"

16 AHAB, King of Israel (d. 853 B.C.) The Hebrew king who made himself notorious by his lapse into paganism was wounded in battle, fighting the Syrians. He ordered his charioteer to withdraw: "Turn me about and carry me out of the battle, for I am wounded."

17 ALBAN (d. 304) A pagan Briton who hid persecuted Christians in his home at the time when people of that faith were being exterminated by the Roman emperor Diocletian, Alban was so impressed by his guests that he himself accepted baptism. Arrested, he was ordered to sacrifice to the Roman gods, and refused, insisting: "These sacrifices, which are offered to devils, are of no avail. Hell is the reward of those who offer them." He was taken out and beheaded by the Roman authorities.

18 ALBERT I, King of Belgians (1875–1934) The popular king, who led his country's army during World War I and guided its postwar recovery, was out for a drive. He told his chauffeur to stop and wait for him while he scaled a cliff: "If I feel in good form, I shall take the difficult way up. If I do not, I shall take the easy one. I shall join you in one hour." His broken corpse was discovered the next morning after several hours' search.

19 ALBERT, Prince Consort of Victoria of Great Britain (1819–1861) The German-born prince who, during his marriage to Britain's queen, was a proponent of strict morality and family values, asked his daughter Alice if her sister Vicky, the Crown Princess of Prussia, had been informed of his worsening illness. When Alice said, "Yes, I told her that you were very ill," Albert answered: "You did wrong. You should have told her that I am dying." Just before he lost consciousness, he pressed his wife's hand and said, in German: "Good little wife!"

20 ALBERT VICTOR, Duke of Clarence and Avondale (1864–1892) The dissipated grandson of Queen Victoria, third in line to the British throne at the time of his sudden death from pneumonia, called out "in a clear, sweet voice," speaking of his younger brother George, who was alive and well and would eventually become king: "Something too awful has happened — my darling brother George is dead." Several hours later, he repeated, over and over: "Who is that?" He repeated the question "every more slowly and faintly" until he became unconscious and died.

21 ALBERTONI, Luisa (1473–1533) The pious Roman widow spent much of her time in prayer and in service to the sick. She was wont to bake big batches of bread with gold and silver coins in them, praying that the largest coins would reach the people with the greatest need when she distributed the food. On her deathbed, the philanthropist prayed the final prayer of Christ: "Father, into Thy hands I commend my spirit."

22 ALCOTT, Amos Bronson (1799–1888) The transcendentalist philosopher said to his daughter, novelist Louisa Mae (who survived

him by only two days): "I am going up. Come with me."

23 ALCOTT, Louisa Mae (1831–1888) The novelist, author of *Little Women*, in poor health for many years, became worse after visiting her dying father and inquired: "Is it not meningitis?" The doctors were not certain, but she died in a few days.

24 ALDRICH, Thomas Bailey (1836–1907) The poet and short-story writer declared: "In spite of it all, I am going to sleep."

25 ALEXANDER I, Emperor of Russia (1777–1825) The monarch who helped to defeat Napoleon was ill with liver disease when his physicians proposed to treat him by applying 35 leeches. The Tsar agreed: "Now, gentlemen, do your work. Give me the remedies you judge necessary."

26 ALEXANDER I, King of Yugoslavia (1888–1934) The monarch who tried unsuccessfuly to establish peace among the quarreling ethnic groups of his nation was murdered by terrorists in Marseilles, France. His last thoughts were of his wife: "Take good care of the queen."

27 ALEXANDER II, Emperor of Russia (1818–1881) The "Tsar Liberator," who freed the serfs and revolutionized his country's legal system, was about to grant a constitution when he was mortally injured by a terrorist's bomb which shattered his legs and caused internal injuries. As he was rushed back to the palace, he murmured: "Home to die. . . . It's cold. . . ." After receiving oxygen and blood transfusions, he opened his eyes as his little granddaughter was brought to his bedside. The child's father said, "Papa, your sunshine is here." Alexander smiled, lifted a finger, but said nothing. A few minutes later he received the last rites and died.

28 ALEXANDER III, King of Macedon (356 B.C.–323 B.C.) Alexander the Great, who extended his empire to the east as far as India, died of a fever in Babylon, failing to name a successor, replying vaguely when pressed to do so: "To the strongest."

29 ALEXANDER III, Emperor of Russia (1845–1894) The son of the murdered Alexander II was criticized for his authoritarian rule. Shortly before he died of chronic interstitial nephritis and heart failure, the tsar told his wife: "I have even before my death got to know an angel." Later, when his doctor, who had ordered him not to leave the bed, found him up, the physician asked the monarch if another medical man had told him that he could be up. The tsar replied: "No! No, doctor, but it was in obedience to the Tsar's own command!"

A few hours before he died, he told his family: "I feel the end approaching. Be calm. I am quite calm." Then, after receiving the last rites of the Orthodox Church, when the priest placed both hands on the sick man's head, Alexander whispered, moments before he died: "How good!"

30 ALEXANDER VI, Pope (1431–1503) Born Rodrigo Borgia in Spain, he presided over an eleven year pontificate that is an embarrassment even to the most orthodox of Roman Catholic historians. The pontiff, who was notorious for his murderous and immoral behavior, allegedly fancied that Satan, in the form of an ape, was running around his sickroom. When a cardinal offered to catch the spectral animal, Alexander warned: "Let it alone, for it is the devil!" Then, evidently to the devil, the Pope said: "I am coming. I am coming. It is just. But wait a little."

31 ALEXANDRA Feodorovna, Empress Consort of Nicholas II of Russia (1872–1918) Forced with her family into the basement of the house where they had been imprisoned by the communists in Siberia, she asked, seeing that the room was empty: "Well, then, is there no chair? Can't we sit down?" Moments after a chair was brought, she and her family and retainers were gunned down by a Red death squad.

32 ALEXIS I, Tsar of Russia (1629–1676) Father of Peter the Great, he died shortly after his second marriage, remarking: "I would never have married had I known that my time would be so brief. If I had known that, I would not have taken upon myself double tears."

33 ALFIERI, Vittorio (1749–1803) The Italian poet said to a friend: "Take my hand, dear friend, for I think I'm dying."

34 ALFONSO XII, King of Spain (1857–1885) The ruler known as "The Romantic King" because of his numerous amorous pursuits, died prematurely, of tuberculosis, telling his wife: "I don't deserve to be cared for as you have cared for me. I know that when I have gone you will care for Spain as I have myself."

35 ALFONSO XIII, King of Spain (1886–1941) Since his father, Alfonso XII, died several months before his birth, Alfonso XIII was king from the instant of his birth until he was deposed in 1931. Dying of heart disease in Italy, Alfonso prayed to the Virgin Mary to save either his life or his soul, whichever would be more to the advantage of Spain. Afterwards he remarked to a friend: "Did Father Lopez tell you of the old gambler's cunning with which I placed my stakes to win on either side of the cloth?" As oxygen was administered, Alfonso protested: "There are so many of the poor who have more need of it than I!" At the very instant of death, the former king kissed the crucifix and exclaimed: "Spain! My God!"

36 ALFONSO, Count of Covadonga (1907–1938) The eldest son of Alfonso XIII, he renounced his right to the succession after his marriage to a Cuban commoner. A historian has described him as "spoiled, mindless, and mercurial" and held that his only interests were nightclubs and fast cars. He was wheeled into the emergency room of a Miami hospital after suffering minor injuries in an automobile accident. To the bewilderment of those treating him, he screamed: "I am going to die! I am going to die!" The emergency room doctors, who were unaware that the count was a hemophiliac, chided him: "Don't be dramatic!" The count then cried out to a friend, mentioning his mother, from whom he was estranged because he blamed her for his hereditary condition: "*Mi madre! Mi madre!* Where is my mother? I'm all alone in this country! Don't leave me, Jack!"

37 ALFRED the Great, King of West Saxons (848–901) The Saxon king, who successfully fought the Vikings, codified the laws of the country that would become England, and founded what became Oxford University. He said to his son Edward: "Thou, dear son, set thee beside me and I will deliver thee true instructions. I feel that my hour is coming. My strength is gone. My countenance is wasted and pale. My days are almost ended. We must now part. I go to another world and thou art to be left alone in possession of all that I have thus far held. I pray thee, dearest child, to be a father to thy people. Be the children's father and the widow's friend. Comfort the poor, protect and shelter the weak, and with all thy might, right that which is wrong. And, my son, govern thyself by law. Then shalt the Lord love thee and God Himself shall be thy reward. Call thou upon Him to advise thee in all thy need, and He shall help thee to com-

pass all thy desires."

38 ALGER, Horatio (1834–1899) The American author of "rags to riches" stories he told his nurse and his sister that he wanted to go to New York. When his sister told him that she would pack his bags, the dying man exclaimed: "Splendid! I'll sleep now. I shall have a nap. Later I can pack and leave on the evening train. But I'm tired. Let me rest."

39 ALICE, Grand Duchess of Hessen (1843–1878) The daughter of Queen Victoria and the mother of the future Empress Alexandra of Russia died of diphtheria, which she caught from her children whom she was nursing. She whispered: "Now I shall go to sleep again."

40 ALLEN, Ethan (1737–1789) The Revolutionary War general from Vermont told the clergyman who was trying to prepare him for death by telling him that the angels were waiting: "Waiting, are they? Waiting, are they? Well, God damn them, let them wait!"

41 ALLEN, Gracie (1895–1964) The comedienne told the paramedics who were placing her in an ambulance: "I'm sorry, boys. I'm all wet."

42 ALLENDE Y GOOSENS, Salvador (1908–1973) The Marxist president of Chile, killed in a right-wing coup, declared: "Long live the workers! Long live Chile!"

43 ALLINGHAM, William (1824–1889) The Irish poet suffered for seven months from what his biographers described as "serious internal trouble." Asked if he had any requests to make, he said: "No. My mind is at rest. . . . And so, to where I wait, come gently on. I thank you. I thank everyone." Just before he died he declared: "I am seeing things that you know nothing of!"

44 ALTGELD, John Peter (1847–1902) Governor of Illinois during the

1890s, he was a well-known advocate of organized labor and social reform. When he collapsed after giving a speech, he said of his wife: "You've got to be careful of her, you know."

45 AMBROSE, Bishop of Milan (ca. 340–397) The renowned theologian and church leader told his colleagues during his last illness: "I have not lived among you in such a way that I would be ashamed to live still longer, but neither do I fear to die, since we have a good Lord." When he heard deacons in the next room discussing possible successors, Ambrose responded when he heard one potential candidate dismissed because he was too old, calling out: "Old, but good!" A few days before his death, as the Bishop of Lodi was praying with him, Ambrose said: "I see the Lord Jesus at my bedside, smiling at me."

46 AMELIA, Princess (1783–1810) The youngest and favorite daughter of King George III died of tuberculosis, telling her weeping parents: "Remember me, but do not grieve for me."

47 ANASTASIA Nicolayevna (1901–1984) Youngest daughter of Nicholas II of Russia, the fact of her survival of the Bolshevik massacre that claimed the lives of her parents is still ridiculed by establishment historians. She died in Charlottesville, Virginia, the wife of a Virginia farmer and genealogist. When the former grand duchess, confined to a nursing home, was told that she would have to go to Martha Jefferson Hospital, she, who for two years had been capable of little more than crying, "Mama Hans!" (her husband was John Manahan), asked lucidly: "Where is Martha Jefferson Hospital?"

48 ANAXAGORAS (ca. 500 b.c.– 428 b.c.) The Greek philosopher urged: "Give the boys a holiday."

49 ANDERSEN, Hans Christian (1805–1875) The Danish author, best known for his fairy-tales, died of cancer at the home of his friends, the Melchiors. A few days before the end, the author remarked to Dorothea Melchior: "If I except my cough, my exhaustion, and my swollen feet, I really feel quite spry. Two things much move me: H.C. Andersen's patience, and Fru Melchior's." Three days later he spoke again, saying: "What a lot of trouble I am giving you! How tired you must be of me!" After two more days of silence, Andersen spoke for the last time, in reply to Fru Melchior, who asked how he felt: "Don't ask me how I am! I understand nothing more!" The next day he breathed his last.

50 ANDERSON, Sherwood (1876–1941) The American author was taken ill on a cruise. Before being taken to a hospital in the Panama Canal zone, where he died four days later, he spoke his last recorded words to a magazine editor who jokingly said, "You can't bear to go down the coast with me!" Anderson answered, "You expect pretty costly tribute from your admirers, don't you, my girl? I'll let them examine me here at the Canal and do what they have to do and then I'll catch the next boat."

ANDRÉ, Brother *see* BESSETTE, André

51 ANDRE, John (1750–1780) A British major hanged as a spy during the American Revolution, he declared on the gallows: "It will be but a momentary pang. I pray you bear witness that I met my fate like a brave man."

52 ANDREWS, Roy Chapman (1884–1960) The American zoologist and paleontologist famed for his discovery of dinosaur fossils in the Gobi Desert of Mongolia said, as he was stricken with a heart attack: "There's that pain again! I can feel it in my arm and in my head."

53 ANNE, Queen of England (1665–1714) "Good Queen Anne," according to some accounts, on her deathbed, called out repeatedly: "Oh, my brother! Oh, my poor brother!" Some attributed this to remorse at her exclusion from the succession of her half-brother, James Edward Stuart, because of his Roman Catholicism.

54 ANNE of Austria, Queen Consort of Louis XIII of France (1601–1666) Regent during the opening years of the reign of her son, Louis XIV, she commented, shortly before she succumbed to breast cancer: "Consider what I owe to God, the favor He has shown to me, and the great indulgence for which I am beholden to Him." Then, gazing at her swollen hands, she commented: "I can see it is time I went."

55 ANNE Boleyn, Queen Consort of Henry VIII of England (ca. 1501–1536) Second wife of Henry VIII and mother of Elizabeth I, Anne was condemned by her husband. The night before her execution, she remarked: "The people will have no difficulty in finding a nickname for me. I shall be Queen Anne Lackhead."

On the scaffold, she told the witnesses: "Good Christian people, I am come hither to die, for according to the law and by the law I am judged to die, and therefore I will speak nothing against it. I am come hither to accuse no man, nor to speak anything of that whereof I am accused and condemned to die. But I pray God save the King and send him long to reign over you. For a gentler nor a more merciful prince was there never: and to me he was ever a good, a gentle, and sovereign lord. And if any person will meddle of my cause I require them to judge the best. And thus I take my leave of the world and of you all, and I heartily desire you all to pray for me."

Some believed that, through such mild and conciliatory words, the rejected queen hoped to win a last-minute reprieve. None was forthcoming. Kneeling down on the block while an executioner from France prepared to sever her head with a sword, she prayed: "To Christ I commend my soul! Jesus, receive my soul! To Christ..." The stroke of the sword cut short her orisons.

56 ANNE Hyde, Duchess of York (1637–1671) Wife of the future King James II and mother of future queens Mary II and Anne of England, she was visited on her deathbed by the Anglican Bishop of Worcester. Having heard that the duchess was a recent, secret convert to Roman Catholicism, the bishop asked her, "I hope you continue still in the truth," to which the sick woman replied: "What is the *truth?*" A little later, the duchess, who suffered from breast cancer, cried out to her husband: "Duke! Duke! Death is terrible!" A witness wrote, "She was full of unspeakable torture and died (poor creature) in doubt of her religion, without the sacrament ... like a poor wretch."

57 ANSELM of Canterbury (1034–1109) An Italian monk who became England's Archbishop of Canterbury, he was one of the most influential theologians of the Middle Ages. He said to his students: "If it be His will that I remain with you yet so long a time as that I may solve a problem which I am turning over in my mind, as to the origins of the soul, I should welcome the delay, because I know not whether, when I am gone, there will be anyone left to solve it. If I could but eat, I think I should pick up a little strength. I feel no pain in any part of my body, only I cannot retain nourishment, and that exhausts me."

58 ANTHONY of the Desert (251–356) The Egyptian Christian hermit was renowned for his life of holy asceticism. To his two companions, he said, among other things: "I am going the way of the fathers, as it is written, for I see myself being summoned by the Lord. Be watchful and do not destroy your lengthy discipline, but as if you were making a beginning now, strive to preserve your enthusiasm.... Strive always to be bound to each other as allies, first of all in the Lord, and then in the saints, so that after death they may receive you into the eternal habitations as friends and companions. Consider these things and turn your minds to them, and if you care for me and remember me as a father, do not permit anyone to take my body to Egypt, lest they set it in the houses. It was for this reason that I went to the mountain and came here. You know how I always corrected the ones who practiced this and ordered them to stop the custom. Therefore, perform the rites for me yourselves, and bury my body in the earth. And let my word be kept secret by you, so that no one knows the place but you alone. For in the resurrection of the dead I shall receive my body incorruptible once again from the Saviour. Distribute my clothing. To Bishop Athanasius give the one sheepskin and the cloak on which I lie, which he gave to me new, but I have by now worn out. And to Bishop Serapion give the other sheepskin, and you keep the hair garment. And now, God preserve you, children, for Anthony is leaving and is with you no longer."

In the words of Bishop Athanasius, "When he had said this, and they embraced him, he lifted his feet, and as if seeing friends who had come to him and being cheered by them (for as he lay there, his face seemed bright), he died and was taken to the fathers."

59 ANTHONY of Padua, (c.1190–1231) Born Fernando de Bulhões, the Portuguese Franciscan was a celebrated preacher known as "The Hammer of the Heretics." Dying suddenly after a heart attack, St. Anthony looked up and said: "I see my Lord!"

60 ANTHONY, Susan Brownell (1820–1906) The suffragette told her friend, Anna Howard Shaw: "Anna, if there is a continuance of life beyond and if I have any conscious knowledge of this world and of what you are doing, I shall not be far away from you, and in times of need I will help you all I can." Anthony seemed to see persons invisible to others in the room. She said: "They are passing before me—face after face, hundreds of them. I know how hard they have worked. I know the sacrifice they have made." Then she raised Shaw's hand to her lips, kissed it, and lost consciousness.

61 ANTONINUS Pius, Emperor of Rome (86–161) One of Rome's "Good Emperors," on his deathbed he was asked for a password. The word he selected was in keeping with the character of his reign: "Tranquillity."

62 ANTONY, Marc (83 B.C.–30 B.C.) Defeated by his archrival Octavian in a power struggle for the control of the Roman world, the political and military leader committed suicide, telling his mistress, the Egyptian queen Cleopatra: "You must not pity me in this last turn of fate. You should be happy that I was once the most powerful, and now have fallen, not dishonorably, a Roman, by a Roman vanquished."

63 APOLLONIA (d. 249) A "wonderful old lady," a pillar of the Christian community in Alexandria, Egypt, she was renowned for her lifelong virginity and for her holiness. When the Roman Emperor Decius decreed the death of all Christians, she was seized by a mob, who prepared a bonfire. After knocking out her teeth, the ringleaders threatened to throw her into the fire unless she renounced Christ. Seeming to waver, Apollonia said: "Take your hands off me and give me a little time to think it over." As soon as she was released, she leapt into the flames.

64 APPHIANUS (286–306) A Christian arrested at Caesarea in Palestine during the persecution of the Roman Emperor Diocletian, he followed a common practice when the authorities demanded his name, his father's name, and his residence. He refused to divulge information that would lead to the arrest of others: "I am a Christian. My father is God." When, even after torture, he refused to reveal any information, he was tied up and thrown into the sea.

65 APPLETON, Jesse (1772–1819) The American clergyman and educator and father of future First Lady Jane Appleton Pierce, he was serving as president of Bowdoin College in Maine when he succumbed to a painful throat affliction, crying: "Glory to God in the highest! The whole earth shall be filled with His glory!"

66 AQUINAS, Thomas (c.1224–1274) The most prominent theologian of the Middle Ages, "The Angelic Doctor" had a mystical experience several months before he died, of which he said, "All I have written seems like so much straw, compared to that which I have seen and what has been revealed to me." He never wrote again. Injured in an accident en route to a General Council in France, he died at a town in Italy called Fossanuova. Speaking of the Eucharist, he declared: "I am receiving Thee, O price of my soul's redemption. All my studies, all my vigils, and all my labors have been for love of Thee. I

have taught and written in the faith of Jesus Christ and of the Holy Roman Church, to whose judgment I offer and submit everything, in the obedience of which I now depart from the world."

Thomas exclaimed: "Soon will the God of all comfort complete His mercies and fulfill my desires. Soon I shall be satisfied in Him and drink of the torrents of His delights. I shall be inebriated in the abundance of His House and in Him, who is the source, I shall behold the Light." He was asked "What is the best way to live without offending God?" The Doctor, with almost his last breath, replied: "He who walks in the presence of God and is always ready to give an account of His actions to Him certainly will never be separated from Him by sin."

67 ARCHIMEDES of Syracuse (287 B.C.–212 B.C.) The Greek philosopher and mathematician refused to accompany the soldier who ordered him to go with him to the quarters of the Roman general who had just conquered Syracuse and wanted to meet the wise man. Archimedes protested: "I really cannot go until I have finished my problem." Enraged, the soldier stabbed the philosopher to death.

68 ARIOSTO, Lodovico (1474–1533) The Italian poet, celebrated for his epic *Orlando Furioso*, reflected: "Several of my friends have already gone. I wish to see them again and languish continually until I attain this happiness."

69 ARMISTEAD, Lewis Addison (1817–1863) The Confederate general, who was one of the leaders of Pickett's Charge that climaxed the battle of Gettysburg, fell mortally wounded after reaching the enemy lines. Speaking of his great friend, Union General Winfield Scott Hancock, who had been wounded in the same battle: "Say to General Hancock for me that I have done him and done you all a grievous injury, which I shall always regret."

70 ARMOUR, Philip Danforth (1832–1901) The American industrialist who built what was at one time the largest meat-packing firm in the world commented shortly before his death: "I am not afraid to die."

71 ARNAULD, Angelique (1591–1661) The abbess of the Cistercian Convent at Port-Royal in France and a leader of what was known as the Jansenist movement within the Roman Catholic Church told her weeping Sisters: "How human you still are!"

72 ARNDT, Johannes (1555–1621) The German Lutheran devotional writer declared: "Oh, what a wonderful glory it is! It is the glory which eye hath not seen nor ear heard, neither hath it entered into the heart of any man!" Then, with his last breath he cried: "I have overcome!"

73 ARNOLD, Benedict (1740–1801) The Revolutionary war general, whose defection from the American to the British side made him a byword for treason on both sides of the Atlantic, died in England. The earliest accounts of his death mention no remarks, but a later biographer stated that in his final illness Arnold insisted: "Let me die in my old uniform. God forgive me for ever having put on another."

74 ARNOLD, Thomas (1795–1842) The British educator, realizing that he was dying and would never complete the book he was writing, conceded: "Ah, very well!"

75 ARNOULD, Sophie (1744–1802) The French opera singer answered her priest, who commented on "the bad times you have gone through": "Oh, the times were good. It was I who was so unhappy."

76 ARTHUR, Chester Alan (1829–1886) The former president, wasted by heart and kidney disease, remarked to a friend shortly before his death: "After all, life is not worth living for, and I might as well give up the struggle for it now as at any other time and submit to the inevitable."

The day before he died, frustrated that he could not be taken to Central Park, which was near his Lexington Avenue residence in New York, because his wheelchair could not negotiate the uneven pavement, he told his doctor: "Doctor, I believe that if I ever get well I shall devote myself to trying to invent some way in which invalids will get able to get to the park without being killed by the pavement." That night, before going to sleep, he told his housekeeper: "Goodnight." When she attempted to wake him the next morning, she found him paralyzed, speechless, and semiconscious. Later that day he died, a smile on his lips.

77 ASTOR, John Jacob (1763–1848) The German immigrant who built an immense fortune in the fur trade was noted for his ruthless behavior and unpleasant personality. The story was told that shortly before his death, Astor, who had vast holdings in real estate in New York, flew into a rage when one of his tenants was behind in her rent. When one of his agents pleaded in behalf of the woman, urging that she be given time, the old man snapped:: "No! No! I tell you that she *can* pay it and she *will* pay it! You don't go the right way to work with her!"

The agent reported the conversation to one of the Astor sons, who provided the sum out of pocket to pacify his father. When the agent showed the cash to the dying capitalist, Astor triumphantly cackled: "There! I told you she would pay if you went the right way to work with her!"

78 ASTOR, William Backhouse (1792–1875) Son of John Jacob, he was known as the "Landlord of New York." On his deathbed he commented: "I might have lived another year if I had not caught this cold, but I am satisfied to go now. I am eighty-four years old — long past the allotted time of man — and at my age, life becomes a burden."

79 ATAHUALLPA, Emperor of the Inca (1502–1533) The monarch, after winning a civil war against his brother, was captured by the Spanish who held him for ransom and finally garroted him after he agreed to become a Christian and was baptized as Juan de Atahuallpa. To Juan Pizarro, the conquistador who ordered his death, the emperor urged: "Show compassion to my children and receive them under your care."

80 ATATURK, Mustafa Kemal (1881–1938) The founder of the modern Turkish republic and its long-time leader, his last word was: "Goodbye."

81 ATTALUS (d. 177) A native of Pergamum in Asia Minor, he was living in Lyon, in what is now France, when the Roman emperor Marcus Aurelius decreed the death of all Christians unwilling to renounce their faith. He was roasted to death in an iron chair, as he shouted to the crowd in the arena, gathered to watch the mass executions: "This thing which you are doing is devouring men, but we do not devour people or do any other wicked thing!" Someone in the crowd roared, "What is God's name?" Attalus, with his last breath, called out: "God doesn't have a name like a man!"

82 ATTLEE, Clement (1883–1967) The British statesman, who served as prime minister during the closing days of World War II, greeted an aide, Charlie Griffiths: "Hullo, Griff. How are you getting on?"

83 ATZERODT, George (Port Tobacco) (1831–1865) The drifter was hanged for complicity in the Lincoln assassination conspiracy. Hanged in Washington, he said to his executioners: "Goodbye, gentlemen. May we all meet in the other world."

84 AUDUBON, John James (1785–1851) The Haitian-born American artist and ornithologist, who painted all known species of American birds, suffered a premature loss of his mental faculties. When his daughter entered his room, he asked, in French: "It is you, my mother, who loved me so? Is it you, Mama?"

85 AUGUSTINE of Hippo (354–430) The African theologian, who wrote *The Confessions*, *The City of God*, and numerous other works that comprise the foundation of Christian thought, mused: "He who is life came down to this earth. He suffered our death for us and He made it die through the abundance of His life. Since life came down to us, why shouldn't we wish to go up to it and live?" Just before the end, he prayed: "Thy will be done. Come, Lord Jesus!"

86 AUGUSTUS (63 B.C.–A.D. 14) Born Octavius, he was the nephew and heir of Julius Caesar, and successfully fought Marc Antony for control of the Roman world, which he ruled for more than 40 years as its first emperor. According to historian Suetonius, Augustus had always prayed to his gods for a *euthanasia*, "a swift and painless death." In his last illness "he gave out one single sign of wandering before he breathed his last, calling out in sudden terror that forty young men are carrying him off." On the last day of his life, Augustus "asked every now and then whether there was any disturbance" in the empire as a result of his illness. Then he "called for a mirror and he had his hair combed and his falling jaws set straight." Then he asked his friends and attendants if he had "played the comedy of life fitly." When they replied in the affirmative, he rhymed: "Since I've played well, with joy your voices raise,/ And from the stage dismiss me with your praise." As the room emptied, Augustus, alone with his relatives, responded to his wife, who covered him with kisses, bidding her: "Live mindful of our wedlock, Livia, and, farewell." He was carried to lie in state by 40 officers of the Praetorian Guard, perhaps the "forty young men" of his dream.

87 AURANGZEB, Emperor of India (1618–1707) The ruler under whom the Mogul Empire reached its greatest extent declared on his deathbed: "No one has seen the departure of his own soul, but I know that mine is departing."

88 AUSTEN, Jane (1775–1817) The British novelist, who suffered from a painful, debilitating disease, told her family: "I cannot tell you what I suffer! I want nothing but death! God grant me patience!" As her agony increased, she pleaded: "Pray for me, oh, pray for me!"

89 AUSTIN, Stephen Fuller (1793–1836) Founder of the American colony of Texas in Mexico, he died shortly after it won its independence but before it was annexed to the United States. In delirium, he imagined that America had recognized Texas' independence: "Texas accepted! Archer told me so! Did you see it in the papers?"

90 BABAR, Emperor of Hindustan (1483–1530) The Moslem Indian emperor told his son Humayun: "I give your brothers to your keeping. Be faithful to them and to all the people."

91/92 BABCOCK, Maltbie Davenport (1858–1901) The clergyman and poet, best remembered for the hymn "This Is My Father's World," drank poison while seriously ill and confided to his wife: "I have swallowed corrosive sublimate."

93 BACHMAN, John (1790–1874) The American clergyman, naturalist, and educator, who helped to found Newberry College and collaborated with Audubon in his *Birds of America*, asked who had come in. Told that it was his daughter, he said to his grandson. "I love her. I love you all."

94 BAER, Max, Sr. (1909–1959) The former heavyweight champion, stricken with a heart attack, cried: "Oh, God, here I go!"

95 BAGEHOT, Walter (1826–1877) The English economist, journalist, and critic insisted on arranging his pillow, declaring: "Let me have my own fidgets."

96 BAKER, Josephine (1906–1975) The American-born entertainer died of a stroke in Paris, the city where she spent most of her life. To the man who took her to her apartment despite her protests that she wanted to stay out longer, she insisted: "Oh, you young people act like old men, you are not fun!" Next morning she was discovered unconscious in bed and never awoke.

97 BALBOA, Vasco Núñez de (1475–1519) The Spanish explorer who became the first European to see the Pacific Ocean was beheaded on charges of rebellion and high treason. On the scaffold he protested the charge upon which he stood condemned: "That is false! I have always served my king loyally and sought to add to his domains!"

98 BALDWIN, James (1924–1987) The American author, dying in France, remarked, the day before he died: "I'm bored."

99 BALDWIN, Stanley (1867–1947) The British Conservative Party leader, who served three times as prime minister, commented, three weeks before his death: "I am ready now." There is no record of his speaking again.

100 BALFOUR, Arthur James (1848–1930) The British statesman and former prime minister who, while serving as foreign secretary during the First World War, issued the proclamation which promised Palestine to the Jews as a national homeland, said to his brother and sister, who sat holding his hands: "Thank you for all that you have done."

101 BALL, Lucille (1911–1989) The comedienne, after heart surgery, replied to her daughter, who asked if there was anything she wanted: "My Florida water."

102 BALZAC, Honoré de (1799–1850) The French author spoke of one of his characters—a physician who worked scientific miracles: "Only Bianchon can save me."

103 BANKHEAD, Tallulah Brockman (1902–1968) Suffering from pneumonia, the actress died in New York, calling for "Codeine! Bourbon!"

104 BANNISTER, John (1760–1836) The British comedian affirmed: "My hope is in Christ."

105 BARBIROLLI, Sir John (1899–1970) The British orchestral conductor, awakened during the night by heart pains, told his wife: "Anyway, I can get a good rest in the morning. There's no rehearsal till three."

106 BARBUSSE, Henri (1873–1935) The French novelist, poet, and editor died in Moscow, speaking of his desire to increase the size of a delegation organized to protest Italy's invasion of Ethiopia: "Telephone and say that they must still enlarge it.... Always larger, broader, more universal.... It's the only means of saving the world."

107 BARING, Maurice (1874–1945) The English novelist, essayist, poet, and diplomat, when asked what he wanted for lunch, responded: "Whatever you would like me to have."

108 BARKLEY, Alben (1877–1956) Majority leader of the United States Senate, he served as vice-president under Truman, then returned to the Senate as a "junior" senator from Kentucky. In a speech in Virginia he declared: "And I am willing to be a junior. I would rather be a servant in the House of the Lord than sit in the seat of the mighty." Then he fell backward, dead.

109 BARNAVE, Joseph (1761–1793) The French statesman who presided briefly over the National Assembly during the Revolution was a constitutional monarchist who was eventually beheaded for treason. Thinking of his service for his country, he complained on the scaffold: "This, then, is my reward?"

110 BARNUM, Phineas Taylor (1810–1891) The American showman was a universalist who believed that all human beings automatically went to heaven. Three years before he died he made a recording in which he spoke of the eventuality of "going to join the great, and I believe happy, majority." During his last illness, referring to death, he said: "It is a good thing, a beautiful thing, just as much so as life, and it is wrong to grieve about it and to look on it as an evil." Shortly before the end he told his wife: "My last thoughts are of you." The last time he spoke he murmured: "I am glad."

111 BARRIE, James Matthew (1860–1937) The British playwright, best known for *Peter Pan*, objected when urged to sleep: "I can't sleep." He did fall asleep but he never woke up again.

112 BARRON, Clarence Walker (1855–1928) The financial editor and publisher demanded: "What's the news?"

113 BARROW, Isaac (1630–1677) The English theologian and mathematician declared: "I have seen the glories of the world!"

114 BARRYMORE, Ethel (1879–1959) The actress, bedridden in the last year of her life, awoke from a nap, took her nurse's hand and, moments before breathing her last, asked: "Is everybody happy? I want everybody to be happy. I know I'm happy."

115 BARRYMORE, John (1882–1942) In delirium, the actor exclaimed: "This is wonderful! What a wonderful place!"

116 BARTH, Karl (1886–1968) The Swiss theologian, working late at night on a lecture, was interrupted by a phone call from a friend. Barth closed the conversation with the words: "Keep your chin up! Never mind! He [God, Christ] will reign!" The next morning his wife found him dead at his desk, his hands folded in prayer.

117 BARTHOU, Jean-Louis (1862–1934) The former French prime minister was serving as foreign minister when he was gunned down along with King Alexander I of Yugoslavia by a Croat terrorist in Marseille. He gasped: "I am suffering. I am thirsty."

118 BARTOK, Bela (1881–1945) The Hungarian composer died in New York while working on a piano concerto. Referring to uncompleted work, he told his doctor just before he died: "I am only sad that I have to leave with a full trunk."

119 BARTON, Clara (1821–1912) The founder of the American Red Cross died in her home near Washington, D.C., pleading: "Let me go! Let me go!"

120 BASEDOW, Johann Bernhard (1723–1790) The German educational reformer who founded the *Philanthropium* as a new model of elementary school insisted: "I want an autopsy made for the benefit of my fellow men."

121 BASHKIRTSEV, Marie Konstantinovna (1859–1884) The Russian writer, best remembered for her autobiography, died of tuberculosis, addressing her last words to a sputtering candle: "We shall go out together."

122 BASS, Sam (1851–1878) The train and stage robber was fatally wounded in an attempt to rob a bank in Round Rock, Texas. When the police urged him to name his accomplices, he answered: "It's agin my trade to blow on my pals. If a man knows anything, he ought to die with it in him. Let me go. The world is bobbing around."

123 BASTIAT, Frédéric (1801–1850) The French political economist said: "I am not able to explain myself."

124 BAUDELAIRE, Charles (1821–1867) The French poet, referring to the Name of Christ, murmured: "Holy Name, oh, Holy Name!"

125 BAUM, Lyman Frank (1856–1919) The author of *The Wizard of Oz* died in Hollywood of heart disease, after a lingering illness. He told his wife: "I just wanted to tell you that I'm going to slip away in a few hours. I feel this is my last farewell. I'm all right. There is little pain now. And there is something that I want you to know — and remember. All my life, since I first met you and fell in love with you — I've been true to you. There has never been another woman in my life or thoughts. This is our house, Maud. I would like to think you are staying here where we have been so happy. The royalties will last for many years. You should have plenty to live on without worry." The next day he whispered to her: "Now we can cross the Shifting Sands."

126 BAXTER, Richard (1615–1691) The English Non-Conformist minister, theologian, and hymnwriter, best remembered for his book, *The Saints' Everlasting Rest*, cried: "Death! Death! Oh, I thank Him! I thank Him! The Lord teach you to die!"

127 BAYARD, George Dashiell

(1835–1862) The 27 year-old Union brigadier general died a day after being struck by shrapnel at Fredericksburg. He dictated: "My black mare and sorrel horse I give to you, father. There are about sixty dollars in my pocketbook. There are papers in my trunk to be turned over to the Department to settle. Once more, goodbye, beloved father, mother, sisters, all. Ever yours, George D. Bayard."

128 BAYARD, Pierre Du Terrail, Chevalier (c.1473–1524) The French soldier called "The Knight Without Fear and Above Reproach," reputed once to have taken 200 Spanish soldiers singlehanded, was mortally wounded fighting in Italy. Bidding farewell to his comrades, he declared: "Weep not, for I die in the bed of honor. I have lived long enough. The only thing that distresses me is that I can no longer serve my prince."

129 BEARD, George Miller (1839–1883) The American physician noted for his work in neurology declared: "Tell the doctors it is impossible for me to record the thoughts of a dying man. It would be interesting to do so, but I cannot. My time has come. I hope others will carry on my work."

130 BEARD, James (1903–1985) The American chef, famous for his cookbooks, after trying to talk to a friend, said: "I can't anymore."

131 BEATON, David Cardinal (1494–1546) The Scots church leader was assassinated by Calvinist radicals in retaliation for his part in the murder of reformer George Wishart. Daring his assailants to attack him, Beaton cried: "I am a priest! I am a priest!" Mortally wounded, he fell to the floor, gasping: "Fie! Fie! All is gone!"

132 BEAVERBROOK, William Maxwell Aitken, First Baron (1879–1964) When told that he needed to rest for a week, the British publisher and statesman responded: "But maybe I wouldn't wake up."

133 BECKET, Thomas (c. 1118–1170) The Archbishop of Canterbury whose independence infuriated his former friend, King Henry II of England (who expected the churchman to function as a rubber stamp), was murdered in a side chapel of his cathedral by henchmen of the king, who sought to curry royal favor by removing the troublesome prelate. As the assassins hacked him, the Archbishop prayed: "To God and Blessed Mary, Denis, and Alphege I commend myself! Into Thy hands, O Lord, I commend my spirit! I accept death for the Name of Jesus and His Church." He slid to the floor, extending his arms in the form of a cross.

134 BEDE the Venerable (673–735) The English monk, theologian, and historian told his scribe: "Take mine head between thy hands and raise me. Full fain would I sit with my face to my holy oratory, where I was ever wont to pray, that sitting so I may call on my Father." Sitting on the floor of his cell, he chanted until he died: "Glory be to the Father and to the Son and to the Holy Ghost!"

135 BEECHER, Henry Ward (1813–1887) The influential Congregational minister, dying after a stroke, remarked: "Now comes the mystery!"

136 BEECHER, Lyman (1775–1863) The minister and writer was known in his days as "the most quoted man since Franklin." For several years he had suffered the eclipse of his mental faculties, but just before he died, he quoted II Timothy 3, asserting: "I have fought the good fight, I have finished the course, I have kept the faith. Henceforth there is laid up for me a crown of righteousness which God, the righteous judge, will give me on that day. That is my testimony! Write it down! That is my testimony!"

137 BEETHOVEN Ludwig van (1770–1827) After receiving the last rites of the Roman Catholic Church, the composer told his priest: "I thank you, Reverend Sir. You have brought me comfort." Shortly afterwards, he lost consciousness. After he had been two days in a coma, a thunderstorm broke over Vienna and a flash of lightning, accompanied by a tremendous thunderclap, illuminated the room. According to a witness, "Beethoven opened his eyes, lifted his right hand upward for several seconds, with his fist clenched, and a very serious threatening expression.... Then he dropped his hand to his bed, his eyes half-closed. My right hand was under his head, my left resting on his breast. Not another breath, not another heartbeat more."

138 BEHAN, Brendan (1923–1964) The Irish playwright, poet, and novelist said to his wife: "You made one mistake. You married me."

139 BELASCO, David (1853–1931) The American playwright and theatrical producer declared: "I'm fighting for my life, doctor!"

140 BELL, Alexander Graham (1847–1922) The inventor of the telephone was urged not to hurry his dictation, but protested: "I have to."

141 BELL, Sir Charles (1774–1842) The Scots psychologist and anatomist bade his wife: "Hold me in your arms."

142 BELLARMINE, Roberto Cardinal (1542–1621) The Italian theologian, later made a saint, was ill with a fever. He was urged to repeat the Nicene Creed and did so, concluding with the words: "...and the Life Everlasting. Amen." Then, until the very instant life departed, when he seemed only to fall asleep, he whispered. "Jesus ... Jesus ... Jesus...."

143 BELLINI, Vincenzo (1801–1835) The Sicilian composer, famed for his operas in the Bel Canto tradition, died of dysentery in France. He mused: "Perhaps some day they will hear my music without even saying, 'Poor Bellini.'"

144 BELLOC, Hilaire (1870–1953) The English author, burned in an accident at home, commented: "Better burn the writer than his work!"

145 BELMONT, Alva Erskine Smith Vanderbilt (1850–1933) Shortly before her death, the society and women's rights leader complained to a friend that her nurses let her hair grow out gray, and commented: "I don't want to die with white hair. It's so depressing. It makes no difference now. The important thing is knowing how to live. Learn a lesson from my mistakes. I had too much power before I knew how to use it and it defeated me in the end. It drove all sweetness out of my life except for the affection of my children. My trouble was that I was born too late for the last generation and too early for this one. If you want to be happy, live in your own time."

146 BENEDICT (c.480–c.550) The abbot of Monte Cassino in Italy is remembered for the rule that he drew up for his monks which, for nearly 1500 years, has been used by countless religious communities. He told his monks: "Don't grieve. I won't leave you alone." He was evidently referring to his rule.

147 BENEDICT XIV, Pope (1675–1758) Born Prospero Lorenzo Lambertini, he was a scholar who, during his 18 year reign, promoted education, literature, and science. Dying of gout, he declared: "Thus passes the glory of the world!"

148 BENEDICT XV, Pope (1854–1922) Born Giacomo Della Chiesa, he tried unsuccessfully to mediate an early conclusion to World War I. The night before he died he offered his life to

God as a sacrifice for world peace, declaring: "I willingly offer my life for the peace of the world." Having predicted his death the next morning, he blessed the church dignitaries who gathered at his bedside: "May the blessing of God Almighty, Father, Son, and Holy Ghost, descend upon you and remain forevermore!" Moments later, at the very hour predicted, he gave up the ghost.

149 BENEZET, Anthony (1713–1783) The French-born American philanthropist and educator said to his wife: "We have lived long in love and peace."

150 BENNETT, Arnold (1867–1931) The English novelist, playwright, and essayist said to his common-law wife: "Everything is going wrong, my girl."

151 BENNY, Jack (1894–1974) According to a tabloid, the comedian, close to death, murmured the name "Lyman Woods." His valet, who knew that Woods, a vaudeville comic, was long dead, questioned Benny, who replied: "I just saw Lyman Woods and he spoke to me. He is going to help me through. He showed me the way, it was beautiful!" Later he repeated: "I was with Lyman. He told me it was beautiful and it was. It was."

152 BENSON, Robert Hugh (1871–1914) The English Roman Catholic church leader prayed: "Jesus, Mary, and Joseph, I give you my heart and my soul!"

153 BENTHAM, Jeremy (1748–1832) The English philosopher told his doctor: "I now feel that I am dying. Our care must be to minimize pain. Do not let the servants come into the room, and keep away the youths. It will be distressing to them and they can be of no use."

154 BENTON, Thomas Hart (1782–1856) The Missouri senator, ill with cancer, told his black house-keeper: "I am comfortable. I am content." Then he bade her put her ear to his chest, commenting: "Kitty, do you hear that? That is the death rattle."

155 BÉRANGER, Pierre-Jean de (1780–1857) The French lyric poet and songwriter prayed: "My God, my God, enlighten us. Inspire in a united mankind the love of the good, the love of well being.... To do good, to live for others—that's happiness. Charity, charity, for all the world to be happy. Widows, small boys—help them."

156 BERENGAR of Tours (c.1000–1088) Canon of the Cathedral of Tours, the French theologian was the author of writings about the Eucharist which were condemned by the pope as heretical. On his deathbed Beranger declared: "Today, on the day of His Epiphany, my Lord Jesus Christ will appear to me, either for glory, as I in my repentance should like, and as I hope, or for condemnation, as others would like, and as I fear."

157 BERG, Alban (1885–1935) The Austrian composer, in delirium, cried: "An upbeat! An upbeat!"

158 BERG, Morris (Moe) (1902–1972) A catcher on several American League baseball teams in the 1920s and 1930s, he was a celebrated linguist who worked as a spy for the United States government during World War II. Minutes before he died, he asked his nurse: "How did the Mets do today?"

159 BERGMAN, Ingrid (1915–1982) The Swedish actress, ill with cancer, responded when told that she had a visitor: "Do I look all right? Give me my brush and makeup."

160 BERLIOZ, Hector (1803–1869) The French composer, speaking to his dead wife, declared, half in French, half in Latin: "Oh, *Mère* Recio, it is finished!"

BERNADETTE, Saint *see* SOUBIROUS, Bernadette

161 BERNADOTTE, Folke, Count (1895–1948) The Swedish nobleman, soldier, and diplomat was assassinated by Jewish extremists while serving as United Nations mediator in Jerusalem. Responding to a reporter who wished him "good luck," he said: "I'll need it."

162 BERNARD of Clairvaux (1090–1153) The abbot of the Cistercian community at Clairvaux, France, St. Bernard was a preacher and theologian who wielded great political and spiritual influence. On his deathbed, paraphrasing Philippians 1:23, Bernard told his monks: "I am in a strait between two things: having a desire to depart and be with Christ, and yet to stay with you." At the very end, he prayed: "Thy kingdom come, Thy will be done."

163 BERNARD, Claude (1813–1878) The French physiologist commented as a traveling rug was put on his legs: "This time it will serve me for the voyage from which there is no return—the voyage of eternity."

164 BERNHARDT, Sarah (1844–1923) When the French actress was told that reporters were outside, waiting for word of her death, she commented: "All my life reporters have tormented me enough. I can tease them now a little by making them cool their heels." But as her suffering dragged on, even she became impatient, complaining: "How slow my death agony is!"

165 BERNSTEIN, Leonard (1918–1990) The American composer and conductor, as if looking into the other world, asked: "What's this?"

166 BÉRULLE, Pierre Cardinal de (1575–1629) The influential French theologian, mystic, and writer, who established 17 colleges for the training of priests and to whom miraculous healings were attributed, prayed: "May Jesus and Mary bless, rule, and govern."

167 BESANT, Annie Wood (1847–1933) The British theosophist died in India, murmuring inconsequentially: "I wonder why so many pretty little animals die so young."

168 BESSARION, Johannes Cardinal (c.1400–1472) The Patriarch of Constantinople, he headed the Eastern Rite of the Roman Catholic Church. He was also a renowned Greek scholar and a collector of ancient manuscripts. On his deathbed he prayed: "Thou art just, O Lord, and just are Thy decrees, but Thou art good and merciful, and Thou wilt not recall our failings."

169 BESSETTE, André (1845–1937) A semiliterate coadjutor brother of the Holy Cross Order, he was renowned as "The Miracle Man of Montreal" because of the healings attributed to his prayers and his application of "Saint Joseph's Oil." He directed the construction of the Oratory of Saint Joseph, one of the largest churches in the world. Hospitalized with multiple ailments, Brother André remarked to his nurse: "How good God is! How powerful! How beautiful! He must indeed be so beautiful, since the soul, which is but a ray of His beauty, is so lovely!" Towards midnight the same day, in severe pain, André prayed: "Mary, sweet mother, mother of my sweet savior, be merciful to me and help me!" The following morning, he tried to say something, but all that could be understood was "Saint Joseph." A few hours later, he moaned: "My God, how it hurts! Oh, I suffer!" The next day, with a peaceful and serene expression, Brother André drew up his feet, yawned, and gave up his spirit.

170 BETHUNE, Mary McLeod (1875–1955) The American educator and civil rights leader, who headed the Negro Division of the National Youth

Administration during the New Deal, said to her family shortly before her death: "Life is wonderful ... I am wonderful...."

171 BEVAN, Aneurin (1897–1960) The coal-miner's son, who became the leader of Britain's Labour Party, served as minister of health and was a founder of his country's national health system. Ill with cancer, he declined to undergo further treatment, insisting: "I will not become a surgeon's plaything!"

172 BEZA, Theodore (1519–1605) The French scholar and theologian referred to Psalm 91, observing: "The Lord has given His angels charge of me. He has satisfied me with a long life. Now I have nothing more to wait for but the fulfillment of the last words of the psalm, 'I will show him my salvation,' for which, with confidence, I have longed."

173 BICKERSTETH, Edward (1786–1850) The English clergyman, who wrote over 700 hymns, said to one of his children: "The Lord bless thee, my child, with overflowing grace, now and forever."

174 BIEDERWOLF, Edward William (1867–1939) The American evangelist died after a long, painful illness, remarking to his wife: "I am soon going to exchange my cross for a crown." Without speaking again he died the next day, holding his wife's hand.

175 BILBO, Theodore Gilmore (1877–1947) The Mississippi senator was an outspoken proponent of white supremacy. He wrote a book called *Take Your Choice — Segregation or Mongrelization* and supported congressional legislation to deport all America's blacks to Africa. Dying of throat cancer, he admitted a black reporter into his room shortly before the end and told him: "I am honestly against the social intermingling of Negroes and whites, but I hold nothing personally against Negroes as a race. God made them as they are and they should be proud of that God-given heritage, as I am of mine." Later, he sat up in bed and said: "I'm feeling fine!" Then he collapsed and lost consciousness. He died the next day.

BILLINGS, Josh *see* SHAW, Henry Wheeler

176 BINGHAM, Sybil Moseley (1792–1848) Missionary for many years in Hawaii, she died in her New England home, saying to her husband: "The Lord be praised! The Lord cares for me! Hiram, almost overcome! Break the bands!"

BIRKENHEAD, Frederick Edwin Smith, First Earl of *see* SMITH, Frederick Edwin

177 BISHOP, Bernice Pauahi (1831–1884) The Hawaiian noblewoman and philanthropist, dying of cancer, told a friend: "Happiness is not money. Having so much I feel responsible and accountable. Pray, and bid all my friends pray, for I need help from on high." She fell into a coma and died a week later.

178 BISMARCK, Otto Eduard Leopold von, Prince (1815–1898) The Prussian prime minister, who built the German Empire in the 1860s, responded to his daughter, who offered him a sip of water: "Thank you, dear child."

179 BIXBY, Bill (1934–1993) The television actor, according to a tabloid, told his wife: "Thanks for the laughter."

180 BIZET, Georges (1838–1875) The French composer died of a heart attack shortly after the premier of his opera *Carmen*. To his wife he said: "My poor Marie, I am in a cold sweat. It is the sweat of death. How are you going to tell my poor father?"

181 BLACK, Hugo Lafayette

(1886–1971) The long-timer Associate Justice of the United States Supreme Court, hospitalized with a stroke, resigned just days before his death. When his wife tried to interest him in a television news broadcast about his resignation, he commented: "It doesn't make any difference."

182 BLACK ELK, Nicholas (1863–1950) The Sioux chief and spiritual leader told his daughter: "I am old, so don't take my death too hard. Do not mourn a long time, you know I will be happy. My sufferings will be over, and I will have no hurt. Pray for me as I taught you to pray in your early days. And pray for me. Do not let a single day pass without praying for me." Speaking of his work as a Roman Catholic catechist, in which he had baptized many dying babies, he continued: "I know I have a lot of little angels up there in heaven watching over me, and one day I'll see them." Then, to his daughter, he spoke of his son: "It seems like I will go any time now, so if your car is all right, go after your younger brother. I want to see him." A few minutes later he died.

183 BLACKIE, John Stuart (1809–1895) The Scots writer and translator, who taught for many years at the University of Edinburgh, murmured: "The Psalms of David and the songs of Burns, but the Psalmist first ... Psalms, poetry."

184 BLAINE, James Gillespie (1830–1893) The American statesman who served as Republican senator from Maine, speaker of the house, and secretary of state, responded to his daughter, who asked, "You had a bad night, didn't you?": "No, I didn't."

185 BLAKE, William (1757–1827) The English poet, dying of "jaundice and torments of the stomach," remarked to his wife: "I am going to the country that all my life I have longed to see. I am happy, hoping for salva-tion through Jesus Christ." A witness recounted, "Just before he died, his countenance became fair. His eyes brightened and he burst into singing of the things he saw in heaven." When his wife asked whose songs he was singing, he answered: "My beloved, they are not mine. No, they are not mine."

186 BLANCHE of Castile, Queen Consort of Louis VIII of France (1188–1252) The influential French queen, the mother of Louis IX, prayed: "Help, ye saints of God! Fly hither, ye angels of the Lord and receive my soul and bear it before the All-High!"

187 BLASCO Ibáñez, Vicente (1867–1928) The Spanish novelist died in France, murmuring: "My garden ... my garden...."

188 BLAURER, Ambrosius (1492–1564) The Swiss leader of the Protestant Reformation prayed: "Oh, my Lord Jesus Christ, this made You in Your great thirst desire nothing, but You were given gall and vinegar."

189 BLAVATSKY, Helena Petrovna (1831–1891) The Russian-born founder of the American Theosophical Society pronounced her "last message" two days before her death: "Keep the link unbroken. Do not let my last incarnation be a failure." Her very last words were: "I do my best, doctor."

190 BLISS, Philipp (1838–1876) The American songwriter and his wife were passengers on a train which wrecked near Ashtabula, Ohio. Escaping unhurt, Bliss returned to the blazing wreckage to search for his wife. Finding her trapped in the ironwork of a seat, he told other survivors, who urged him to save himself: "If I cannot save her, then I will perish with her."

191 BLOCH, Marc (1886–1944) The French historian and economist was shot by the Nazis along with 26 other prisoners. A teenaged boy said to him: "This is going to be bad." Bloch responded: "No, son, it's not bad." Just before he fell, he cried: "Long live France!"

192 BLOMFIELD, Charles James (1786-1857) Bishop of London for 28 years, the Anglican priest, scholar, and editor said simply: "I am dying."

193 BLÜCHER, Gebhard Leberecht, Prince of Wahlstatt (1742-1819) The Prussian field marshal who helped defeat Napoleon at Leipzig and Waterloo told an aide: "You have learned many a thing for me. Now you are to learn how peacefully a man can die."

194 BLUM, Léon (1872-1950) Suffering a heart attack, the French statesman said: "It's nothing. Don't worry about me."

195 BLUNTSCHLI, Johann Kaspar (1808-1881) The Swiss jurist, whose writings on international law were instrumental in codifying the laws of war, declared: "Glory be to God in the highest, peace on earth, good will towards men!"

196 BOAS, Franz (1858-1942) The German-born anthropologist, who taught for many years at Columbia University in New York, remarked on his deathbed: "It isn't necessary to wear oneself out repeating that racism is either a monstrous error or a shameless lie. The Nazis themselves have recently had to appreciate the accuracy of the facts that I have brought together on the European emigrants of America."

197 BOGART, Humphrey de Forest (1899-1957) The actor, suffering from throat cancer, told his physician: "Doc, last night was the worst night of my life — I don't want to go through that again." When his wife, Lauren Bacall, asked if he was feeling better, he answered: "It's always better in the daylight." As she left to bring

their children home from Sunday school, he told her: "Goodbye, Kid. Hurry back." When she returned, he had fallen into a coma from which he never awoke.

BOLEYN, Anne *see* ANNE Boleyn

198 BOLINGBROKE, Henry Saint John, First Viscount (1678-1751) The British statesman and historian remarked to his friend, Lord Chesterfield: "God, who placed me here, will do what He pleases with me hereafter, and He knows best what to do."

199 BOLÍVAR, Simon (1783-1830) The "Liberator," who led the struggle against Spanish rule that resulted in the independence of several South American nations, died of tuberculosis in Colombia, saying in delirium: "Let's go. Bring my luggage on board. They don't want us in this country. Let's go."

200 BONAPARTE, Elisabeth Patterson (1785-1879) The former wife of the brother of the first French emperor, the Baltimore socialite died in relative poverty in the city of her birth, responding to someone who commented, "Nothing is so certain as death": "Except taxes."

201 BONAPARTE, Letizia Ramolino (1750-1836) The mother of Napoleon I, *Madame Mère* spoke of her birthplace: "I leave my heart to Corsica."

BONAPARTE, Louis Napoleon *see* Napoleon III

202 BONAPARTE, Mathilde (1820-1904) Niece of Napoleon I, she was famed as a hostess. She died on the anniversary of one of her uncle's greatest victories. Looking at the sky, she observed: "Ah, it is the sun of Austerlitz!"

BONAPARTE, Napoleon *see* NAPOLEON I

203 BONAPARTE, Napoleon-Joseph-Charles-Paul (1822-1891)

Known as "Plon-Plon," the nephew of Napoleon I sought in vain to claim the imperial throne of France after the deposition of his cousin Napoleon III. Dying, he pompously insisted: "I do not profess the atheistic sentiments attributed to me. I am inclined towards Rousseau's doctrines. I would like to die like an emperor, adhering to the principles of the Concordat, and fully imbued with all the religious sentiments of the Bonapartes." He was referring to a concordat, or agreement, which Napoleon I had made with the pope.

204 BONAPARTE, Pauline, Duchess of Guastalla (1780–1825) Sister of Napoleon I, she died in Florence, of cancer. Holding up a mirror, she remarked of herself: "She may be dying, but she was always beautiful!"

205 BONHOEFFER, Dietrich (1906–1945) The German theologian, prior to his summary trial for plotting against the Hitler regime, asked a friend to convey a message to English Bishop George Bell: "Tell him that for me this is the end, but also the beginning. With him I believe in the principle of universal Christian brotherhood, which rises above national interest, and that our victory is certain. Tell him, too, that I have never forgotten his words at our last meeting."

After the trial, of which no record or recollection has been preserved, Bonhoeffer was taken out and hanged. According to a prison doctor, "He . . . said a short prayer and climbed the steps of the gallows, brave and composed. His death ensued after a few seconds. In the almost fifty years that I worked as a doctor, I have hardly ever seen a man die so entirely submissive to the will of God."

206 BONNET, Charles (1720–1793) The Swiss naturalist and philosopher, who taught what was known as the "catastrophe theory" of evolu-

tion, was convinced that a servant had stolen some important papers. His wife, to humor the old man, promised to bring the offender into the sickroom to acknowledge his guilt. Bonnet murmured: "So he repents? Let him come and all will be overlooked."

207 BOONE, Daniel (1734–1820) The woodsman and pioneer told his family: "Do not grieve. I have lived to a good old age and am going to a world of happiness. I am going. My time has come."

208 BOOTH, Catherine Mumford (1829–1890) Co-founder, with her husband William, of the Salvation Army, she died of breast cancer after a two-year illness. Her son-in-law recalled that during her last days, "At times she would gaze upward intently, as though able to see some wonderful vision, the dim reflection of which would illuminate her face." Several times she declared: "I see!" But she was too weak to describe what she saw.

As the end approached, her husband took her hand and her children kissed her. She looked at her husband and whispered: "Pa." After she kissed him, "Fainter and fainter grew the breathing, while more and more clearly were assurances of peace written upon the . . . countenance, till at length, with one deep sigh, without a struggle, the silver cord was loosed."

209 BOOTH, Edwin (1833–1893) The celebrated American actor died in New York after a long illness. He answered a grandson who asked him how he was feeling: "How are you yourself, old fellow?"

210 BOOTH, John Wilkes (1838–1865) Brother of Edwin, the actor is best remembered as Lincoln's assassin. Dragged from a barn in Bowling Green, Virginia, he died on the porch of the farmhouse from a bullet wound in the head. He murmured: "Tell my mother I died for my country. I did

what I thought was for the best."
Then, looking at his paralyzed hands,
he mumbled: "Useless. Useless."

211 BOOTH, Junius Brutus, Sr.
(1796–1852) Father of Edwin and John
Wilkes, the British-born actor collapsed and died on a steamboat near
Cincinnati. To those who tried to
assist him he pleaded: "Pray! Pray!
Pray!"

212 BOOTH, William (1829–1912)
Co-founder, with his wife, of the Salvation Army, General Booth told his
son to do more for the homeless:
"Mind you, if you don't, I'll come back
and haunt you!" Later he said to him:
"Bramwell, the promises! The promises! The promises of God are sure if
you will only believe!" Then, speaking
of an official in the organization whom
he expected to prove troublesome, he
added: "I'm leaving you a bonnie
handful. Railton will be with you."

213 BOOTHBY, Robert John
Graham, Baron of Buchan and Rat-
tanhead (1900–1986) The British politician died after making this curious
remark to his wife: "I love you so
much; look after the dogs."

214 BORAH, William Edgar
(1865–1940) The influential Republican senator from Idaho died a few
days after suffering a brain hemorrhage after a fall in his bathroom.
Drifting in and out of consciousness,
he whispered his wife's name: "Mary."

215 BORIS Godunov, Tsar of
Russia (c. 1551–1605) The Russian
nobleman who seized the throne was
constantly beset, in his seven-year
reign, by challenges to his rule. In the
midst of an insurrection he suddenly
died, directing: "I leave Russia to
God's will and to the Council."

216 BÖRNE, Ludwig (1786–1837)
The German satirist and political
writer cried: "Pull back the drapes! I'd
gladly see the sun! Flowers! Music!"

217 BORODIN, Alexander (1833–
1887) The Russian composer was attending a party in traditional costume.
When a friend commented to him that
she preferred modern evening dress,
the musician commented: "If you are
really so fond of evening dress, I will
in the future always wear my frock
coat whenever I come to see you, so
that you should never have any cause
for displeasure." No sooner had he uttered these words than he suffered a
heart attack and dropped dead at her
feet.

218 BORROMEO, Carlo Cardi-
nal (1538–1584) The influential archbishop of Milan and one of the leaders
of the Counter-Reformation, he died
of fever, crying: "Behold, Lord, I
come!"

219 BOSCO, Giovanni (1815–
1888) Founder of the Order of Salesian Fathers in the Roman Catholic
Church, Don Bosco is celebrated for
his work with boys. On his deathbed
he said of his boys: "Tell them that I
shall wait for them all in paradise. Frequent Communion and devotion to
Our Lady will be their safeguard."
Concerned that he might become too
weak to impart his dying blessing to
callers, Don Bosco asked a fellow
priest: "When I can no longer speak
and someone comes to ask my blessing, lift up my hands and make it with
the sign of the cross. I will make the
intention." Then he prayed: "Jesus,
Mary, and Joseph, I give you my
heart and soul!"

220 BOSSUET, Jacques-Bénigne
(1627–1704) The French historian,
preacher, and theologian, who served
as Bishop of Meaux, prayed: "Lord, I
suffer grievously, but I am not confounded, for I know in Whom to trust.
Thy will be done."

221 BOUFFLERS, Stanislas-Jean,
Marquis de (1738–1815) The French
author insisted: "Friends, believe that
I sleep."

222 BOUHOURS, Dominique (1628–1702) The French grammarian commented: "I am about to—or I am going—to die. Either expression is used."

223 BOULANGER, Lili (1893–1918) The French composer, dying after years of suffering, told her family: "I offer to God my sufferings so that they may shower down on you as joys."

224 BOULANGER, NADIA (1887–1979) When Leonard Bernstein asked the dying organist, conductor, and teacher what music was playing in her memory, she answered: "A music that has neither beginning nor end." Shortly afterwards she fell into a coma that persisted until her death a month later.

225 BOWDITCH, Henry Ingersoll (1808–1892) The American physician and author replied when he was asked if he were in pain: "No, dear . . . wish that the end would come."

226 BOWDITCH, Nathaniel (1773–1838) The American mathematician and astronomer who served as president of the American Academy of Arts and Sciences, commented after taking a sip of water: "How delicious! I have swallowed a drop from Siloa's brook that flowed fast by the oracle of God!"

227 BOWLES, Samuel (1851–1915) The editor of the *Springfield Republican* and a director of the Associated Press told his nurse: "You may be sure that in another world there will be always one soul praying for you."

228 BRADBURY, William Batchelder (1816–1868) The American composer, conductor, and piano-builder, several weeks before his death from tuberculosis, told his friend, hymn-writer Fanny Crosby: "I am going to be forever with the Lord and I will await you on the bank of the River. Take up my life work where I lay it

down and you will not indeed lose a friendship, though I am going away from you, but rather strengthen it by striving to carry out my own ideals."

229 BRADDOCK, Edward (1695–1755) Ambushed by French and Indians near what is now Pittsburgh, Pennsylvania, the British general, mortally wounded, cried: "Is it possible? All is over."

230 BRADFORD, John (c. 1510–1555) The Protestant minister served as chaplain to the Protestant King Edward VI, only to be burnt at the stake by Edward's sister and successor, the Roman Catholic Mary I. To the man on the stake next to his, Bradford said: "Be of good comfort, brother, for we shall have a merry supper with the Lord this night. . . . Straight is the way and narrow the gate that leadeth to eternal salvation and few there be that find it."

231 BRADFORD, William (1590–1657) Governor of Plymouth Colony, Bradford died after an illness of several months. According to an early biographer, the night before he died, "the God of heaven so filled his mind with ineffable consolations that he seemed little short of Paul, rapt up into the unutterable entertainments of Paradise." The next morning the governor told his family and friends: "The good Spirit of God has given me a pledge of my happiness in another world and the first-fruits of my eternal glory." Several hours later he died.

232 BRADY, James Buchanan (1856–1917) Symbol of America's "Gilded Age," "Diamond Jim" amassed a fortune selling railroad equipment, much of which he spent on food, jewelry, and lavish entertainments. Dying in Atlantic City, he told his physician: "Some day, doctor, you'll understand how much I appreciate your interest in me."

233 BRAHE, Tycho (1546–1601)

The Danish astronomer prayed: "Let me not seem to have lived in vain."

234 BRAHMS, Johannes (1833–1897) The German composer, after taking a sip of wine, murmured: "Thanks, thanks."

235 BRAINERD, David (1718–1747) A Presbyterian minister who served as a missionary to the Indians of Massachusetts, New Jersey, and Pennsylvania and was a key figure in the religious revival in America known as "The Great Awakening," died of tuberculosis, after a long and agonizingly painful illness. The day before he died he told a friend: "It is impossible for anyone to conceive of the pain I suffer." Next day, a few hours before he expired, he affirmed: "It is another thing to die than people imagine!"

236 BREITINGER, Johann Jakob (1701–1776) The Swiss literary critic declared: "Living or dying, we are the Lord's."

237 BREMER, Fredrika (1801–1865) The Swedish author and feminist declared: "Ah, child, let us speak of Christ's love—the best, the highest love!"

238 BRIDGET of Sweden (1303–1373) The Swedish noblewoman who founded the religious Order of the Holy Saviour and was famed for her visions and prophecies died in Rome, praying: "Into Thy hands, O Lord, I commend my spirit."

239 BRIDGMAN, Laura Dewey (1829–1889) One of the first blind, deaf and mute pesons to be successfully educated, she taught at the Perkins Institute for the Blind in Boston, where she died of pneumonia, spelling into the hand of a friend: "Mother."

240 BRIGGS, George Nixon (1796–1861) The lawyer and statesman, known as a devoted opponent of slavery and an advocate of temperance, served as governor of Massachusetts in the 1840s. He died a week after an accidental gunshot injury, telling his son: "You won't leave me again, will you?"

241 BRIGHT, John (1811–1889) The English orator, reformer, and statesman, known as "the personification of his country's conscience," remarked: "There is nothing in the world that gives as much pleasure as poetry—except little children."

242 BRISBANE, Albert (1809–1890) The American social reformer and writer who embraced and advocated what was known as Utopian Socialism said to his wife: "My love, turn me over . . . towards you."

243 BRISBANE, Arthur (1864–1936) The American newspaperman, who edited for many years the New York *Evening Journal* and whose column "Today" was syndicated in newspapers all over the country, commented: "This is the best of all possible worlds."

244 BRITTEN, Benjamin (1913–1976) The English composer spoke for the last time to a friend, Mike Petch: "Goodnight, Mike."

245 BRODERICK, David Colbreth (1820–1859) The controversial California senator died in a duel with California chief justice David Terry, exhorting his friends: "I die! Protect my honor!"

246 BRONTË, Anne (1820–1849) Author of *Agnes Grey* and *The Tenant of Wildfell Hall*, she died of tuberculosis only months after the deaths of her brother Branwell and her sister Emily. When a friend asked, "Are you comfortable?" Brontë replied: "It is not you who can give me ease, but soon all will be well, through the merits of Our Redeemer." To her sole surviving sibling, Charlotte, who was weeping bitterly, she said: "Take courage, Charlotte, take courage!"

247 BRONTË, Charlotte (1816–1855) The English novelist, author of

Jane Eyre, died of complications relating to pregnancy. Awakening from a coma to find her minister-husband praying beside her, she said to him: "Oh, I'm not going to die, am I? He would not separate us. We have been so happy."

248 BRONTË, Emily Jane (1818–1848) Author of *Wuthering Heights*, she suffered, like most of her family, from tuberculosis. After refusing for weeks to see a doctor, she told her sisters just before she died: "If you will send for a physician, I will see him now."

249 BRONTË, Maria Branwell (1783–1821) Mother of the literary Brontë sisters, she died while her children were very young, lamenting: "Oh, God! My poor children!"

250 BRONTË, Patrick (1777–1861) The Anglican rector of Haworth, father of the famous Brontë family, outlived all six of his children, dying at eighty-four, insisting: "While there is life, there is will!"

251 BRONTË, Patrick Branwell (1817–1848) The alcoholic brother of the Brontë sisters whispered, at the conclusion of the prayers for the dying: "Amen."

252 BROOKE, Rupert (1887–1915) The English poet died of blood poisoning on a hospital ship during World War I. To a friend he whispered: "Hallo."

253 BROOKE, Stopford Augustus (1832–1916) The British clergyman, critic, and biographer mused when the newspaper was read to him: "It will be a pity to leave all that."

254 BROOKINGS, Robert Somers (1850–1932) The woodenware manufacturer and philanthropist who founded the Brookings Institute for research in the social sciences declared: "I have done everything I wanted to do. This is the end."

255 BROOKS, Phillips (1835–1893) Episcopal Bishop of Massachusetts, best remembered for his hymn, "O Little Town of Bethlehem," died in his residence in Boston, crying in delirium: "Take me home. I must go home."

256 BROUN, Heywood (1888–1939) The American journalist, hospitalized with pneumonia, told his wife: "I've been pretty sick, Connie, but now I'm going to be all right."

257 BROWN, John (1800–1859) The radical abolitionist was hanged at Charlestown, Virginia, after his attempt to seize the federal arsenal at Harpers Ferry and incite a slave revolt. He wrote a final note which read: "I, John Brown, am now quite certain that the crimes of this guilty land will never be purged away but with blood. I had, as I now think, vainly flattered myself that without my bloodshed it might be done." When the sheriff asked, "Shall I give you the signal when the trap is to be sprung?" Brown replied "in an even voice": "No, no. Just get it over quickly."

258 BROWNING, Elizabeth Barrett (1806–1861) The English poet died in Italy, remarking to her husband Robert: "Our lives are held by God." When asked if she was comfortable she replied: "Beautiful!" Minutes later she died.

259 BROWNING, Robert (1812–1889) The English poet said to his son: "I'm dying. My dear boy, my dear boy!"

260 BROWNSON, Orestes Augustus (1803–1876) The American editor and philosopher was frustrated because he was unable to make his point understood in a theological argument with his son. When his daughter-in-law knocked on the door of his room to bring him his evening meal, the sick man remarked: "If that is Henry, I'm too tired to make it plainer tonight." Shortly afterwards he became unconscious, and two days later he died.

261 BRUCH, Max (1838–1920) The German composer died in Berlin, expressing his desire to return to his home. He asked his daughter: "Can I not go to my home once again by flying there in a zeppelin?"

262 BRUNO, Giordano (1548–1600) The Italian philosopher was burnt as a heretic, and, refusing to kiss the crucifix that was offered to his lips, he cried: "I die a martyr and my soul will ascend in the smoke to paradise!"

263 BRUTUS, Marcus Junius (85 B.C.–42 B.C.) The Roman senator, who led the conspiracy that engineered the assassination of Julius Caesar in hopes of restoring the Roman Republic, committed suicide after his defeat at the hands of Antony and Octavius at Philippi. Before stabbing himself, he declared: "We must flee indeed, but it shall be with our hands."

264 BRYAN, William Jennings (1860–1925) The American statesman, who thrice ran unsuccessfully for president and later served as secretary of state under Wilson, died a few days after the conclusion of Tennessee's notorious "Monkey Trial," in which, despite illness, he served as a witness for the prosecution. Suffering from diabetes, before going upstairs to a sleep from which he never awakened, Bryan told his son: "Seems there's hardly time enough for resting, none at all for dying."

265 BRYNNER, Yul (1920–1985) Asked by a hospital chaplain a few weeks before he died whether he was a believer, the singer and actor replied: "Yes, I am a man of faith. I believe in a higher organization. You can call it God. You can call it Allah. You can call it Mohammed. You can call it anything you want. But I believe. Yes, absolutely!" Just before he lost consciousness for the last time, Brynner, who suffered from lung cancer, re-marked to his son, who announced that he had just given up smoking: "About time!"

266 BUBER, Martin (1878–1965) The Jewish philosopher and theologian declared: "I am not afraid of death, but of dying."

267 BUCER, Martin (1491–1551) The German Protestant reformer died in England, praying: "Cast me not off, O God, in my old age, when my strength faileth me. He hath afflicted me sore, but He will never cast me off. I am wholly Christ's and the devil hath nothing to do with me. God forbid that I should not now have experience of the sweet consolation of Christ!"

268 BUCHANAN, George (1506–1582) The Scots humanist replied to an officer of the Court of Sessions who came to issue him a summons to court to answer for breaking the censorship laws: "Tell the people who sent you that I am summoned to a higher tribunal."

269 BUCHANAN, James (1791–1868) The American statesman and diplomat who served a single term as president just before the outbreak of the Civil War, died at his estate, Wheatland, near Lancaster, Pennsylvania, praying: "O Lord God Almighty, as Thou wilt."

270 BUCHANAN, Robert William (1841–1901) The ailing Scottish poet and novelist, after returning from a bicycle ride, remarked to his daughter: "I should like to have a good spin down Regent Street." Minutes later he suffered a stroke and died eight months later without speaking again.

271 BÜCHNER, Georg (1813–1837) The short-lived, but prolific German poet and playwright, dying of typhus, remarked: "We do not suffer too much, we suffer too little, for it is through suffering that we attain God. We are death, dust, ashes — how should we complain?"

272 BUCK, Pearl Sydenstricker (1892–1973) The American author, famous for her novel *The Good Earth* and other books about China, commented to her nurse a few nights before she died: "Look at me. Look at the way I'm living here. There are children hungry and crying in China, and I have all this here. This isn't what I want."

273 BUCKINGHAM, George Villiers, Duke of (1592–1628) The English statesman, whom many believed to be the power behind the thrones of James I and Charles I, was stabbed to death in France by a disgruntled army officer. Before taking two or three steps towards his assailant, then falling dead against a table, he cried: "God's wounds! The villain hath slain me!"

274 BUCKLAND, Francis Trevelyan (1826–1880) The British scientist and author, who served as inspector of Salmon Fisheries, commented just before his death from cancer: "God is so good to the little fishes. I do not believe He would let their inspector suffer shipwreck at last."

275 BUDDHA (568 B.C.–488 B.C.) Prince Siddhartha Gautama, the Indian philosopher known as the "Enlightened One" (Buddha), exhorted his followers: "Behold now, brethren, decay is inherent in all component things. Work out your salvation with diligence."

276 BUGEAD, Thomas-Robert, Marquis de Piconnerie, Duc de (1784–1849) The French soldier who held the position of marshal of France was instrumental in the conquest of Algeria. Dying, he exclaimed: "It is all over with me."

277 BULLINGER, Heinrich (1504–1575) The Swiss Protestant reformer declared: "If the Lord will make any further use of me and my ministry in His Church I shall willingly obey Him, but if He shall please— which I much desire—to take me out of this miserable life, I shall exceedingly rejoice, as I shall be taken from a wretched old age to go to my Saviour Christ. Socrates was glad when death approached because he hoped to go to Homer, Hesiod, and other learned men. How much more do I rejoice, who am sure that I shall see my Saviour Christ, the saints, patriarchs, prophets, apostles, and all the holy men who lived from the beginning of the world. Since I am sure to see them and partake of their joys, why should I not willingly die to be a sharer in their eternal society and glory?"

278 BULOW, Hans Guido von (1830–1894) The German pianist and conductor was asked how he felt and answered: "Bad."

279 BUNCHE, Ralph Johnson (1904–1971) The American diplomat and founder of the United Nations, answered, when his nurse, who saw he was developing a blood clot, told him that she was going to summon a doctor: "By all means!" When the doctor arrived, he asked Bunche, "Are you all right?" The sick man replied: "Yes." When asked if he were in pain, Bunche said: "No." Then he gave a deep sigh and died.

280 BUNKER, Chang (1811–1874) One half of the celebrated Siamese twins, he suffered a heart attack at one of their North Carolina homes and told his brother, who wanted to go to bed: "My breathing is so bad it would kill me to lie down."

281 BUNKER, Eng (1811–1874) He persuaded his brother to lie down and they both went to sleep. Later he awoke to find Chang dead. To one of their many children he said: "I must go also. My last hour is come. Move Chang nearer to me. Straighten his limbs. May God have mercy on my soul." By the time a surgeon arrived to separate the twins Eng too was dead.

282 BUNSEN, Christian Karl Josias, Baron von (1791–1860) The Prussian scholar and diplomat who served as minister, first to Switzerland and then to Great Britain, said as he took the hand of a visitor: "Very kind, very kind."

283 BUNYAN, John (1628–1688) The English Baptist minister who wrote *The Pilgrim's Progress* caught his death of pneumonia walking through a storm to settle a family quarrel. He told his family: "Weep not for me, but for yourselves. I go to the Father of Our Lord Jesus Christ, who will, no doubt, through the mediation of His blessed Son, receive me, though a sinner, where I hope we shall ere long meet to sing the new song and remain for everlastingly happy, world without end. Amen."

284 BURBANK, Luther (1849–1926) The American horticulturalist, who developed more than 800 new strains and varieties of plants, told his doctor: "I'm a very sick man."

285 BURDETT-COUTTS, Angela (1814–1906) The English philanthropist said: "Tell the Vicar and Mrs. Twining I am so grievously sorry for what I did over the schools and to the Church and that I behaved so badly to the Vicar who did all in his power to help me. They were both such true and good friends to me."

286 BURGHLEY, William Cecil, First Baron (1520–1598) The British statesman, who served as Chief Minister to Elizabeth I and later, for many years, as her Lord High Treasurer, prayed, in agony: "Lord, have mercy! Oh, what a heart is this that will not die! Come, Lord Jesus! One drop of death, Lord Jesus!" Asked if there was anything anyone could do for him, Lord Burghley snapped: "Oh, ye torment me! Let me die in quiet!"

287 BURKE, Edmund (1729–1797) The British statesman and political theorist, shortly before his death from cancer and heart disease, declared: "I hope to obtain the divine mercy through the intercession of the Blessed Savior, which I have long sought with unfeigned humiliation and to which I look with a trembling hope." He last spoke when, being helped to bed, he murmured thickly: "God bless you."

288 BURNETT, Frances Eliza Hodgson (1849–1924) The novelist best remembered for *Little Lord Fauntleroy* and *The Secret Garden*, commented shortly before she succumbed to a long illness: "With the best that was in me I have tried to write more happiness into the world."

289 BURNEY, Charles (1726–1814) The British composer and musical historian declared: "All this will soon pass away as a dream."

290 BURNS, Robert (1759–1796) The Scottish poet, suffering from a heart condition, declared: "I am much better today. I shall be well again, for I command my spirits and my mind. But yesterday I resigned myself to death." The next day he died, whispering his brother's name: "Gilbert."

291 BURNSIDE, Ambrose Everett (1824–1881) The Civil War Union general who later served as governor of Rhode Island and then as U.S. senator, died suddenly of a heart attack, demanding: "Something must be done at once!"

292 BURR, Aaron (1756–1836) The New York politician best remembered for killing former Treasury Secretary Alexander Hamilton in a duel when the former was serving as Jefferson's vice-president refused to comment on his expectations regarding the next world. Asked if he expected to be saved, he answered: "On that subject, I am coy." A few hours later, just before he breathed his last, he looked at his nurse and whispered: "Madame."

293 BURR, Raymond (1917–1993) The actor told a friend: "I think the worst is over. One day we'll be together again."

294 BURROUGHS, John (1837–1921) The American naturalist died on a train passing through Ohio en route from California, where he had become ill, to New York, where he had his home. He asked: "How far are we from home?"

295 BURTON, Sir Richard Francis (1821–1890) The British explorer and author called to his wife: "Quick, Puss, chloroform! Ether! Or I am a dead man!"

296 BUSHNELL, Horace (1802–1876) The influential Congregationalist minister and Yale professor who founded the University of California told his family, who were gathered around his bedside: "Well, now we are all going home together, and I say, the Lord be with you — and in grace and peace and love — and that is the way I have come along home."

297 BUSONI, Ferruccio Benvenuto (1866–1924) The Italian pianist and composer told his wife: "I thank you for every day we have been together."

298 BUTLER, Arthur John (1844–1910) The British scholar, educator, and translator murmured brokenly: ". . . where the larks sing. . . ."

299 BUTLER, Benjamin Franklin (1818–1893) The controversial Union general who served as governor of Massachusetts in the 1880s told his valet, who helped him to bed: "That's all, West. You need do nothing more." A half hour later the valet, returning to the room, found him dead.

300 BUTLER, Joseph (1692–1752) Bishop of Durham in England, he is best remembered for his *Analogy of Religion, Natural and Revealed*. When his chaplain read from the sixth chapter of the Gospel of St. John, Butler commented: "I am surprised that though I have read that Scripture a thousand times over, I never felt its virtue till this moment, and now I die happy."

301 BUTLER, Samuel (1835–1902) The English writer, author of *Erewhon* and *The Way of All Flesh*, ill with cancer, asked his valet: "Have you brought the checque-book, Alfred?"

302 BYNG, Julian Hedworth George, Viscount of Vimy (1862–1935) The British soldier and statesman who served as governor-general of Canada in the 1920s called out: "My God! My God!" This prompted his nurse to ask if he were religious. He failed to respond to that question, but, later, to his wife, who took his hand, he spoke her pet-name: "My Pog."

303 BYRON, George Gordon Lord (1788–1824) The British romantic poet died of fever, fighting for Greek independence against the Turks. Speaking of Greece, he said: "There are things that make the world dear to me. For the rest, I am content to die. I have given her my time, my means, my health, and now I give her my life. Now I shall go to sleep."

304 CABRINI, Frances Xavier (1850–1917) Mother Cabrini, founder of the Missionary Sisters of the Sacred Heart, came from Italy to America in 1889 to establish schools and hospitals. She became the first American citizen to be named a saint. She died suddenly in Chicago, after telling a sister: "Sweep the dust from the floor, especially in front of my rocker, where I will sit and receive [in a Christmas party]. I am a bit weary and later will rise anew."

305 CAESAR, Gaius Julius (100 B.C.–44 B.C.) The Roman general and political leader, stabbed to death in the Capitol by senators who wanted to restore the republican form of government, said in Greek to Decimus Brutus: "You, too, son?"

306 CAJETAN (1480–1547) The Italian scholar and priest founded the congregation called the Theatines to redress the numerous abuses that abounded in the Church of Rome of his day. Urged to lie on a mattress, he insisted: "My Saviour died on a cross. Allow me at least to die on wood."

307 CALHOUN, John Caldwell (1782–1850) The South Carolina senator, regarded as the foremost spokesman for the interests of the South before the Civil War, died in Washington of tuberculosis. When a minister urged him to accept Christ as Saviour, Calhoun snapped: "I won't be told what to think!" He dismissed the clergyman and told his son: "I desire to die in the discharge of my duty. I have an unshaken reliance on the providence of God." Later, he mused: "If I had my health and strength to devote one hour to my country in the senate, I could do more than in my whole life." Then, when his son asked him how he felt, he answered: "I am perfectly comfortable."

When his doctor arrived, Calhoun held out his arm for him to take the pulse. After feeling for several minutes, the physician said, "You are pulseless, sir." He gave the sick man a sip of wine, hoping to stimulate his circulation. Having felt again for a pulse, he told the patient, "The wine has produced no effect." According to witnesses, Calhoun gave the doctor a long, searching look, and leaned back, adjusting his head on his pillow, and placing his hand on his chest, waiting in silence.

308 CALLAS, Maria (1923–1977) After receiving a few spoonfuls of coffee, the operatic soprano, suffering from a heart attack, insisted: "I've had enough. I feel better."

309 CALVIN, John (1509–1564) The French religious reformer, suffering from a painful and debilitating illness, prayed: "Lord, I opened not my mouth, because Thou didst it. . . . I did mourn like a dove. . . . Thou, Lord, bruiseth me, but I am abundantly satisfied, since it is Thy hand." Calvin asked to carried into his dining room to greet friends who had come to see him. Before returning to his bed, he told them: "I came to see you, brothers, for the last time, never more to sit down with you at table. This intervening wall [between the dining room and the bedroom] will not prevent me from being present with you in spirit, though absent in body." He soon lost the power of speech and died several days later.

310 CAMBRONNE, Pierre-Jacques-Étienne, Comte de (1770–1842) The French general mused on his deathbed: "Man is thought to be something, but he is nothing."

311 CAMPAN, Jeanne-Louise-Henriette Genet (1752–1822) The French educator commented after making a peremptory demand of her caregivers: "How imperious one is when one no longer has time to be polite!"

312 CAMPBELL, Thomas (1777–1844) The Scots poet, who helped to found the University of London and was famous for his patriotic lyrics, replied, after being given a drink: "Thank you. Much obliged."

313 CANDY, John (1950–1994) The Canadian-born comedian told a watchman at the house where he was staying in Mexico during the filming of a movie, before retiring to bed for a sleep from which he never awoke: "I'm so tired, all I want to do is go home and be with my family."

314 CANITZ, Friedrich Rudolf Ludwig von (1654–1699) The German poet, helped to the window, looked out at the sunrise and exclaimed: "Oh, if the appearance of this earthly and created thing is so beautiful and quickening, how much more shall I be enraptured at the sight of the unspeakable glory of the Creator Himself!"

315 CANNING, George (1770–1827) The British statesman who served seven years as foreign minister died after only four months as prime minister, murmuring, in delirium: "Spain and Portugal. . . ."

316 CANOVA, Antonio (1757–1822) The Italian sculptor, dying after a lingering illness, repeated several times: "Pure and beautiful spirit!"

317 CARDOZO, Benjamin Nathan (1870–1938) The last recorded words of the associate supreme court justice, several weeks before his death after a long illness, were to Chief Justice Hughes: "They tell me I am going to get well, but I file a dissenting opinion."

318 CAREY, William (1761-1834) The English Baptist missionary to India joked with his colleague, Joshua Marshman: "After I am gone, Brother Marshman will turn the cows into the pasture."

CARL XII, King of Sweden
see CHARLES XII

CARLOS III, King of Spain
see CHARLES III

CARLOS IV, King of Spain
see CHARLES IV

319 CARLYLE, Thomas (1795–1881) The Scottish historian and philosopher commented calmly: "So, this is death! Well. . . ."

320 CARNEGIE, Andrew (1835–1919) The millionaire philanthropist told his wife, who suggested that he might feel better after taking a little sleep: "I hope so, Lou."

321 CARNOT, Marie-François-Sadi (1837–1894) President of France, he left a banquet at the Exhibition of Arts, Sciences, and Industries at Lyon and walked to his carriage. Just as he sat down, an anarchist leaped into the carriage, and, taking a knife out of a newspaper that he was carrying, plunged it into the president's abdomen. Carnot slumped and became immediately unconscious, but was revived a few hours later. His doctor asked, "Do you know your state," and the president answered: "Yes. I am dying." When the Archbishop of Lyon said, "Your friends are around you," Carnot responded: "I am glad to find my friends here." A half hour later he died.

322 CAROLINE of Brandenburg, Queen Consort of George II of Great Britain (1683–1737) When the dying queen told her husband that he ought to remarry, only to be told that he would rather have mistresses, she retorted: "That shouldn't stop you." Asking her servants to remove the candles around her bed, she told George: "I would spare you the affliction of seeing me die." Struggling for breath, she announced: "I now have an asthma. Open the window." Taking the king's hand, she whispered: "Pray!"

323 CAROLINE of Brunswick, Queen Consort of George IV, King of Great Britain (1768–1821) Detested by her husband, who barred her from his coronation, she died shortly after his unsuccessful attempt to divorce her, insisting that her public humiliation was the cause of her final illness. Pointing to her heart, she said: "The doctors do not understand my malady. It is here. But I will be silent. My lips will never make it known."

324 CARROLL, Charles (1737–1832) The former senator from Maryland and the last surviving signer of the Declaration of Independence, the American statesman and diplomat told his priest shortly before he died: "I have lived to my ninety-sixth year. I have enjoyed continued health. I have been blessed with great wealth, prosperity, and most of the good things that the world can bestow — public approbation, esteem, applause. But what I now look back on with greatest satisfaction to myself is that I have practiced the duties of my religion."

On the day of his death, he told the priest, who had come to administer the last rites of the Roman Catholic Church: "You find me very low. I am going, sir, to the tomb of my fathers." Later, he told his physician, who pressed him to eat: "Thank you, doctor, not just now. This ceremony is so deeply interesting to the Christian that it supplies all the wants of nature. I have no more desire for food." Lifted from a chair to his bed by his doctor and granddaughter, he said: "Thank you. That is nicely done." When the doctor lifted him to an easier position in bed, the dying man whispered: "Thank you, doctor."

CARROLL, Lewis *see* DODSON, Charles Lutwigg

325 CARSON, Christopher (Kit) (1809–1868) The celebrated American frontiersman, suffering from a hemorrhage, took the hand of a friend and whispered in Spanish: "Farewell, my friend."

326 CARSTARES, William (1649–1715) The leader of the Church of Scotland and the head of the University of Edinburgh, he declared: "I have peace with God through our Lord Jesus Christ."

327 CARUSO, Enrico (1873–1921) The Italian operatic tenor died of blood poisoning in a hotel in Naples after telling his American wife: "Let me sleep."

328 CARVER, George Washington (1861–1943) The American agricultural chemist, who devised some 300 uses for the peanut, said to his secretary before retiring to a sleep from which he never awoke: "I think I'll sleep now."

329 CARY, Alice (1820–1871) The American writer and women's rights advocate, dying of tuberculosis, told her sister Phoebe: "I want to go away."

330 CARY, Phoebe (1824–1871) The American poet died a few months after her sister Alice, crying out in pain: "Oh, God, have mercy on my soul!"

331 CASALS, Pablo (1876–1973) The celebrated Spanish cellist, en route to hospital in an ambulance, commented: "The driver's a maniac! He'll kill us all!"

332 CASANOVA, Giovanni Giacomo (1725–1798) The Venetian author, famed for his accounts of his romantic exploits, declared: "I have lived as a philosopher and I am dying a Christian."

333 CASAUBON, Isaac (1559–1614) The French classicist, who was a Protestant, was asked by a messenger from the French ambassador in what religion he professed to die. He answered: "Then you think, my lord, that I have been all along a dissembler in a matter of the greatest moment!"

334 CASEY, Hugh Thomas (1913–1951) A star relief pitcher for the Brooklyn Dodgers, he shot himself in the head after being named a defendant in a paternity suit. He shouted over the phone: "So help me God, I am innocent of that charge!"

335 CATHERINE II, Empress of Russia (1729–1796) Catherine the Great, who vastly expanded the territory of her country at the expense of Poland and Turkey, died several days after suffering a stroke while on her toilet. The only word she uttered during her illness was: "Water."

336 CATHERINE de'Medici, Queen Consort of Henry II of France (1519–1589) The mother of three kings who succeeded each other without issue tried unsuccessfully to maintain peace in a land torn by civil and religious strife. Referring not only to the turmoil in France but also to the imminent extinction of the House of Valois, Catherine lamented: "I am crushed in the ruins of the House!"

337 CATHERINE of Aragon, Queen Consort of Henry VIII of England (1485–1536) Rejected and divorced by the king, she died of cancer, praying: "Into thy hands, O Lord, I commend my spirit."

338 CATHERINE of Genoa (1447–1510) Born Caterina Fieschi, St. Catherine was an Italian mystic who wrote *The Treatise on Purgatory*. Terrified by a vision of Satan, she cried: "Drive away the beast that is looking for food!"

339 CATLIN, George (1796–1872) The American painter, renowned for his portraits of Indians, expressed concern over the fate of his works: "What will become of my gallery? What will become of my gallery?"

340 CATO, Marcus Porcius the Elder (234 B.C.–149 B.C.) The Roman statesman, who fought to preserve traditional Roman customs and morals against foreign influences and who successfully urged his country into war against Carthage, died making a prediction in verse about Scipio, a soldier who would eventually conquer and destroy the Carthaginians: "The only wise man of them all is he,/ The others e'en as shadows flit and flee."

341 CATO, Marcus Porcius the Younger (95 B.C.–46 B.C.) The Roman statesman, soldier, and philosopher backed Pompey in the civil war with Caesar. When Caesar won, Cato stabbed himself to death, declaring: "Now I am master of myself."

342 CAUCHY, Augustin-Louis (1789–1857) The French mathematician and poet invoked the names of: "Jesus! Mary! Joseph!"

343 CAVELL, Edith Louise (1865–1915) The British nurse, executed during World War I by the Germans, for assisting the escape of Allied prisoners, told her chaplain: "Standing as I do in view of God and eternity, I realize that patriotism is not enough. I must have no hatred or bitterness towards anyone." When the chaplain said, "We shall always remember you as a heroine and martyr," Cavell replied: "Don't think of me like that. Think of me only as a nurse who tried to do her duty. We shall meet again." As she approached the place where she would meet the firing squad, Cavell said to the chaplain: "Ask Mr. Gahan to tell my loved ones that my soul, I believe, is safe, and that I am glad to die for my country."

344 CAVOUR, Camillo Benso, Conte di (1810–1861) The statesman who worked to build a united Italy died only three months after the establishment of his new nation, telling the priest who administered the last rites: "I must prepare myself for that great passage into eternity. I want the good people of Turin to know that I die like a good Christian. I am tranquil. I have never done harm to anyone." Just before he lost consciousness he said to the priest: "Friar! Friar! A free church in a free state!"

345 CAYCE, Edgar (1877–1945) The American psychic, known as "The Sleeping Prophet," died of a stroke at his Virginia Beach, Virginia, home, asking his wife: "Who is that man? He looks like a musical conductor. It's beautiful music." When his wife asked, "What is he playing?" Cayce replied: "Oh, I don't know. I don't know much about music."

346 CAZOTTE, Jacques (1719–1792) The French author, guillotined during the Reign of Terror, cried: "I die as I have lived, faithful to God and my king!"

347 CECELIA (d. 177) A wealthy Roman who opened her home for use as a Christian church, she was arrested and ordered to sacrifice to the gods of Rome. Refusing, she declared: "Are these the gods that you worship, or are they blocks of wood and pieces of stone?" After attempting to scald her to death in her bath, the authorities beheaded her.

348 CERMAK, Anton Joseph (1873–1933) Mayor of Chicago, he was killed in Miami by bullets intended for president-elect Franklin Roosevelt. His much-publicized words, immediately after the shooting, "I'm glad it was me and not you," were not his last. Dying in a hospital some days later, Cermak said to his wife: "Kiss me."

349 CERRETTI, Bonaventura Cardinal (1872–1933) The influential Italian churchman, told that the Pope was praying for him, said brokenly: "The Holy Father . . . I am truly moved . . . I would say to the Holy Father all my. . . ." As the final prayers were offered, he responded to each petition with a whispered: "Pray for us."

350 CERVANTES, Miguel de (1547–1616) The Spanish writer, famed for his *Don Quixote*, unable to speak, wrote: "Goodbye, all that is charming. Goodbye, wit and gaiety. Goodbye, merry friends, for I am dying and wish to see you contented in another life."

351 CÉZANNE, Paul (1839–1906) The French painter spoke the name of his son: "Paul."

352 CHALIAPIN, Feodor Ivanovich (1873–1938) The Russian operatic basso asked his wife: "Why is it so dark in this theatre, Masha? Turn up the lights!"

353 CHALMERS, Thomas (1780–1847) The Scottish minister, educator, and theologian, who founded the Free Church of Scotland, bid his family: "A general goodnight."

354 CHAMFORT, Sébastien-Roch-Nicolas (1741–1794) The French playwright commented before taking his life: "At last I am about to leave this world, where the heart must be broken or be brass."

355 CHANEL, Gabrielle (Coco) (1883–1971) The French fashion designer, helped into bed by a servant, observed: "So this is how they let you die."

356 CHANNING, William Ellery (1780–1842) The founder of the Unitarian Church commented, shortly before his death: "I have received many messages from the Spirit."

357 CHAPMAN, John Jay (1862–1933) The essayist stroked his wife's fingers as if they were the strings of a harp and declared: "I want to play on the open strings."

358 CHARLEMAGNE (Charles Augustus, Emperor of Romans) (742–814) The Frankish ruler, who ruled over much of western and central Europe, caught a chill while hunting, which developed into pleurisy. He dismissed his doctors, insisting: "Leave me. I'll die well enough without your remedies!" Then, speaking to himself about two deceased children, he said: "Patience, I'll soon join them."

359 CHARLES I, Emperor of Austria-Hungary (1887–1922) The last kaiser of his multi-national central European state, he was deposed and his empire dismantled after World War I. Dying in exile of pneumonia, he prayed: "Oh, God, Thy will be done. . . . Into Thy hands I commend my spirit and the care of my wife and children . . . I offer Thee my life as a sacrifice for my people." He then whispered to his wife Zita: "I love you so much." With his last breath he said: "Jesus."

360 CHARLES I, King of England (1600–1649) Beheaded after losing a civil war against a Parliament dominated by the Puritans, Charles said to his valet on the morning of his execution: "I will get up, having a great work to do this day. This is my second marriage day. I would be as trim today as may be, for before tonight I hope to be espoused to my blessed Jesus." He put on an extra shirt, lest he shiver in the January cold and create the impression that he was afraid: "I would have no such imputation. I fear not death. Death is not terrible to me. I bless my God I am prepared."

After Charles dressed, his valet brushed his hair and attached his pearl earrings. The king then prayed with the Bishop of London and received the Eucharist. He then told the bishop that he wanted no other food, but was convinced that he should eat something, lest he faint on the scaffold. When a soldier entered to advise the condemned man that it was time to go, Charles knelt in prayer, took the bishop's hand, and walked slowly to the place of execution, his dog following behind.

Standing before the block, Charles declared to the spectators: "I die a Christian, according to the profession of the Church of England. I have a good cause and a gracious God. I have no fear, for I pass from a corruptible crown to an incorruptible one, where no disturbance can be, no disturbance in the world, but peace and joy forevermore." Tucking his long hair under his white satin nightcap, he stood praying silently, looking heavenwards. Then, lying down on the block, he told the executioner: "Stay for the sign." When Charles extended his arms in the form of a cross, he was dispatched to his "incorruptible crown."

361 CHARLES II, King of England (1630–1685) Son of Charles I, he was restored to the throne in 1660 and adopted a lifestyle that earned him the soubriquet "The Merry Monarch." Apologizing for his lingering illness, he told family and attendants: "I have been most unconscionably long a-dying."

Asking that provision be made for his current mistress, Nell Gwynn, he pleaded: "Let not poor Nellie starve." Then he asked: "Draw back the curtain, that I might once again behold the light of day." The king's final words were: "That clock must be wound tomorrow."

362 CHARLES III, King of Spain (1716–1788) One of Spain's most successful and respected rulers, he asked his friend, Count Floridablanca: "Did you think I was going to live forever?" To the Patriarch of the Indies, who asked him if he forgave his enemies, Charles replied: "I did not need this extremity to forgive them. They were forgiven the moment of doing me injury."

363 CHARLES IV, King of Spain (1748–1819) The ineffectual ruler, deposed by Napoleon, died in exile in Naples, speaking the name of his brother, the King of Naples: "Fernando."

364 CHARLES V, Holy Roman Emperor (1500–1558) The Hapsburg prince, who headed an empire that extended over much of Europe and the New World, spent most of his reign fighting the French, the Turks, and the Protestants. He retired to a monastery, where he died two years after his abdication, gazing at a silver crucifix and sighing: "Ah, Jesus!"

365 CHARLES V, King of France (1337–1380) Known as Charles the Wise, he was noted as a scholar and administrator. Dying of gout, after blessing his courtiers, he directed: "Withdraw, my friends, withdraw and go away a little, so I can rest from the bother and labor I did not shirk."

366 CHARLES VI, King of France (1368–1422) Called Charles the Mad, the schizophrenic monarch spoke the name of his mistress, Odette de Champdivers: "Odette. Odette."

367 CHARLES VII, King of France (1403–1461) The king who regained the throne that his father, Charles the Mad, had lost to Henry V of England and his heirs, noted that it was the feast of St. Mary Magdalene: "I thank God that I, the greatest of sinners, should die on this day."

368 CHARLES VIII, King of France (1470–1498) The monarch, who died of accidental head injuries after a short reign, cried: "My God, the Virgin Mary, my lord St. Claude, and my lord St. Blaise, they help me!"

369 CHARLES IX, King of France (1550–1574) The weak, vacillating monarch who ordered the Massacre of St. Bartholomew's Eve in 1572, in which thousands of French Protestants were butchered, was haunted for the brief remainder of his life by this act. Dying of tuberculosis, the king moaned: "Blood, blood, rivers of blood! So much blood! Ah, nurse, what bad advice I listened to! Ah, God forgive me! I don't know where I am anymore. What will become of me and my people? I am lost, lost! Thank God I have no son to succeed me!"

Told of some official business he needed to transact, Charles responded: "It doesn't matter. Nothing on earth matters anymore." After making his confession and receiving Communion, Charles said wistfully: "If only Jesus my Saviour would number me among His redeemed!" Shortly after that he died tranquilly, holding his mother's hand and whispering: "Mother."

370 CHARLES X, King of France (1757–1836) The former king, deposed in 1830 after attempting to restore absolute monarchy, died of cholera, telling his grandchildren: "May God protect you, my children. Walk in the paths of justice. Do not forget me.

Pray for me sometimes."

371 CHARLES XII, King of Sweden (1682–1718) The soldier king, known as "The Lion of the North," spent much of his reign in conflict with Peter the Great of Russia, and was killed while attempting an invasion of Norway. Standing on a breastwork, he was urged by his officers not to expose himself to enemy fire. The king called down to them: "Don't be afraid." Moments later a shot took out his brains.

372 CHARLOTTE of Mecklenberg, Queen Consort of George III of Great Britain (1744–1818) Her attendants thought she was in a coma when one of them remarked, "This is a life of toil and trouble, but there is another beyond it, in which none shall know trouble." The queen, who had been listening all the time, added: "Very true."

373 CHARLOTTE Augusta, Princess of Wales (1796–1817) The only child of the prince who became George IV, and heir to the British throne, Princess Charlotte died in childbirth. Referring to the drink of hot wine and brandy that she had been given, she said to her doctor, Baron Stockmar: "They have made me tipsy . . . Stocky! Stocky!"

374 CHARLOTTE Augusta Matilda, Queen consort of Frederick I, King of Württemberg (1766–1828) Daughter of Britain's George III, she said: "I hear your voice, but I don't see you anymore."

375 CHASE, Harold Homer (Hal) (1883–1947) Star first baseman for the New York Yankees for many seasons, he fell into disgrace because of his gambling activities. Dying, he mused: "I came to know a good many years ago and I know more clearly now, that my life has been one great mistake after another."

376 CHASE, Salmon Portland

(1808–1873) The former Ohio governor, who served as secretary of the treasury during the Civil War, was America's chief justice when, seeking treatment for a wasting, debilitating disease, he stopped at his daughter's house in New York, en route from Washington to Boston. Awakening from sleep, the sick man motioned to the fireplace in his bedroom and said to his servant: "Fire!" Moments later, seized with spasms of pain, he went into convulsions, and died three hours later.

377 CHATEAUBRIAND, François-René, Vicomte de (1768–1848) The French author and statesman died a natural death during the revolution that swept away the regime of King Louis Philippe I and set up a Republican government. Told that there was fighting in the street, he said: "I want to go there."

378 CHEKHOV, Anton Pavlovich (1860–1904) The Russian author, dying of tuberculosis, commented: "It has been some time since I have drunk champagne."

379 CHÉNIER, André (1762–1794) The French poet, guillotined during the Reign of Terror, placed his hand on his heart and said: "And yet, I *did* have something here!"

380 CHESTERTON, Gilbert Keith (1874–1936) The English writer greeted first his wife, then their friend Dorothy Collins, who entered his sickroom: "Hallo, my darling! Hallo, my dear!"

381 CHEVALIER, Maurice (1888–1972) The French entertainer's last words were the name of a song: "There's fun in the air" ("Y'a d'la Joie").

382 CHOATE, Joseph Hodges (1832–1917) The American lawyer and diplomat who served as ambassador to Great Britain and later represented the United States at the Second Hague Peace Conference, died suddenly of a heart attack after complaining to his wife: "I am feeling very ill. I think this is the end."

383 CHOATE, Rufus (1799–1859) The American lawyer who served as a senator from Massachusetts, died suddenly, like his younger cousin Joseph, after saying: "I don't feel well. I feel faint."

384 CHOPIN, Frédéric François (1810–1849) The French-Polish pianist and composer, dying of tuberculosis, said to his sister: "I love God and man. I am happy so to die; do not weep, my sister." He exhorted the friends around his bedside: "My friends, do not weep. I am happy. I feel that I am dying. Farewell. Pray for me."

He begged his doctors: "Let me die. Do not keep me longer in this world of exile. Let me die; why do you prolong my life when I have renounced all things and God has enlightened my soul? God calls me; why do you call me back?" Frustrated at continued efforts to prolong his life, he reflected: "O lovely science, that only lets one suffer longer! Could it give me back my strength, qualify me to do any good, to make any sacrifice — but a life of fainting, of grief, of pain to all who love me, to prolong such a life — O lovely science!" Again he complained to his doctors: "You let me suffer cruelly! Perhaps you have erred about my sickness. But God errs not. He punishes me and I bless Him therefore. Oh, how good is God to punish me here below! Oh, how good God is!"

A few hours before the end he prayed: "Without You I should have croaked like a pig!" At the point of death, Chopin kissed the crucifix, pressed it to his heart, and cried: "Jesus! Mary! Joseph! Now I am at the source of blessedness!"

385 CHRISTIAN IV, King of

Denmark and Norway (1577–1648) During a 60 year reign, he founded a number of cities, including what is now Oslo, and involved his country in the Thirty Years War. Taking the hand of his pastor, he declared: "Now comes the fight."

386 CHRISTIAN IX, King of Denmark (1818–1906) After a reign of more than four decades, the popular, democratically-minded monarch, whose children included two kings, a queen, and an empress, died suddenly at a party. He announced: "I'll go into the next room and fetch a cigar. I'll be back in a moment." When his daughter, the Russian dowager empress, asked if she could get the cigar for him, Christian replied: "No, certainly not." When the king returned he was pale and sweating. Helped to his bedroom, he lay down and said: "I think I can sleep a little." Moments later he was dead.

387 CHRISTIAN X, King of Denmark (1870–1947) The six foot seven inch monarch, who strenuously resisted Nazi rule and helped to thwart German attempts to massacre his Jewish subjects, died after a heart attack, declaring: "My task on this earth is over. I am at peace with my God and myself. I am so tired."

388 CHRYSIPPUS (c.280 B.C.–207 B.C.) The Greek Stoic philosopher saw a donkey solemnly eating human food and, bursting into laughter, told his servant: "Give him a bumper of wine!" He continued to laugh until he suffered an apparent heart attack and died.

389 CHURCH, Frank (1924–1984) Senator from Idaho for many years, he answered a cousin who asked him, "How are you doing, Frank—I mean spiritually?" The dying man opened his eyes and said: "John, it is very, very interesting."

390 CHURCHILL, Jennie Jerome (1854–1921) The American-born social-ite who was the mother of future British prime minister Winston Churchill died of a hemorrhage after a leg amputation: "Nurse! Nurse! I'm pouring blood!"

391 CHURCHILL, John, Duke of Marlborough (1650–1722) The British soldier and statesman, asked if he was aware of the prayers that had been offered for him, replied: "Yes, and I joined in them." Asked if he wanted to be lifted from his chair to bed, he answered: "Yes." A few hours later he died in his sleep.

392 CHURCHILL, Randolph Frederick Edward Spencer (1911–1968) The English journalist, author, and politician, son of Winston Churchill, was asked, shortly before he died, if he believed in God, and replied: "No, I don't think I do. But I believe that when you die all the goodness in you comes together as a force."

393 CHURCHILL, Sir Winston Leonard Spencer (1874–1965) The British statesman who led his country through most of World War II sighed: "I am bored of it all."

394 CHYTRÄEUS, David (1531–1600) Born David Kochhafe, the author of Biblical commentaries, who is known as one of the "Fathers of the Lutheran Church," died shortly after completing a history: "I have concluded the history of this century and put the finishing touches to it, and not another word will I write."

395 CICERO, Marcus Tullius (106 B.C.–43 B.C.) The Roman statesman, author, and orator was murdered during the civil war that followed the assassination of Julius Caesar. Overtaken as he fled, he opened the curtains of his litter to his assassins, pointed to his neck, and told their leader: "Strike here, veteran, if you think it right."

396 CLANTON, William Harrison (1862–1881) The Arizona cowboy, mortally wounded in the gunfight at the OK Corral with the Earp brothers and Doc Holliday in Tombstone, Arizona, pleaded: "I don't want to die with my boots on!"

397 CLARE of Assisi (1193–1253) Founder of the Franciscan Order of Poor Ladies (Poor Clares), the protégé of St. Francis, dying after a long illness, prayed softly: "Go forth, Christian soul. Go forth without fear, for thou hast a good guide for thy journey. Go forth without fear, for He that created thee hath sanctified thee, always hath protected thee, and He loveth thee with the love of a mother." When a nun asked her to whom she was speaking, Clare replied: "I am talking to my own soul." Just before she breathed her last, the abbess asked: "Can you see the King of Glory, whom I see?"

398 CLARE, John (1793–1864) The British poet said: "I have lived too long. I want to go home."

399 CLARK, George Rogers (1752–1818) The Revolutionary War officer, who won important victories over the British in what is now the American Midwest, died after a lingering illness. Told of the death of a friend, he complained: "Everybody can die but me!"

400 CLAY, Henry (1777–1852) The influential Kentucky statesman who served at various times as speaker of the house, secretary of state, and U.S. senator, and who three times forged compromises to avoid civil war, died of tuberculosis in a Washington hotel. Shortly after being shaved, Clay called his son Thomas and insisted: 'Sit near me, my dear son. I do not wish you to leave me for any time today." An hour later he said: "Give me some water." Then he whispered: "I believe, my son, I am going." After indicating that he wanted his shirt collar unbuttoned, he grasped his son's hand.

Moments later his grip relaxed and he was gone.

401 CLEMENCEAU, Georges (1841–1929) The French statesman who served as premier during World War I was drifting in and out of consciousness, suffering from kidney failure. Coming to his senses, he asked a friend: "What has happened, Pietri?" When told, "You have had an attack," Clemenceau responded: "This time it will be a long one." He never spoke again and died the next day.

402 CLEMENS, Olivia Langdon (1845–1904) According to one tradition, the wife of "Mark Twain" responded to her husband, who asked her, as she lay in agony, "Why don't you call on the resources of your great religion?": "I don't have them any more. You made certain of that."

403 CLEMENS, Samuel Langhorne (1835–1910) The American author who wrote under the pen name "Mark Twain" said to his daughter Clara Gabrilowitsch: "Goodbye, dear. Then, if we meet . . . ."

404 CLEMENT XI, Pope (1649–1721) Born Giovanni Francesco Albani, he reigned for more than 20 years. He told his nephew, who was a cardinal: "See how all the honors of the world come to an end. Only that is great which is great in God's sight. Make it your endeavor to be a saint."

405 CLEMENT XII, Pope (1652–1740) Born Lorenzo Corsini, he was totally blind during most of his pontificate during which he struggled to increase the power of the papacy. To Father Barberini, who offered to hear his confession, Clement insisted: "I have no fault of any kind." When the priest suggested, "Even popes may have some omissions to repent of," Clement responded: "No, neither on that point do we feel any remorse of conscience."

406 CLEMENT XIV, Pope (1705–

1774) Born Giovanni Vincenzo Antonio Ganganelli, he reigned for five years, during which he dissolved the Jesuit Order. On his deathbed he was pressed by his cardinals to name 11 more princes of the Church. When he refused and they still insisted, the dying man said: "We cannot and we will not do it. The Lord will judge our reasons." The cardinals knelt on the floor and repeated their request, prompting the exasperated invalid to complain: "I'm on my way to eternity and I know why!"

407 CLEMENTE, Roberto (1934–1972) The star outfielder for the Pittsburgh Pirates insisted on accompanying a planeload of supplies to victims of an earthquake in Nicaragua. When friends protested that the plane was not safe, Clemente, just before boarding, declared: "If you're going to die, you're going to die." The plane crashed into the sea.

408 CLEOPATRA VII, Queen of Egypt (69 b.c.–30 b.c.) After her defeat by Octavian and the suicide of her lover Marc Antony, she avoided capture by offering her breast to the bite of a poisonous snake. When the asp was brought to her, she murmured: "So, then, here it is."

409 CLEVELAND,   Stephen Grover (1837–1908) The New Jersey governor who served two nonconsecutive terms as president was a man renowned for his honesty and integrity, and, a few hours before his death after a lingering illness, he is said to have insisted: "I tried so hard to do right."

410 CLIVE, Robert, Baron of Plassey (1725–1774) The British soldier and statesman who was instrumental in colonizing India in the 1750s was suffering from illness and depression when a visitor to his home asked him if he would be so kind as to make a pen for her. Taking a penknife and preparing a quill for writing, he

answered: "To be sure." Shortly afterwards he went into the bathroom and slit his throat with the same penknife.

411 COCHISE (c.1812–1874) The Apache leader, wasted by a painful, debilitating illness, asked his friend, Indian agent Tom Jeffords, who was leaving: "Do you think you will see me alive again?" When Jeffords indicated that he did not, Cochise added: "I think I will die about ten o'clock tomorrow morning. Do you think we will see each other again?" When Jeffords answered, "I don't know. What do you think about it?" Cochise replied: "I don't know. It is not clear to my mind, but I think we will, somewhere up there."

412 COCTEAU, Jean (1889–1963) The French poet and playwright remarked: "The boat is going down."

413 CODY, William Frederick (Buffalo Bill) (1846–1917) Informed by his doctor that he had but 36 hours to live, the American showman replied: "Thirty-six hours? That's all! Well, let's forget about it and play High-Five."

414 COFFIN, Charles Carleton (1823–1896) The American journalist and author, famous for his lectures and travel books, reflected: "If it were not for this pain I should get up and write."

415 COFFIN, Robert Peter Tristram (1892–1955) The American poet and educator died of a heart attack while attempting to deliver a lecture in Portland, Maine. Unable to continue, he explained before collapsing: "The cold air caught my breath. Just let me sit down for a moment."

416 COGHILL, George Ellett (1872–1941) The American anatomist, zoologist, and educator complained to his nurse, who was trying to get him to swallow a spoonful of peppermint water: "Why, that's what we used to give to babies!"

417 COHAN, George Michael (1878–1942) The American songwriter, speaking of his wife, asked: "Look after Agnes."

418 COKE, Sir Edward (1552–1634) The British jurist and statesman, as the Our Father was prayed, mumured: "Thy kingdom come, Thy will be done...."

419 COLBERT, Jean-Baptiste (1619–1683) Finance minister of Louis XIV and first comptroller general of France, he responded to his wife, who asked if he had answered a letter from the king: "It is the King of Kings that I should be thinking about."

420 COLE, Nathaniel Adams (Nat King) (1919–1965) Two days before he died, the singer and entertainer, suffering from lung cancer, told a friend: "My future is now in the hands of Jesus and God. I'm ready for whatever happens." A few hours before he died he whispered his wife's name: "Maria."

421 COLE, Thomas (1801–1848) The American landscape painter, dying of pneumonia, said after receiving Holy Communion: "I want to be quiet."

422 COLERIDGE-TAYLOR, Samuel (1875–1912) The British composer died of pneumonia, informing his wife that he looked forward to heaven, because: "I look forward to meeting such a crowd of musicians." The musician, whose father was African, reflected on the content of his obituaries: "All the papers will call me a Creole."

423 COLETTE, Sidonie-Gabrielle (1873–1954) The French novelist, who was invalid the last five years of her life, pointed to a box of butterflies and fluttered her hands like wings, calling to her husband: "Look, Maurice, look!"

424 COLIGNY, Gaspard de (1519–1572) Admiral of France, the Huguenot leader died in the St. Bartholo-

mew's Day Massacre of Protestants. He told his assassin: "Oh, my brother, I now perceive that I am beloved of God, seeing that for His most holy name's sake I suffer these wounds."

425 COLT, Samuel (1814–1862) The American gun manufacturer, succumbing to gout and rheumatic fever, told his wife: "It's all over now."

426 COLUMBA (521–597) The Irish missionary to the Picts of Scotland, a man who was characterized as "loving to everyone, happy-faced, rejoicing in his inmost heart with the joy of the Holy Spirit" died in his monastery on the island of Iona, enjoining his religious: "Dear children, this is what I commend with my last words— let peace and charity that is mutual and sincere reign always among you. If you act thus, following the example of the saints, God who strengthens the just will help you, and I, who shall be near Him, will intercede on your behalf, and you shall obtain of Him not only the necessities of the present life in sufficient quantity, but still more the rewards of eternal life, reserved for those who keep His law."

427 COLUMBUS, Christopher (c.1450–1506) The discoverer of the New World prayed: "Into Thy hands, O Lord, I commend my spirit."

428 COMBE, Andrew (1797–1847) The British physician and physiologist was, along with his brother George, a proponent of phrenology, the "science" of determining personality characteristics from the study of the contours of the head. Asked how he felt, Combe answered: "Happy! Happy!"

429 COMBE, George (1788–1858) The British phrenologist remarked: "From my present sensations I should say I was dying — and I am glad of it."

430 COMPTON, Spencer Cavendish, Duke of Devonshire (1833–1908) The British statesman conceded: "The game is over and I am not sorry."

431 COMTE, Auguste (1798–1857) The French philosopher, considered a founder of sociology and positivism, lamented his approaching death: "What an irreparable loss!"

432 CONAN DOYLE, Sir Arthur (1859–1930) The English author best known for his Sherlock Holmes stories, told his nurse: "There ought to be a medal struck for you, inscribed, 'To the best of all nurses.'"

433 CONFUCIUS (c.551 B.C.– 478 B.C.) The Chinese philosopher complained: "There is none who knows me. No intelligent ruler arises to take me for his master."

434 CONKLING, Roscoe (1829–1888) The influential Republican senator from New York murmured in delirium: "I will supply the vitality!"

435 CONNELLY, Cornelia (1809–1879) She and her husband were converts to Roman Catholicism from the American Episcopal Church. He became a priest and then renounced the faith. She became a nun and founded the Society of the Holy Child Jesus which established schools in England, America, and France. Dying in England, she declared: "In this flesh I shall see my God!"

436 CONRAD, Joseph (1857–1924) The Polish-born British author, suffering from a heart condition, called to his wife: "You, Jess! I'm better this morning! I can always get a rise out of you." A few minutes later he died.

437 CONSALVI, Ercole Cardinal (1757–1824) The Vatican statesman, noted for his moderation in accommodating the political reforms of his day and his efforts to achieve good relations with the governments of the European nations, declared: "My mind is at rest."

438 CONSTANTINE I, Emperor of Rome (c.272–377) The ruler who proclaimed religious tolerance throughout his realm was baptized a Christian just before he died. After receiving Holy Communion, he declared: "Now I know in very truth that I am blessed. I have the confidence that I am a partaker of divine light. I have the assurance that I have been found worthy of eternal life. My only anxiety now is to hasten my journey to God."

439 CONSTANTINE XI Palaeologus (1404–1453) The last Byzantine emperor fell defending the walls of Constantinople from the Turks. As his comrades fell around him, he cried out: "So there is no Christian who wishes to free me from this life?" A few minutes later he was killed by two soldiers of the enemy army.

440 COOK, Frederick Albert (1865–1940) The explorer of the Arctic, near death from a stroke, was told that the president had pardoned his conviction for mail fraud. Cook roused himself briefly from a coma to murmur: "Great ... happy day ... pardon...." He died two months later. There is no record of him speaking again.

441 COOKE, Jay (1821–1905) The American financier who managed United States war loans during the Civil War, responded, after his pastor offered the prayers for the dying: "Amen. That was the right prayer."

442 COOKE, Terence Cardinal (1921–1983) The archbishop of New York told his weeping secretary: "Maura, you were always so good and kind to me. You've got to be very brave, just like my sister."

443 COOKMAN, Alfred (1828–1871) The American Methodist minister was famous as a camp-meeting preacher. Dying of a excruciatingly painful illness diagnosed as "mialgia" he said to his sister-in-law: "This is the sickest day of my life, but all is well. I am so glad I have preached full salvation. What would I do without it now? If you forget everything else, remember my testimony — washed in the blood of the Lamb! Jesus is drawing me closer and closer to His great heart of infinite love."

He said to his wife: "I am Christ's little infant. Just as you fold your little babe on your bosom, so I am nestled close to the heart of Jesus." To his son he declared: "My son, your papa has been all day sweeping close by the gates of death." As he was moved in bed, he commented: "How sweet and quiet everything now seems. I feel like resting now." A few minutes later he vomited and became unconscious, dying four hours later.

444 COOLIDGE, John Calvin (1872–1933) The popular Republican president died in retirement at his home, "The Beeches," in Northampton, Massachusetts. "Silent Cal" said nothing in the last moments of his life to undermine his reputation as a man of few words. Speaking to a handyman, he said: "Good morning, Robert." Then he went into his bathroom, where his wife found him dead of a heart attack.

445 COOPER, Gary (1901–1961) The movie actor, dying of cancer, affirmed: "It is God's will."

446 COPLESTON, Edward (1776–1849) The British churchman and author, who served as Bishop of Landaff in the Church of England declared: "I expect soon to die, and I die in the firm faith of the redemption wrought by God in man through Christ Jesus, assured that all who believe in Him will be saved."

447 COPLEY, John Singleton (1738–1815) The American painter died in England, after a series of strokes. Just before he lost consciousness, he told his daughter that he was "perfectly resigned and willing to die," and "expressed his firm trust in God, through the merits of the Redeemer." When she asked him how he felt, he answered: "Happy! Happy! Supremely happy!"

448 CORBET, Richard (1582–1635) The English poet and clergyman who served as Bishop of Norwich bade his chaplain: "Goodnight, Lushington."

449 CORBULO, Gnaeus Domitius (d. A.D. 67) The general, who restored Roman control over Armenia, was accused of plotting the overthrow of Nero, and committed suicide, blaming himself for his failure to depose the tyrant: "Well deserved!"

450 CORDAY, Charlotte (1768–1793) The assassin of the French revolutionary Marat spoke to her executioner about the guillotine that would soon sever her head: "I have a good right to be curious, for I have never seen one before."

451 COROT, Jean-Baptiste-Camille (1796–1875) The French landscape painter commented: "I hope with all my heart there will be painting in heaven."

452 CORRIGAN, Michael Augustine (1839–1902) Archbishop of New York for 17 years, he died suddenly of "fatty degeneration of the heart," while recovering from pneumonia. Clutching a crucifix, he whispered: "I feel very weak."

453 CORYAT, Thomas (c.1577–1617) The former English court jester was renowned as a world traveler. He published a book called *Coryat's Crudities*, and is credited with introducing the fork to England. Dying of fever in India, he cried for a drink: "Sack! Sack! Is there any such thing as sack? I pray you give me some sack!"

454 COTTON, John (1585–1652) The Puritan leader, pastor of Boston's First Church, answered a friend who promised to pray that God would grant him "the light of His countenance": "God hath done it already, brother."

455 COUZENS, James Joseph,

Jr. (1872–1936) The Republican senator from Michigan, who was an enthusiastic supporter of Roosevelt's New Deal, reassured his wife and son before undergoing an operation, after which he would never regain consciousness: "Don't worry. They can't kill an old dog like me. I'll see you later, Mother. Don't worry."

456 COWLES, Anna Roosevelt (1855–1931) Theodore Roosevelt's sister and advisor, of whom it was said, "If she had been a man she would have been president," patted the hand of a cousin who was distressed at seeing her in great pain: "Never mind. It's all right."

457 COWPER, William (1731–1800) The British poet was offered some refreshment by his nurse, and then asked what difference it made: "What does it signify?"

458 CRABBE, George (1754–1832) The English poet said to his loved ones: "God bless you. God bless you."

459 CRANE, Hart (1899–1932) The American poet and his girlfriend were on a ship in the Caribbean. He had been drinking heavily, when he entered her room in his pajamas and said despondently: "I'm not going to make it, dear. I'm utterly disgraced." When she told him that he would feel better, once he changed into clean clothes, he left, saying: "All right, dear. Goodbye." Moments later, he jumped into the sea.

460 CRANE, Stephen (1871–1900) The American author, who succumbed to tuberculosis, told a friend during his final illness: "When you come to the hedge we must all go over, it isn't so bad. You feel sleepy and you don't care. Just a little dreamy anxiety ... which world you're really in ... that's all...."

461 CRANMER, Thomas (1489–1556) Archbishop of Canterbury for more than 30 years, he was the first Protestant primate of England. When Mary I, who reestablished Roman Catholicism, confined him in the Tower of London, the Archbishop signed seven recantations of his theological positions in an attempt to save his life. When he was nonetheless condemned to the stake, Cranmer showed remorse for his lack of courage and, as the flames leaped up around him, he thrust his right hand, with which he had signed the recantations, into the fire and cried: "This hath offended, oh, this unworthy hand!" As he was enveloped in the fire, he prayed: "Lord Jesus, receive my spirit!"

462 CRAWFORD, Francis Marion (1854–1909) The American novelist, dying in Sorrento, Italy, commented: "I love to see the reflection of the sun on the bookcase."

463 CRAWFORD, Joan (1908–1977) The actress, when she saw her nurse praying, snapped: "Damn it! How dare you ask God to help me!"

464 CRAZY HORSE (c.1842–1877) The Oglala Sioux chief was stabbed to death by a soldier while trying to escape the prison at Fort Robinson, Nebraska, where he was confined by the U.S. Army. To a relative who had been trying to restrain him, he said reproachfully: "Cousin, you killed me! You are with the white people!" Some accounts say that when his parents came to see him, he told his father: "Father, it is no use to depend on me. I am going to die." Most contemporary accounts state, however, that by the time the parents arrived, Crazy Horse was dead.

465 CRISTINA, Queen Consort of Ferdinand VII of Spain (1806–1878) The Neapolitan princess, who ruled as Queen Regent for her young daughter for eight years after her husband's death, died in France, speaking of her grandson who was now the Spanish king: "Tell my Alfonso he must console himself and make Spain flourish."

466 CRITTENDEN, John Jordan (1787–1863) The Kentucky senator, who tried to arrange a compromise to avoid the Civil War, told his son: "Tom, come and raise me up and arrange my pillow. That's right, Tom."

467 CROLL, James (1821–1890) The Scots geologist asked for a teaspoon of whiskey, commenting: "I'll take a wee drop o' that. I don't think there's much fear o' me learning to drink now!"

468 CROME, John (1768–1821) The English landscape painter, ill with a fever, made motions as if he were painting, and murmured: "There — there — there's a touch — that will do — now another — that's it. Beautiful!" Five minutes before he died, referring to a seventeenth century Dutch landscape painter, Crome cried: "Oh, Hobbema, my dear Hobbema! How I have loved you!"

469 CROMWELL, Oliver (1599–1658) The Parliamentary leader who defeated and finally executed King Charles I in England's Civil War and then ruled as Lord Protector of the Commonwealth until his death, was pressed to drink something, but answered: "It is not my design to drink or to sleep, but my design is to make what haste I can to be gone." Next morning the Protector told his doctors: "You physicians think I shall die. I tell you I shall not die this hour. I am sure on't. I speak the words of truth upon surer grounds than Galen or your Hippocrates furnish you with." Later the same day he told his friends: "Go on cheerfully. Banish sadness altogether and treat my death as no more to you than that of a serving man." Then, just before slipping into a coma, he affirmed: "My own faith is all in God."

470 CROMWELL, Thomas, Earl of Essex (c.1490–1540) The English

statesman, beheaded on order of Henry VIII, prayed: "Lord, into Thy hands I commend my spirit. Lord Jesus, receive my spirit."

471 CROSBY, Frances Jane (Fanny) (1820–1915) The American author, blind from infancy, served as a teacher and administrator at the New York Institute for the Blind before attaining a reputation as a hymn-writer. The night before she died she dictated the last of her approximately 9000 poems: "In the morn of Zion's glory,/ When the clouds have rolled away,/ And my faith has dropped its anchor/ In the vale of perfect day,/ Then, with all the pure and holy,/ I shall strike my harp anew,/ And with power no arm can sever,/ Love will hold me fast and true.

After she retired for the night, her nephew looked in on her and she said: "All right, Governor." A few hours later she arose, collapsed in the hallway in her niece's arms, was carried back to bed, and died a half hour later of a cerebral hemorrhage, with a smile on her lips.

472 CROSBY, Howard (1826–1891) The American Presbyterian minister, educator, and author who served as chancellor of the University of New York affirmed: "I place my hand in the hand of Jesus."

473 CROWFOOT, Joseph (c.1825–1890) Born Sapo Omarxika, the Blackfoot chief, dying after a lingering illness, addressed the leading men of his tribe: "A little while and Crowfoot will be gone from among you. Whither, we cannot tell. From nowhere we come, into nowhere we go. What is life? It is as the flash of a firefly in the night. It is as the breath of a buffalo in winter time. It is as the little shadow that runs along the grass and loses itself in the sunset. I have spoken."

474 CROWLEY, Aleister (1875–

1947) The British cultist, described as a satanist and "the wickedest man alive," died weeping. He moaned: "I am perplexed."

475 CURIE, Marie Skłodowska (1867–1934) Co-discoverer of radium, with her husband Pierre, the Polish-born scientist died of a blood disorder caused by prolonged exposure to the substance with which she had worked so long. When a nurse attempted to give her an injection, Curie objected: "I don't want it. I want to be left alone."

476 CURLEY, James Michael (1874–1958) Former mayor of Boston and governor of Massachusetts, the colorful political boss, wheeled off a hospital elevator after surgery, remarked to his son: "I wish to announce the first plank in my campaign for re-election — we're going to have the floors in this goddamned hospital smoothed out!"

477 CUSHING, Harvey William (1869–1939) The leading brain surgeon of his time, he told his nephew, who was treating him: "Pat, you have the touch. You're a good doctor."

478 CUSHMAN, Charlotte (1816–1876) The American actress, ill with cancer and pneumonia, responded to a nephew who had said, "Come, Auntie, here is your milk punch": "Punch, brothers! Punch with care!"

479 CUSTER, George Armstrong (1839–1876) The military officer, who perished with a command of some 250 men at Little Big Horn, was overheard by his Indian scouts, as they withdrew before the clash with the Sioux, exhorting his men: "Courage, boys! We'll get them! And, as soon as we do, we'll go home to glory!"

480 CUTHBERT (c.634–687) The English monk, missionary, and church leader died while serving as Bishop of Landisfarne. He told his religious: "Although during my life

some have despised me, yet after my death you will see what sort of a man I was and that my doctrine was by no means worthy of contempt."

481 CUVIER, Georges, Baron (1769–1832) The French naturalist whose book, *The Animal Kingdom* was, in its day, considered the highest authority on zoology and who has been called "the father of vertebrate palaeontology" handed back to his sister-in-law the glass of lemonade she had offered him: "It is delightful to me to see those I love still able to swallow."

482 CYPRIAN (c.200–258) Thascius Ciprianus, the Bishop of Carthage, a noted theologian and leader of the early Christian Church, was condemned because he refused to sacrifice to the gods of Rome. He told his executioner: "Hurry up and get it over with."

483 CYRUS THE GREAT (c.600 B.C.–529 B.C.) The founder of the Persian empire, who styled himself "King of the World," was mortally wounded fighting the Scythians, and exhorted his sons and his comrades: "Remember my last saying: show kindness to your friends, and then you shall have it in your power to chastise your enemies. Goodbye, my dear sons, bid your mother goodbye for me. And all my friends, who are here or far away, goodbye."

484 CZOLGOSZ, Leon (1873–1901) The anarchist who murdered President McKinley at a reception in Buffalo, New York, was electrocuted six weeks after the president's death, after an eight hour trial in a verdict that was not appealed. As he was strapped into the chair he declared: "I killed the President because he was the enemy of the good people, the good working people. I am not sorry for my crime."

485 DALBERG, Karl Theodor

Anton Maria von (1744–1817) Archbishop-Elector of Mainz and Grand Duke of Frankfurt, he was renowned as a patron of the arts. Dying, he murmured: "Love ... life ... God's will...."

DAMIEN, Father *see* DE-VEUSTER, Damien

486 DAMROSCH, Walter Johannes (1862–1950) The composer and conductor was in late years deprived of his mental faculties. Imagining that he was still on tour, he told a former colleague who came to visit: "Just back from Japan. They loved us in Tokyo. Rave reviews everywhere! Marvelous! Marvelous!"

487 DANCOURT, Florent Carton (1661–1725) The French playwright kept reproaching himself for the sins of his early life. When his daughter told him, "Father, a man who dies well is half saved," he answered: "May God's will be done. My grave is dug. My last bed is made. You have to lie on the bed you have made."

488 D'ANNUNZIO, Gabriele (1863–1938) The Italian poet and politican was talking about a trip he planned to make to Rome and commented: "I want to see again in springtime the city that I love. I have been thinking about this trip with joy and with trembling." He retired to rest and was found shortly afterwards dead in bed.

489 DANTE Alighieri (1265–1321) The Italian poet and philosopher, best known for his *Divine Comedy*, exiled from his native Florence, died at the court of Guido of Polenta in Ravenna. Replying to a request for political advice, Dante said: "You ask too much of me. Dedicate your strength and your spirit to your prince and your country, and leave to God the mysterious balance of fortune. Every banner that is not borne by a traitor leads to virtue."

490 DANTON, Georges-Jacques (1759–1794) The French revolutionary leader was arrested by his former friend Robespierre on charges of disloyalty, and beheaded. He told his executioners: "Above all, don't forget to show my head to the people. It's well worth having a look at!"

491 DARWIN, Charles (1809–1882) The English naturalist, author of *The Origin of Species* and *The Descent of Man*, commented: "I am not the least afraid to die. I am only sorry that I haven't the strength to go on with my research."

492 DAVID, King of Israel (c.1040 B.C.–970 B.C.) The former shepherd who made Israel the leading power in the Middle East advised his son and successor Solomon to reward his supporters and kill his enemies. He spoke of Shimei, who had supported David's son Absalom in his rebellion against his father. After Absalom's defeat and death, Shimei begged David's forgiveness and the king promised not to kill him. However, he told Solomon: "Hold him not guiltless, for you are a wise man. You will know what you ought to do to him, and you shall bring his gray head down with blood to Sheol."

493 DAVID, Jacques-Louis (1748–1825) The French painter was indicating corrections to be made on a copy of his "Leonidas at Thermopylae": "Too dark ... too light.... The dimming of the light is not well enough indicated.... This place is blurred.... However, I must admit, that's a unique head of Leonidas...." Then he dropped dead.

494 DAVIS, Cushman Kellogg (1838–1900) The influential Republican senator from Minnesota exclaimed: "Oh, that I might live five more years for my country's sake!"

495 DAVIS, David (1815–1886) The longtime friend and advisor of

Lincoln was serving as associate justice of the U.S. Supreme Court when he succumbed to diabetes, calling out the childhood name of his son George: "Geordie!"

496 DAVIS, Jefferson Finis (1808–1889) The former president of the Confederate States of America refused medication: "Pray excuse me, I cannot take it."

497 DAVIS, Bette (Ruth Elizabeth) (1908–1989) The American actress, dying in Paris, spoke of her estranged daughter: "Tell B.D. I'm sorry. I loved her. I really did love her."

498 DAVIS, Sammy, Jr. (1925–1990) According to a tabloid, the American entertainer told his son: "Don't cry for me. I'll be dancing in heaven."

499 DAVIS, Varina Anne Banks Howell (1826–1906) The First Lady of the Confederacy spent her final years in New York City, writing a column for the New York *World* under the name "V. Jefferson-Davis." On her deathbed she told her daughter Margaret, her oldest child and the only one of her six to survive her: "My darling child, I am going to die this time, but I'll try to be brave about it. Don't wear black. It is bad for your health and it will depress your husband." Just before the end, she repeated the closing words of the liturgical prayer "Te Deum Laudamus": "O Lord, in Thee have I trusted. Let me never be confounded."

500 DAVY, Sir Humphrey (1778–1829) The British chemist told his servants: "I am dying, and when it is all over I desire that no disturbance of any kind be made in the house. Lock the door and let everyone retire quietly to his apartment."

501 DAY, Dorothy (1897–1980) A founder of the Catholic Workers Movement and a passionate advocate of social justice, she took her daughter's hand and, a few minutes before she died, observed: "How good life can be at certain moments."

502 DAYAN, Moshe (1915–1981) The Israeli soldier and statesman was annoyed when his daughter told him, "Just be strong," and that he would "be all right." He answered: "You are such an idiot! Philosophy shit! Thank God I'm leaving this place!"

503 DECATUR, Stephen (1779–1820) The American naval officer, celebrated for his exploits in the Barbary Wars and the War of 1812 was serving as U.S. naval commissioner when he was mortally wounded in a duel with another naval officer at Bladensburg, Maryland. Dying at his home in Washington, he said: "I did not believe it possible to endure so much pain. I am a dying man. I do not so much regret my death as I deplore the manner of it. Had it found me on the quarter deck it would have been welcome."

504 DECIUS, Emperor of Rome (c.195–251) Ruler of the Roman Empire for two years, the military leader is best remembered as a persecutor of Christians. He died fighting the Ostrogoths in the swamps where the Danube empties into the Black Sea. After seeing his son felled by a javelin, Decius shouted: "The loss of one soldier is not important to the Roman state. Let no man mourn the emperor's son!" A few minutes later the emperor himself was killed.

505 DEFOE, Daniel (1660–1731) The English author who wrote *Robinson Crusoe* reflected: "I do not know which is more difficult in a Christian life, to live well or to die well."

506 DE GAULLE, Charles (1890–1970) The French statesman, shortly after leaving the presidency, suffered a heart attack and cried out to his wife: "Yvonne, I hurt on my right side! Call a doctor! Oh, how it hurts!"

507 DELACROIX, Eugène (1799–1863) The French romantic painter insisted: "Oh, if I get well, I will do wonderful things! My mind is bubbling with ideas!"

508 DELAHANTY, Edward Joseph (1867–1903) The star outfielder for the Washington Senators baseball team was put off a train because of disorderly conduct. Shortly afterwards a railroad watchman found him standing on a bridge, looking over the side at the water. When he shone a light on him, the ballplayer said threateningly: "Take that light away or I'll knock your damned brains out!" Later, the watchman thought he heard someone call for help from the water below. Delahanty was found drowned several days later.

509 DELANE, John Thadeus (1817–1879) The editor of *The Times of London*, dying after a lingering illness, commented: "It is better for me to die than to live."

510 DE MILLE, Cecil Blount (1881–1959) The night before he died, the movie producer penned his last thoughts: "'The Lord giveth and the Lord taketh away. Blessed be the Name of the Lord.' It can only be a short time until those words, the first in the Episcopal funeral services, are spoken over me. After those words are spoken, what am I? I am only what I have accomplished. How much good have I spread? How much evil have I spread? For whatever I am a moment after death—a spirit, a soul, a bodiless mind—I shall have to look back and forward, for I have to take both with me."

511 DE MOLAY, Jacques (1243–1314) Grand Master of the Knights Templar, a mediaeval crusading order, he was burnt at the stake by Philip IV of France after Pope Clement V denounced and disbanded the Knights. His prophecies were, incidentally, fulfilled. He declared: "We die innocent. The decree which condemns us is an unjust decree, but in heaven there is an august tribunal to which the weak never appeal in vain. To that tribunal I summon the Roman Pontiff within forty days. Oh, Philip, I pardon thee in vain, for thy life is condemned. At the tribunal of God, within a year, I await thee."

512 DE MORNAY, Philippe (1549–1623) The French Protestant leader, called "The Huguenot Pope" cried: "I am flying! I am flying! I am flying to heaven! Let angels bear me to the Saviour's bosom! I know that my Redeemer lives! With these eyes I shall see Him! With these eyes! With these eyes!"

513 DEMOSTHENES (c.384 B.C.–322 B.C.) The Athenian statesman and orator took poison rather than submit to arrest by Archias, an officer of the army of the Macedonians, who had overrun his city-state. To Archias, who was a former actor and who had defiled the temple of Poseidon, where the orator had sought sanctuary, Demosthenes said: "Now you can play the part of Creon in the tragedy as soon as you like and cast forth my body unburied. But I, gracious Poseidon, quit thy temple while I yet live. Antipater and his Macedonians have done what they could to pollute it."

514 DE PORRES, Martin (1579–1639) A Peruvian lay brother in the Dominican Order, he was known for his mystical gifts. When his prior, who had come to see him, asked why he had made the Viceroy wait, Martin, who had been in ecstasy, replied: "Near that altar there was the Most Holy Virgin Mary, my patron and advocate, and my father Saint Dominic, with St. Vincent Ferrer and many other saints and angels, and I was so occupied with those holy visitors that I could not receive any others at that moment."

When, after the administration of the last rites, he was urged, in his agony, to invoke St. Dominic, he answered: "It would be useless to ask him to come. He is aleady here with St. Vincent Ferrer." Martin soon lost the power of speech. The community recited the prayers for the dying, then chanted the Salve Regina. Then, as the prior intoned the Credo, with the community responding in unison, Martin died, "without a tremor, without a sound," seeming only to fall asleep.

515 DE QUINCEY, Thomas (1785-1859) The British writer, author of *Confessions of an English Opium-Eater,* murmured: "Sister ... sister ... sister...."

516 DE RESZKE, Jean (1850-1925) The Polish operatic tenor died in retirement in Paris. Suffering from pneumonia, he told his wife: "Let me lie quietly. I am very tired." Then, in delirium, he sang passages from his favorite opera, *Tristan.* Finally, he sang a chromatic scale. He died several days later without speaking or singing again.

517 DESCARTES, René (1596-1650) The French philosopher died in Stockholm, Sweden. Two days before the end he remarked: "Soul, thou hast long been held captive. The hour has now come for thee to quit thy prison, to leave the trammels of this body. Suffer, then, this separation with joy and courage." After lying quietly for two days, the philosopher asked his valet to help him to an armchair by the fire. There he fainted. Revived, he declared: "Ah, my dear Schluter, this is the fatal stroke! I must leave now." Carried to bed, he lost the power of speech and died a few hours later.

518 DE SMET, Pierre-Jean (1801-1873) The Beglian missionary to the Flathead and Blackfoot tribes in the American Northwest, he was wasted by a long illness and commented on how his clothing no longer fit him. When reminded, "You forget how fat you used to be," he answered: "Too fat for comfort. It's better to be thin." A little later, when a lay brother was attending him, the dying priest declared: "I am a lazy old fool after all!"

519 DESMOULINS, Lucie-Simplice-Camille-Benoist de (1760-1794) The French journalist was beheaded for criticizing the revolutionary leader Robespierre. On the scaffold he shouted: "I am the first apostle of liberty! Do not let them murder me! Help!"

520 DE STAËL—HOLSTEIN, Anne-Louise-Germaine Necker, Baroness (1766-1817) The French author, paralyzed by a stroke, requested opium to help her sleep. After being administered a generous dose, she was asked, "Will you sleep now?" and replied: "I'll sleep as soundly as any old peasant woman." She never awoke.

521 DE VEUSTER, Damien (1840-1889) The Belgian priest, who devoted many years to a ministry at the leper colony on the Hawaiian island of Molokai, eventually became afflicted with leprosy himself. Shortly before he died he reflected: 'Well, God's will be done. My work, with all its faults and failures, is in His hands, and before Easter I shall see my Saviour."

522 DEWEY, George (1837-1917) Hero of the Battle of Manila in the Spanish-American War, the American admiral murmured: "The battle is done. The victory is ours."

523 DIAGHILEV, Sergei Pavlovich (1872-1929) The Russian ballet producer, ill with diabetes, whispered to a friend: "Catherine, how beautiful you are! I am happy to see you. How sick I am! I am very, very sick ... I feel as if I were drunk."

524 DICKENS, Charles (1812-1870) The English novelist suffered a stroke at the dinner table. Asked if he wanted to lie down, he answered: "Yes, on the ground." He became unconscious immediately and died a few hours later.

525 DICKINSON, EMILY (1830–1886) The eccentric and reclusive poet died of a stroke and kidney disease in her Massachusetts home. Her mind wandered to her childhood, to her mother, who used to call her indoors for the reason: "It's already growing damp." The last time Dickinson spoke, she said: "I must go in, for the fog is rising."

526 DIDEROT, Denis (1713–1784) The French philosopher, renowned for his editorship of the celebrated *Encyclopedia*, was warned by his wife not to eat the apricot he had in hand. Diderot protested: "But, what the devil is it going to do to me?" He ate the fruit, had a heart attack, and dropped dead.

527 DIETRICH, Marlene (1901–1992) Shortly before the end, the entertainer confided: "I lost my faith in the war and can't believe they are all up there, flying around or sitting at tables, all those I've lost. All, all, all. I suppose I'm jealous I can't believe, but I can't. If it were true, Rudi [her husband] would be there and would give me a message." Just before she breathed her last, Dietrich whispered her daughter's name: "Maria."

528 DIGBY, Sir Everard (1578–1606) The English landowner was hanged, drawn, and quartered for his part in a plot to blow up the Parliament building and overthrow King James I. When the executioner cut out his heart and cried, "Here is the heart of a traitor," the dying man retorted: "Thou liest!"

529 DIOGENES (413 B.C.–323 B.C.) The Greek philosopher, who spent much of his life in pursuit of the "Honest Man," wanted to be placed in an open field after his death. When his disciples objected that birds would eat his remains, he argued: "If that is the case, it is no matter whether they eat me or not, seeing that I shall be insensible to it."

530 DISNEY, Walter Elias (1901–1966) The movie producer, ill with lung cancer, requested: "Raise my bed, so I can look out the window and see my studio."

531 DISRAELI, Benjamin, Earl of Beaconsfield (1804–1881) The British statesman, who twice served as prime minister, declared: "I had rather live, but I am not afraid to die." He then lifted himself from his pillow, leaning forward as if he were about to speak. His lips moved silently and he sank back. Ten minutes later he died.

532 DIX, Dorothea Lynde (1802–1887) The American reformer, who worked for the improvement of conditions in prisons and mental hospitals, told her doctor: "Don't give me anything. None of those anodynes to dull the senses or relieve pain. I want to feel it all. And—please tell me when the time is near. I want to know."

533 DIXON, Henry Hall (1822–1870) The English novelist and sportswriter who used the penname "The Druid" remarked when told that he was dying: "Oh, God, I thank Thee! I could not bear much more!"

534 DODGE, Grace Hoadley (1856–1914) The American social welfare worker, educator, and philanthropist who served as president of the National Board of the YWCA regretted her inability to see her guests: "And were they happy?"

535 DODSON, Charles Lutwigg (1832–1898) The English mathematician, who wrote *Alice in Wonderland* and *Through the Looking-Glass* under the penname of Lewis Carroll, died of pneumonia, insisting: "Take away the pillows. I shall need them no longer."

536 DOLET, Étienne (1509–1546) The French scholar and printer was hanged for disseminating atheistic materials. On the gallows he punned: "This is not doleful for Dolet, but it means dole for the good people."

537 DOLFUSS, Engelbert (1892–1934) The Austrian chancellor told the policemen who assisted him after he was mortally wounded by Nazi gunmen: "Children, you are so good to me. Why aren't the others like you? I only wanted peace. We never attacked, we only had to defend ourselves. May the Lord forgive them. Give my regards to my wife and children."

538 DOMINIC de Guzmán (1170–1221) The Spanish friar who founded the Order of Preachers told his disciples: "Do not weep. I may be more useful to you where I am going than I could be here." Then he prayed: "Come to my aid, saints of God, and bear my soul into the presence of the Most High."

539 DOMITIAN, Emperor of Rome (51–96) The unpopular emperor perished in a palace coup, just after telling an aide: "Hand me the dagger under my pillow, and call the servants!"

540 DONIZETTI, Gaetano (1797–1848) The Italian composer who wrote nearly 70 operas, died a lingering death from syphilis. During one of his last lucid intervals, he spoke of his dead wife: "I shall be miserable until she intercedes with God for my death and our eternal reunion." In the last days before he lost the power of speech, he told a visitor: "Donizetti ... Donizetti.... Don't you know that poor Donizetti is dead?"

541 DONN-BYRNE, Brian Oswald (1889–1928) The novelist and journalist died in an auto crash near his home at Coolmain Castle in County Cork, Ireland, after announcing: "I think I'll go for a drive before dinner. Anyone come along?"

542 DONNE, John (1573–1631) The English poet and clergyman died after a lengthy illness. According to his earliest biographer, "In the last hour of his last day, as his body melted away into spirit, his soul having, I verily believe, some revelation of the Beatific Vision," Donne said: "I were miserable if I might not die." Later, "he closed many periods of his faint breath by saying": "Thy kingdom come, Thy will be done." He died quietly, apparently caught up in a vision of heaven.

543 DOOLEY, Thomas Anthony (1927–1961) The American medical missionary and author spoke of the birthday cake brought into his room in the hospital in New York, where he was being treated for cancer: "I'll have a piece of that in about two hours."

544 DORSEY, Thomas Francis (1905–1956) The American bandleader wrote a note to his estranged wife: "Dear Janie, Thank you for the dinner. It was wonderful and be sure to thank your mom. I'm leaving early in the morning. Kiss Susie for me before she leaves for school." Just before retiring for the night, he told a friend: "I plan to sleep late." Next morning he was discovered dead in bed.

545 DOS PASSOS, John (1896–1970) The American author told his wife: "I think I'd like to read the paper now." She went out to get the paper and found him unconscious when she returned.

546 DOSTOEVSKY, Feodor Mikhailovich (1821–1881) The Russian novelist, dying of emphysema, said to his wife: "My poor darling, my dearest ... what am I leaving you with? My poor girl, how hard it will be for you to live!" A little later he gasped, repeatedly: "Call the children." Then, after giving his New Testament to his son, he peacefully died.

547 DOUGLAS, ALFRED

BRUCE, Lord (1870–1945) The English poet loved horse-racing, and just before he died he asked his friend to place a bet for him with the bookmaker: "Mixed bark doubles — Nicholson's mounts."

548 DOUGLAS, Sir James (c.1286–1330) Known as "Black Douglas," the Scots nobleman and military leader was one of the heroes of the Battle of Bannockburn, in which his country won her independence from England. He died fighting for the King of Castile and Leon, against the Moslems of Spain. Greatly outnumbered, he rode into the enemy lines shouting: "A Douglas! A Douglas! I follow or die!"

549 DOUGLAS, Stephen Arnold (1813–1861) When his physician asked why all the windows were open in his bedroom, the Illinois senator answered: "So that we can have fresh air." When the doctor remarked to Mrs. Douglas, who sat holding her husband's hand, "I'm afraid he does not lie comfortably," the statesman whispered brokenly: "He is very comfortable." He never spoke again.

Four hours later, when his wife asked, "Do you know me? Will you kiss me?" the senator opened his eyes, smiled, and moved his lips as if he were trying to comply with her request. An hour later he died. The *New York Herald* reported, "His death was calm and peaceful; a few faint breaths . . . , a slight rattling of the throat; a short, quick, convulsive shudder, and Stephen A. Douglas passed into eternity."

550 DOUGLASS, Frederick (1818–1895) The abolitionist, editor, and diplomat died at Cedar Hill, his estate across from Washington, D.C. He was entertaining his wife by imitating a speaker at a meeting from which he had just returned, when he gasped: "What's that?" Then he fell dead.

551 DOWSON, Ernest (1867–1900) The poet, short-story writer, and translator said to his nurse: "You are like an angel from heaven. God bless you."

DOYLE, Sir Arthur Conan *see* CONAN DOYLE, Sir Arthur

552 DRAKE, Sir Francis (c.1540–1596) The English sea captain and explorer died of dysentery on shipboard while on an expedition to the Caribbean. In delirium, he demanded of an aide: "Help me dress and buckle on my armor, that I might die like a soldier!"

553 DREISER, Theodore (1871–1945) The American novelist told his wife: "You are beautiful."

554 DREW, Samuel (1765–1833) The English philosopher, told that he would be with the Lord Jesus that very day, responded: "Yes, my good sir, I trust I shall."

555 DREXEL, Katharine (1858–1955) The American nun and philanthropist who founded the Sisters of the Blessed Sacrament for Indians and Colored People, as well as 145 missions, 12 schools for Indians and 50 for blacks, including Xavier University in New Orleans, and gave away 20 million dollars of her personal fortune to various charities, said to the priest who came to administer the last rites: "You've come early."

556 DRUMMOND, Henry (1851–1897) The Scots evangelist and educator, who tried to reconcile the theory of evolution with Christian belief, died of cancer. He recited a portion of his favorite hymn to a friend: "I'm not ashamed to own my Lord/ Or to defend His cause,/ Maintain the glory of His cross,/ And honor all His laws." Then he added: "There's nothing to beat that, Hugh."

557 DU BARRY, Jeanne Bécu, Comtesse (1743–1793) Mistress of King Louis XV, she survived him by nearly two decades, to die on the scaffold during the Reign of Terror. She pleaded with the executioner: "Give me just a few minutes more!" When he threw her onto the block, she screamed: "You're going to hurt me! Oh, please don't hurt me!"

558 DU BOIS, William Edward Burghardt (1868–1963) The American civil rights leader, who helped to organize the NAACP, embraced communism late in life and moved to Ghana, where he died. He told his wife: "Now sit here beside me. Rest your little self. Don't bother with supper or anything else. Just stay here with me." A few minutes later he whispered her name: "Shirley."

559 DU BOS, Jean-Baptiste (1670–1742) The French historian declared: "Death is a law and not a punishment. Three things ought to console us for giving up life: the friends whom we have lost, the few persons worthy of being loved whom we leave behind us, and, finally, the memory of our stupidities and the assurance that they are now going to stop."

560 DUCOS, Jean-François (1765–1793) A leader of the Girondist faction in the French Revolution, he was guillotined during the Reign of Terror. He joked on the scaffold: "The Convention has forgotten one decree: a decree on the indivisibility of heads and bodies."

561 DU GUESCLIN, Bertrand (c.1320–1380) The French military leader, who held the title Constable of France, told those gathered at his bedside: "Remember that your business is only with those who carry arms. The churchmen, the poor, the women and children are not your enemies ... I commend to the king my wife ... my brother.... Farewell, I am at an end."

562 DUKE, James Buchanan (1857–1925) The American industrialist and philanthropist, who built a

fortune through the manufacture of tobacco products, and who endowed the university in North Carolina that bears his name, remarked to his lawyer from his hospital bed a few days before he died: "I have not provided sufficient funds for carrying out the complete plans I have in mind for the university. I want to arrange to give an additional seven million to complete the building program."

563 DULLES, John Foster (1888–1959) U.S. secretary of state under Eisenhower, he remarked to a friend a few days before he died: "Bill, just remember this. If the United States is willing to go to war over Berlin, there won't be war over Berlin." He never spoke again.

564 DUMAS, Alexandre, fils (1824–1895) The novelist and playwright, best remembered for his novel *Camille*, was ill with a brain tumor when he told his daughters: "Go and have lunch and leave me to get some rest." When they returned, he was unconscious.

565 DUMAS, Alexandre, père (1802–1870) The French writer, author of *The Count of Monte Cristo* and *The Three Musketeers*, suffering from the effects of a stroke, showed his son two coins and said: "Alexandre, everybody has said that I was prodigal. You yourself wrote a play about it. And so, do you see how you were mistaken? When I first landed in Paris, I had two 'louis' in my pocket. Look! I still have them."

566 DUMAS, Thomas Alexandre (1762–1806) One of Napoleon's generals, he was a black Haitian and the father of Alexandre Dumas, père. Dying, the general raged: "Oh, must a general who, when he was no more than thirty-five, had already been commander-in-chief of three armies, die at forty, like a coward, in his bed? Oh, my God, my God, what have I done that You should condemn me so young to leave my wife and children?"

567 DUNANT, Jean-Henri (1828–1910) The Swiss philanthropist who founded the Red Cross wrote his executor a testament just before his death: "I wish to be carried to my grave like a dog, without a single one of your ceremonies, which I do not recognize. I trust to your goodness to respect my last earthly request. I count upon your friendship that it shall be so. Amen. I am a disciple of Christ as in the first century and nothing more."

568 DUNBAR, Paul Laurence (1872–1906) The American poet famed for his verse in Negro dialect died of tuberculosis, murmuring a portion of Psalm 23: "Through the valley of the shadow."

569 DUNCAN, Isadora (1878–1927) The American dancer, who lived in France, said to her friends as she stepped into a chauffeured car: "Farewell, my friends, I go to glory." As the car pulled away, Duncan's head suddenly slumped against the rim of the door. The chauffeur, sensing that something was wrong, got out and found that Duncan's long scarf, hanging outside the door, had caught in the spokes of the wheel and broken her neck when the vehicle began to move.

570 DUNCAN, Joseph (1794–1844) Congressman and then governor of Illinois, he supported the interests of frontiersmen. Asked on his deathbed if Christ was precious to him, he answered: "Ever precious. Ever precious."

571 DUPONT, Alfred Irenée (1864–1935) The American industrialist said: "I thank you, doctors. I thank you, nurses. I'll be all right in a few days."

572 DUSE, Eleanora (1859–1924) The Italian actress died of pneumonia while performing in Pittsburgh. Horrified at the possibility of dying in so horrid a place as Pittsburgh, she insisted: "At dawn we must leave.... Hurry, we must leave!"

573 DUVEEN, Joseph, Baron (1869–1939) The British art dealer died of cancer, after a five year illness, during which the doctors warned him several times that he had but months to live. Just before he finally succumbed, he told his nurse: "Well, I fooled them for five years!"

574 DWIGHT, Timothy (1752–1819) President of Yale, the clergyman, poet, and theologian, dying of cancer, commented on the eighth chapter of Saint John, which had just been read to him: "What triumphant truths!"

575 EADS, James Buchanan (1820–1887) The American engineer and inventor died while working on a plan to construct a canal across the isthmus of Tehuantepec in Mexico, lamenting: "I cannot die. I have not finished my work."

576 EAGELS, Jeanne (1890–1929) The American actress died of a drug overdose in New York. As friends were taking her to a hospital, she said: "I'm going to Dr. Caldwell's for one of my regular treatments."

577 EARLY, Jubal Anderson (1816–1894) The Confederate general said to a friend: "I want to tell you goodbye, Major. Don't leave the room. I want to talk to you about certain arrangements." He was then seized with such pain that he could not speak.

578 EARP, Baxter Warren (1855–1900) The gunfighter came to an inglorious end in a barroom, after he shouted a drunken challenge: "Johnny, go get your gun this time! We're going to shoot it out!"

579 EARP, Celia Ann Blaylock ("Mattie") (1850–1888) Wife of gunfighter Wyatt Earp, she died after mixing liquor and laudanum. To the friend who brought her the drugs, she said: "I think I can sleep."

580 EARP, Morgan S. (1851-1882) The gunfighter, shot through the spine while he played billiards in Tombstone, Arizona, summoned his brother Wyatt. Some years before, the brothers had made an agreement that the first to die was to relate to the other whether he had any visions of the world to come. Wyatt had always been skeptical of deathbed visions. Asking Wyatt to bend down close to him, he declared: "I guess you were right, Wyatt. I can't see a damned thing." After a few minutes he said: "Take care of yourself Wyatt. They got me, Wyatt. Don't let them get you. Tell Ma and Pa goodbye. I expect to meet you in heaven." Then, according to a sister-in-law, he "drew a deep, ragged breath and never breathed again."

581 EARP, Wyatt Berry Stapp (1848-1929) The gunfighter died of a prostate condition in a Los Angeles motel. He said to his wife and a friend: "What are you two coyotes cooking up?" Later he called for: "Water!" Shortly afterwards, in the words of his widow, he died "peacefully, without a struggle, like a baby going to sleep."

582 EATON, Margaret O'Neale Timberlake (Peggy) (1799-1879) A Washington tavern-keeper of questionable reputation, her marriage to Secretary of War John Henry Eaton caused a major scandal in the Jackson Administration. Dying in Washington many years later, she declared: "I am not in the least afraid to die, but this is such a beautiful world to leave." Then, quoting her favorite hymn, she recited: "I would not live alway, I ask not to stay/ Where storm after storm rises dark o'er the way;/ The few lurid mornings that dawn on us here/ Are enough of life's woes, full enough of its cheer."

583 EDDY, Mary Baker (1821-1910) Unable to speak, the founder of the Christian Science religion scrawled on a piece of paper: "God is my life."

584 EDDY, Nelson (1901-1967) The American baritone celebrated for his performances in movies and on radio and television, was singing in a nightclub when he suddenly stopped and dropped dead after telling his audience: "Something has happened. I'm so dry."

585 EDGEWORTH, Richard Lovell (1744-1817) The British author and inventor declared: "I die with the soft feeling of gratitude to my friends and submission to the God who made me."

586 EDISON, Thomas Alva (1847-1931) The inventor, dying at his mansion in West Orange, New Jersey, was asked if he had thought of the life to come. He replied: "It doesn't matter. No one knows." Asked if he were suffering, he responded: "No. Just waiting." Later, emerging from a coma, he told his wife, referring to no one knew just what—possibly to the other world, possibly to the autumn foliage: "It's very beautiful over there."

587 EDWARD I, King of England (1239-1307) The mediaeval king who conquered the Welsh and strengthened the power of Parliament at the expense of the feudal nobles, died fighting the Scots. He instructed his officers: "Wrap my bones in a hammock and have them carried before the army, so that I may still lead the way to victory."

588 EDWARD III, King of England (1312-1377) The monarch who began the Hundred Years' War with France reigned 50 years. Deserted, in his last illness, by his courtiers and by his mistress, he was left alone with a single priest, who told him, "You have grievously sinned against God, and you need to ask his mercy." The dying king whispered, in Latin: "Jesus, have mercy." When asked if he forgave his enemies, Edward extended his hand.

Then when the priest held out the cross, Edward pressed it to his lips and died.

589 EDWARD VI, King of England (1537–1553) England's first Protestant king, under whom the Reformation began in earnest in his country, died at 15, of a lingering illness which turned his skin black and caused his extremities to rot. Edward prayed: "Lord, deliver me from this miserable and wretched life and take me among Thy chosen. Howbeit, not my will, but Thy will be done. I commit my spirit to Thee. Yet, for Thy chosen's sake, send me life and health, that I may truly serve Thee. O Lord God, bless Thy people and save Thine inheritance. O my Lord God, defend this realm from papistry and maintain Thy true religion, that I and my people may praise Thy holy name, for Thy son Jesus Christ's sake. Amen."

To one of his physicians, Edward said: "I had not perceived thee so nigh. I had thought thee further off." When his lips moved and he was asked what he wanted, Edward replied: "I was praying to God." Seized with convulsions, the king cried: "Lord, have mercy! Take my spirit!"

590 EDWARD VII, King of Great Britain (1841–1910) The monarch, whose love of women, food, races, and other material pleasures came to symbolize the period sometimes called "La Belle Epoche," collapsed while playing with his canaries. As he sat slumped in an armchair, his son told him that one of his horses had won the Spring Two Year Old Plate by half a length. He responded: "I am very glad."

591 EDWARD VIII, King of Great Britain (1894–1972) Forced to abdicate because of his determination to marry divorcée, he died in France as Duke of Windsor, mumbling: "Mama, Mama, Mama, Mama."

592 EDWARD the Confessor, King of England (1002–1066) The Saxon ruler, renowned for his great piety, lectured his courtiers: "Dear loyal friends, it is a folly to lament my death. When God wills it, one cannot remain. Weep not, dear ones, grieve not for my death, since after this my death, I shall arrive at the sure port where I shall live with my Lord, always in joy and happiness. Now I pray all who are here, my loyal people and friends, bear loyal company to the queen, who is my wife, whose virtues I cannot number, and who has been to me a sister and dear. She has been my daughter and my wife, and of very precious life. Honor her as befits so good and exalted a matron. Let her have her dowry in full, and her manors and her people, be they English, be they Norman, honor them all their life. In the Church of Saint Peter, to whom of old I made my vow, let me be buried. To him I give myself, both living and dead, who was to me both aid and comfort."

593 EDWARD THE MARTYR, King of England (964–979) The Saxon king was hacked to death in a coup, crying: "Jesus!"

594 EDWARD, Prince of Wales (1330–1376) Known as the "Black Prince," the son of Edward III was hero of the battles of Crecy and Poitiers in the Hundred Years' War. He never lived to succeed his father to the throne. Dying after a long illness, he prayed: "I thank Thee, O Lord, for all Thy benefits. With all my power I ask for Thy mercy, for Thou wilt forgive me for all the sins that I, in my wrong-doing, have committed against Thee. And I ask with my whole heart the grace of pardon from all men whom I have knowingly or unwittingly wronged."

595 EDWARD, Duke of Kent (1767–1820) Fourth son of King George III and father of the future

Queen Victoria, he died of pneumonia, whispering to his wife: "Do not forget me."

596 EDWARDS, Jonathan (1703–1758) The American philosopher, Congregational minister, and theologian died shortly after taking office as president of the College of New Jersey (now Princeton), after a smallpox inoculation. To his family, who feared that his death, coming so soon after his installation, would be seen as a reflection of God's displeasure, Edwards said: "Trust in God and ye need not fear."

597 EICHMANN, Adolf (1906–1962) The German official, who once boasted that he would step into eternity proud of his role in the liquidation of five million Jews, was captured in Argentina by Israeli agents and, after a trial, hanged in Jerusalem. Asked if he had any last words, he declared: "My belief was correct. After a short time, gentlemen, we shall all meet again. So is the fate of all men. I have lived believing in God and I die believing in God. Long live Germany! Long live Argentina! These are the countries with which I have been most closely associated and I shall not forget them. I greet my wife and my friends. I had to obey the rules of war and my flag. I am ready."

598 EINSTEIN, Albert (1879–1955) The physicist celebrated for his Theory of Relativity declined risky heart surgery, insisting, a few days before his death: "I want to go when I want. It is tasteless to prolong life artificially. I have done my share. It is time to go. I will do it elegantly." The night before he died, he told his son: "If only I had more mathematics!" As the son left the hospital room, he told his father to get some sleep. Einstein smiled and said: "Your presence won't stop me from going to sleep." A few hours later his nurse heard him murmur something she could not understand and went to fetch a doctor. When they returned, Einstein was dead.

599 EISENHOWER, Dwight David (1890–1969) The supreme commander of the Allied Expeditionary Forces in Europe in World War II served two terms as president. Dying in Walter Reed Army Medical Center, he commanded: "Lower the shades! Pull me up! Two big men! Higher!" Then he prayed: "I want to go. God, take me."

600 ELDON, John Scott, First Earl of (1751–1838) Lord Chancellor of England for more than 20 years, when told that it was cold outside he said: "It matters not to me, where I am going, whether the weather here be hot or cold."

601 ELIJAH of Tishbe (d. c.850 B.C.) When the Hebrew prophet announced his imminent departure from the world to his disciple Elisha, the younger man asked him for "a double share of your spirit," to which Elijah responded: "You have asked a hard thing; yet, if you see me as I am being taken from you, it shall be so for you; but if you do not see me, it shall not be so." A few minutes later "a chariot of fire and horses of fire" separated the two prophets as Elijah mounted heavenward "in a whirlwind."

602 ELIOT, Charles William (1834–1927) President of Harvard for 40 years and author of numerous books on education declared: "I see Mother."

603 ELIOT, George (1819–1880) The English novelist, whose real name was Mary Ann Evans, died suddenly, telling her American banker husband: "Tell them that I have a great pain on the left side."

604 ELIOT, John (1604–1690) The Puritan minister who translated the Bible into Mohican, converted over 3000 Indians to the Christian faith, trained a number of native preachers, and was known as "The Apostle to the Indians of North America," exclaimed: "Welcome, joy!"

605 ELIOT, Thomas Stearns (1888–1965) The poet, playwright, and essayist, a native of St. Louis, lived most of his life in England, where he died, his wife's name on his lips: "Valerie."

606 ELISABETH, Empress Consort of Francis Joseph of Austria-Hungary (1837–1898) The eccentric empress was stabbed by an anarchist in Geneva, Switzerland. Believing that she had only been punched, she boarded a boat on Lake Geneva, where she collapsed. Revived momentarily, she asked: "Thank you. Whatever happened to me?" It was then that it was noticed that she had been stabbed. She was rushed to a nearby hotel, where she died.

607 ÉLISABETH of France (1764–1794) Madame Élisabeth, sister of the murdered Louis XVI of France, she was on the scaffold when the executioner's assistant noticed the outline of a religious medal beneath the cape that covered her shoulders. He ripped off the garment in order to seize the medallion, prompting the outraged princess to protest: "Sir, in the name of your mother, cover me!"

608 ELISABETH, Queen Consort of Carol I of Romania (1843–1916) The queen was famous for her poetry, written under the pseudonym "Carmen Sylva." Dying of pneumonia, she told her daughter-in-law, Queen Marie: "You're supposed to say beautiful things, and you can't." She complained to her doctors: "Stop giving me injections! Let me go!"

609 ELISABETH Christine of Brunswick-Wolfenbüttel, Queen Consort of Frederick II of Prussia (1715–1797) The widow of Frederick the

Great told those around her bedside: "I know you will not forget me."

610 ELISABETH Kaahumanu, Queen Regent of Hawaii (1770–1832) The monarch, who introduced Christianity and western culture to her islands, died after a long and painful illness. She murmured: "The way that I am going — the habitation is prepared — send the thoughts thither with joyfulness." After a severe paroxysm of pain, her pastor suggested, "Elisabeta, this is perhaps your departure. We think the Lord will soon take you from us." The queen responded: "I will go to Him and shall be comforted." Then she sang a few words from a Hawaiian hymn: "Lo, here I am, O Jesus,/ Grant me Thy gracious smile."

Kaahumanu looked up and asked: "Is this Bingham?" When the American missionary who functioned as her spiritual director answered in the affirmative, the queen whispered: "I am going now." Then, without speaking again, she died ten or fifteen minutes later.

611 ELIZABETH I, Queen of England (1533–1603) "Good Queen Bess," under whom England became a world power, told the Archbishop of Canterbury: "I have been a great queen, but I am about to die and must yield an account of my stewardship to the great King of Kings." She died holding the archbishop's hand.

612 ELIZABETH I, Empress of Russia (1709–1762) Daughter of Peter the Great she told her nephew and successor: "Be kind to your subjects. Live in peace with your wife. Cherish your son."

613 ELIZABETH of Hungary (1207–1231) Daughter of King Andrew II of Hungary, she was married to Landgrave Ludwig IV of Thuringia, who died on crusade. After his death, she was expelled from the Wartburg

Castle and lived the rest of her life as a Franciscan tertiary, dying at Marburg at the age of 24. St. Elizabeth became a folk heroine because of her concern for the poor and sick. On her deathbed she declared: "This is the moment when Almighty God calls His friends to Himself."

614 ELIZABETH, Queen Consort of Denis of Portugal (1271–1336) The grandniece of Elizabeth of Hungary and the wife of the Portuguese king, she was renowned for her concern for the unfortunate. She founded hospitals, orphanages, and homes for abandoned women. She died shortly after mediating a peace treaty between her son and the King of Castile. Favored with a vision of the Virgin Mary, St. Elizabeth said to her attendants: "Draw up a chair for the radiant lady in white who is coming! . . . O Mary, Mother of Grace!"

615 ELIZABETH of the Trinity (1880–1906) A French Carmelite nun, she is renowned for her spiritual writings. A few days before her death after a lingering illness, she declared: "Everything passes. In the evening of life, love alone remains." Moments before she breathed her last, Elizabeth declared: "I am going to light, to love, to life!"

616 ELLIOTT, Ebenezer (1781–1849) The English poet, called the "Corn Law Rhymer" because of his poems opposing the English corn laws, commented: "A strange sight, sir: an old man unwilling to die."

617 ELLIS, Havelock (1859–1939) The English psychologist famous for his seven-volume *Studies in the Psychology of Sex* told his nurse: "You must go to bed, you are so tired, and I feel better. Perhaps I may sleep a little. I shall ring if I need you."

618 EMERSON, Ralph Waldo (1803–1882) The American poet and philosopher, a few hours before his

death, perhaps referring to a long-dead son, murmured wistfully: "Oh, that beautiful boy!"

619 EPAMINONDAS (c. 418 b.c.– 362 b.c.) The Theban general, mortally wounded at the Battle of Mantinea, where his troops defeated the Spartans, tore the fatal spear from his chest and declared: "I have lived long enough, since I die unconquered."

620 EPICURUS (341 b.c.–270 b.c.) The Greek philosopher, who taught that happiness was to be obtained through a life of temperance and simplicity, took leave of his disciples with simple advice: "Now, farewell. Remember all my words."

621 ERASMUS, Desiderius (1466–1536) The Dutch scholar and writer succumbed after a long illness, praying: "Lord, free me! Lord, pity me! Lord, bring the end! Lord, have mercy! Dear God!"

622 ERICSSON, John (1803–1889) The Swedish-born engineer, who invented the screw propeller and designed the ironclad *Monitor* for the Union Navy during the Civil War, commented: "The rest is magnificent, more beautiful than words can tell."

623 ERNST August, Prince of Hanover (1887–1953) The son-in-law of Germany's last Kaiser said to his wife, Princess Viktoria Luise: "Now I must jump the final hurdle, but God will help me over it."

624 ESSEX, Robert Devereux, Second Earl of (1566–1601) A former favorite of Elizabeth I of England, he was executed for treason after leading a rebellion. On the scaffold, he exhorted God and the spectators: "O God, give me true humility and patience to endure the end, and I pray you all to pray with me and for me, that when you shall see me stretch out my arms and neck on the block and the stroke ready to be given, it would please the everlasting God to send down His angels to carry my soul before His mercy seat. Lord, as unto Thine altar do I come, offering up my body and soul for a sacrifice, in humility and obedience to Thy commandment, to Thine ordinance, and to Thy good pleasure. O God, I prostrate myself to my deserved punishment. Have mercy upon me, O God, according to Thy loving kindness, according to the multitude of Thy compassions, put away mine iniquities. Wash me thoroughly from mine iniquity and cleanse me from my sin."

Turning to the headsman, he cried: "Executioner, strike home!" Then he prayed: "Come, Lord Jesus! Come, Lord Jesus and receive my soul! Oh, Lord, into Thy hands I commend my spirit!"

625 EUGENE IV, Pope (1383–1447) Born Gabriele Condulmaro, the mediaeval pontiff told those around his bed: "Pray only that God will perform His will. We have often begged in our prayers for what would have been better not to have prayed ... I do not desire to live long, but to die quickly, and that my soul may return to God."

626 EUGÉNIE, Empress Consort of Napoleon III of France (1826–1920) The once-beautiful widow of France's second emperor survived, not only her husband, but also her son, by 40 years, and died in England after a brief illness. She felt ill, went to bed, and told a friend: "It will soon be over." A few hours later it was.

627 EULER, Leonhard (1707–1783) The mathematician collapsed, declaring: "I am dying!"

EVANS, Mary Ann *see* ELIOT, George

628 EVARTS, Jeremiah (1781–1831) The American lawyer, editor, and philanthropist strenuously opposed the government's plans to deport the eastern Indian tribes beyond the Mississippi. As he succumbed to tuberculosis, he exclaimed: "Wonderful, wonderful, wonderful glory! We cannot understand — we cannot comprehend — wonderful glory — I will praise Him, I will praise Him! Who are in the room? Call all in. Call all. Let a great many come. I wish to give directions. Wonderful! Glory! Jesus reigns!"

629 EVERS, Medgar Wiley (1925–1963) The field secretary of the Mississippi NAACP was assassinated by a white supremacist. In the ambulance en route to the hospital he cried: "Lift me up! Turn me loose!"

630 EWELL, Richard Stoddert (1817–1872) The Confederate general died of pneumonia at his estate in Maury County, Tennessee, blaming his fatal chill on his wearing a pair of lightweight trousers in mid–January: "After fighting against the United States so long, it is strange that an old pair of pantaloons should kill me at last!"

631 FAIRBANKS, Douglas, Sr. (1883–1939) The actor and movie producer, hospitalized after a heart attack, responded when his nurse asked him how he felt: "I've never felt better!" He fell asleep and never awoke.

632 FANON, Frantz (1925–1961) The French social philosopher was ill with leukemia. A dark-skinned native of Martinique, he insisted that the frequent blood transfusions to which he was subjected were part of a plot on the part of his doctors to make him white. In this spirit he told a friend: "They put me in the washing machine again last night!"

633 FARADAY, Michael (1791–1867) The British chemist, who made important discoveries in the field of electricity, declared: "He hath set His testimony in the heavens."

634 FARLEY, John Cardinal (1842–1918) The Archbishop of New

York, asked if he wanted anything, replied: "Water."

635 FAULKNER, William (1897–1962) The American novelist, hospitalized with a heart attack, answered a nephew who urged him to let him know when he was ready to come home: "Yes, Jim, I will."

636 FAURÉ, Gabriel (1845–1924) The French composer, organist, and teacher, speaking to his sons, spoke of a day when his work would fall out of favor, and urged them not to be distressed: "There is always a moment of oblivion. All that is unimportant. I did what I could. May God be the judge."

637 FAWCETT, John (1740–1817) The English Methodist minister and hymnwriter, best remembered for writing the words to "Blest Be the Tie That Binds," prayed: "Come, Lord Jesus, come quickly! Oh, receive me to Thy children!"

638 FEBRONIA (286–304) A member of a religious community in Sibapte, Syria, she was arrested during the attempt by the Emperor Diocletian to eradicate the Christian faith throughout the Roman Empire. When she refused to renounce her religion, Febronia was publicly tortured. After the executioner cut off one of her breasts, she prayed: "My Lord! My Lord! My God, see what I am suffering and receive my soul into Thy hands!"

639 FÉNELON, François de Salignac (1651–1716) The French author and theologian, who served as Archbishop of Cambrai, was a leader of a spiritual movement known as "Quietism." On his deathbed he declared: "I am on the cross with Christ. Three times he prayed the same prayer: 'Father, if it be possible, let this cup pass from me; nevertheless, not as I will, but as Thou wilt.'"

640 FERDINAND I, King of Romania (1865–1927) The monarch, who allied his country with the Allied cause in World War I and considerably expanded his territory, died after a long illness, whispering to his wife, Queen Marie: "I am so tired."

641 FERRIER, Kathleen Mary (1912–1953) The English contralto, famed for her performances in opera, oratorio, and concert, was ill for many months with cancer. She told her nurse: "Wouldn't it be lovely if I could go to sleep and not wake up again?"

642 FICHTE, Johann Gottlieb (1762–1814) The German philosopher said to his son, who was trying to give him some medicine: "Leave it alone. I need no more medicine. I am well."

643 FIELD, Cyrus West (1819–1892) The businessman who organized and directed the company which laid the Atlantic Cable relived, in delirium, his activities of some 20 years earlier: "Hold those ships! Don't let them sail! I must make further experiments first!"

644 FIELD, Eugene (1850–1895) The popular American poet died suddenly in his sleep after telling his family: "Goodnight."

645 FIELDS, William Claude (1878–1946) The comedian counseled his companion: "Grab everything and run. The vultures are coming." Then he said: "Chinaman . . . Goddamn it! Goddamn! Goddamn the whole friggin' world and everybody in it, but you, Carlotta.

646 FILLMORE, Millard (1800–1874) The former U.S. president who, in later years served as chancellor of the University of Buffalo, died a few days after suffering a paralytic stroke, remarking to a nurse, who was trying to feed him: "It tastes good."

647 FINNEY, Charles Grandison (1792–1875) The American evangelical preacher, abolitionist, and college president, dying of a heart attack, commented: "Perhaps this is the thirst of death ... I am dying."

648 FISH, Albert (1870–1936) A serial killer and child molester who allegedly kidnapped, dismembered, and ate several boys and girls, said of the electric chair: "It will be the supreme thrill — the only one I haven't tried."

649 FISHER, John (1469–1535) Bishop of Rochester, beheaded for his opposition to the policies of Henry VIII, he prayed on the scaffold: "O Lord, in Thee have I trusted. Let me never be confounded."

650 FISK, James, Jr. (1835–1872) The American business leader, dying of gunshot wounds, told his doctors, after the painkillers they administered failed to take effect: "I'm as strong as an ox, and it takes four times as much medicine to affect me as an ordinary man."

651 FISK, Wilbur (1792–1839) The Methodist minister, who served as first president of Wesleyan University, responded, when his wife asked him if he knew her: "Yes, Love, yes!"

652 FITZGERALD, Edward (1809–1883) The British poet, best remembered for his translation of the "Rubaiyat" of Omar Khayyam, announced before his sudden death: "I will go to bed."

653 FITZGERALD, Francis Scott Key (1896–1940) The novelist died of a heart attack in a Hollywood hotel, after telling a friend, who offered to buy him some Hershey bars, instead of the ice cream he requested: "Good enough. They'll be fine."

654 FLAGSTAD, Kirsten (1895–1962) The Norwegian operatic soprano told her daughter: "I know this is the end, Elsa, but you mustn't be sad. It is best so. You must be a brave, strong girl and take it calmly and naturally." Then she said to a friend: "No, you mustn't cry. You must be

strong, like Elsa. There's nothing to cry about. I have sung my song."

655 FLAUBERT, Gustave (1821–1880) The French author, dying of a stroke, mumbled disjointedly. The Hellot he mentioned was a physician. He murmured: "Rouen ... we're not far from Rouen ... Hellot ... I know the Hellots...."

656 FLEMING, Sir Alexander (1881–1955) The British bacteriologist, who developed penicillin, died of a heart attack: "I'm covered in a cold sweat. And I don't know why I've got this pain in my chest. It's not the heart. It's going down from the esophagus to the stomach."

657 FLINT, Frank Sylvester (1855–1892) Star catcher of the Chicago White Stockings, he died of complications from alcoholism shortly after his career ended. To his former teammate Billy Sunday, now a preacher, he said: "There's nothing in the life of years ago I care for now. I can hear the bleachers cheer when I make a hit that wins the game. But there is nothing that can help me now. And if the Umpire calls me out now, won't you say a few words over me, Bill?"

658 FLOYD, Charles Arthur (Pretty Boy) (1901–1934) Asked if he were indeed "Pretty Boy" Floyd, the bankrobber answered one of the FBI agents who had shot him: "Who the hell tipped you off? I'm Floyd, all right. You got me this time."

659 FONTANELLE, Bernard Le Bovier, Sieur de (1657–1757) The centenarian French scientist and author told his doctor: "I feel nothing, except a certain difficulty in continuing to exist."

660 FOOT, Solomon (1802–1866) Senator from Vermont, he was known for his parliamentary skills and for his opposition to slavery. Dying of a painful "internal inflammation" after a month's illness, he told another senator, who was leaving: "Oh, yes, we shall meet again in heaven, and the time will not be long. Farewell, dear friend. God bless you forevermore." He then asked to be lifted up in bed so that he could see the capitol dome. Embracing his wife, he cried: "What, can this be death? Is it come already? I can see! I can see it! The gates are wide open! Beautiful! Beautiful!"

661 FORD, Arthur (1897–1971) The medium called "The Man Who Talks to the Dead," died of heart disease, crying: "Oh, God, I can't take any more! God, help me!"

662 FORD, Henry (1863–1947) The automobile manufacturer told his maid: "I'll sleep well tonight. We're going early to bed."

663 FORD, Paul Leicester (1865–1902) The American novelist, historian, and genealogist, was fatally shot by his brother in a family quarrel. He gasped: "I want to die bravely."

664 FORREST, Nathan Bedford (1821–1877) The Confederate cavalry general helped to found the Ku Klux Klan, which he later renounced. He underwent a religious conversion before his death, which followed a lingering illness. A few days before the end he told his pastor: "Just here I have an indescribable peace. All is peace within. I want you to know that between me and ... the face of my heavenly Father not a cloud intervenes. I have put my trust in my Lord and Saviour." His very last words were the innocuous request: "Call my wife."

665 FORRESTAL, James Vincent (1892–1949) The first U.S. secretary of defense, suffering from depression, was a patient at the Bethesda Naval Medical Center when he copied a poem by Greek author Sophocles about the hero Ajax, who was contemplating suicide: "Woe to the mother in her close of day,/ Woe to her desolate heart and temples gray/

When she shall hear/ Her loved one's story whispered in her ear!/ 'Woe! Woe!' will be the cry —/ No quiet murmur like the tremulous wail/ Of the lone bird, the querulous night...."/ Before he completed the word "nightingale," he put the paper in the book of poetry, walked across the hall to the diet kitchen, and leaped out of the window, falling 13 stories to instant death.

666 FORSTER, Edward Morgan (1879–1970) The British author, after lying silently through the visit of a garrulous friend, commented after the man left: "He's really nice, that old bore."

667 FOSDICK, Harry Emerson (1878–1969) The Baptist minister and theologian told his daughter: "I'll be waiting for you at the bottom steps of the pearly gates." When she asked, "Why at the bottom?" he replied: "Because you'll need someone to guide you up and by St. Peter."

668 FOSTER, Stephen Collins (1826–1864) The American songwriter, an alcoholic, died in a charity ward of New York's Bellevue Hospital after injuries sustained in a fall. He complained to a friend: "Nothing has been done for me. I can't eat the food they bring me." According to one account, his final words were to a nurse: "God bless you."

669 FOX, Charles James (1749–1806) The British statesman was serving as foreign secretary at the time of his death. Told that he might not live another day, Fox replied: "God's will be done. I have lived long enough and I shall die happy." When his wife asked him to repeat what he had been trying to say, Fox, in an eighteenth century figure of speech, told her that it did not matter, that it was not important: "It don't signify, dearest Liz."

670 FOX, George (1624–1691) The founder of the Quakers (Society of

Friends) collapsed and died at a meeting, telling those who came to his assistance: "Never heed. The Lord's power is over all weakness and death."

671 FOX, Henry (1705–1774) The British statesman spoke of the expected visit of a friend: "If I am alive, I shall be glad to see him, and if I am dead, he would like to see me."

672 FRANCE, Anatole (1844–1924) The French novelist, poet, and playwright, whose real name was Jacques Anatole Thibault, murmured: "Mama."

673 FRANCIS I, King of France (1494–1547) Best remembered as a patron of the arts and a pursuer of women, the king died of a disease that left "his stomach abscessed, his kidneys shriveled, his entrails putrefied, his throat corroded, and one of his lungs in shreds." Not surprisingly, Francis announced: "I am ready to go. I have had my full life and I am glad to die." He then prayed: "Into Thy hands, O Lord, I commend my spirit." And then, clasping his hands and lifting his eyes to heaven, he gasped: "Jesus!" Minutes later he was gone.

674 FRANCIS of Assisi (c.1181–1226) The "Little Poor Man" who renounced the lifestyle of a wealthy merchant to live in poverty and humility, ministering to the poor, died after a long, painful illness. One of his earliest biographers records that Francis "spent the few days that remained before death in praise, teaching his companions . . . to praise Christ with him." He told his doctor: "Tell me bravely, Brother Doctor, that death, which is the gateway of life, is at hand." When, reluctantly, the physician concurred, Francis told his friars: "When you see that I am brought to my last moments, place me naked upon the ground, just as you saw me the day before yesterday, and

let me lie there, after I am dead, for the length of time it takes to walk one mile unhurriedly."

After he was placed on the ground, he moved his lips silently, as if in prayer, while one of his friars read a passage from the Gospel of Saint John. During the reading, Francis breathed his last. During his last moments, he seemed lost in the contemplation of heaven.

675 FRANCES of Rome (1384–1440) A wealthy married woman of Rome, where she was renowned as a mystic and visionary, she established a community of Benedictine nuns. On her deathbed she announced: "The angel has finished his task. He beckons me to follow him."

676 FRANCIS de Sales (1567–1622) The Roman Catholic Bishop of Geneva, Switzerland, author of a number of devotional books, of whom a Protestant minister once said, "If we honored any man as a saint, I know of no one since the days of the Apostles more worthy of it than this man," clasped the hand of a friend and said: "It is towards evening and the day is far spent." Asked if he were afraid of Satan, he replied: "I place all my trust in the Lord, who will know how to deliver me from all my enemies." With his very last breath he gasped: "Jesus!"

677 FRANCIS Ferdinand, Archduke of Austria-Hungary (1863–1914) Heir to the throne of his multinational empire, he was assassinated along with his wife on a goodwill visit to the city of Sarajevo, in Bosnia, which was then a province of the Austro-Hungarian Empire. His wife Sophie, herself mortally wounded by the gunshots a terrorist fired into their open car, saw blood pouring out of the archduke's mouth, and cried: "My God! What has happened to you?" She then collapsed. Francis Ferdinand pleaded:

"Sophie darling, Sophie darling, don't die! Live for our children!" Rushed into surgery, he murmured six or seven times: "It is nothing."

678 FRANCIS Joseph, Emperor of Austria-Hungary (1830–1916) The kaiser who reigned 68 years became ill in his office and was taken to bed. When his valet asked him when he wanted him to return, the kaiser said: "Tomorrow morning, half past three." After drinking some tea, Francis Joseph murmured: "Fine." Then he fell into a coma and died three hours later.

679 FRANCIS Solano (1549–1610) The Spanish Franciscan toiled for many years as a missionary to Indians and Spanish colonists in Peru and was known as "The Wonder-Worker of the World." His last words were of praise: "Glory be to God!"

680 FRANCIS Xavier (1506–1552) The Jesuit missionary to India and Japan died on a journey to China, praying: "Jesus, Son of David, have mercy on me. O Virgin Mother of God, remember me."

681 FRANCK, August Hermann (1663–1727) The German clergyman, educator, and philanthropist responded to his wife, who inquired if the Saviour was still with him: "Of that there is no doubt."

682 FRANCK, César (1822–1890) The Belgian-born composer died in Paris several months after being struck by a bus. He murmured: "My poor children, my poor children!"

683 FRANCO, Francisco (1892–1975) The Spanish general, who ruled his nation with an iron hand for four decades, complained about the measures undertaken by his doctors to prolong his life: "Please let me be. . . . How hard this is to bear! . . . My God, how hard it is to die!"

684 FRANK, Hans (1900–1945) Nazi governor of Poland during the German occupation, he was hanged as a war criminal after trial at Nuremberg. He declared: "I am thankful for the kind treatment I have received. I pray God to receive me mercifully."

685 FRANKFURTER, Felix (1882–1965) The retired associate justice of the U.S. Supreme Court died minutes after telling an aide who was visiting him in the hospital: "I hope I don't spoil your Washington's Birthday."

686 FRANKLIN, Benjamin (1706–1790) The American philosopher, scientist, and statesman commented: "These pains will soon be over. They are for my good. What are the pains of a moment compared with the pleasures of eternity?" When someone expressed the hope that he would recover from his illness and live many years more, Franklin responded: "I hope not!" Urged to roll over so as to be able to breathe more easily, Franklin said: "A dying man can do nothing easily."

FRANZ Ferdinand *see* FRANCIS Ferdinand

FRANZ Joseph *see* FRANCIS Joseph

687 FRANZ, Robert (1815–1892) The German composer, best remembered for his *lieder* and his editing of the works of Bach and Handel, referred to a portrait of his dead wife and told a friend: "There, take a good look at that! Such a face you will never see again!"

FREDERICK, Empress Consort of Frederick III of Germany *see* VICTORIA, Empress Frederick of Germany

688 FREDERICK II, King of Prussia (1712–1786) Frederick the Great, who made his German nation a European power, remarked, just before his death from pneumonia: "The mountain is passed. We shall go better now."

689 FREDERICK III, Emperor of Germany (1831–1888) Suffering from throat cancer at his accession, the kaiser reigned only three months. When asked if he were tired, he responded: "Very. Very."

690 FREDERICK VIII, King of Denmark (1843–1912) The monarch suffered a heart attack on a Hamburg street, and sat down on the steps of a butcher shop. A physician, passing by, noticed that he was ill and offered to get him to a hospital. The king refused, saying: "I am staying at the Hamburger Hof. I feel better. I will go on foot." He got up, staggered a few steps, and then dropped dead on the street.

691 FREDERICK Lewis, Prince of Wales (1707–1751) Son of George II of Great Britain and father of George III, he never lived to be king. Dying suddenly of an abscess in his chest, he gasped, in French: "I feel death."

692 FREDERICK William I, King of Prussia (1688–1740) The eccentric king, famous for organizing a regiment of the tallest men he could recruit or kidnap, died of gout, praying: "Lord Jesus, in Thee I live, in Thee I die. Thou art my prize."

693 FRELINGHUYSEN, Frederick Theodore (1817–1885) The American statesman, who served as Republican senator from New Jersey, and later as U.S. secretary of state, replied, when asked how he felt: "All peace. More than ever before."

694 FRÉMONT, John Charles (1813–1890) The American explorer and military officer, who led expeditions through the Rocky Mountains to the Pacific coast, died in New York, telling his physician: "If I continue as free from pain, I can go home next week." When the doctor asked which home he meant, Frémont replied: "California, of course!"

695 FRENCH, Daniel Chester (1850–1931) The American sculptor, best known for his statue of Lincoln in the celebrated memorial to the Civil War president in Washington, told his nurse: "You're very good to me."

696 FREUD, Sigmund (1856–1939) The Viennese psychiatrist, who suffered from oral cancer for many years, had an agreement with his physician that the doctor would administer a lethal dose of painkiller when Freud's suffering became unsupportable. And so, close to death in England, Freud said: "My dear Schur, you certainly remember our first talk. You promised me then not to forget me when my time comes. Now it's nothing but torture and makes no sense anymore. I thank you. Tell Anna about this." The next day the physician complied with Freud's wishes.

697 FRICK, Henry Clay (1849–1919) The American steel manufacturer and art collector told his nurse, after she brought him a glass of water: "That will be all. Now I think I'll go to sleep."

698 FROEBEL, Friedrich Wilhelm August (1782–1852) The German educator, who founded the kindergarten, asked to be placed before an open window. When his doctor objected to his request, Froebel insisted: "I have peeked at lovely nature all my life. Permit me to pass my last hours with this enchanting mistress."

699 FROHMAN, Charles (1860–1915) The American theatrical manager, aboard the liner *Lusitania* when it was torpedoed by a German submarine, declared before he perished in the waters off the coast of Ireland: "Why fear death? It is the most beautiful adventure of life! Why fear death?"

700 FROST, Robert Lee (1874–1963) The American poet observed, when his physician, who was usually accompanied by interns, arrived alone in his hospital room: "Traveling light today, aren't you?" Later in the day he told friends: "I feel as though I were in my last hours."

701 FROUDE, James Anthony (1818-1894) The British historian cried out: "Shall not the judge of all the earth do right?"

702 FRY, Elizabeth Gurney (1780-1845) The English philanthropist and prison reformer prayed: "Oh, my dear Lord, help and keep thy servant!"

703 FULLER, Melville Weston (1833-1910) Chief justice of the U.S. Supreme Court for 22 years, he was famous as a defender of the concept of states' rights. His last words were: "I am very ill."

704 GABRILOWITSCH, Ossip Solomonovich (1878-1936) The pianist and conductor, suffering from cancer and delirious, told his wife Clara Clemens (daughter of Mark Twain): "You must not think I am crazy, but I am not as crazy as you think because I know that I am crazy."

705 GAINSBOROUGH, Thomas (1727-1788) The English painter, ill with cancer, spoke to his friend Sir Joshua Reynolds about Sir Anthony Van Dyke, a portrait painter of the previous century: "We are all going to heaven and Van Dyke is of the company."

706 GAITSKELL, Hugh Todd Naylor (1906-1963) The British Labour Party leader remarked to his wife about the team of doctors who appeared in his room: "Here come the plumbers!"

707 GAIUS (Caligula), Emperor of Rome (12-41) The detested ruler was killed, along with his wife and daughter, in a palace coup. As he lay writhing on the ground, he called out: "I still live!" Thereupon the rebellious officers proceeded to finish their work of hewing him to pieces.

708 GALGANI, Gemma (1878-1903) The Italian servant girl, noted for her mystical gifts, including the "Stigmata" (wounds suggestive of Christ's crucifixion), died of tuberculosis, praying to Jesus and Mary: "O Jesus, You see that I am at the end of my strength. I can bear no more. If it be Your holy will, take me. Mother, I commend my soul into your hands. Do ask Jesus to be merciful to me."

709 GALLAUDET, Thomas Hopkins (1787-1851) The educator of the deaf announced to his family: "I will go to sleep."

710 GALLI-CURCI, Amelita (1882-1963) The operatic soprano, dying in retirement in California, wrote a last message for her friends shortly before her death: "I am learning to make peace with my handicaps. I read a lot. I still have much to learn, and I enjoy fully this final, fascinating cycle of my life that prepares me for the exodus — The Great Adventure!"

711 GALLO, Maria Francesca (1715-1791) A Neapolitan mystic who exhibited the "Stigmata" (spontaneous wounds in the hands, feet, and side suggestive of Christ's passion), she was depressed by the French Revolution and lamented: "Troubles in the present! Greater troubles in the future! I pray God that I may not live to witness them."

712 GALOIS, Evariste (1811-1832) The French mathematician, wounded in a duel, said to his friends, "Don't cry. I need all my courage to die at twenty."

713 GAMBETTA, Léon Michel (1838-1882) The French president died in office, after a long, painful illness: "I am lost and there is no use denying it. I have suffered so much that death will be a relief."

714 GANDHI, Kasturbhai Makanji (1869-1944) The wife of India's founder told her husband and sons: "There must be no unnecessary weeping and mourning for me." Then she prayed: "O God, give me Thy mercy and Thy forgiveness. Give me faith and infinite devotion. My death should be an occasion for rejoicing. O Lord, I have filled my belly like an animal! Forgive me. All I desire is to love Thee and be devoted to Thee — nothing more." When her husband asked, "What is the matter? What do you feel?" she answered: "I don't know. I am going now. No one should cry after I am gone. I am at peace."

715 GANDHI, Mohandas Karamchand (1869–1948) The father of modern India, the spiritual and political leader known as the Mahatma or "Great Soul" was shot to death by a Hindu extremist, after ending a fast undertaken to reconcile Moslems and Hindus. Slumping to the ground, Gandhi gasped: "Oh, God! Oh, God!"

716 GARFIELD, James Abram (1831–1881) After only four months as president, the long-time Republican congressman from Ohio was gunned down at a railway depot on the Mall in Washington. Lying incapacitated at his summer home in Elberon, New Jersey, two months later, he asked an aide, Colonel Rockwell: "Do you think my name will have a place in human history?" When Rockwell replied, "Yes, and a grand one. But you musn't talk like that. You have great work yet to perform," Garfield shook his head, insisting: "No. My work is done."

Later that day Garfield was stricken with a heart attack and cried to his chief-of-staff: "Oh, Swaim! Swaim! I am in terrible agony! Can't you do anything to relieve me? Can't you stop this? Oh, my heart! The terrible pain! Oh, Swaim! Swaim!"

717 GARIBALDI, Giuseppe (1807–1882) The Italian military and political leader who helped to unify his country told his nurse not to drive away the two little birds that perched on his window-sill: "Let the little birds in. Feed them when I am gone. Perhaps they are the spirits of my little Anita and Rosa, come to bear their father away."

718 GARNER, John Nance (Texas Jack) (1868–1967) Democratic representative from Texas for 30 years, he served as vice-president during the first two terms of Franklin D. Roosevelt. The man who once declared that the vice-presidency was not worth a bucket of warm spit (or something less mentionable) told his family: "I love you."

719 GARRETT, Patrick (1849–1908) The frontier lawman who slew "Billy the Kid" was killed on his New Mexico ranch in an argument with a stockman. Garrett threatened: "God damn you! If I can't get you off my property one way, I will another!"

720 GARRISON, William Lloyd (1805–1879) Asked, "What do you want?" the abolitionist replied: "To finish it up!" After he lost the power of speech, he listened as his children sang his favorite hymns while he beat time with his hands and feet.

721 GASSENDI, Pierre (1592–1655) The French scientist, philosopher, and mathematician said to his priest, who offered to pray the Psalms aloud: "I pray you, say them softly, because speaking out loud disturbs me."

722 GEER, Louis, Baron de (1811–1896) Swedish premier in the 1870s, the statesman prayed: "My God, have pity on me. Do not visit on me suffering beyond my strength. Oh, Christ, Thou hast suffered still more for me!"

723 GEHRIG, Henry Louis (Lou) (1903–1941) The Hall of Fame first baseman of the New York Yankees, debilitated by a neuromuscular disease, insisted, the day before he died: "I'm going to beat this!" Later, speaking of his job as a parole commissioner, he promised his wife: "I'll be back on the parole board yet. I've still got a fifty-fifty chance!" The next day, unable to speak, he voicelessly mouthed his final words to his wife: "Fifty-fifty! Eleanor!"

724 GELLERT, Christian Fürchtegott (1715–1769) The German poet, told that he had but one hour to live, declared: "God be praised! Only one more hour!"

725 GEMELLI, Agostino Gerardo (1878–1959) The Italian physician, psychologist, and theologian, founder of Milan's Catholic University, he was bothered by the lamp in his hospital room and asked: "Please put out that light."

726 GENGHIS KHAN (1162–1227) The Mongol leader, who forged an empire extending from China to the Adriatic Sea, died in northwestern China while warring with a local ruler. He told his sons: "I have almost come to my end. For you I have created this empire. To the north, south, east, and west my dominions extend for a year's journey. My last will and testament are these. If you want to retain your possessions and conquer your enemies, you must make your subjects submit willingly and unite your enemies to one, as in that way you can continue to hold your power. When I am gone, you must recognize Ugedey as my successor. Further, let each see to his own affairs. During many years I have enjoyed a great name and I die without regrets, but my spirit wishes to return to my native land. Although Jaghatay is not present to hear my wishes, I do not think he will disobey my wishes and create a disturbance. I die in the territory of my enemy, and though the ruler of Hsi Hsia has submitted, he has not yet arrived. Hence, after I am dead, conceal my death and kill him when he comes."

727 GEORGE I, King of Great Britain (1660–1727) The first British king from the House of Hanover spoke no English and left the conduct of affairs largely in the hands of his ministers, beginning the tradition of a sovereign disengaged from the direction of national policy. Dying of a heart attack in Germany, he said in French: "It's all over with me."

728 GEORGE I, King of the Hellenes (1845–1913) The Danish prince who reigned as Greek king for 50 years was assassinated while taking a stroll with an aide down the streets of Salonika. As he was starting on his walk, an army officer warned him about his lack of security, prompting the response: "My dear General, don't let me have that sermon over again. I am a fatalist. When my hour comes, it will be of no use, even if I immure myself in my house and put a thousand Evzones on guard outside." A few minutes later, as the king passed a cafe, a madman leaped out and shot him in the back.

729 GEORGE II, King of Great Britain (1683–1760) Son of George I, he is perhaps best remembered as the king who began the practice of rising during the "Hallelujah Chorus" of *The Messiah*. Like his father, he died suddenly. During his fatal heart attack, in his bathroom, he called for his daughter: "Call Amelia!"

730 GEORGE II, King of the Hellenes (1890–1947) The Greek king during World War II whose later years on the throne were marred by strife between left and right wing elements, died suddenly of a heart attack after asking his maid: "Get me a glass of water."

731 GEORGE III, King of Great Britain (1738–1820) The monarch who lost the American colonies reigned for nearly 60 years. During his last years he was physically and mentally incapacitated. Shortly before he died, when his nurse wet his lips with a sponge, he fussed: "Do not wet my lips but when I open my mouth." Then he mumbled: "I thank you. It does me good."

732 GEORGE IV, King of Great Britain (1762–1830) The unpopular and eccentric king held the hand of a friend, Sir Wathen Waller, and exclaimed: "My dear boy, this is death!" When his doctor came in a few minutes later, George held out his hand, said nothing, gave several short gasps, and died.

733 GEORGE V, King of Great Britain (1865–1936) The monarch who reigned during World War I was given a lethal injection of cocaine and morphine by his physician, with the queen's approval. Shortly before he lost consciousness, he looked at those around his bedside and cursed: "God damn you!"

734 GEORGE VI, King of Great Britain (1895–1952) The World War II monarch retired to bed after a day of hunting, telling his valet: "I'll see you in the morning." Next morning the king, who had been in ill health, was found dead in bed.

735 GEORGE, Henry (1839–1897) The American economist dropped dead after telling his wife: "I don't feel well, but I suppose it doesn't amount to much."

736 GERONIMO (c.1823–1909) The Apache medicine man, on his deathbed, had a vision of his dead grandson and a friend who had recently died, who chided him for his hesitancy to accept the Christian faith and his refusal to listen to the missionaries. Asking why they had not come sooner, the dying man protested: "I have been unable to follow The Path in my life and now it is too late!"

737 GERSHWIN, George (1898–1937) The American composer, suffering from a brain tumor, mumbled to his brother, before falling into a coma from which he never emerged: "Astaire."

738 GERTRUDE of Delft (d. 1358) The Dutch mystic and stigmatic declared: "I am longing, longing to go home."

739 GERTRUDE of Helfta (1256–1302) The German nun was famed as a scholar, mystic, and writer. She prayed: "When wilt Thou come? My soul thirsteth for Thee, O loving Father."

740 GETULIUS (d. 124) A wealthy Roman who was the host of a house church and instructed inquirers in the Christian faith, he was ordered to sacrifice to Jupiter and Mars or die. He retorted: "My life will not be extinguished, and I rejoice with joy unspeakable to refuse to sacrifice to the gods." He was told, "Do not despise the commands of the emperor. Obey the mighty gods." Getulius answered: "I thank my God, the Father Almighty, that I am able to offer Him an acceptable sacrifice." When asked, "What sacrifice?" the martyr replied: "The sacrifice of a broken and contrite heart." His head was battered in with an uprooted fence-post.

741 GIACOMETTI, Giovanni Alberto (1901–1966) The Swiss sculptor and painter told his doctor: "Soon again I'll see my mother." A little later, just before he lost consciousness, he told his wife: "Till tomorrow."

742 GIBBON, Edward (1737–1794) The British historian who wrote *The History of the Decline and Fall of the Roman Empire* said to his physician (in French): "Dussaut, you're leaving me?"

743 GIBBONS, James Cardinal (1834–1921) The Archbishop of Baltimore for more than three decades told some of his aides a few days before he died: "You do not know how I suffer. The imagination is a powerful thing.

My reason tells me that the images which rise before me have no foundation in fact. Faith must ever be the consolation of all men. Without faith we can accomplish little. Faith bears us up in our trials." After blessing a group of priests, the dying prelate remarked: "What a loyal, devoted band of priests!" Reviving after two days in a coma, he declared: "I have had a good day!"

744 GIBRAN, Kahlil (1883-1931) The Lebanese-American poet and philosopher, famous for *The Prophet*, declared: "Don't be troubled. All is well."

745 GIDE, André (1869-1951) The French novelist and publisher said: "It is well."

746 GILBERT, Sir Humphrey (c.1539-1583) The English explorer and navigator drowned in a storm near the Azores while returning from a voyage to Newfoundland. He was last seen and heard shouting: "We are as near to heaven by sea as by land!"

747 GILBERT, Sir William Schwenk (1836-1911) The English dramatist, who collaborated with composer Sir Arthur Sullivan to produce a series of light operas, swam to the aid of a young girl who seemed to be drowning and bade her: "Put your hands on my shoulders and don't struggle!" The 75 year-old writer suffered a heart attack and sank. The girl was saved.

748 GILBERT of Sempringham (1085-1189) The centenarian founder of the now-defunct Gilbertian Order in England exhorted his religious: "Three maxims I have always tried to observe I now commend to you: first, never to hurt anyone, and, if injured, never to seek revenge; secondly, to bear patiently whatever suffering God may inflict, remembering that He chastens every one whom He receives; and, finally, to obey those in author-

ity, so as not to be a stumbling block for others."

749 GIPP, George (1895-1920) The star halfback of the Notre Dame football team responded to Coach Knute Rockne: "What's tough about it? I've got no complaint. I've got to go, Rock. It's all right. I'm not afraid. Will you do one last thing for me? Some time, when the team's up against it and things aren't breaking right, tell the boys to go out and win just one for the Gipper. Wherever I'll be, Coach, I'll know about it and it'll make me very happy."

750 GISSING, George Robert (1857-1903) The English novelist murmured: "Patience ... patience ... God's will be done."

751 GIUSTINIANI, Lorenzo (1381-1456) The Patriarch of Venice responded to attendants who wanted to place him on a more comfortable bed: "My Saviour did not die on a featherbed, but on the hard wood of the cross!"

752 GLADSTONE, William Ewart (1809-1898) The four-time British prime minister, dying of cancer, blessed his daughter and told her: "God bless you. God bless you. May a good and silver light shine down upon your path. I am quite comfortable, quite comfortable. I am only waiting, only waiting, but it is a long time, the end. Kindness, kindness, nothing but kindness on every side."

753 GLEASON, Henry John (Jackie) (1916-1987) The comedian remarked shortly before he died:"If God wants another joke man, I'm ready."

754 GLINKA, Mikhail Ivanovich (1804-1857) The Russian composer, on his deathbed, thought about the idea of eternal life, then commented: "It is nonsense! I do not believe in eternity!"

755 GODET, Frédéric (1812-1900)

The Swiss Protestant theologian, best known for his commentaries on the New Testament, told his family: "I have carried you in my heart all my life, and I hope I will still be permitted to do the same up there."

756 GOEBBELS, Joseph Paul (1897–1945) The Nazi propaganda minister and governor of Berlin poisoned his children and committed suicide along with his wife rather than fall into the hands of the Soviet army when German defeat in World War II became apparent. Speaking of Karl Doenitz, the naval commander who succeeded Hitler as führer of the dying Reich, he said to a friend: "Tell Doenitz that we understood not only how to live and fight, but also how to die."

757 GOERING, Hermann Wilhelm (1893–1946) A few hours before he was to be hanged as a war criminal, the Nazi leader who commanded the German air force during World War II told a chaplain, who urged him to accept Christ as his Saviour: "I am a Christian, but I cannot accept the teachings of Christ. But I feel at ease." Shortly after that he bade his doctor: "*Gute Nacht.*" Then he swallowed poison.

758 GOETHALS, George Washington (1858–1928) The American army engineer who directed the construction of the Panama Canal and afterwards served as governor of the Canal Zone died in New York. He commented: "Let me stay here. If I stay here, I'll be much nearer to West Point."

759 GOETHE, Johann Wolfgang von (1749–1832) The German poet, novelist, and dramatist asked his valet to: "Open the shutter in the bedroom so that more light can come in."

GOGH, Vincent Van *see*
VAN GOGH, Vincent

760 GOGOL, Nikolai Vasilyevich (1809–1852) The Russian author, in delirium, murmured: "Go on! Rise up! Charge, charge the mill!"

761 GOLDBERGER, Joseph (1874–1929) The Austrian-born medical researcher who did extensive studies of the disease pellagra said to his wife just before he died in Washington, D.C.: "Mary, don't leave me. You have always been my rock, my strength. Mary, we must have patience."

762 GOLDSBOROUGH, Fitzhugh Coyle (1880–1911) An eccentric musician and poet, he killed novelist David Phillips because he believed that an offensive character in one of Phillips' novels was based on his sister. He shot Phillips, shouting: "Here you go!" Then he shot himself in the head, crying: "Here I go!"

763 GOLDSBY, Crawford (1876–1896) "Cherokee Bill," a robber and murderer executed at Fort Smith, Arkansas, was asked if he had any last words, and answered: "No! I came here to die, not to make a speech!"

764 GOLDSMITH, Oliver (1728–1774) The English author is said to have lived his last years in "squalid distress and squalid dissipation" and to have "died wretchedly." Asked, "Is your mind at ease?" Goldsmith replied: "No, it is not!"

765 GOMPERS, Samuel (1850–1924) The labor leader who organized the American Federation of Labor declared: "God bless our American institutions. May they grow better day by day."

766 GONZAGA, Aloysius (1568–1591) An Italian nobleman who became a Jesuit priest, he died while nursing victims of plague in Rome. He remarked to the priest who was hearing his confession: "We are going, Father, we are going." When the priest asked him where they were going, Aloysius responded: "To heaven." As the other priest continued his prayers, the sick man murmured: "Into Thy hands . . . ."

767 GORDON, Charles George (1833–1885) The colorful English general was serving as governor-general of the Sudan when he was killed trying to defend the city of Khartoum from native insurgents. Just before the army of the Mahdi burst into the town, Gordon calmly told an aide: "Now leave me to smoke these cigarettes."

768 GORETTI, Maria (1890–1902) An 11-year-old Italian girl killed resisting a would-be rapist, she came to be known as a "martyr of purity." Dying in a hospital of multiple stab wounds, she was asked by the chaplain, "Do you forgive your murderer with all your heart?" "Mariettina" answered: "Yes, yes, I too, for the love of Jesus, forgive him and I want him to be with me in paradise. May God forgive him, because I have already forgiven him."

In her delirium she relived the crime: "What are you doing, Alessandro? You will go to hell!" The last time she spoke she cried: "Carry me to bed! Carry me to bed, because I want to be nearer to the Madonna!" As for her murderer, Alessandro Serenelli, released eventually from prison, he died in 1970 at the age of 88, declaring: "I killed a saint, but now I go to meet her in heaven."

769 GORGAS, William Crawford (1854–1920) U.S. surgeon-general, he made the construction of the Panama Canal possible by eradicating the yellow fever mosquito. Dying in a London hospital of kidney disease, complicated by a stroke, Gorgas, after receiving the last rites of the Church of England, told his wife: "Well, if this is dying, dying is very pleasant."

770 GORKI, Maxim (1868–1936) The Russian novelist and playwright, born Alexei Maximovich Peshkov, prophesied: "There will be wars. We have to prepare. We have to button all our buttons."

771 GOULD, Glenn (1932–1982) The Canadian pianist, suffering from a stroke, asked a friend: "Ray, where are you?"

772 GOULD, Jay (1834–1892) The American financier who, at one time, owned approximately one out of every ten miles of railroad track in the United States, was worth $72 million at the time of his death of tuberculosis. He insisted: "I wish to have all my family present."

773 GOUNOD, Charles François (1818–1893) The French composer, a few days before his death told a reporter: "When I look at you in this way I see but half of your face. I know I look robust, but, as St. Paul says in his epistle to Timothy, 'I am now ready to be offered and the time of my departure is at hand. I have fought the good fight, I have finished the course, I have kept the faith.' I have had several attacks already. The next—"

The day of his death he saw a friend to the door of his house and bid him: "*Au revoir.*" Minutes later he suffered a final stroke and died.

774 GRABLE, Ruth Elizabeth (Betty) (1916–1973) The American actress commented, as her family gathered around her bedside, on the apparent absence of a sister (who was, in fact, present): "Marjorie isn't here."

775 GRADY, Henry Woodfin (1850–1889) The editor of the *Atlanta Constitution*, who advocated the industrial development of the South, was read a description of the funeral of Jefferson Davis, and repeated to himself the last words of the account: "And the little children cried in the streets!"

776 GRAINGER, Percy Aldridge (1882–1961) The Australian-American pianist and composer confided to his wife: "You're the only one I like."

777 GRANT, Cary (1904–1986) The actor, suffering from the effects of a stroke, tried to reassure his wife: "I love you, Barbara. Don't worry."

778 GRANT, Ulysses Simpson (1822–1885) The Union Army commander, a failure as president and in business, spent his last days, ill with throat cancer, at work on his memoirs in the hope that the royalties would provide for his family. A few days before he died he wrote: "I do not sleep, though sometimes I doze a little. If up, I am talked to and in my efforts to answer cause pain. The fact is, I think I am a verb instead of a personal pronoun. A verb is anything that signifies to be, to do, or to suffer. I signify all three." The day before he died, Grant was asked by his son if he were in pain and replied: "No." Later that night, when asked if he wanted anything, he said: "Water." The next morning he breathed his last.

779 GRANVILLE, John Carteret, First Earl of (1690–1763) The British statesman commented, when the preliminaries of the Treaty of Paris (which ended the Seven Years War and secured for Britain most of France's former possessions in the New World) were read to him, commented: "It has been the most glorious war and it is now the most honorable peace this nation ever saw."

780 GRAY, Thomas (1716–1771) The English lyric poet, best known for "Elegy Written in a Country Churchyard," suffered a heart attack and told a relative: "Molly, I shall die!"

781 GREELEY, Horace (1811–1872) The founder and editor of the *New York Tribune*, shortly after running unsuccessfully for president against Grant on the Democratic ticket, died of what was diagnosed as an inflammation of the brain. When an old friend asked, "Do you know who this is?" Greeley replied: "Yes." He held up his hands in greeting. A few minutes later, when his doctor asked him, "Do you know that you are dying?" Greeley whispered: "Yes." When asked if he were in pain, the invalid simply laid his hand on his chest. He lay still, with closed eyes and twitching hands, then began to murmur indistinctly. One witness understood him to say: "I know that my Redeemer liveth." Another thought he was cursing. His daughter thought he asked: "Lift my head higher." She put an additional pillow under his head, and 15 minutes later the journalist died, "settling into a look of perfect peace."

782 GREEN, Hetty Howland Robinson (1834–1916) "The Witch of Wall Street," a financier who built a large fortune through stocks and real estate and became, reputedly, the richest woman in the world, declared: "I am not worrying. I don't know what the next world is like, but I do know that a kindly light is leading me and that I shall be happy after I leave here."

783 GREGOIRE, Henri (1750–1831) The French statesman and cleric, who served as Bishop of Blois, supported the moderate faction in the French Revolution and was an advocate of religious freedom and racial equality. In delirium he murmured: "I have been tormented for eight days. I see a whole population of blacks isolated on an island, which serves as their refuge. They are going to die of hunger. I was told that some Protestants and Jews came to see me. Although they are not of my church, I desire to make acknowledgments to them. Let someone send theological books to Haiti. The poor Haitians!" Then he said: "I see that my last hour is come. Do not desert me in my last moments."

784 GREGORY I, Pope (540–604) Saint Gregory the Great strengthened the power and prestige of the papacy and sent missionaries to Britain. Dying after a long illness, Gregory prayed: "I pray that the hand of Almighty God raise me from the sea of this present life and let me rest on the shores of eternal life."

785 GREGORY VII, Pope (1020–1085) Born Hildebrand of Soana, he forbade secular rulers to appoint bishops and abbots, an action that enraged Holy Roman Emperor Henry IV, who was convinced that such an action limited his ability to control Central Europe and Italy. The emperor declared Gregory deposed, and the pope died in exile in Salerno. He told his attendants: "I am going up there, and I commend you with fervent supplication to the mercy of God."

Then, in a bitter paraphrase of Psalm 45:7 (which reads, "Thou lovest righteousness and hated wickedness: therefore God, thy God, hath anointed thee with the oil of gladness above thy fellows"), he declared: "I have loved justice and hated iniquity. Therefore I die in exile."

786 GREGORY XV, Pope (1554–1623) Born Alessandro Ludovisi, he vigorously resisted the Protestant Reformation. Dying of "the stone," he told the cardinals assembled at his bedside: "We shall die with one consolation. Our successor may correct some errors in the administration of the Christian Republic. It will not be possible, my beloved brothers, for a successor to us to be chosen who will not be more worthy of the authority than we and who will not better fill the exalted pontifical office."

787 GREGORY XVI, Pope (1765–1846) Born Bartolomeo Alberto Cappellari, he was a member of a very strict monastic order before his election in 1831. During his reign he attacked such evils as slavery, democracy, and modern theology. On his deathbed he insisted: "I wish to die as a monk and not as a sovereign."

788 GREGORY, Isabella Augusta Persse, Lady (1853–1932) The Irish playwright and poet, who directed the Abbey Theatre of Dublin for many years, was a Protestant who reacted strongly to the attempts of her nurse to convert her to Roman Catholicism: "Never!"

789 GREY, Zane (1875–1939) The New York dentist, famed for his novels about the American West, dismissed his heart pains as: "A slight case of indigestion."

790 GRIEG, Edvard (1843–1907) The Norwegian composer, when told that he was unlikely to survive his heart attack, conceded: "Well, if it must be so."

791 GRIMALDI, Joseph (1778–1837) The British comedian, who performed as "Joey the Clown," died of a heart attack in his sleep after telling his driver: "God bless you, my boy. I shall be ready for you tomorrow night."

792 GRISI, Giulia (1811–1869) The Italian operatic soprano, dying in England, answered her daughter, who asked her if she wanted anything, saying in Italian: "Beautiful . . . my beautiful. . . ."

793 GRISWOLD, Rufus Wilmot (1815–1857) The American critic and editor commented: "I may not have always been a Christian, but I am very sure that I have been a gentleman."

794 GROTIUS, Hugo (1585–1643) The Dutch lawyer and statesman, who is considered the father of international law, compared himself to Jan Urich, a religious mystic who spent eight hours a day in prayer: "I have spent my life laboriously doing nothing. I would give all my learning and honor for the plain integrity of Jan Urich." Just before the end he commented to his doctor: "I hear your voice well, but understand with difficulty what you say."

795 GUEVARA de la Serna, Ernesto (Ché) (1928–1967) The Argentine-born revolutionary was captured and shot by the Bolivian army, while leading a guerrilla movement in South America. Professing shame at having been taken alive, he said: "Do not worry, Captain. It is all over. I have failed."

796 GUITEAU, Charles Julius (1842–1882) The eccentric drifter shot President Garfield and, after a long trial in which his lawyers tried to prove him insane, was executed for the murder. Hanged in the District of Columbia jail, Guiteau read a poem he composed for the occasion: "I saved my party and my land;/ Glory, halleluiah!/ But they have murdered me for it,/ And that is the reason/ I am going to the Lordy./ Glory, halleluiah!/ Glory, halleluiah!/ I am going to the Lordy!/ I wonder what I will do when I get to the Lordy./ I guess that I'll weep no more when I get to the Lordy./ Glory, halleluiah!/ I wonder what I will see when I get to the Lordy./ I expect to see the most splendid things beyond all earthly conception when I am with the Lordy./ Glory, halleluiah!/ Glory! Glory! Glory!"

797 GUIZOT, François-Pierre-Guillaume (1787–1874) The French statesman and historian, a few days before his death, told his daughter: "Ah, my child, how little do we know. However, I shall soon enter the light!" The day of his death the daughter told him, "We shall meet again, my father," prompting the response: "No one is more convinced of that than I am." Then, discussing his funeral arrangements, he dismissed the idea of speeches and eulogies: "God alone should speak by the side of the grave."

798 GURNEY, Joseph John (1788–1847) The British philanthropist told

his wife: "I think I feel a little joyful, dearest."

799 GUSTAV II Adolph, King of Sweden (1594–1632) Called "The Lion of the North," Gustav Adolph, or Gustavus Adolphus, is considered one of Sweden's greatest leaders, a king who fostered economic growth and made his nation a European power. Mortally wounded in the Battle of Lützen in the Thirty Years War, a victory which saved the Protestant cause in Germany, the king told an aide: "I am gone. Look to your own life."

800 GUSTAV III, King of Sweden (1746–1792) The monarch who encouraged agriculture, commerce, and science, and promoted religious toleration, died several days after being shot at a masked ball. A few minutes before he died, he conceded: "'T is all over."

801 HAAKON VII, King of Norway (1872–1957) Prince Carl of Denmark was elected by the Norwegian Parliament as that nation's first modern king, after its separation from Sweden in 1905. Haakon always suspected that he was not fully accepted by the people of his adopted country. His last recorded words, addressed to his doctor, were: "When I am gone, Norway will get its first Norwegian king."

802 HADLEY, Samuel Hopkins (1842–1906) A former alcoholic, he devoted his life to the homeless of New York City, where he operated the Water Street Mission. Dying after surgery for appendicitis, he cried in despair: "My poor bums! My poor bums? Who will look out for them for me?"

803 HADRIAN, Emperor of Rome (76–138) One of the five "Good emperors," he is remembered best for his mausoleum in Rome and the wall he built to separate Britain from Scotland. Shortly before his death, suffering from a lingering illness, he recited a poem of his own composition: "Soul of mine, pretty one, flitting one,/ Guest and partner of my clay,/ Whither wilt thou hie away—/ Pallid one, rigid one, naked one—/ Never to play again, never to play?"

804 HALDANE, Robert (1764–1842) The Scots philanthropist and Baptist theologian murmured: "Forever with the Lord ... forever ... forever...."

805 HALE, George Ellery (1868–1938) The American astronomer famed for his studies of the sun spoke, on his deathbed, of the subject of his life's work and of the California observatory where a telescope of his design was being constructed: "It is a beautiful day. The sun is shining and they are working on Palomar."

806 HALE, Nathan (1755–1776) The Long Island school master and army captain was hanged as a spy by the British during the American Revolution. He is supposed to have quoted from Addison's play *Cato*, declaring: "I only regret that I have but one life to lose for my country." According to Captain Frederick MacKenzie, a British officer who witnessed the execution in New York City, Hale's last words were actually: "It is the duty of every good officer to obey an order given him by his commander-in-chief."

807 HALÉVY, Jacques (1799–1862) The French composer, best remembered for his opera *La Juive*, asked his daughter to help him onto a couch in musical terms, referring to a scale of notes: "Lay me down like a gamut." Minutes later, singing musical scales, he died.

808 HALL, John Vine (1774–1860) The English bookseller and temperance advocate murmured: "Passing away, passing away ... Jesus, Jesus.... He is, He is ... pray ...

Amen."

809 HALLECK, Fitz-Greene (1790–1867) The American poet, remembered for his patriotic poem "Marco Bozzaris" and for his lines, frequently cut on nineteenth century tombstones—"Green be the turf above thee/ Friend of my early days/ None knew thee but to love thee/ None named thee but to praise"—said to his sister: "Maria, hand me my pantaloons, if you please."

810 HALLER, Albrecht von (1708–1777) The Swiss physiologist, anatomist, botanist, and poet commented: "Now I am dying."

811 HAMER, Fannie Lou Townsend (1917–1977) The Mississippi civil rights leader told friends: "I'm so tired. I want you all to remember me and keep up the work. I've taken care of business. My house is in place. Everything is in order with God."

812 HAMILTON, Alexander (1755–1804) America's first secretary of the treasury and the founder of the Federalist Party was wounded in a duel with Vice-President Aaron Burr, who blamed him for his defeat in his campaign for the New York statehouse. Dying the next day, Hamilton exhorted his weeping wife "in a pathetic and impressive manner": "Remember, my Eliza, you are a Christian." After Episcopal Bishop More of New York administered the last rites, with his wife, seven children, and his doctor beside him, Hamilton expired "without a struggle and almost without a groan."

813 HAMILTON, Edith (1867–1963) The American author and educator confided to a friend shortly before her death: "You know, I haven't felt up to writing, but now I think I am going to finish that book on Plato."

814 HAMMERSTEIN, Oscar II (1895–1960) The American playwright, best known for his collaboration with Richard Rodgers in the creation of several celebrated Broadway musicals, was ill with cancer. When his son began to weep, Hammerstein snapped: "God damn it! I'm the one who's dying, not you!" Then he mused: "I've had a happy childhood. I've had a good time as a young man. And I've had a terrific middle age. The only thing I'm disappointed in is that I was looking forward to having a really good old age, too." He told his daughter: "I know I'm going to die. I don't want to die but I know I'm going to. But I've been a very lucky man. I've had the work that I wanted to do. I've been married to the woman I love and I've had a good life. I've had everything. I'd like it to last longer, but since it isn't, I'm not dissatisfied."

Still later he remarked: "There's a game that people are playing now as to who would you rather be than yourself if you had your life to live over. I'm actually dying, so I should play the game better than anybody. Yet I can't figure out whether I'd be Albert Einstein or Babe Ruth. Einstein's mind and feeling for people, his sense of music, makes me feel he's the most sensitive and best man of this country. But as soon as I think of that—just the feel and hearing the ball hit the bat and see it go over the fence.... So, I don't know." Two days later Hammerstein, a great baseball fan, died murmuring the names of his favorite players: "Ruth ... Gehrig ... Rizzuto...."

815 HAMPDEN, John (1594–1643) A member of the British Parliament who led the opposition to King Charles I, he was mortally wounded at Chalgrove Field as Puritan forces battled armies loyal to the king. Dying a few days later Hampden prayed: "Oh, Lord, save my country. Lord, be merciful, too."

816 HAMPTON, Wade (1818–1902) The Confederate cavalry general, in a long post-war political career as governor of South Carolina, and later as U.S. senator, worked for racial reconciliation. With his last breath, he prayed: "All my people, black and white, God, bless them all!"

817 HANCOCK, Winfield Scott (1824–1886) The Union general, who ran unsuccessfully for president in 1880 on the Democratic ticket, died of diabetes, calling to his wife, as she left the room: "O Allie, Allie, Myra.... Good...."

818 HANDEL, George Frideric (1685–1759) The British composer collapsed after conducting a performance of his famous oratorio, *The Messiah*, a week before Easter. After signing his will, he remarked: "I want to die on Good Friday, in hopes of rejoining my good God, my sweet Lord and Savior, on the day of His Resurrection." He died early on the morning of Holy Saturday.

819 HANNA, Marcus Alonzo (1837–1904) The American industrialist, who bankrolled the presidential campaign of William McKinley, was serving as senator from Ohio when he died of typhoid. When offered a handkerchief, he joked: "I would like one, but I suppose I cannot have it. My wife takes them all."

820 HANNIBAL (247 B.C.–183 B.C.) The Carthaginian general, who was defeated by the Romans as he led his North African nation in its vain struggle for the control of the Mediterranean, later met defeat again, while leading a Syrian fleet against his old enemy. He fled to Bithynia in Asia Minor (modern Turkey), where the Roman general Flaminius demanded his surrender. Rather than give himself up, Hannibal took poison, declaring: "It is time now to end the great anxiety of the Romans, who have grown weary in waiting for the death of a hated old man."

821 HARDING, Florence Kling de Wolfe (1860–1924) The widow of President Warren Harding survived her husband by only 15 months. A few days before she lost consciousness, she said to her husband's secretary, George Christian, who came to see her: "I am glad you are here, George. I want you to take care of all this mail and see that every letter is acknowledged, and thank them for their kind interest." Her last conscious act came after a message of concern from President and Mrs. Coolidge was read to her. Unable to speak, she smiled and nodded her head.

822 HARDING, Warren Gamaliel (1865–1923) Ill with a bad heart and depressed by scandals in his administration, the president lay in bed in a San Francisco hotel while his wife read him a magazine article that was favorable to him. He told her: "That's good. Go on. Read some more." When she finished reading, Florence Harding left the room. When the night nurse entered a few minutes later, the president was having a heart attack. The two doctors who reached his bedside seconds later pronounced him dead.

823 HARDY, Oliver Norvell (1892–1957) After losing more than 100 pounds on a diet, the comedian suffered an incapacitating stroke that deprived him of the ability to communicate. Not long before his death, however, his wife saw him move his lips as if to mouth the words: "I love you."

824 HARDY, Thomas (1840–1928) The English poet and novelist called his sister-in-law, inquiring (about what, no one knew): "Eva, Eva, what is this?"

HARI, Mata *see* MATA Hari

825 HARLAN, John Marshall (1833–1911) Associate justice of the U.S. Supreme Court for more than three decades, he was known as "The Great Dissenter." Dying of pneumonia, he told his family: "Good-bye. I am sorry that I kept you all waiting for so long."

826 HARLAN, John Marshall (1899–1971) Associate justice of the U.S. Supreme Court, the grandson of the jurist by the same name was, in his last months, nearly blind and afflicted with a very painful spinal cancer. Shortly before he died he asked an assistant: "Why did this have to happen to me?"

827 HARLOW, Jean (1911–1937) The movie actress, known as the "Blond Bombshell," dying of kidney failure, said: "Where is Aunt Jetty? Hope she didn't run out on me."

828 HAROUN AL RASCHID, Caliph of Baghdad (c.765–809) The Moslem leader died of a stroke while on a military campaign and declared: "Haroun is prince of the believers, those of the race that know how to die."

829 HARRIS, Joel Chandler (1848–1908) The Atlanta journalist who created the Uncle Remus stories succumbed to a lingering illness. Asked if he felt better, Harris replied: "I feel about the extent of a tenth of a gnat's eyebrow better."

830 HARRISON, Benjamin (1833–1901) The soldier and attorney, who served a term as U.S. president, died of pneumonia at his Indianapolis home. The day before he died, he asked his wife: "Are the doctors present?" Later a friend thought that he was trying to comment on the plight of South Africa when he seemed to say: "Pity . . . hopeless. . . ." When his aunt arrived, she thought she could make out: "Doctor . . . my lungs. . . ." Harrison last showed signs of consciousness when his three-year-old daughter was brought into the room. Opening his eyes, he smiled, took the child's hand, then dropped it.

831 HARRISON, Caroline Lavinia Scott (1832–1892) The artist, musician, and civic leader, who was the first wife of Benjamin Harrison and the first president-general of the Daughters of the American Revolution, died in the White House of tuberculosis, answering her husband, who asked if he could do anything for her: "No, dear."

832 HARRISON, Carter Henry (1825–1893) Mayor of Chicago, he was shot in his home by an embittered ex-policeman. When a friend told him that he would soon recover, Harrison retorted: "I have been shot in the heart and I know I cannot live."

833 HARRISON, Sir Rex (1908–1990) The British actor said to his wife (presumably as a compliment): "What did I do to deserve you?"

834 HARRISON, William Henry (1773–1841) The American soldier, political leader, and diplomat served as president for only a month before he succumbed to lung, stomach, and intestinal problems. After hearing Psalm 103 read, Harrison commented: "I thank the Lord for all His goodness." Then, to his nurse, he said: "Ah, Fanny, I am ill, very ill, much more so than they think!" Complaining of the painful treatments to which he was subjected by his doctors, he cried: "It is wrong! I won't consent! It is unjust! These applications, will they never cease? I cannot stand it! I cannot bear this! Don't trouble me." Then, in delirium, thinking that he was talking to his vice-president (who was in Virginia), he said: "Sir, I wish you to understand the true principles of government. I wish them carried out. I ask nothing more."

835 HART, Bret (1836–1902) The American poet and short-story writer died in England, telling his nurse: "That is fine. Very fine."

836 HART, Lorenz Milton (1895–1943) The author of the lyrics of many successful Broadway musicals asked despondently: "What have I lived for?"

837 HARVEY, William Henry (1811–1866) The Irish botanist, an authority on algae, commented: "Yet it has been a pleasant world to me."

838 HASSLER, Ferdinand Rudolph (1770–1843) The Swiss-born engineer, who taught at West Point and served as superintendent of the United States Coast Survey during the last 11 years of his life, mumbled: "My children, my papers!"

839 HASTINGS, Warren (1732–1818) The first British governor of India commented: "Surely, at my age it is time to go. God only can do me good. My dear, why wish me to live to suffer thus? None of you know what I suffer."

840 HAUFF, Wilhelm (1802–1827) The short-lived but prolific German novelist and poet, famous for his fairy tales, died of typhoid after a trip to Italy, praying: "Father, into Thy hands I commend my immortal spirit."

841 HAVELOCK, Sir Henry (1795–1857) The English general told his son: "Come, my son and see how a Christian can die."

842 HAVERGAL, Frances Ridley (1836–1879) The English poet and musician reacted, a few days before her death, when her physicians told her that her lingering illness would soon terminate fatally: "It's home the faster! God's will is delicious! He makes no mistakes!" She lingered in agonizing pain that no drugs could alleviate. Once, while her sister was fanning her, Havergal commented: "Maria, you have made this last year of my life the brightest."

When her doctor visited her, he told her that she would likely die in 24 hours and she said: "Beautiful! Too good to be true!" A few hours later she exclaimed: "Splendid to be so near the gates of heaven! So beautiful to go! There is no bottom to God's mercy and love. All His promises are true. Not one thing hath faileth!"

As her pain grew worse, she asked her sister and brother for permission to groan. When they told her how very patient she had been throughout her long, painful illness, she responded: "Oh, I'm glad you tell me this. I did want to glorify Him every step of the way, and especially in this suffering. I hope none of you will have five minutes of this pain." Several times, in spasms of pain, she cried: "Come, Lord Jesus, come and fetch me! Oh, run! Run!" To her sister she spoke of other relatives: "I want *all* to come to me in heaven. Oh, don't, *don't* disappoint me. Tell them, 'Trust Jesus.'" Finally, seized with violent convulsions, she gasped: "There! Now it is all over! Blessed rest!"

Her sister Maria recounted, "She now looked up steadfastly as if she saw the Lord; and surely nothing less heavenly could have reflected such a glorious radiance upon her face. For ten minutes we watched the almost invisible meeting with her King, and her countenance was so glad, as if she were already talking to Him. Then she tried to sing, but after one sweet high note, 'He,' her voice failed, and as her brother commended her soul into her Redeemer's hands, she passed away."

843 HAWTHORNE, Nathaniel (1804–1864) The American novelist and short-story writer, in failing health, remarked to his friend, former president Franklin Pierce, just a few hours before dying in his sleep: "What a boon it would be, if when life draws to its close, one could pass away without a struggle."

844 HAWTHORNE, Sophia Amelia Peabody (1809–1871) The artist and writer, widow of Nathaniel Hawthorne, died in London of typhoid pneumonia, telling her children: "I only wanted to live for you children, you know. I never wanted anything for myself, except to be with your father."

845 HAY, John (1838–1905) The American statesman was serving as secretary of state under Theodore Roosevelt when, recovering from prostate surgery, he suffered a pulmonary embolism and died shortly after telling his nurse: "Come!"

846 HAYDN, Franz Joseph (1732–1809) The Austrian composer, called "Father of the Symphony" died after several years' illness and inactivity, during the bombardment of Vienna by the armies of Napoleon. To his household staff he said: "Children, be comforted. I am well." He never spoke again and three days later, in the words of his doctor, "went blissfully and gently to sleep."

847 HAYES, Patrick Cardinal (1867–1938) The New York archbishop died in his sleep of a heart attack after cheerfully bidding his secretary: "Goodnight!"

848 HAYES, Rutherford Birchard (1822–1893) The American lawyer, soldier, and politician, who served as governor of Ohio before his single term as president, died of a heart attack at his home. His last thoughts were of his dead wife as he told his doctor: "I know tht I am going where Lucy is."

849 HAYWARD, Susan (1917–1975) The American movie actress died of cancer, telling her son: "I love you."

850 HAYWORTH, Rita (1918–1987) The actress lost her mental faculties in her last years. Before she ceased entirely to speak, she mumbled to herself, perhaps speaking of her father: "He used to do that. He told me how to do that."

851 HAZLITT, William (1778–1830) The English essayist and critic declared: "I have led a happy life."

852 HEALY, George Peter Alexander (1813–1894) The American portrait painter, sometimes called "the painter of the presidents," exclaimed to his daughter: "Happy! So happy!"

853 HEALY, James Augustine (1830–1900) A former slave from Georgia, he became the first African American to be appointed bishop in the American Catholic Church, when he was installed as bishop of Portland, Maine. Dying after a long and painful illness, he commented: "I wonder if heaven is worth it all? Yes! Yes! It is worth all this and infinitely more still!"

854 HEARN, Patrick Lafcadio (1850–1904) The Irish-Greek author, who lived for some years in America, died in Japan of a heart attack, devastated at the number of projected books that he would never write: "Because of sickness!"

855 HEARST, William Randolph (1863–1951) The newspaper publisher spoke about his magnificent estate to a friend: "Please stop at San Simeon and look the place over. I want to be sure everything is all right there."

856 HECKEWELDER, John Gottlieb Ernestus (1743–1823) The American Moravian missionary to the Indians of Ohio murmured: "Golgotha . . . Gethsemane. . . ."

857 HEGEL, Georg Wilhelm Friedrich (1770–1831) The German philosopher died of cholera in Berlin, brooding: "Only one man ever understood me. And he really didn't understand me."

858 HEINE, Heinrich (1797–1856) The German poet suffered for many years from a neuromuscular disease that caused progressive paralysis. He is supposed to have quipped: "God will pardon me. It's his profession." According to contemporary accounts of his passing, the last thing he said was: "I'm dying! I'm dying!"

859 HEMANS, Felicia Dorothea Browne (1793–1835) The English romantic poet, dying after a long, painful illness, commented: "I have been making peace with God. I feel all at peace within my bosom."

860 HEMINGWAY, Ernest Miller (1899–1961) The American author, on the night before he shot himself in the head, told his wife: "Goodnight, my kitten."

861 HENDRICKS, Thomas Andrew (1819–1885) The Democratic senator from Indiana who became Cleveland's first vice-president died in office of heart disease, telling his doctor: "I'm free at last . . . I mean, at last I'm free of pain."

862 HENIE, Sonja (1912–1969) The Norwegian figure skater, actress, and art collector died of leukemia on a plane flying from Paris to Oslo. She told her husband: "Oh, Niels, I am so tired."

863 HENRIETTA Maria, Queen Consort of Charles I of England (1609–1669) The widow of the murdered king died in her native France. She sent word to her physician: "Tell Duquesne that I cannot sleep and that I would like him to take me some new medicine." She took the sleeping potion and never awoke.

864 HENRY II, King of England (1133–1189) The monarch, who at one time controlled not only England, but northern France, Scotland, Wales, and parts of Ireland, tried to limit the power of the nobles and the Church. In the last years of his reign, his sons rebelled against him. Told that his favorite son John was also in revolt he said: "Let the rest go as it will. Now I care not what becomes of me. Shame, shame on a conquered king!"

865 HENRY II, King of France (1519–1559) The monarch who spent most of his reign fighting the English, the Spanish, and the Holy Roman Empire was fatally injured in a tournament. He told his son and heir: "My boy, you are going to be without your father, but not without his blessing. I pray God to make you more fortunate than I have been."

866 HENRY III, King of France (1551-1589) Fatally stabbed by a monk in the midst of the religious strife that had raged in France during the entirety of his reign, he was asked by his confessor if he forgave his enemies, and replied: "I forgive them with all my heart." When asked if he included those who brought about his death, the king replied: "Yes, even them. I pray God that He may pardon them their sins as I hope He will pardon mine."

867 HENRY IV, Holy Roman Emperor (1050-1106) The European ruler, who struggled throughout a long reign against the power of the pope in German politics, was eventually deposed by one of his sons. He felt it necessary to justify his life on his deathbed: "Oh, how unhappy I am who squandered such great treasures in vain! How happy I could have been if I had given those things to the poor! But I swear before the eye of the All-Knowing that all my efforts have been only for the advancement of my Church."

868 HENRY IV, King of England (1367-1413) Dying after a long illness, he expressed his feeling of guilt for his overthrow of his cousin Richard II 14 years earlier. He told his son and heir: "Well, fair son, what right I had to it, God knoweth. I commit all to God and remember you to do the same."

869 HENRY IV, King of France (1553-1610) The sovereign who ended France's religious wars and promoted tolerance was stabbed to death by a Roman Catholic terrorist. Trying to

reassure his aides, the wounded monarch insisted: "It is nothing."

870 HENRY V, King of England (1387-1422) The victor over the French at Agincourt, who made plans to unite the two kingdoms upon the eventual succession of his son, died of dysentery at 34, leaving an infant heir from whom the French would soon recover their independence. As if talking to the devil, Henry cried: "Thou liest! Thou liest! My portion is with the Lord Jesus!" Clutching a crucifix he prayed: "Into Thy hands, O Lord; Thou hast redeemed my end."

871 HENRY VII, King of England (1457-1509) Victor over the detested Richard III in the Battle of Bosworth, Henry founded the Tudor dynasty. Dying of tuberculosis, he told his attendants: "If it should please God to send me life, you should find me a new changed man."

872 HENRY VIII, King of England (1491-1547) The sovereign who severed his country's ties with the pope, when he divorced the first of his six queens, repented of his cruel and dissipated life as he lay dying: "I have abused my life. Yet is the mercy of Christ able to pardon me all my sins, even though they were greater than they be." When his attendants urged him to summon the Archbishop of Canterbury to administer the last rites, Henry replied: "Cranmer, but not yet. First I will take a little sleep, then, as I feel myself, I will advise upon the matter."

When the king awoke and felt worse, the archbishop was summoned. Henry sighed: "All is lost!" When Cranmer arrived, Henry could not speak. The archbishop bade Henry squeeze his hand as a sign that he put his faith in Christ. The dying king wrung Cranmer's hand with all his might.

873 HENRY, Matthew (1662-1714)

The Welsh Biblical commentator declared: "A life spent in the service of God and communion with Him is the most comfortable and pleasant life that anyone can live in this world."

HENRY, O. *see* PORTER, William Sydney

874 HENRY CHRISTOPH I, King of Haiti (1767–1820) Ruler of the northern part of Haiti, he committed suicide with a silver bullet during a revolt, declaring: "Since the people of Haiti no longer have faith in me, I know what to do!"

875 HENRY FREDERICK, Prince of Wales (1594–1612) The eldest son of King James I and heir to the English throne died of typhoid, calling out: "Where is my dear sister?"

876 HENRY, Patrick (1736–1799) The revolutionary era statesman who served five terms as Virginia's governor was given a draught of liquid mercury by his physician, who told him that it would either cure his cancer or kill him. Henry pulled his nightcap over his face and prayed for his family and country, and declared: "I am thankful for the goodness of God, which, having blessed me all my life, thus permits me now to die without pain." He told his doctor: "Behold the benefit and the reality of the Christian religion to one about to die."

877 HEPBURN, Audrey (1929–1993) The actress, dying of cancer in Switzerland, told her bachelor sons: "Fellas, your old Ma needs a kiss. Forget the movies — you two are the best work I ever did. I always thought I'd make a wonderful granny. But I guess God had other plans." Referring to her humanitarian work with the starving children of East Africa, she said: "Remember the children when I'm gone. Please make sure those poor starving babies get enough to eat."

878 HERBERT, Edward, First Baron of Cherbury (1583–1648) The English philosopher, diplomat, and historian asked the time, and when told, commented: "Then an hour hence I shall depart."

879 HERBERT, George (1593–1632) The English clergyman and poet, dying of tuberculosis, prayed: "I am now ready to die. Lord forsake me not, now that my strength faileth me, but grant me mercy, for the merits of my Jesus. And now, Lord — Lord, receive my spirit."

880 HERDER, Johann Gottfried von (1744–1803) The German poet, concerned about his unfinished work, begged his doctor: "My friend, my dearest friend, preserve me still, if that is possible."

881 HERZL, Theodor (1860–1904) The Austrian playwright, who worked to create a national Jewish state and is known as the founder of modern Zionism, died of heart disease, telling his children: "Well, my dear ones, you saw me, I saw you. Now go home."

882 HESSUS, Helius Eobanus (1488–1540) The German scholar, known in his day as "The King of Poets" declared: "I want to ascend to my Lord."

883 HEWART, Gordon (1870–1943) The retired Lord Chief Justice of England, annoyed by the sound of a bird outside, complained: "Damn it! There's that cuckoo again!"

884 HEWITT, Abram Stevens (1822–1903) The American philanthropist and politician, who served as mayor of New York in the 1880s, snatched the oxygen tube from his mouth and declared: "And now I am officially dead!"

885 HEYLIN, Peter (1600–1662) The English church historian told his pastor: "I know it is church time with you and I know this is Ascension Day. I am ascending to the Church Triumphant. I go to my God and Savior, unto joys celestial and to hallelujahs eternal."

886 HILARION (d. 303) A little African boy, who was ordered to renounce his Christianity by a Roman governor who threatened to cut off his hair, nose, and ears, replied: "Do as you please. I am a Christian." As he was led off to torture and death, he cried: "Thanks be to God!"

887 HILL, Ambrose Powell (1825–1865) The Confederate general, trying to force the surrender of two federal soldiers, leveled his pistol at them and, reining his horse, shouted: "Surrender!" Both men shot him, and he fell mortally wounded.

888 HILL, Benjamin Harvey (1823–1882) The Democratic senator from Georgia suffered from cancer of the tongue, which limited his speech, but the day before he died he called out in a clear voice: "Almost home!"

889 HILL, Daniel Harvey (1821–1889) The Confederate general, dying of stomach cancer, murmured: "Nearly there."

890 HILL, Joe (Joel Emmanuel Hägglund) (1879–1915) The Swedish-born labor leader and songwriter, who helped organize the International Workers of the World, was sentenced to the firing squad in Utah for murder. As he was strapped in the chair, he told the witnesses: "I will show you how to die. I will show you how to die. I have a clear conscience. I am going now, boys. Goodbye. Goodbye, boys. Fire! Go on and fire!"

891 HILLMAN, Sidney (1887–1946) The labor leader, president of the Amalgamated Clothing Workers and a founder of the Congress of Industrial Organizations, commented: "I feel like hell. I'm going to lie down again."

892 HILTON, Conrad Nicholson (1887–1979) The American businessman, who built a hotel empire, allegedly said, when asked if he had a last message for the world: "Leave the shower curtain on the inside of the tub."

893 HIMMLER, Heinrich (1900–1945) The Nazi leader, who supervised Hitler's extermination camps, committed suicide after his capture by the British. Ordered by an officer to strip, Himmler snarled: "He does not know who I am!" When the order was repeated, Himmler bit down on a vial of cyanide concealed in his teeth.

894 HINDENBURG, Paul von (1847–1934) Germany's top military commander in World War I was elected President of the German Republic in 1925 and served until his death — a year after he approved the appointment of Adolf Hitler as chancellor. Referring to death as "Friend Hein," Hindenburg said to his doctor: "It's all right, Sauerbruch. Now tell Friend Hein he can come in now."

895 HITCHCOCK, Alfred Joseph (1899–1980) The movie and television director commented: "One has to die to know exactly what happens after death, although Catholics have their hopes."

896 HITLER, Adolf (1889–1945) Faced with imminent defeat and unwilling "to be put on exhibition in a Russian wax-museum," the German leader prepared to take his life. When an aide urged him to attempt an escape, the führer refused, declaring: "One must have the courage to face the consequences. I am ending it all here. I know that by tomorrow millions of people will curse me. Fate wanted it that way."

Just before Hitler and his wife retired to their room in the bunker beneath Berlin, where the dictator and his goverment had taken refuge during the latter days of the war, the tyrant insisted: "Death for me means only freedom from worries and a very difficult life. I have been deceived by my best friends and have experienced treason. Now it has gone so far. It is finished. Goodbye." Minutes after the Hitlers had closed the door to their room, Adolf was told by the soldier guarding the door that the wife of propaganda minister Joseph Goebbels wanted to see him. He replied: "I do not want to see her." Minutes later he shot himself.

897 HITLER, Eva Braun (1912–1945) Long-time mistress of the German strongman and his bride for but a day, she took her life by poison. Before withdrawing with her husband to their room, she embraced one of the secretaries and told her: "Greet Munich for me. Take my fur coat. I've always liked well-dressed people."

898 HOBBES, Thomas (1588–1679) The English rationalist philosopher is said to have remarked: "Now I am about to take my last voyage, a great leap in the dark."

899 HODGE, Charles (1797–1878) The Presbyterian clergyman, theologian, and educator, who taught for many years at Princeton and was famous as a conservative Biblical commentator, told his daughter: "Why should you grieve, daughter? To be absent from the body is to be with the Lord, to be with the Lord is to see the Lord, to see the Lord is to be like Him."

900 HODGES, Gilbert Ray (1924–1972) Star first baseman of the Brooklyn (and later Los Angeles) Dodgers and afterwards manager of the Washington Senators and New York Mets, he was asked by one of his coaches when they would meet for dinner. Hodges replied, seconds before dropping dead on the sidewalk: "Let's say, 7:30."

901 HOFFMAN, Ernst Theodor Amadeus (1776–1822) The German short-story writer conceded: "It is time to think a little bit about God."

902 HOGG, Ima (1882–1975) The Texas philanthropist who, among other things, organized the Hogg Foundation for Mental Health and founded the Houston Symphony Orchestra, died in London where she went "to hear the greatest music in the world one last time." Her last recorded words, after suffering a broken hip five days before her death, were: "It's going to be all right."

903 HOGG, James (1770–1835) The Scots poet known as the "Ettrick Shepherd" succumbed to a liver disease, one of the symptoms of which was severe hiccoughing: "It is a reproach to the faculty that they cannot cure the hiccough."

904 HOKUSAI, Katsushika (1760–1849) The Japanese artist, famed for his wood-block prints, lamented: "If heaven had only granted me five more years I could have become a real painter."

905 HOLLIDAY, John Henry (1851–1887) The gunfighting dentist died of alcoholism and tuberculosis in Colorado, telling the friend who was nursing him: "This is funny."

906 HOLMES, John (1812–1899) The American intellectual worked for a living for very little of his long life and published nothing, but was known as the brother of poet Oliver Wendell Holmes, Sr. and uncle of the jurist, Oliver Wendell Holmes, Jr. His reputation as a wit extended even to his deathbed. When his nurse reached under the covers and, after feeling his feet, remarked, "Nobody ever dies with their feet warm," the old man, referring to an English clergyman burnt at the stake in the sixteenth century, quipped: "John Rogers did!"

907 HOLMES, Oliver Wendell, Jr. (1841–1935) Associate justice of the U.S. Supreme Court for 30 years, he was celebrated for his liberal interpretation of the Constitution. Dying at his home in Washington, he was irritated at efforts to prolong his life and complained, as oxygen was administered: "Lot of damned foolery!"

908 HOLTBY, Winifred (1898–1935) The English journalist, poet, and novelist, dying of a heart condition, spoke to her mother about her fiancé: "Mummie, when I'm better, Bill and I are going to get married. It's just an understanding between us — not really an engagement. You don't mind, do you, darling? Not an engagement, just an understanding."

909 HOOD, John Bell (1831–1879) The Confederate general, who commanded the Texas Brigade, died shortly after his wife in an epidemic of yellow fever, leaving minor children, of whom he said: "The Texas Brigade will take care of them, for that is what I wish."

910 HOOD, Thomas (1799–1845) The British poet, humorist, and editor, dying after a lingering illness, told his wife: "I forgive all, *all*, just as I hope to be forgiven." He then prayed: "O Lord, say, 'Arise, take up thy cross and follow me.'" Just before he lost consciousness he murmured: "Dying ... dying...."

911 HOOKER, Richard (c.1553–1600) The Anglican priest and theologian, best known for his *Laws of Ecclesiastical Polity*, told his doctor: "Good Doctor, God had heard my daily petitions, for I am at peace with myself and from that blessed assurance I feel that inward joy which this world can neither give nor take from me: my conscience beareth me this witness and this witness makes the thoughts of death joyful. I could wish to live to do the Church more service, but cannot hope it, for my days are past as a shadow that returns not."

912 HOOKER, Thomas (1586–1647) One of the founders of Connecticut, he was told, "You are going to receive the reward of all your labors,"

and answered: "Brother, I am going to receive mercy!"

913 HOOVER, Herbert Clark (1874–1964) When his nurse announced the visit of an old friend, Admiral Strauss, the former president roused himself and murmured: "Lewis Strauss was one of my best friends."

914 HOPE, John (1868–1936) The African American leader who served as president of Morehouse College, then, up to the time of his death, of Atlanta University, died of pneumonia shortly after remarking: "I'd like to live long enough to tell my successor what I'm trying to do."

915 HOPKINS, Gerard Manley (1844–1889) The English clergyman and poet, dying of typhoid, remarked, after receiving the last rites of the Roman Catholic Church: "I am happy, so happy!"

916 HOPKINS, Harry Lloyd (1890–1946) Aide to Franklin Delano Roosevelt and one of the most influential administrators of the New Deal, he died after a lingering illness, commenting: "You can't beat destiny."

917 HOPKINS, Johns (1795–1873) The American merchant and philanthropist who endowed the university and hospital in Baltimore that bear his name spoke to his nephew about the habit of living: "Joe, it is very hard to break up an old habit. I've been living for seventy-eight years now and I find it hard to make a change in my ways."

918 HOPKINS, Samuel (1721–1803) The Congregationalist pastor and theologian taught that Christians should be willing to be damned for the glory of God. When a fellow minister asked him why he was groaning, Hopkins replied: "It is only my body. All is right in my soul."

919 HORNEY, Karen Danielson (1885–1952) The German-born American psychoanalyst, ill with cancer, declared: "I am at last content to be leaving. There is just no point going on."

920 HOUDINI, Harry (1874–1926) The American illusionist, born Ehrich Weiss, confided to his wife: "Dash, I'm tired of fighting. I guess this thing is going to get me."

921 HOUSMAN, Albert Edward (1859–1936) The English poet was visited by his physician the night before he died. The author laughed heartily at a dirty joke that the doctor told and said: "That's a good one, and tomorrow I shall be telling it on the golden floor!"

922 HOUSTON, Samuel (1793–1863) The soldier and statesman who served as president of the Republic of Texas and later, when Texas was made a state, as senator, was serving as governor when he was removed from office because of his opposition to secession. Two years later he died of pneumonia. An hour before he died he said to his son-in-law: "Charlie, have you an American flag? Bring it out. I want to die under its glorious folds. I am sorry that it is the will of God that I cannot see that flag float again. Do you be faithful and true to it forever." A few minutes later he said to his wife: "Texas ... Texas ... Margaret...."

923 HOW, William Walsham (1823–1897) The English clergyman, poet, and hymnwriter who served as Anglican bishop of Wakefield told his family: "Goodnight, I don't want anything, thank you."

924 HOWARD, Moses (Moe) (1897–1975) The leader of the Three Stooges comedy team spoke his last recorded words to former Stooge Joe Besser five days before he died. Concluding a telephone conversation, Moe, who had lung cancer, confided: "I've been really sick lately, so I'm sorry that I have answered yours and Ernie's letters, but I think about you daily."

925 HOWARD, Oliver Otis (1830–1909) The Union general, who later served as director of the Freedmen's Bureau and superintendent of West Point, founded Howard and Lincoln universities, for the education of African Americans. He was stricken at his office with heart pains and returned home with his son, and promptly collapsed and died. Speaking of his heart, he told his son: "Some day it will just stop and I will be on the other shore."

926 HOWE, Julia Ward (1819–1910) The American poet and suffrage leader, famous for her words to "The Battle Hymn of the Republic," commented as she died of pneumonia: "God will help me. I'm so tired."

927 HUDSON, Rock (1925–1985) When a friend asked him if he wanted another cup of coffee, the ailing actor answered: "No, I don't believe so." A few minutes later he quietly died.

928 HÜGEL, Friedrich, Baron von (1852–1925) The Roman Catholic Old Testament scholar bade his nurse: "Pray for me."

929 HUGHES, Charles Evans (1862–1948) The American statesman served, at various stages of his career, as governor of New York, associate justice of the Supreme Court, secretary of state, and, for 11 years, chief justice. He was also Republican candidate for president in 1916. On his deathbed he remarked: "I've been the luckiest man in the world. I've had everything. I've drunk the wine of life to the bottom of the glass. Now only the dregs are left."

Just before he lost consciousness, he was asked if he would like to see his children. He answered: "You bet I do!" A few minutes later he changed his mind and said: "I would rather be alone."

930 HUGHES, John (1797–1864) The first archbishop of New York, dying after a lingering illness, was told that his doctors had concluded that there was no hope for his recovery. He responded: "Did they say so?"

931 HUGO, Victor-Marie (1802–1886) The French author and statesman murmured: "I see black light."

932 HULL, Isaac (1773–1843) The American naval officer who commanded the *U.S.S. Constitution* ("Old Ironsides") during the War of 1812 declared: "I strike my flag."

933 HUMBERT I, King of Italy (1844–1900) The second king of Italy was shot in his carriage while leaving an athletic event. Ordering his coachman to drive away, he told his aides: "It is nothing." Minutes later he died.

934 HUMBERT II, King of Italy (1904–1982) Italy's last king reigned for but a month before his subjects voted to abolish the monarchy. Dying in exile, he whispered: "Italy!"

935 HUMBOLDT, Alexander, Baron von (1769–1859) The German naturalist, explorer, and geographer commented when the blinds were opened: "How grand those rays! They seem to beckon earth to heaven!"

936 HUME, David (1711–1776) The Scots philosopher told the physician who was treating him for cancer: "Doctor, as I believe you would not choose to tell me anything but the truth, you had better say that I am dying as fast as my enemies, if I have any, could wish, and as easily and cheerfully as my best friends could desire."

937 HUMPHREY, Hubert Horatio (1911–1978) The Democratic senator from Minnesota, who served as vice-president under Lyndon Johnson and was his party's candidate for president in 1968, died of cancer after a lingering illness. He said to a friend: "I feel I have so much to do yet."

938 HUNT, James Henry Leigh (1784–1859) The English poet and editor commented: "I don't think I shall get over this."

939 HUNTER, William (1718–1783) The British physician, anatomist, physiologist, and obstetrician to Queen Charlotte commented: "If I had strength enough to hold a pen I would write how easy and pleasant a thing it is to die."

940 HUSS, John (1369–1415) The Czech priest was burned at the stake at Constance, Switzerland by church authorities who were enraged by his teaching that obedience to the pope is not necessary for salvation. Huss declared: "In the truth of the Gospel, of which I have written, taught, and preached, I will die today with gladness." As the flames sprang up, he prayed: "Oh Christ, Thou son of the living God, have mercy on me!"

941 HUSSERL, Edmund (1859–1938) The German phenomenologist philosopher experienced a religious conversion during his last illness. On Good Friday he exclaimed: "Good Friday! What a day! Christ has forgiven us everything!" Later that evening he commented: "I have fervently prayed to God to let me die, and he has given His consent. I find it a great disappointment that I am still alive. God is good — yes, good, but so incomprehensible. It is a heavy trial for me. Light and darkness ... deep darkness, and again light." For the next few days he was silent, then, minutes before his death, he told his nurse: "Oh, I have seen something so wonderful! Quick, write it down!" The nurse ran to fetch writing materials, but when she returned, Husserl was dead.

942 HUXLEY, Aldous Leonard (1894–1963) The British novelist and critic, best remembered for his *Brave New World*, murmured: "Who is eating out of my bowl?" Then he wrote on a tablet: "LSD — try it/ intermuscular/ 100 mm." His doctor gave him the injection and the author, who had been ill with throat cancer, died peacefully.

943 HYDE, John Nelson (1865–1912) The American Presbyterian missionary to India was celebrated for his mystical and ascetical life and was given the soubriquet "Praying Hyde." Dying of cancer, he cried: "Shout the victory of Jesus Christ!"

944 IBSEN, Hendrik (1828–1906) The Norwegian dramatist known as "The Colossus of the North" replied to his wife, who whispered to his nurse, "You see, the Doctor will be well again": "On the contrary!"

945 IGNATIUS of Antioch (c.30–107) The early Christian leader, brought to Rome for execution, was thrown to the lions. When he heard the animals roar, he cried: "I am the wheat or grain of Christ. I shall be ground with the teeth of wild beasts, that I may be found pure bread!"

946 IGNATIUS of Loyola (1491–1556) The Spanish military officer who became a priest and founded the Society of Jesus (Jesuit Order) collapsed with a heart attack, crying: "Oh, my God!"

947 INGERSOLL, Robert Green (Colonel Bob) (1833–1899) The American philosopher and lecturer, called "The Great Agnostic" by some, was asked how he felt and replied: "Oh, better."

948 INNOCENT X, Pope (1572–1655) Born Giambattista Pamfili, he was the head of the Roman Catholic Church for 11 years. After the last rites were administered, he told Cardinal Sforza: "You see where the grandeurs of the sovereign pontiff must end!"

949 INNOCENT XI, Pope (1611–1689) Born Benedetto Oedescalchi, he died after a reign of 13 years. When an ambassador assured him that he would look after his relatives, the pontiff retorted: "We have no house or family! God gave us the pontifical dignity, not for the advantage of our kindred, but for the good of the Church and nations."

950 INNOCENT XIII, Pope (1655–1724) Born Michelangelo Conti, he reigned for but two years before dying of a strangulated hernia. Urged to create more cardinals, he demurred, protesting: "We are no longer of this world."

951 IQBAL, Muhammed (1876–1938) The poet and statesman from what is now Pakistan said of his 14-year-old son Javid: "Please see to it that he learns the passage, 'Addressed to Javid,' which appears near the end of my Javid-Namah [i.e. Book of Eternity]."

952 IRENE (d. 304) A Greek Christian in the city of Thessalonica, she was asked by the governor if she had the temerity to refuse to offer sacrifice to the gods of Rome. She answered: "It is not temerity, but divine piety. In that I still persist." She was burnt at the stake.

953 IRVING, Sir Henry (1838–1905) The British Shakespearean actor prayed: "Into Thy hands, O Lord, into Thy hands...."

954 IRVING, Washington (1783–1859) The American author, best remembered for his stories "Rip Van Winkle" and "The Legend of Sleepy Hollow," was tortured by heart disease. He told his niece, who was helping him into bed: "You cannot tell how I have suffered! When will this ever end?" He sobbed, then pressed his hand to his side, then sank to the floor, dead.

955 ISABELLA I, Queen of Spain (1451–1504) The "Catholic Monarch" who, with her husband Ferdinand V, created a united Spain and sponsored the voyages of Columbus, told her family: "Do not weep for me nor waste your time in fruitless prayers for my recovery, but pray rather for the salvation of my soul."

956 ISABELLA II, Queen of Spain (1833–1904) The controversial ruler, deposed more than three decades earlier, died in Paris of a heart attack. She told her son-in-law: "Take my hand and pull my right arm as hard as you can. There is something very strange in my chest. I think I am going to faint."

957 JACKSON, Andrew (1767–1845) The former president died after a lingering and excruciatingly painful illness. After receiving the last rites of the Presbyterian Church and Holy Communion, he told his family: "When I have suffered sufficiently, the Lord will then take me to Himself. But what are all my sufferings? Compared to those of the Blessed Savior who died upon that cursed tree for me, mine are nothing." He lingered a week more, but it was noted that in the most extreme suffering "not a groan escaped his lips." He never mentioned his pain, but spent most of his time in silent prayer.

On the last day of his life he assembled his family. He kissed and blessed each of his grandchildren, telling each: "Keep holy the Sabbath Day and read the New Testament." He proceeded to give his family and household staff what his physician, Dr. Esselman, described as "one of the most impressive lectures on the subject of religion that I have ever heard," speaking for a half hour, urging everyone to: "Look to Christ as your only Savior." To his slaves he counseled: "Do your duty. As much is expected of you, according to your opportunities, as from whites. You must try to meet me in heaven."

After greeting more relatives and friends, he told everyone assembled around his bed: "God will take care of you for me. I am my God's. I belong to Him. I go but a short time before you, and I want to meet you all in heaven, both white and black." To his slaves, who were now all in tears, Jackson said: "What is the matter with my dear children? Have I alarmed you? Oh, do not cry. Be good children and we will all meet in heaven." He smiled at his favorite granddaughter. Seconds later, his body twitched, his head fell forward onto his chest, and he was gone.

958 JACKSON, Helen Hunt (1830–1885) The American novelist and poet, who described the unhappy plight of the American Indian, mused: "You know, as I lie here and fancy myself a ghost, it doesn't seem strange or alarming."

959 JACKSON, Joseph Jefferson (1887–1951) The star outfielder for the Chicago White Sox was banned from his sport because of his alleged complicity in the "Black Sox Scandal," in which he and seven other team members were accused of taking bribes to "throw" the 1919 World Series. Jackson maintained his innocence literally to his dying day. Stricken with a final heart attack, less than 20 minutes before he breathed his last he told his brother Dave: "Buddy, I'm going to face the Umpire now. I'm not guilty of that charge."

960 JACKSON, Rachel Donelson Robards (1767–1828) The wife of Andrew Jackson, she had been deeply shocked by charges about her moral character made by her husband's opponents during the election campaign. A month after the election, as she sat by the fire at her estate, The Hermitage, she turned to her maid and said of the White House: "I'd rather be a doorkeeper in the House of God than live in that palace." Twenty minutes later she cried: "I'm fainting." She died in the arms of her maid.

961 JACKSON, Thomas Jonathan

(Stonewall) (1824–1863) The Confederate general, mortally wounded by friendly fire during his great victory at Chancellorsville, died several days later, murmuring: "Let us cross over the river and rest under the shade of the trees."

962 JACOB (16th century B.C.) The Hebrew patriarch on whom the Lord bestowed the name Israel died in Egypt at the age of 147, instructing his twelve sons: "I am about to be gathered to my people. Bury me with my fathers in the cave in the field of Ephron the Hittite, the cave in the field of Machpelah, near Mamre in Canaan, which Abraham bought as a burial place from Ephron the Hittite, along with the field. There Abraham and his wife Sarah were buried, there Isaac and his wife Rebekah were buried, and there I buried Leah. The field and the cave in it were bought from the Hittites." Jacob then "drew up his feet into the bed, breathed his last, and was gathered to his people."

963 JAMES I, King of England (1566–1625) King of Scotland from infancy, he succeeded Elizabeth I of England and ruled both kingdoms (as James I and VI) until his death. Best remembered for his colonization of America and his authorization of the translation of the Bible which bears his name, the king died of "a terrible dysentery." After Bishop Williams prayed the Creed, James cried: "There is no other belief, no other hope!" After receiving absolution for his sins, the king remarked: "But in the dark way of the Church of Rome, I do defy it!"

964 JAMES II, King of England (1633–1701) The former king, deposed by Parliament in the "Glorious Revolution" of 1688, died in exile in France. A devout Roman Catholic, he exclaimed to his wife: "Think of it Madam, I am going to be happy!"

965 JAMES V, King of Scotland (1513–1542) Demoralized by the defeat of his army by the forces of English king Henry VIII at Solway Moss, James collapsed and took to his bed. Informed that his queen had given birth to a girl, who as his only living child would survive him, he alluded to the marriage of Marjorie Bruce and Walter Stewart, which had commenced the Stewart dynasty of Scotland. He made a prophecy which was never fulfilled: "Adieu, fare well, it came with a lass, it will pass with a lass." Six days later he died, without saying anything else that was recorded.

966 JAMES, Bishop of Jerusalem (d. A.D. 62) Known as "The Brother of the Lord," the leader of the Christian community in Jerusalem was killed by a Jewish mob, infuriated when James, standing on the pinnacle of the Temple, proclaimed Jesus as Lord. Thrown to the ground and battered to death, he prayed: "I beseech Thee, O Lord God, Father, forgive them, for they know not what they do."

967 JAMES the Dismembered (d. A.D.421) A Persian army officer who professed Christianity, St. James was sawn alive into 28 pieces. After his limbs were completely removed, he told his executioners, who were preparing to amputate his head: "Now the boughs are gone. Cut down the trunk."

968 JAMES the Great (d. A.D. 44) Son of Zebedee and brother of St. John the Evangelist, St. James was killed during a persecution of Christians by the Palestinian King Herod Agrippa I. The man who denounced James to the authorities as a Christian was so moved by his composure during his trial that he himself was converted and was, in turn, condemned to die. On the way to the place of execution, the informer begged James to forgive him. The apostle, silent for a few minutes, embraced him and said: "Peace be with you, brother."

969 JAMES, Alice (1848–1892) The American diarist (daughter of Henry James, Sr. and sister of Henry, Jr. and William) murmured the words of a telegram she wanted sent to family members: "Tenderest love to all. Farewell. Am going soon."

970 JAMES, Henry, Sr. (1811–1882) The American philosopher spoke of his dead wife: "There's my Mary."

971 JAMES, Henry (1843–1916) The American novelist, who became a British subject shortly before he died, cried out to his sister-in-law: "Stay with me, Alice! Stay with me! This is the end!"

972 JAMES, Jesse Woodson (1847–1882) The famous bandit was killed in his home by one of his own men, who was motivated by the $10,000 reward offered by the state of Missouri for the capture of the outlaw, dead or alive. Looking at a picture of Stonewall Jackson, the brigand commented: "That picture's awfully dusty." As he stood on a chair to dust the picture Bob Ford shot him in the back of the head.

973 JAMES, William (1842–1910) The American psychologist and philosopher (brother of Henry), dying of a heart condition, said to his wife: "I can't stand this again—cruel, *cruel!* This has come so rapidly, rapidly!" Then, speaking of his brother Henry he said: "Go to Henry when his time comes." (She did.)

974 JANÁČEK, Leoš (1854–1928) When his nurse asked him if he wanted to make his peace with God, the Czech composer said indignantly: "Nurse, you probably don't know who I am!"

975 JANE GREY, Queen of England (1537–1554) The dying Edward VI, a devout Protestant, passed over his halfsisters in naming his successor and designated as his heir his cousin, Lady Jane Grey, whose religious position was similar to his own. After nine days in power, Jane was deposed by Edward's sister Mary. A few months later Jane and her husband, Guilford Dudley, were beheaded. As she saw her husband's body taken away, she cried: "Oh, Guilford, Guilford! The antepast that you have tasted and I shall soon taste is not so bitter as to make my flesh tremble! For all this is nothing to the feast that you and I shall partake this day in paradise!"

On the scaffold the "Nine Day Queen" declared: "Good people, I come hither to die, and by law I am condemned to the same. The fact against the queen's highness was unlawful and the consenting thereof by me; but touching the procurement and desire thereof by me or on my behalf, I do wash my hands in innocency before God and the face of you, good Christian people, this day. I pray you all to bear witness that I die a true Christian woman and that I do look to be saved by no other means but the mercy of God in the blood of His only son Jesus Christ, and I confess that when I did know the word of God, I neglected the same, loved myself and the world, and therefore this plague and punishment is happily and worthily happened to me for my sins. And yet I thank God that of His goodness He hath thus given me a time and respite to repent. And now, good people, I pray you assist me with your prayers."

On her knees, Jane repeated the penitential Psalm 51. Then, standing, she gave her gloves and handkerchief to her maid and her prayer book to another attendant. After she was blindfolded she forgave the executioner, who knelt down to ask her pardon, telling him: "I pray you dispatch me quickly." Groping towards the block, she asked him: "Will you take it off before I lay me down? What shall I do? Where is it?" After the executioner guided her to the block, Jane prayed: "Lord, into Thy hands I commend my spirit."

976 JEANNE d'Albret, Queen of Navarre (1528-1571) Ruler of a territory later absorbed by France, she was the mother of the man who became French king Henry IV. A devout Protestant, she declared as she lay on her deathbed, ill of a lung tumor: "Death is not terrible to me. It is the way we pass to eternal rest." She prayed: "Oh, my God, in due time deliver me from this body of death and from the miseries of this present life, that I may no more offend Thee. Grant me to attain that felicity which Thou hast promised in Thy word to those that love Thee." Then she told her ladies: "I pray you not to weep for me. God, by this sickness, has called me to the enjoyment of a better life. Now I am about to enter the desired haven, toward which this frail vessel hath been so long steering." Asked, "Are you willing to die?" she replied: "Yes, more willing than to linger here in this world of vanity."

977 JEFFERSON, Thomas (1743-1826) The former president died on the fiftieth anniversary of the signing of the Declaration of Independence. A few days earlier, Jefferson, ill with urinary and intestinal problems, told a grandson: "Do not imagine for a moment that I feel the smallest solicitude about the result. I am like an old watch, with a pinion worn out here and a wheel here, until it can go no longer."

On July 2, he began to slip in and out of a coma. By the next day, he was almost continuously unconscious, but at seven in the evening he awoke to find his physician at his bedside. He asked: "Ah, Doctor, are you still there? Is it the Fourth?" The physician told him that it soon would be. Later that evening Jefferson asked a grandson: "This is the Fourth?" The younger man lied and said it was, prompting the response: "Just as I wished."

Jefferson was comatose most of the last 16 hours of his life. His grandson recalled that at 4 A.M. the dying man "called the servants" and was "perfectly conscious of his wants." Later his hands moved as if he were writing, as he mumbled, delirious: "Warn the committee to be on the alert!" Although an account was published shortly after his death which alleged that Jefferson, who seemed to reject traditional Christian belief and practice, suddenly sat up in bed and began piously praying in Latin, his doctor and other witnesses denied that this happened.

978 JEHORAM, King of Israel (d. 841 B.C.) The monarch was overthrown and killed by Jehu, one of his generals who was commanding his troops against the Syrians. In the company of Azariah, King of Judah, Jehoram went out to meet Jehu, without suspecting the general's intentions. When Jehu denounced Jehoram for the "harlotries and sorceries" of his mother Jezebel, Jehoram shouted to the King of Judah: "Treachery, O Azariah!" He attempted to flee, but Jehu shot him in the back, killing him instantly. The King of Judah was also fatally wounded.

979 JEROME of Prague (c.1360-1416) The Czech religious reformer, burnt by church authorities at Constance, Switzerland, he prayed: "This soul in flames I offer, Christ, to Thee!"

980 JERROLD, Douglas (1803-1857) The English playwright, journalist, and humorist commented, as his sons took each hand: "This is as it should be."

981 JESUS of Nazareth (c.7 B.C.-A.D. 33) The four Gospels record seven statements made on the cross, the "Seven Last Words of Christ," which, over the centuries, have been set to music and made the basis of sermons and essays. In reference to his tormentors, Jesus prayed: "Father, forgive them, for they know not what they do." To a bandit dying on a nearby cross who expressed sorrow over his sins, he promised, "Today shalt thou be with me in paradise." Entrusting his mother to the care of his cousin John, he said: "Woman, behold thy son! ... Behold thy mother!" Praying the opening words of Psalm 22, he cried: "My God, my God, why hast thou forsaken me?" Then he commented: "I thirst." In a loud voice he exclaimed: "It is finished." He also prayed: "Father, into thy hands I commend my spirit."

The last words Jesus spoke on earth, however, would have been after his resurrection when, according to the *Acts of the Apostles*, he told his disciples: "It is not for you to know the times or dates [i.e., for his return] the Father has set by his own authority. But you will receive power when the Holy Spirit comes on you; and you will be my witnesses in Jerusalem and in all Judaea and Samaria, and to the ends of the earth."

982 JEWEL, John (1522–1571) The Anglican bishop of Salisbury, who promoted the religious policies of Queen Elizabeth I, prayed: "O Lord, confound me not. This is my 'today.' This day quickly let me come unto Thee. This day let me see the Lord Jesus."

983 JEZEBEL, Queen Consort of Ahab, King of Israel (d. 841 B.C.) The Israelite queen who tried to stamp out the worship of Yahweh and promote pagan cults was killed by Jehu, a general who murdered her son Jehoram and seized the throne. Referring to an earlier king who usurped the throne, she demanded of Jehu: "Did Zimri have peace, who murdered his master?" Jehu then ordered her thrown out of the window. While Jehu feasted in the palace, horses trampled the queen's blood-spattered corpse and dogs consumed her mangled flesh.

984 JINNAH, Mahomed Ali (1876–1948) The founder of the nation of Pakistan, suffering from cancer, tuberculosis, and pneumonia, whispered his sister's nickname: "Fati."

985 JOACHIM Frederick, Elector of Brandenburg (1546–1608) The German prince advised his heir: "Don't blow up what doesn't burn you."

986 JOAN of Arc (1412–1431) The peasant girl, who led French troops to victory over the English at Orleans and helped secured the independence that her people had lost during the Hundred Years War, was captured by the enemy and burnt at the stake. Enveloped in flames, Joan called upon God, St. Michael, and St. Catherine, begged for holy water, and cried: "Jesus!"

987 JOFFRE, Joseph-Jacques-Césaire (1852–1931) The French general who commanded his country's armies during the first two years of World War I and then served as a military advisor to his government commented: "I have not done much evil in my life and I have sincerely loved my wife."

988 JOHN XXIII, Pope (1881–1963) Born Angelo Giuseppe Roncalli, the pope who began the Second Vatican Council said to his family, who were gathered at his bedside: "Do you remember how I never thought of anything else in life but being a priest? ... I embrace you and bless you ... I am happy, because in a little while I shall see our mother and father in heaven.... Pray ... I wish to be dissolved and be with Christ.... Into Thy hands, O Lord, I commend my spirit."

989 JOHN the Almsgiver (c.560–619) A layman known for his philanthropy, at 50 he was named Patriarch of Alexandria, Egypt, and spent the next decade working in behalf of the poor and dispossessed. By the time he died he had completely exhausted his once considerable private fortune. He commented: "I always wanted to possess, at death, nothing but a bedsheet. And now this sheet can be given to the poor!"

990 JOHN of the Cross (1542–1591) Born Juan de Yepes, the Spanish Carmelite monk is famous for his mystical writings, *Ascent of Mount Carmel* and *Dark Night of the Soul*. The day before he died he predicted that "at midnight I will be before God Our Lord, saying Matins." When the bell was heard signaling Matins, the first office of prayer of the monastic day, John exclaimed: "Glory be to God! For I must go to say Matins in heaven!" Then he prayed: "Into Thy hands, O Lord, I commend my spirit." He died at the hour he foretold.

991 JOHN the Evangelist (c.3–c.101) The last survivor of the Twelve Apostles of Jesus died a natural death in Ephesus in Asia Minor (now Turkey), blessing his disciples, who had carried him, at his request, outside the city gates to die. Making the sign of the cross, John prayed: "Be with me, Lord Jesus Christ." Blessing his followers, he declared: "Peace and grace be with you, my brothers!"

992 JOHN, King of England (1167–1216) The monarch's attempt to weaken the power of the feudal nobility resulted in his being forced to sign the *Magna Carta*, which later became the foundation of the English constitution and the tradition of limited government. Dying of dysentery a year later, while at war with France, he referred to an eleventh century bishop of Worcester: "To God and St. Wulfstan I commend my body and soul."

993 JOHN of Kronstadt (1829–1908) The influential Russian Orthodox priest, renowned for his holiness and mystical life, was in severe pain during the last months of his life as the result of a bladder ailment. He declared: "I thank God for my sufferings, sent me to purify my sinful soul before death ... Holy Communion revives me." A little later, after being told the date, he said: "Thank God, two more days. We'll have time to do everything." Two days later, after receiving Communion, he died, after commenting: "I cannot breathe."

994 JOHN Chrysostom (344–407) Patriarch of Constantinople, the "Golden-Mouthed" preacher was banished to exile in Asia Minor after repeatedly denouncing the lax morality of his city. He died proclaiming: "Glory be to God for all things!"

995 JOHN PAUL I, Pope (1912–1978) Born Albino Luciani, he died suddenly after a reign of only a month. Before retiring for the night he said to an aide: "Now, goodnight. Until tomorrow, if God is willing."

996 JOHNSON, Andrew (1808–1875) The former president, impeached and almost removed from office in a struggle with Congress over Reconstruction, was serving as senator from Tennessee when overtaken by his final illness. He remarked to a friend: "I am winding up my personal affairs. I wish to be my own executor. I have had a bad feeling in my head, which makes me fear apoplexy, and a man liable to that never knows how suddenly he may be cut off."

A few hours later he fell from his chair to the floor. When his granddaughter rushed to his aid, the ex-president said "indistinctly": "My right side is paralyzed." When she went to send for a doctor, he said: "I need no doctor. I can overcome my troubles." To the horror of the physicians who were eventually called, Johnson's family obediently waited 24 hours, until the sick man lost consciousness, to summon medical help. In the meantime, Johnson "conversed imperfectly," but, even before he fell completely silent, nobody could understand "the particulars of what he said."

997 JOHNSON, John Albert (1861–1909) The popular Democratic governor of Minnesota, dying after a long, painful illness, told his wife: "Well, Nora, I guess I am going, but I've made a good fight."

998 JOHNSON, John Arthur (Jack) (1878–1946) The former heavyweight boxing champion, injured in an automobile accident, begged a friend: "Call my wife. Stick by me."

999 JOHNSON, Lyndon Baines (1908–1973) The former president, seized with a heart attack at his ranch in Texas, called for help over the intercom: "Send for Mike immediately!" Moments later he was found dead in his room.

1000 JOHNSON, Samuel (1709–1784) The English lexicographer told his servant: "Attend, Francis, to the salvation of your soul, which is the object of greatest importance." Later, to a friend who came to request his dying blessing, he said: "God bless you, my dear."

1001 JOHNSON, Tom Loftin (1854–1911) Mayor of Cleveland, Ohio, during the first decade of the twentieth century commented: "It's all right. I'm so happy."

1002 JOHNSON, Walter Perry (1887–1946) The Hall of Fame pitcher of the Washington Senators, famed for his incomparable fastball and his 414 victories, was semiconscious for months, suffering from a brain tumor. Several weeks before he died, shortly before losing the power of speech altogether, when a relative asked him if he knew which team had won the World Series, he whispered: "The Cardinals."

1003 JOHNSTON, Albert Sidney (1803–1862) The Confederate general, mortally wounded in the Battle of Shiloh, replied, when asked if he were injured: "Yes, and I fear seriously."

1004 JOKAI, Mor (1825–1904) The Hungarian novelist said: "I want to sleep."

1005 JOLSON, Asa (Al) (1886–1950) The singer and actor died shortly after his return to the United States from Korea, where he had been entertaining American troops. Stricken with a heart attack, he told his doctors: "I'm a real important guy. Hell, Truman had only one hour with MacArthur. I had two!" Seconds later he moaned: "Oh! Oh, I'm going!"

1006 JONES, Robert Reynolds Davis (Bob) (1883–1968) The clergyman and educator who founded the conservative college in South Carolina that bears his name cried out, in delirium: "Get my shoes! I must go preach!"

1007 JONES, Robert Tyre (Bobby) (1902–1971) The celebrated golfer converted to Roman Catholicism on his deathbed to please his wife. He told his priest: "You know, if I'd known how happy this had made Mary, I would have done it years ago."

1008 JOPLIN, Janis (1943–1970) The rock star died from a drug overdose after wishing a friend: "Goodnight."

1009 JORTIN, John (1698–1770) The English church historian told a servant who was trying to get him to eat: "No, I have had enough of everything."

1010 JOSEPH (16th century B.C.) The Hebrew patriarch who became the minister of the Egyptian pharaoh died at the age of 110, exhorting his family: "I am about to die, but God will visit you and bring you up out of this land to the land which he swore to Abraham to Isaac and to Jacob. God will visit you and you shall carry my bones from here."

1011 JOSEPH II, Emperor of Austria (1741-1790) The brother of Marie Antoinette of France was an "enlightened despot" who abolished serfdom and feudalism, promoted education, and set up institutions to benefit the poor, yet saw all his reforms eclipsed by civil strife. Succumbing to a long illness, Joseph told the president of the War council: "Give me your hand. I will no longer have the pleasure of pressing it. Adieu, my dear Haddick. We are seeing each other for the last time."

A little later Joseph mused: "I do not know whether the poet who writes, 'Fearful is the step from the throne to the grave' is right. I do not miss the throne. I feel at peace, but only a little hurt with so much painful effort to have made so few happy and so many ungrateful. But then, such is the fate of men on the throne. Now I see that the Almighty is destroying all my works in my lifetime." He never spoke again and died two days later.

1012 JOSEPH of Cupertino (1603-1663) Born Giuseppe Desa, the Franciscan friar's life was characterized by intense spirituality and by abundant mystical phenomena, such as healings and levitations. He died praising God: "Say that again! Say that again! Praised be God! Blest be God! May the holy will of God be done!"

1013 JOSEPHINE, Empress of France (1763-1814) Napoleon's first wife, whom he divorced to marry the Austrian princess Marie-Louise, died while her former husband was in exile on the island of Elba in the Mediterranean. She murmured: "Napoleon . . . Elba . . . Marie-Louise. . . ."

1014 JOSHUA (13th century B.C.) After eliciting from the Israelites, whom he had led into Canaan, the promise that they would obey the Lord, he took a large stone and set it up under an oak tree and said: "See! This stone will be a witness against us. It has heard all the words the Lord has said to us. It will be a witness against you if you are untrue to God." He sent the people away and shortly afterwards died at age 110.

1015 JOWETT, Benjamin (1817-1893) The English writer and classical scholar exclaimed: "I bless God for my life! I bless God for my life! I bless God for my life! Mine has been a happy life! I praise and bless God for my life!"

1016 JOYCE, James (1882-1941) The Irish writer, regaining consciousness after surgery, was told that he was receiving blood donated by two soldiers from Neuchâtel, Switzerland. He replied: "A good omen. I like Neuchâtel wine."

1017 JUÁREZ, Benito (1806-1872) The Mexican president, dying of a heart condition, asked his physician: "Doctor, is my disease mortal?"

1018 JUDAS Iscariot (d. A.D. 33) The apostle who betrayed Jesus hanged himself in remorse and despair after returning to the Jewish religious leaders the money they had given him for betraying his master: "I have sinned in betraying innocent blood!"

1019 JUDSON, Adoniram (1788-1850) The American Baptist missionary to Burma told a servant: "Take care of poor mistress."

1020 JULIAN the Apostate, Emperor of Rome (331-363) The ruler who tried unsuccessfully to restore the worship of old gods to the Roman Empire after Christianity became predominant was killed fighting the Persians and died conceding: "Thou hast conquerered, O Galilean!"

1021 JULIUS II, Pope (1443-1513)

Born Giuliano Della Rovere, the patron of Michelangelo was called "The Terrible Pope" because of the continual wars he waged as temporal head of the Papal States. On his deathbed Julius lamented: "Would to God that we had never been pope, or at least that we could have turned all the arms of religion against the enemies of the Holy See."

1022 JUNG, Carl Gustav (1875–1961) The Swiss psychiatrist insisted: "Help me get out of bed. I want to look at the sunset."

1023 JUSTIN MARTYR (c.100–166) A philosopher in the Greek tradition, he was a convert to Christianity who, through his writings and teachings, attempted to explain Christianity to the pagan world. Denounced as a Christian during the reign of Marcus Aurelius, he answered the prefect who examined him in Rome and threatened to kill him unless he sacrificed to the gods of Rome: "Even when we have been punished, through prayer we can be saved through our Lord Jesus Christ, Our Savior. He has guaranteed salvation for us and will give us confidence when we appear before His fearful and universal judgment seat."

KAAHUMANU *see* Elisabeth Kaahumanu

1024 KAFKA, Franz (1883–1924) The Czech author, dying of tuberculosis, begged his doctor for more painkiller. After he was given an injection of morphine, he said: "Don't try to fool me. You're giving me an antidote. Kill me, or else you are a murderer!" He then begged his doctor: "Don't leave me." When the physician assured him that he was not leaving, Kafka answered: "But I am leaving you." Confusing the doctor with his sister, whom he did not want close to him because of the contagious nature of his malady, the writer warned: "Don't

come so close, Elli. Not so close. Yes, this is better."

KAIULANI *see* VICTORIA Kaiulani

1025 KALAKAUA, King of Hawaii (1836–1891) Dying of kidney disease in San Francisco, the monarch, after days in a coma, suddenly awoke and whispered to an aide: "Well, I am a very sick man." As an episcopal bishop administered the last rites, the king "babbled" incomprehensibly in Hawaiian.

1026 KAMEHAMEHA I, King of Hawaii (c.1753–1819) The chieftain who united the Hawaiian islands into a consolidated kingdom was asked by his courtiers for "a word" and replied: "I have given you the greatest good: peace and a kingdom that is all one — a kingdom of all the islands. That is all. It is finished."

1027 KAMEHAMEHA V, King of Hawaii (1831–1872) The childless sovereign, dying of pleurisy, was urged to name as his successor his sister-in-law, Queen Emma, but objected, explaining: "She was merely queen by courtesy, having been the wife of a king."

1028 KANT, Immanuel (1724–1804) The Prussian philosopher, celebrated for his *Critique of Pure Reason*, declared: "It is well."

KARL I, Emperor of Austria-Hungary *see* Charles I

1029 KATHERINE, Grey, Countess of Hertford (1540–1568) A younger sister of the "Nine Day Queen," she was imprisoned by Elizabeth I, who considered her a rival to the throne. Dying at 27, she cried: "Lo, He comes! ... Yea, even so, come Lord Jesus! ... Welcome, death! ... O Lord, for Thy manifold mercies, blot out of Thy book all of my offenses." When the nobleman in whose custody she was kept under house arrest suggested that arrangements be made for the bell of the local church to be rung to toll her passing, the countess said: "Good Sir Owen, let it be so." Then, awaking as if from a dream an hour later, she prayed: "Lord, into Thy hands I commend my spirit."

1030 KAUFMAN, Angelica (1741–1807) The Swiss artist, noted for her decorative wall paintings, died in Rome, directing a cousin, who was trying to read "a hymn for the dying": "No, Johann, I will not hear that. Read me the 'hymn for the sick' on page 128."

1031 KAUFMAN, George Simon (1889–1961) The American playwright and director, after a long illness, remarked: "I'm not afraid any more."

1032 KAZANTZAKIS, Nikos (1883–1957) The Greek author died in Germany. When his wife asked if he were suffering, he answered: "No. No. I'm thirsty." Asked if his lips were irritated, he replied: "Yes."

1033 KEAN, Edmund (1787–1833) The English Shakespearean actor relived the death of Richard III, one of his greatest roles. He called out in delirium: "A horse! A horse! A kingdom for a horse!"

1034 KEARNS, Jack (Doc) (1882–1963) The fight manager who managed boxing champion Jack Dempsey died in Florida, telling his son: "We have got to get ready and get on the ball and go to Nevada."

1035 KEARNY, Philip (1814–1862) The American soldier, who lost an arm in the Mexican War, was killed when, serving as a Union major general, he was caught behind the lines at Chantilly, Virginia. Attempting to ride to safety, he responded contemptuously to a Confederate officer who warned, "You are a crazy man! You can't get ten feet! Don't be foolish!": "You couldn't hit a barn!" Within seconds he was slumped on his horse,

riddled with 20 bullets.

1036 KEATS, John (1795–1821) The English romantic poet died in Rome of tuberculosis. He told a friend: "Lift me up, Severn. Don't be afraid. Thank God it has come."

1037 KEELER, William Henry (Wee Willie) (1872–1923) The Hall of Fame baseball outfielder died of heart disease just after midnight on New Year's Day, a few hours after declaring: "I know that I am fighting a losing fight, but I want to live to see 1923 ushered in." At the stroke of midnight he sat up in bed, rang a bell to welcome in the new year, and, shortly afterwards, died.

1038 KELLY, Michael Joseph (King) (1857–1894) The star catcher of the Chicago White Stockings became an alcoholic. He caught pneumonia on a train. En route to Boston Emergency Hospital, he whispered: "This is me last ride."

1039 KEMBLE, John Philip (1757–1823) The British tragic actor told his wife: "Don't be alarmed, my dear. I have had a slight attack of apoplexy."

1040 KEN, Thomas (1637–1711) Bishop of Bath and Wells, the Anglican prelate is best remembered for his hymns, several of which conclude with the famous "doxology" ("Praise God from whom all blessings flow . . ."). Ken's last words were praises to God: "All glory be to God!"

1041 KENNEDY, John Fitzgerald (1917–1963) Riding in an open car through Dallas the President responded to the wife of the Texas governor, who told him, "You can't say Dallas hasn't been friendly to you." He replied: "I certainly can't." Almost at the same moment, shots rang out, and Kennedy, clutching his wounded throat, gasped: "My God, I've been hit!" Seconds later, shot through the head, he slumped, dying, into his wife's arms.

1042 KENNEDY, Robert Francis (1925–1968) Shot by a Palestinian nationalist while celebrating his victory in the California presidential primary, the former Attorney General and incumbent New York senator said to those who tried to assist him: "Don't lift me."

1043 KENNY, Elisabeth (1880–1952) The Australian nurse who was famed for the therapy she developed to treat victims of polio died after suffering a stroke. Most of those at her bedside thought her last word was: "America." One witness, however, thought she was trying to say: "Mother."

1044 KENT, James (1763–1847) The justice of the Supreme Court of New York, who wrote the authoritative *Commentaries on American Law*, told his children: "On this point my mind is clear: I rest my hopes of salvation on the Lord Jesus Christ."

1045 KEPLER, Johannes (1571–1630) The German mathematician and astronomer who developed laws of planetary motion was asked how he hoped to attain salvation and replied: "Solely by the merits of Jesus Christ, Our Savior."

1046 KERR, Michael Crawford (1827–1876) The Democratic congressman from Indiana served as speaker of the house for but a year before he succumbed to consumption of the bowels, after a long and agonizing illness. The day before his death he dictated a message to his law partner: "The end of it all is near at hand. I wish it could be painless, but I fear not. When the news comes to you at home, bear it bravely and resignedly, for I will. My heart turns to you with warmest love."

The next day a minister called on him, asking him if he expected to go to heaven. The speaker nodded. But when asked if he trusted in the merits of Jesus, Kerr paused and then slowly shook his head in denial. Later he told his son: "I have nothing to leave you, my son, except my good name. Guard it and your mother's honor and live as I have lived. Pay all my debts, if my estate warrants it, without leaving your mother penniless. Otherwise, pay what you can and then go to my creditors and tell them the truth, and pledge your honor to wipe out the indebtedness."

1047 KETCHEL, Stanley (1887–1910) The American middle-weight champion, known as "The Michigan Assassin," was shot while eating breakfast at his home in Conway, Missouri, by a jealous farmhand. He lived long enough to name his murderer: "It is Hurz who has shot me."

1048 KEYSERLING, William (1869–1951) The Russian-born businessman and philanthropist was stricken with a heart attack at a special session of the United Jewish Appeal at the Commodore Hotel in New York. Before clutching the microphone and slumping, dead, to the floor, he said: "We must save Jewish lives!"

1049 KIDD, William Captain (c.1645–1701) The Scots naval officer, hanged as a pirate, went to the gallows protesting his innocence, declaring: "This is a very fickle and faithless generation."

1050 KIERKEGAARD, Søren Aabye (1813–1855) The Danish philosopher and theologian, dying in a Copenhagen hospital, responded when a minister told him that he looked well enough to go home: "Yes, but there is only one thing in the way, and that is I cannot walk. But there are other means of conveyance. I can be lifted. And I have had the feeling of becoming an angel and getting wings. And that is what will happen! I shall ride astride a cloud. All else is evil. I do not mean that what I said is evil. I said it to get rid of evil and so come to halle-luiah. Of course, every idiot can say that, but it all depends on how it is said."

When asked if he prayed, Kierke-gaard replied: "Yes, indeed! I pray first for the forgiveness of my sins, that everything may be forgiven me. Next, I pray that I may be free from despair at the hour of death. And then, too, I pray for something I dearly want, that I may know a little beforehand when death is coming." Asked if most of his life had turned out satisfactorily, he answered: "Yes. That's why I'm very happy; and very sad that I cannot share this happiness with anyone." Shortly afterwards he lost the power of speech. Two weeks later he died.

1051 KING, Martin Luther, Jr. (1929–1968) The American civil rights leader called from the balcony of his motel in Memphis, Tennessee to a musician who was to sing at the dinner he planned to attend that evening: "Ben, be sure to sing 'Precious Lord, Take My Hand.' Sing it real pretty." Shortly afterwards, still on the balcony, he replied to a friend who suggested that he wear an overcoat: "Okay, I will." Seconds later a shot rang out and King, mortally wounded, fell backward onto the floor of the balcony.

1052 KINGSLEY, Charles (1819–1875) The English novelist, ill with pneumonia, whispered: "It is all right. All under rule."

1053 KIPLING, Rudyard (1865–1936) The British poet, novelist, and writer of stories was suffering from a perforated ulcer and answered a doctor who asked him what was wrong: "Something has come adrift inside."

1054 KIRKPATRICK, William Jaaaph (1030 1091) The Amorioan composer of church music was seated at his desk at 2 A.M. and wrote: "Just as Thou wilt, Lord, which shall it be?/ Life everlasting, waiting for me?/ Or shall I tarry here at Thy feet?/ Just as Thou wilt, Lord, whatever is meet." The next morning, his wife found him dead, there at his desk.

1055 KLOPSTOCK, Friedrich Gottlieb (1724–1803) The German poet quoted from his epic *Der Messias*: "Can a woman forget her child, that she should not have pity on the fruit of her womb? Yes, she may forget, but I will not forget thee!"

1056 KNOX, John (1505–1572) The Presbyterian minister who led the Reformation in his native Scotland died of a stroke. The day before he died he commented: "I have been in heaven and have possession, and I have tasted of those heavenly joys where I presently am." Next day, just before he died, he asked his wife to read him the seventeenth chapter of the Gospel of John: "Go, read where I cast my first anchor." When she had done so, Knox prayed: "Lord Jesus, receive my spirit."

1057 KNOX, Ronald Arbuthnott (1888–1957) The English Roman Catholic priest, famed for his transla-tion of the Bible, was asked if he wanted to be read to from his own translation of the New Testament. He replied: "No. Awfully jolly of you to suggest it, though."

1058 KOSSUTH, Lajos (1802–1894) The Hungarian statesman, who fought unsuccessfully for his nation's independence from Austria, died in exile in Italy. When his sister told him that he was the most popular Hun-garian, he answered: "Only your van-ity holds this."

1059 KRAUTH, Charles Porter-field (1823–1883) The American Lu-theran clergyman, administrator, educator, and theologian withdrew from communication with his family and friends in his last illness, insisting, a few days before he died: "I want to be left alone with my God."

1060 KUHLMAN, Kathryn (1907–1976) The American evangelist, to whose ministry many miraculous cures were attributed, died after heart surgery, murmuring: "Love! Love! Love!"

1061 LABOUCHERE, Henry Dupré, Baron Taunton (1831–1912) The British statesman and publicist remarked when an oil lamp beside his bed flared up: "Flames? Not yet, I think."

1062 LABOURÉ, Catherine (1806–1876) A sister of St. Vincent de Paul in Paris, she was renowned for her visions of the Virgin Mary. She told her niece, who promised to return in the morning: "You shall see me, but I shall not see you, for I won't be here."

1063 LACÉPÈDE, Bernard-Germain-Étienne, Comte de la Ville-sur-Illon (1756–1825) The French naturalist and political leader asked his son to write on an unfinished manuscript: "Charles, write in large letters the word 'end' at the foot of the page."

1064 LACORDAIRE, Jean-Baptiste-Henri (1802–1861) The French preacher and theologian cried: "My God, open to me!"

1065 LAENNEC, René-Theophile-Hyacinthe (1781–1826) The French physician who invented the stethoscope took off his rings and said: "It would be necessary soon that another do me this service. I do not want anyone to have the bother of it."

1066 LAFAYETTE, Maria-Joseph-Paul-Yves-Roch-Gilbert Du Motier, Marquis de (1757–1834) The French soldier and statesman who served as a general in the American Revolution commented: "Life is like a flame. Out, light! When there is no oil — zest! — it goes out and all is over."

LA FLESCHE, Susette *see* TIBBLES, Susette La Flesche

1067 LA FOLLETTE, Robert Marion, Sr. (1855–1925) The Progressive Republican senator from Wisconsin told his son: "I am at peace with the world, but there is still a lot of work I could still do. I don't know how the people will feel toward me, but I shall take to the grave my love for them, which has sustained me through life." After taking a sip of milk, the senator commented: "It is good." Two hours later he was dead.

1068 LAHARPE, Jean-François de (1739–1803) The French poet and literary critic told his priest: "I am grateful to Divine Mercy for having left me sufficient recollection to feel how consoling these prayers are to the dying."

1069 LAKANAL, Joseph (1762–1845) The educator who reformed the French school system during the Revolution told his physician: "Your attentions will not save me. I feel that there is no more oil in the lamp."

1070 LALANDE, Joseph-Jérôme-François de (1732–1807) The French astronomer told his caregivers: "Withdraw. I no longer have need of anything."

1071 LAMAR, Lucius Quintus Cincinnatus (1825–1893) The American statesman who served as senator from Mississippi, secretary of the interior, and, finally, associate justice of the Supreme Court, gasped: "I am suffocating!"

1072 LAMBALLE, Marie-Thérèse-Louise de Savoie-Carignan, Princess de (1749–1792) Superintendent of the household of the doomed Queen Marie Antoinette, she was ordered by revolutionaries to swear an oath of allegiance to liberty and equality and an oath renouncing her allegiance to the king and queen. She agreed to do everything except denounce her sovereigns. As she was dragged into a back alley to be hacked to pieces, the princess cried: "Fie on the horror!"

1073 LAMMENAIS, Hugues-Félicité-Robert de (1782–1854) The French clergyman and political and religious philosopher, who advocated freedom of conscience, assembly, and press, commented on the sunlight: "Let it come. It is coming for me."

1074 LAMY, Jean-Baptiste (1814–1888) The first Roman Catholic archbishop of Santa Fe was ill with pneumonia. To those around his bed he said: "Keep praying for me, for I feel that I am going."

1075 LANDIS, Kenesaw Mountain (1866–1944) The American judge, who became famous for fining the Standard Oil Company of Indiana in 1908 for accepting freight rebates served as baseball's first commissioner from 1920 until his death. When his nurses told him that his friends wanted to know how he was, the judge answered: "The Judge is doing all right."

1076 LANDON, Michael (1936–1991) The actor, ill with cancer, spoke to his dead parents: "Dad, you'll have to wait. I'll be with you in a minute. Oh, Mom, it's so pretty here." When his daughter told him that his loved ones were awaiting him on the other shore, Landon conceded: "Yes, I've got to go." When his son told him, "It's time to move on," the dying man agreed: "You're right. It's time. I love you all."

1077 LANGTRY, Lily (1852–1929) The British actress known as "The Jersey Lily" told a friend: "I know that I am at the end. I shall never get better, dear. I am going, dear. I am very sorry, but I am going."

1078 LANIER, Sidney (1842–1881) The American poet and musician died of tuberculosis, which he had contracted in a Union prisoner-of-war camp during the Civil War. Declining further medication, he insisted: "I

can't."

1079 LANSKY, Meyer (1902–1983) The reputed gangster, dying of cancer, begged his doctors: "Let me go! Let me go!"

1080 LANZA, Mario (1921–1959) The American tenor who starred in many motion pictures died while a patient at a weight-loss clinic in Rome. He told his chauffeur of his decision to leave the establishment: "Go to the house. Don't let anyone know what you're up to. Bring me something to wear and let's get the hell out of here before they kill me with all these injections." Shortly afterwards, he was found dead.

1081 LAPLACE, Pierre-Simon, Marquis de (1749–1827) The French mathematician, astronomer, and physicist commented: "What we know is of small amount. What we do not know is enormous."

1082 LARCOM, Lucy (1824–1893) The American editor and writer, famous in her day for her poems about New England life, whispered the word: "Freedom."

1083 LA SALLE, Jean-Baptiste de (1651–1719) The French priet and educator, asked if he accepted his sufferings with joy, replied: "Yes, I adore in all things the designs of God in my regard."

1084 LASKI, Harold Joseph (1893–1950) The British political scientist died unexpectedly of a lung infection, after a brief illness, telling his wife: "Isn't this incredible?"

1085 LATIMER, Hugh (1485–1555) The Protestant Bishop of Worcester was burnt alive during the reign of England's "Bloody" Mary I. Chained to the same stake was Nicholas Ridley, Bishop of London. After bags of gunpowder were attached to the necks of the prisoners, to ensure a speedy death, and a lighted faggot was thrown onto the logs around the victims' feet, Latimer called out: "Be of good comfort, Master Ridley, and play the man. We shall this day light such a candle, by God's grace, in England, as I trust shall never be put out." As the flames shot upward, he prayed: "O Father in heaven, receive my soul." The fire ignited the gunpowder and he died instantly.

1086 LATROBE, John Hazelhurst Boneval (1803–1891) The American lawyer and philanthropist who served as president of the American Colonization Society, which settled freed slaves in Africa before the Civil War, commented: "The machine is worn out."

1087 LAUD, William (1573–1645) Archbishop of Canterbury during the English Civil War, his open hostility to the Puritans led to his condemnation by Parliament. On the scaffold he prayed: "Lord, I am coming as fast as I can. I know that I must pass through the shadow of death before I can come to Thee, but it is but an *umbra mortis*, a mere shadow of death, a little darkness upon nature. But thou, by Thy merits and passion hast broken through the jaws of death. So, Lord, receive my soul and have mercy upon me and bless this kingdom with peace and plenty and brotherly love and charity, that there might not be this effusion of Christian blood amongst them, for Jesus Christ, His sake, if it be Thy will. Amen."

1088 LAUGHTON, Charles (1899–1962) The British character actor called out: "Am I dying? What's the matter? Am I dying?"

1089 LAUREL, Stanley (1890–1965) The comedian remarked to the nurse who was giving him an injection: "I wish I were skiing now." Asked, "Oh, are you a skier, Mr. Laurel?" He answered: "No, but better be doing that than having those needles stuck into me."

1090 LAURENCIN, Marie (1883–1956) The French painter and lithographer insisted: "Let no one come to see me when I am dead."

1091 LAURIER, Sir Wilfred (1841–1919) The Canadian statesman who served as prime minister between 1896 and 1911 said to the nun who was nursing him: "Well, it is the bride of the Divine Husband who comes to help a great sinner." Asked if he wanted a priest, Laurier responded: "Very well, but I am not so sick as you think. Only a little weak." When the last rites were concluded, he died, saying: "It is finished."

1092 LAVAL, Pierre (1883–1945) The French political leader who served as premier of the pro–German puppet Vichy Republic after his country was invaded during World War II was shot as a traitor shortly after the war. He cried: "Long live France!"

1093 LAWRENCE (d. 258) A Roman deacon in the Christian Church, he perished during the persecution of the Emperor Valerian, who ordered the death of all Christian clergy. Roasted alive on a grid, Lawrence suggested to his torturers: "My flesh is well-cooked on this one side. Turn the other, and eat."

1094 LAWRENCE, David Herbert (1885–1930) The English writer, dying of tuberculosis, commented: "I am better now. If I could sweat, I would be better. I am better now."

1095 LAWRENCE, Ernest Orlando (1901–1958) The American physicist who developed the first cyclotron told his wife: "I'm ready to give up now. Molly, I can't make it."

1096 LAWRENCE, Gertrude (1898–1952) The English actress died of cancer while starring in the musical, *The King and I*. She directed: "About the play—see that Connie Carpenter steps in. She has waited so long for the chance. See that she gets the role. And see that Yul [Brynner] gets star billing. He has earned it."

LEADBELLY *see* LEDBETTER, Huddie

1097 LEAR, Edward (1812–1888) The British painter and author of "nonsense verse" died in Italy, dictating to his valet a last message for his friends: "My good Giuseppe, I feel that I am dying. You will render me a sacred service in telling my friends and relations that my last thought was for them, especially the judge and Lord Northbrook and Lord Carlingford. I cannot find words sufficient to thank my good friends for the good they have always done me. I did not answer their letters because I could not write, as no sooner did I take a pen in my hand then I felt as if I were dying."

1098 LECOUVREUR, Adrienne (1692–1730) The French actress became ill during a performance and died five days later. The priest who came to administer the last rites urged her to "make an act of repentance of the scandal of your profession," angering Lecouvreur, who pointed to her lover, Count Maurice de Saxe and declared: "There is my universe, my hope, and my god!"

1099 LEDBETTER, Huddie (Leadbelly) (1888–1949) The American folk singer, hospitalized with a neuromuscular disease, objected when his doctor wanted him to go to bed: "You put me in that bed and I'll never get out."

1100 LEE, Charles (1731–1782) Secondly only in rank to George Washington at the start of the American Revolution, Lee was court-martialed and dismissed from the army for refusing to obey orders at the Battle of Monmouth. Dying in Philadelphia, he relived the scenes of battle: "Stand by me, my brave grenadiers!"

1101 LEE, Gypsy Rose (1914–1970) The strip-tease dancer clung to life after a long illness with cancer. She was complaining to her son of severe pains when he tried to reassure her by saying, "It'll be over soon." Somewhat shocked, she responded: "What do you mean?"

1102 LEE, Robert Edward (1807–1870) The Confederate's military commander was serving as president of what is now Washington and Lee University in Lexington, Virginia, when he suffered a stroke after a lengthy church vestry meeting. A few days before he died he was told by his doctor, "Make haste and get well. Traveler has been standing so long in the stable he needs exercise." The general shook his head. When his son spoke of his recovery, Lee again shook his head and pointed to heaven. When his daughter tried to give him some medicine, he whispered: "It is of no use."

The next day he was in great pain, but was unable to speak. The following day his suffering was even more intense. Then, after he became delirious, his wife heard him reliving "those dreadful battlefields." First Lee cried: "Tell Hill he *must* come up!" Then he gave the order: "Strike the tent!" He never spoke again. Next day, shortly after the prayers for the dying were offered, he died.

1103 LEEUWENHOEK, Antonie van (1632–1723) The Dutch scientist, who designed the first microscope and became the first to observe and describe bacteria, directed a friend: "Be so good as to have these two letters on the table translated into Latin. Send them to London to the Royal Society."

1104 LEHAR, Franz (1870–1948) The Hungarian composer, best remembered for his operetta *The Merry Widow*, told his housekeeper: "Now I have finished with all earthly business. High time, too. And now, my dear child, now comes death."

1105 LEKEU, Guillaume (1870–1894) The Belgian composer, dying of typhoid, cried in despair: "So many works unfinished! My quartet!"

1106 LENIN, Vladimir Ilich (1870–1924) The Communist revolutionary, who founded and ruled the Soviet Union, was disabled, during his last years, by a series of strokes. The day he died he was bundled up and placed on a sleigh, so that he could watch his friends hunt. When a retriever brought back a bird to one of his friends, the dictator raised his hand and said: "Good dog!" A few hours later he died.

1107 LEO X, Pope (1475–1521) Born Giovanni de' Medici, he was made a cardinal at 15 and elected pope at 38. He was renowned as a patron of the arts and for his attempt to suppress the teachings of Martin Luther. Dying after a sudden illness, the pope looked around the room and said "to no one in particular": "Pray for me. I want to make you all happy."

1108 LEO XI, Pope (1535–1605) Born Alessandro Ottaviano de' Medici, he died of a fever after a reign of less than a month. Urged to name one of his nephews a cardinal, he told family members: "Do not suggest to us any care for earthly interests. You must speak to us now only about eternal things."

1109 LEO XIII, Pope (1810–1903) Born Gioacchino Vincenzo Rafaello Luigi Pecci, he wore the papal tiara for 25 years and is remembered as a scholar and statesman and the founder of the Catholic University in Washington. Emerging from a coma, he told his doctors: "This time you will not win your brave fight with death." Later, to one Cardinal Oreglia, he said: "To Your Eminence, who will so soon seize the reins of supreme power, I confide the church in these difficult times." Then to Monsignor Bisleti,

who asked for a blessing, Leo said: "Be this my last greeting." After blessing those around his bedside, the pontiff declared: "This is the end." Then he lapsed into a coma from which he never awoke.

1110 LEONARDO da Vinci (1452–1519) The artist and scientist, who lived in France during his last years, during his final illness told King Francis I: "I have offended God and mankind in not having labored at my art as I ought to have done."

1111 LEOPARDI, Giacomo (1798–1837) The consumptive Italian romantic poet told his friend Antonio Ranieri: "I am suffocating, Totonno. Give me light."

1112 LEOPOLD I, King of Belgians (1790–1865) The German prince who was elected first king of Belgium after his nation was created in 1831. He remarked to his chaplain: "May God pardon all my sins."

1113 LEOPOLD II, King of Belgians (1835–1909) The monarch who organized and ruled the Congo Free State in Africa complained to his doctor: "I am suffocating, doctor, I am suffocating!"

1114 LESPINASSE, Julie-Jeanne-Eleonore de (1732–1776) The French letter writer and society leader emerged from a coma and asked: "Am I still alive?"

1115 LEWIS, Clive Staples (1898–1963) The British author, ill with heart and kidney problems, remarked, two days before he died: "I have done all that I was sent into the world to do, and I am ready to go." He spoke for the last time when his brother brought him tea, responding perfunctorily: "Thank you." A few minutes later he was dead.

1116 LEWIS, George (1900–1968) The jazz clarinetist died in his native New Orleans, telling a friend who placed a crucifix in his hands: "Departings are too hard. I'll be back after you."

1117 LEWIS, Joy Davidman Gresham (1915–1960) The American author who married C.S. Lewis was ill with cancer for several years. The day she died she told her priest: "Don't get me a posh coffin. Posh coffins are all rot." Shortly before she died she told her husband: "You have made me happy." Then, to the priest she confided: "I am at peace with God."

1118 LEWIS, Meriwether (1774–1809) Private secretary to Thomas Jefferson and explorer of the Louisiana Territory, he was serving as governor of Louisiana when he was found dying of gunshot wounds in a hotel room. He murmured: "I am no coward, but I am so strong! It is so hard to die!"

1119 LEWIS, Sinclair (1885–1951) The American novelist died in Rome, telling his nurses: "I am happy. God bless you all."

1120 LIBERACE, Walter Valentino (1919–1986) When asked if he wanted to go to church, the entertainer answered: "I wish I could. I'll just stay here and watch my shows."

1121 LIGNE, Charles-Joseph, Prince de (1735–1814) The Belgian military officer, diplomat, and author who commanded Austrian troops as field marshal in many important engagements in the late eighteenth century cried: "Close the doors! Away with it! There is the monster, the Gray Comrade!"

1122 LIGUORI, Alphonsus (1696–1787) The Italian bishop and theologian who founded the Redemptorist Congregation asked: "Give me the picture of Our Lady." Gazing at the likeness of the Virgin Mary, he prayed the *Ave Maria*, concluding: "Holy Mary, Mother of God, pray for us sinners, now and at the hour of our death. Amen."

1123 LILIUOKALANI, Queen of Hawaii (1838–1917) The last monarch of Hawaii, deposed after a reign of two years, after she challenged the power of the American business establishment in her realm, died in Honolulu after a long illness. She murmured to a friend: "Thank you. How are you?"

1124 LINCOLN, Abraham (1809–1865) Sitting in a box at Ford's Theatre in Washington, he took his wife's hand. When Mrs. Lincoln expressed concern about their shocking display of intimacy, asking what their guest, Clara Harris, would think of her hanging onto her husband in such a way, Lincoln answered: "She won't think anything about it." A few minutes later he was shot by an assassin and spoke no more.

1125 LINCOLN, Abraham II (1873–1890) The only grandson of the famous president developed a tumor in his armpit and died several months later in London, trying to reassure his weeping nurse: "It's all right."

1126 LINCOLN, Mary Todd (1818–1882) The widow of the assassinated president spent her last months in a darkened room of her sister's house in Springfield, Illinois. Several days before she died, she insisted: "I want to walk across the floor and look out of the window." After making the effort, she suffered a stroke and was unable to speak again.

1127 LINCOLN, Nancy Hanks (1784–1818) The mother of the future president summoned her two children to her bedside, and, according to her cousin, Dennis Hanks, who was also present, bade them: "Be good and kind to your father, to one another, and to the world. I hope you live as I have taught you. Love men and love, reverence, and worship God."

1128 LIND, Jenny (1820–1887) The Swedish soprano died at her home in England. As her daughter opened the blinds, the dying woman burst into the opening bars of Schumann's "Sunshine Song": "O sun so bright! O sun so bright!/ Thou fillest my heart with sweet delight!" Then she prayed: "Dear Lord, You did not let me be made a sacrifice, in any part, in any way. Dear Lord, how beyond all understanding has been Your goodness to me."

1129 LINDBERGH, Charles Augustus (1902–1974) The aviator, dying in Hawaii, told the doctor that once he had been afraid of death, but: "This time I am not apprehensive or frightened." He commented to his wife: "It's a natural thing. It's harder on you, watching me die, than it is on me."

1130 LINDSAY, Vachel (1879–1931) The eccentric American poet told his wife that he had drunk Lysol, then declared: "They tried to get me! I got them first!"

1131 LISZT, Franz (1811–1886) The Hungarian pianist and composer died of pneumonia after attending, against his doctor's orders, a performance of the opera *Tristan and Isolde*. After the doctor refused to allow him a sip of brandy, Liszt whispered: "Tristan."

1132 LIVINGSTONE, David (1813–1873) The Scots physician, missionary, and explorer of Africa died on the shores of Lake Bangweolo. After an attendant brought him water, he said: "All right. You can go out now." Next morning he was found kneeling beside his bed, dead.

1133 LLOYD GEORGE, David (1863–1945) The British statesman, who served as prime minister during and immediately after World War I, remarked wistfully a few days before his death: "I wish I could have the blind faith of the Catholic." Religion was still on his mind when he spoke his last words to his doctor: "Have you been to chapel?"

1134 LOCKE, John (1632–1704) The English philosopher whose writings influenced Jefferson and other political thinkers declared: "I have lived long enough and I thank God I have enjoyed a happy life. But, after all, this life is nothing but vanity."

1135 LOEWE, Frederick (1901–1988) The Austrian-born composer who collaborated with lyricist Alan Jay Lerner in writing *My Fair Lady*, *Camelot*, and other Broadway musicals, murmured, in German: "I want to die."

1136 LOGAN, John Alexander (1826–1886) The Union general and three-term senator from Illinois died in Washington from "congestion of the brain," whispering his wife's name: "Mary."

1137 LOMBARDI, Vincent Thomas (1913–1970) The football coach who led the Green Bay Packers for many years was head coach of the Washington Redskins when he died from cancer. A few days before the end, he told his priest: "I'm not afraid to die. I'm not afraid to meet my God now. But what I do regret is that there is so damned much left to be done on earth!" He spoke for the last time when he whispered to his wife: "Happy anniversary! I love you."

1138 LONDON, Jack (1876–1916) The American writer, suffering from kidney disease, remarked to his wife as he went to his study to work: "Thank God you're not afraid of anything!" After she went to bed, he took an overdose of painkiller and died.

1139 LONG, Huey Pierce (1893–1935) The Louisiana political leader who proposed to confiscate the wealth of the rich and guarantee all Americans a basic income died two days after being gunned down in the state capitol, weeping: "God, don't let me die! I have so much to do!"

1140 LONGFELLOW, Henry Wadsworth (1807–1882) After several days in delirium the beloved American poet suddenly became lucid and looked up and saw his sister from Portland, Maine, sitting beside his bed. He told her: "Anne, my dear! If they have sent for you, I know I must be very ill."

1141 LONGFELLOW, Mary Storer Potter (1812–1835) First wife of the poet, she died in Rotterdam, Holland, after a miscarriage: "Dear Henry, do not forget me! Tell my dear friends at home that I thought of them at the last hour."

1142 LONGFELLOW, Samuel (1819–1892) The Unitarian minister and poet, brother and biographer of Henry, repeated lines from Whittier's "Hampton Beach" as he succumbed to a lingering illness: "The soul may know no fearful change/ Nor sudden wonder,/ Nor sink the weight of mystery under,/ But up with the upward rise/ And with the vastness grow,/ Familiar as our childhood's stream/ Or pleasant memory of a dream." Then he reapted the last lines again: "Familiar as our childhood's stream/ Or pleasant memory of a dream."

1143 LONGSTREET, James (1821–1904) The Confederate general called his third wife Louise by the name of his second, promising: "Helen, we shall be happier in this post."

1144 LÓPEZ, Francisco Solano (1826–1870) President of Paraguay, he ruled as a dictator and led his country into a protracted war with Brazil, Argentina, and Uruguay. Killed in battle by a Brazilian force in northern Paraguay, he cried: "I die with my country!"

LORENZO, the Magnificent
see MEDICI, Lorenzo de'

1145 LOUIS I the Pious, Emperor of Franks (778–840) Son of Charlemagne, he died while trying to quell a rebellion raised by one of his sons: "I pardon him, but let him know that it is because of him that I am dying."

1146 LOUIS VI the Fat, King of France (1081–1137) The mediaeval king who strengthened the power of the French crown, was allegedly virtually immobilized by his weight, and, according to one chronicler, "disappeared in rolls of flesh." He exhorted his son: "Remember, my son, that kingship is a public charge, for which you will have to render a strict account in another world."

1147 LOUIS VIII, King of France (1187–1226) Dying of dysentery after a reign of only three years, he spoke to a young girl who had been brought to his bedside by superstitious courtiers who insisted that he could be cured through sex with a virgin: "Ah, no! It will not be so, young lady! I will not commit mortal sin for whatever reason!"

1148 LOUIS IX, King of France (1214–1270) Saint Louis, one of the most famous of mediaeval kings, was renowned for his justice and piety, as well as for his skill as a military commander. Dying of dysentery while on crusade in Africa, he told his son: "My own dear child, I give you all the blessings a good father can give to his son. May the Blessed Trinity and all the saints keep and defend you from all evils and may God grant you grace to do His will always, so that He may be honored through you, so that you and I, after this mortal life is ended, may both be with Him together and join in praising Him through all eternity."

After the last rites were administered, Louis prayed psalms until he felt that death was near and then he prayed: "O God, be the sanctifier and guardian of Thy people. O Lord God, grant that we may so despise the prosperity of this world that we stand in no fear of adversity." He asked to be placed on a bed covered with ashes. When this was done, he crossed his hands on his chest, looked heavenward, and prayed: "I will enter into Thy temple! I will adore Thee in Thy holy house! I will confess Thy name!"

1149 LOUIS XI the Spider, King of France (1423–1483) He was called "the terrible king" because of the ruthlessness with which he broke the power of the nobility. He prayed: "In Thee, Lord, have I trusted. Let me not be confounded. I shall sing forever of the Lord's mercies."

1150 LOUIS XII, King of France (1462–1515) The gout-ridden monarch, sentenced by his doctors to a "horrifying diet," departed from it when he married the teenaged sister of Henry VIII of England. Dying less than three months after their wedding, on New Year's Day, he told his bride, whom he knew was repelled by him: "Darling, as a New Year's present, I give you my death."

1151 LOUIS XIII, King of France (1601–1643) Dominated by Cardinal Richelieu during most of his 30-year reign, he died of tuberculosis. A few days before he died he asked his physicians if there were any hope of his recovery. When they were silent, he said: "Your silence tells me that I must die. God is my witness that I have never liked life and that I shall be overjoyed to go to Him."

The day he died, Louis heard laughter from an adjoining room and told his confessor about his suspicions concerning his wife's fidelity. When the priest rebuked him for harboring such thoughts, Louis answered: "In my present condition, I am obliged to forgive her, but I am not obliged to believe her."

1152 LOUIS XIV, King of France (1638–1715) The "Sun King," who reigned 72 years, was a great patron of the arts, but nearly bankrupted his country through ruinous wars, was dying of diabetes when he summoned his little great-grandson, who was heir to the throne. He said to him: "Sweet child, you are about to be a great king, but your whole happiness will depend on your submission to God, and on the care you take to relieve the people of their burden. In order to do this you must, whenever you can, avoid making war: it is the ruin of the people. Do not follow the bad example I have given you on this point. Often, I have started wars without sufficient cause and continued them to satisfy my pride. Do not imitate me, be a peaceful ruler, and let your main object be to look after your subjects. Take advantage of the education the Duchess of Ventadour is giving you, obey her and follow the advice of Father Le Tellier when it comes to serving God. I give him to you as your confessor."

After giving more instructions to relatives and staff, he assembled his courtiers, who crowded around the bed to hear the king's final exhortation: "Messieurs, I am pleased with your services; you have served me faithfully and with the desire to please. I am sorry I could not reward you better; these last few years have not allowed me to do so. Serve the Dauphin with the same affection you have shown me; he is only a five-year-old child who may have many setbacks, for I remember having had many myself when I was young. I am going, but the State will remain. Be faithful to it and let your examples inspire all my other subjects. Always remain united and in accord—that is the strength of a state—and always obey the orders my nephew will give you; he will govern the kingdom. I hope that you will do your duty and also that you will remember me sometimes."

The next day Louis told his 80-year-old wife: "The thought which consoles me in parting from you is the hope that, considering your age, we will soon be reunited." Seeing two valets in tears, he declared: "Why are you crying? Did you think me immortal? As for me, I knew I was not and you must have been prepared to lose me, considering my age." Later that night he was asked if he were in great pain and answered: "No, and that annoys me. I would like to suffer more for the expiation of my sins."

Two days later, he spoke of the Dauphin—the heir to the throne—as "the king," creating a visible reaction among those in the room. Louis said: "But why? It does not worry me at all." The next few days the king was in and out of a coma. After the prayers for the dying was offered, the king said to Cardinal Rohan: "Those are the last blessings of the Church." Then he prayed: "O God, come to my help. Please relieve me soon." A few hours later he died.

1153 LOUIS XV, King of France (1710–1774) Remembered more for his colorful mistresses than for his successes as a monarch, he died of smallpox after a reign of 59 years. After the administration of the last rites, Louis said: "I have never felt better, or more at peace."

1154 LOUIS XVI, King of France (1754–1793) The well-meaning but ineffectual monarch perished during the Reign of Terror that climaxed the French Revolution. On the scaffold, he shouted to the crowds: "People, I die innocent! Gentlemen, I am innocent of all that I am accused of! I hope my blood will cement the happiness of the French people!" He tried to continue, but the executioners ordered the drummers who stood by to drown out, with a loud roll of drums, the final words of the condemned king.

1155 LOUIS XVII, Dauphin of France (1785–1795) The only surviving son of the murdered Louis XVI and Marie Antoinette, he was imprisoned in a building called The Temple, where he died of tuberculosis of the bones at the age of ten. When one of the child's attendants expressed regret at seeing him suffer, the boy replied: "Be comforted. I shall not always suffer." As his pain increased, he begged: "Put me where I shall not suffer so much." One of the attendants held the child in his arms. Shortly before he died, the dauphin declared: "I suffer much less. The music is so beautiful. Listen. In the midst of all those voices, I recognize my mother's."

1156 LOUIS XVIII, King of France (1755–1824) Brother of the murdered Louis XVI, he headed the restored Bourbon monarchy from the fall of Napoleon until his death from diabetes. Awakening to hear a priest offering the prayers for the dying, Louis said: "Continue, since you have thought it necessary to begin. I am not afraid of death. It is only a bad king who does not know how to die."

As family members presented themselves at his bedside for a last blessing, he said: "Farewell, my children. May God be with you." Then, to the young Duke of Bordeaux he said: "Poor child! May you be happier than we were!" Next day, after hours in a coma, he awoke and was able to respond playfully when a guard asked him for the password for the day. Making a pun on the words "J'y vais," which means, "I'm going," he gave the password: "Saint Denis-Givet."

1157 LOUIS, Joe (1914–1981) The former boxing champion, dying after years of illness, told his doctor: "I'm ready whenever God wants to take me. I've lived my life and I've done what I needed to do."

1158 LOUIS PHILIPPE I, King

of France (1773-1850) Known as "The Citizen King" because of his sympathy with some of the ideas of the French Revolution, he was deposed, after a reign of 18 years. He died two years later in England, declaring: "Now I go where God calls me."

1159 LOUISE, Madame (1737-1787) A daughter of King Louis XV of France, she died in a Carmelite convent. Impatient for death, she cried, as if she were urging on a coachman: "To heaven, at a gallop! To heaven, at a gallop!"

1160 LOUISE, Princess, Marchioness of Lorne and Duchess of Argylle (1848-1939) Daughter of Queen Victoria and widow of the governor-general of Canada, she commented, when flowers were brought to her: "You will never need to bring any more flowers for me."

1161 LOUISE of Mecklenburg-Strelitz, Queen Consort of Frederick William III of Prussia (1776-1810) The popular queen, dying of pneumonia, told her husband: "Do not fear, dear friend. I am not going to die." A few minutes later, however, choking with spasms, she cried: "I am dying! Jesus, make it short!"

1162 LOUISE of Savoy (1476-1531) The mother of French king Francis I was ill and bedridden when her room was brightened one night by the light of a comet, prompting her to remark: "Ah, that is a sign that does not appear to people of low degree. God causes it to appear for the nobility. Close the window. The comet announces my death and I must prepare." When her doctors tried to assure her that she was not seriously ill, she answered: "If I had not seen the sign of my death, I would believe what you say, for I do not feel that bad." Three days later she was dead.

1163 LOWELL, Amy (1874-1926) The American poet and biographer died suddenly of a stroke, telling her secretary: "My arm hurts. It's numb. I can't use it. Pete, a stroke! Get Eastman [her doctor]!"

1164 LOWELL, James Russell (1819-1891) The American poet, critic, and diplomat, ill for months with cancer, asked his doctors: "Oh, why don't you let me die?"

1165 LOWRY, Robert (1826-1899) The American minister, musicologist, and composer told a friend: "I am going to join those who have gone before, for now my work is done."

1166 LUCE, Henry Robinson (1898-1967) The publisher of *Time* and *Life* magazines, stricken with a heart attack in the bathroom, gasped: "Oh, Jesus!"

1167 LULLY, Jean-Baptiste (1632-1687) The French composer, dying of gangrene, apparently caused by a misplaced blow of the long heavy stick with which he beat time while conducting, was told by his confessor that his illness was God's punishment for composing music for the theater. The priest withheld absolution until the dying composer caused the opera score that lay beside the bed to be burnt in his presence. When the priest left, a friend expressed horror that Lully had destroyed his own work, prompting the response: "That's nothing to worry about. You see, I had another copy in my desk."

1168 LUNA, Álvaro de (c.1390-1453) The Spanish statesman, who served for three decades as constable of Castile, fell out of favor with the queen and was executed. On the block he declared: "It does not matter what they do with my body and head after my death."

1169 LUNALILO, King of Hawaii (1835-1874) William Charles Lunalilo reigned for only 14 months before his death of tuberculosis. To one of his attendants, he said, in Hawaiian: "I am now dying." Then, according to a newspaper report, he "turned his head, closed his eyes, and calmly expired."

1170 LUTHER, Katharina von Bora (1499–1550) The widow of the Protestant reformer died three months after a fall from a horse, telling her children: "I'll cling to Christ like a burr to a topcoat."

1171 LUTHER, Martin (1483–1546) The German priest and religious reformer died of a heart attack while mediating a political dispute in the town of Eisleben in Saxony. He prayed: "Dear Lord, I am in much pain and fear. I am on my way. I shall probably now remain in Eisleben." When a friend expressed the hope that he would soon feel better, Luther replied: "Yes, it is a cold, deathly sweat. I shall give up the ghost, because the illness has become more severe."

The reformer then prayed: "O heavenly Father, God and Father of Our Lord Jesus Christ, God of all consolation, I thank Thee that Thou hast revealed Thy son Jesus Christ to me, in whom I believe, of whom I have preached, and to whom I have confessed, whom I have loved and praised, and who is abused, persecuted, and mocked by the insufferable pope and by all those who are without God. I beg Thee, my Lord Jesus Christ, command my poor soul. O Heavenly Father, though I shall have to leave this body and be torn from this life, I know for certain that I shall remain with Thee eternally and that no one can tear me from Thy hands."

Quoting St. John's Gospel, he declared: "God so loved the world that He gave it His only son, so that none who believe in Him should perish, but enjoy life everlasting." Then from Psalm 118 he quoted: "We have a God of salvation and a Lord who leads us away from death." Speaking to his doctors, Luther insisted: "I'm on my way. I shall give up the ghost." Then he prayed: "Father, into Thy hands I commend my spirit. Thou has redeemed me, God of Truth."

He lost consciousness, but revived when the doctors massaged his heart. When one of his colleagues asked him if he wished "to die standing up for Christ and for the teaching you have preached," Luther gasped: "Yes." Turning onto his right side, he slept for 15 minutes and then, in the words of a witness, he "drew a deep, but soft breath, and with this he gave up the ghost, quietly and with great forbearance, without moving so much as a finger. No one observed . . . any kind of disquiet, bodily suffering, or pain of death."

1172 LYON, Mary (1797–1849) The American educator, who founded Mount Holyoke Female Seminary in Massachusetts, died after a stroke, remarking: "I should love to come back to watch over the seminary, but God will take care of it."

1173 LYTTLETON, George, Baron (1709–1773) The English statesman and writer told a friend: "Be good, be virtuous, my lord. You must come to this."

1174 MABIE, Hamilton Wright (1845–1916) The American editor and essayist commented: "I have had a quiet but very happy Christmas."

1175 MACARTHUR, Douglas (1880–1964) Emerging from anesthesia after an operation a few days before he died, the military commander of World War II and Korea renown promised his wife and doctor: "I am going to do the very best I can." Shortly afterwards he fell into a coma.

1176 MACAULAY, Thomas Babington (1800–1859) The British historian, poet, and statesman, who suffered from a heart condition, told his butler: "I am very tired." At the butler's suggestion, he sat down on a sofa. Seconds later he died.

1177 MCAULEY, Jeremiah (1839–1884) A reformed alcoholic, he founded the Water Street Mission in Manhattan's Bowery district, where he and his wife ministered to the homeless and down-and-out. Dying of tuberculosis, he grasped his wife's hand and pointed upward: "It's all right up there!"

1178 MCCARTY, Henry (1859–1881) The notorious bandit of the American Southwest, known as "Billy the Kid," entered his room, where lawman Pat Garrett crouched in the darkness. The Kid called out, in Spanish: "Who is it?" Garrett opened fire and killed him.

1179 MCCLELLAN, George Brinton (1826–1885) The Union general, whom Lincoln twice dismissed as commander of the Army of the Potomac because of his apparent unwillingness to fight, served, in later years, as governor of New Jersey. Stricken with a heart attack, he spoke of his wife: "Tell her I feel better now."

1180 MCCLOSKEY, John Cardinal (1810–1885) New York's archbishop became America's first cardinal. Before he lapsed into a coma two weeks before he died, he answered a churchman who expressed the hope that the archbishop would be able to join him in Atlantic City that year: "No, Father. I am going on a longer journey. God has been good to me all my life and I hope He will be good enough now to take me home."

1181 MCCORMACK, John Francis (1884–1945) The Irish tenor said (presumably in jest) to his nurse: "So, you're here! In my opinion all women should be strangled at birth!" He fell into a coma and died two days later.

1182 MCCORMICK, Cyrus Hall (1809–1884) The American industrialist who invented the mechanical reaper

told his family: "It's all right. It's all right. I only want heaven."

1183 MCDANIEL, Hattie (1895–1952) The last coherent words of the movie actress were to a friend whom she reassured: "I'll be all right. I'll soon be up and back in harness."

1184 MACDONALD, George (1824–1905) The Scottish author suffered the complete loss of his mental faculties during the last years of his life. He seems to have spoken for the last time a couple of years before his death when taken out in his wheelchair. He seemed to awake, as if from a dream, and, referring to his wheelchair, asked "Whose is this machine?"

1185 MACDONALD, Jeanette Anna (1903–1965) The American singer and actress, dying after heart surgery, told her husband: "I love you."

1186 MACDONOUGH, Thomas (1783–1825) The U.S. Navy commodore, celebrated for his victory over the British on Lake Champlain during the War of 1812, was commanding the U.S. Mediterranean Squadron when he became ill. Sailing for home, he died 600 miles off the American coast, telling his physician: "I have an aversion to being thrown into the sea. I wish my body taken home for interment."

1187 MCGRAW, John Joseph (1873–1934) Manager of the New York Giants baseball team for 30 years, he whispered to his wife: "I love you."

1188 MCGUFFEY, William Holmes (1800–1873) The American educator, best known as the author of the popular *Eclectic Readers*, spoke of his students at the University of Virginia, where he taught Moral Philosophy: "Oh, that I might once more speak to my dear boys! But Thy will be done."

1189 MCINTYRE, Oscar Odd

(1884–1938) The American journalist, author of the column, "New York, Day by Day," which was carried by over 500 newspapers, told his wife: "Snooks, will you please turn me this way? I like to look at your face."

1190 MACKENZIE, Alexander (1822–1892) The former Canadian prime minister begged: "Take me home, oh, take me home."

1191 MACKENZIE, Sir Morell (1837–1892) The British laryngologist asked for his brother, who was also a physician: "Yes, send for Stephen."

1192 MCKINLEY, Ida Saxton (1847–1907) The physically and emotionally fragile widow of President McKinley, dying after a long illness, was frustrated by the efforts of her doctors to prolong her life: "Why should I linger? Please God, if it be Thy will, why defer it? He is gone and life is dark to me now."

1193 MCKINLEY, William (1843–1901) Dying several days after being shot by an anarchist at the Pan American Exposition in Buffalo, New York, the president who acquired Puerto Rico, Guam, and the Philippines through war with Spain told his doctors: "It is useless, gentlemen. I think we ought to have prayer."

Later his wife entered the room and stood beside him, holding his hands and kissing him. He said: "Goodbye, goodbye all. It is God's way. His will, not ours, be done." When she sobbed, "I want to go too! I want to go too!" he answered: "We are all going. We are all going." Then he sang: "Nearer, my God, to Thee,/ Nearer to Thee,/ E'en though it be a cross/ That raiseth me..." The McKinleys silently held hands for several hours until Ida was led out. Afterwards the president spoke again only once, when he murmured, as if in pain: "Oh, dear!"

1194 MACKINTOSH, Sir James (1765–1832) The Scots philosopher

whispered: "Happy."

1195 MCLAURY, Thomas Clark (1853–1881) The Arizona cowboy killed by the Earp Brothers and Doc Holliday in the "Gunfight at the OK Coral," according to witnesses, protested when the lawmen insisted that he surrender his firearms. Throwing open his coat, he insisted: "I have got nothing." Two of his companions were armed; there were shots exchanged, and Tom was killed.

1196 MCLOUGHLIN, John (1784–1857) The Canadian-American physician and fur trader known as "Father of Oregon" was asked, "*Comment-allez-vous*," and answered: "To God."

1197 MACMILLAN, Harold (1894–1986) The former British prime minister announced: "I think I will sleep now."

1198 MCPHERSON, Aimee Semple (1890–1944) The Pentecostal evangelist who founded the Four Square Gospel Church in Los Angeles died of an accidental overdose of sleeping pills. Before retiring to bed, on hearing the sound of an airplane, she had remarked: "I wonder if we'll be flying around in airplanes when we die."

1199 MCQUEEN, Terrence Steven (Steve) (1930–1980) The American actor, dying in Mexico after an operation, murmured: "Ice cubes ... ice cubes ... I want more ice cubes." Later he called the names of his daughter, son, and wife: "Terry ... Chad ... Barbara...."

1200 MADISON, Dorothea Payne Todd (1768–1849) The former first lady died in her home on Lafayette Square, across from the White House. When her nurse begged her pardon for some minor annoyance, she replied: "Don't trouble about it, dear. There is nothing in this world worth really caring for. Yes, believe me, I, who have lived so long, repeat to you, there is nothing in this world below worth really caring for."

1201 MADISON, James (1751–1836) The "Father of the Constitution," who wrote the Bill of Rights and served as the United States' fourth president, died at Montpelier, his estate in Orange County, Virginia. When his niece noticed that he did not look well and asked him what the matter was, the statesman replied: "Nothing more than a change of mind, my dear." The niece left the room for a few minutes, returning to find Madison slumped dead in his chair.

1202 MAETERLINCK, Maurice (1862–1949) The Belgian dramatist, essayist, and poet told his wife: "For me this is quite natural. It is for you that I am concerned."

1203 MAGINOT, André (1877–1932) The French political leader who sponsored the fortification system against Germany that came to be called the "Maginot Line" told Labor minister Laval: "For me, this is the end, but you—continue."

1204 MAHAN, Alfred Thayer (1840–1914) The American naval officer and historian, whose writings about sea power inspired the United States and other nations to build up their navies, looked at a tree outside his hospital window and commented to a nurse: "If a few more quiet years were granted me, I might see and enjoy these things, but God is just and I am content."

1205 MAHLER, Gustav (1860–1911) The composer and conductor, dying in Vienna, cried: "Mozart! Mozart!"

1206 MAIN, Sylvester (1817–1873) The New York music publisher said to his wife and son: "The dear Lord is about to give me rest. If you love me, do not weep, but rejoice."

1207 MAINTENON, Françoise

D'Aubigné, Marquise de (1635–1719) The second wife of Louis XIV of France responded when her daughters asked her to bless them: "I am not worthy."

1208 MALCOLM X (1925–1965) Born Malcolm Little, the civil rights leader tried to calm the audience he was about to address when a disturbance broke out. Seconds before he fell dead in a burst of gunfire he called out: "Brothers and sisters, stay cool!"

1209 MALHERBE, François de (1555–1628) The French poet complained to a priest who was trying to describe heaven: "Do not speak of it any more. Your bad style leaves me disgusted."

1210 MALIBRAN, Maria Felicita (1808–1836) The Spanish operatic soprano, injured in a riding accident, died of complications, complaining to her physician: "I am a slain woman! They have bled me!"

1211 MANET, Édouard (1832–1883) The French painter, considered one of the founders of the Impressionist school, was tormented by phantom limb pain after a leg amputation. When his friend Claude Monet put his cap down on the bed, Manet cried: "Take care! You'll hurt my foot!"

1212 MANN, Horace (1796–1859) The Massachusetts legislator and educator, often called the father of American public education, died while serving as president of Antioch College in Ohio, telling his family: "Now I bid you all goodnight."

1213 MANNING, Henry Edward Cardinal (1808–1892) The English church leader, who vigorously defended the doctrine of papal infallibility, handed a friend a book which had belonged to his wife (who died before he became a Roman Catholic priest). Manning said: "I know not to whom to leave this. I leave it to you. Into this little book my dearest wife wrote her prayers and meditations. Not a day has passed since her death on which I have not prayed and meditated from this book. All the good I may have done, all the good I may have been, I owe to her. Take precious care of it." Then, in Latin, the cardinal declared: "I have laid down the yoke. My work is done."

MANOLETE *see* RODRÍ-GUEZ, Manuel Laureano

1214 MANSFIELD, Katherine (1888–1923) The British short-story writer, whose real name was Kathleen Beauchamp Murry, died of tuberculosis in France, gasping: "I believe I am going to die."

1215 MANSFIELD, Richard (1854–1907) The British actor answered his wife, who whispered, "God is life": "God is love."

1216 MANZONI, Alessandro (1785–1873) The Italian writer, author of the celebrated novel *I Promessi Sposi*, answered a friend who asked him why he was mixing up his words: "If I knew why it was, I wouldn't get them mixed up."

1217 MAO ZEDONG (1893–1976) The Chinese dictator, shortly before his death, told a group of Communist Party officials who were gathered around his bedside: "Few live beyond seventy, and as I am more than eighty, I should have died already. Are there not some among you who hoped I would go to see Marx sooner?" When told that there were none, he replied: "Really? No one? I don't believe it!"

1218 MARCIAN (d. 304) A Roman soldier sentenced to death for being a Christian, he told a friend to keep his wife away: "Keep her away until it is all over. File must not and we die." When his son came to him, just before he was beheaded, he blessed him and said: "Lord Almighty, take this child into Thy special care."

1219 MARCONI, Guglielmo (1874–1937) The Italian engineer who developed wireless telegraphy asked his physician how he could have no pulse and still be alive. When the doctor hedged, Marconi told him that he knew that he was dying and added: "But I don't care. I don't care at all."

1220 MARCUS AURELIUS, Emperor of Rome (121–180) Remembered for his book of *Meditations* as well as for his vicious persecution of Christians, he died in Vienna after a long illness. According to historian Dio Cassius, the emperor said to an aide who asked for a password: "Go to the rising sun, for my sun is setting."

1221 MARGARET Mary Alacoque (1645–1690) The French nun is famous for her visions of the Sacred Heart of Jesus. Dying, she professed: "I need nothing but God and to lose myself in the heart of Jesus."

1222 MARGARET of Scotland (c.1419–1445) Daughter of King James I of Scotland, she was rejected by her husband, the future Louis XI of France, when she failed to produce children. Dying of pneumonia, she cried: "Fie on the life of this world! Do not speak to me more about it!"

1223 MARIA THERESA, Empress of Austria (1717–1780) The Hapsburg monarch who ruled over much of central Europe was urged to sleep by one of her numerous children. She replied: "You want me to sleep? While any moment I must be called before my Judge, I am afraid to sleep. I must not be taken unawares. I wish to see death coming." When one of her sons asked if she were comfortable, the empress replied: "No, but comfortable enough to die."

1224 MARIAM of Jesus Crucified (1846–1878) Born Maria Baouardy, the illiterate Galilean Carmelite nun was known for her visions, ecstasies, prophecies, and for her ability to read the thoughts of others. She was reputed to levitate at times from the ground. She died of gangrene after breaking her arm. She prayed: "Oh, yes, mercy!"

1225 MARIE, Queen Consort of Ferdinand I of Romania (1875-1938) The popular dowager queen told her dissipated son: "Be a just and strong king."

1226 MARIE ANTOINETTE, Queen Consort of Louis XVI of France (1755-1793) Pale and haggard, the queen stared silently ahead as she rode in the tumbrel to the guillotine. As she mounted the stair, she accidentally stepped on the foot of the executioner and said: "I beg your pardon, sir. I didn't do it on purpose."

1227 MARIE LECZINSKA, Queen Consort of Louis XV of France (1703-1768) The queen had suffered the death of six of her ten children and had recently lost her father in a fire. She told her physicians: "Give me back my father and my children and I will get well."

1228 MARIE LOUISE, Empress Consort of Napoleon I of France (1791-1847) The second wife of Napoleon died in her native Austria, telling her attendants: "Go on praying."

1229 MARIE Thérèse Charlotte, Duchess of Angoulême (1778-1851) The last surviving child of the murdered Louis XVI and Marie Antoinette, she was known as Madame Royale. On her deathbed she prayed: "God, I ask pardon for my sins. Assist Thy humble servant in this moment which will decide her eternity."

1230 MARIE Thérèse of Austria, Queen Consort of Louis XIV of France (1638-1683) The Spanish princess who became the first wife of France's Sun King commented, as she succumbed to the effects of bleeding and purging to treat an abscess in her armpit: "Since I became queen, I have

not known a single happy day."

1231 MARION, Francis (1732-1795) The American general, whose successful guerrilla tactics against the British in the Carolina swamps during the Revolution earned him the soubriquet "Swamp Fox," declared: "Thank God, I can lay my hand upon my heart and say: Since I came to man's estate, I have never intentionally done wrong to any."

1232 MARIS, Roger Eugene (1934-1985) The baseball outfielder, who while a New York Yankee, set a record of 61 home runs during the 1961 season, died of cancer, making the request: "I want a radio in my room."

1233 MARK the Evangelist (d. c.67) The early Christian leader, author of the Gospel in the New Testament that bears his name, was, according to tradition, beheaded in Alexandria, Egypt, during the reign of Emperor Nero. Mark prayed: "Into Thy hands, O Lord, I commend my spirit."

1234 MARQUETTE, Jacques (1637-1675) The Jesuit priest and missionary, who explored the Mississippi River, died in what is now Michigan, praying: "Jesus ... Mary...."

1235 MARSH, Othniel Charles (1831-1899) The paleontologist, who unearthed the fossils of many dinosaurs and other prehistoric animals, told Hugh Gibb, one of his colleagues at Yale, a few days before his death: "Goodbye, Gibb."

1236 MARSHAL, William, Third Earl of Pembroke (1145-1219) The English political and military leader who, in the last three years of his life, served as regent for the young King Henry III, told his wife, son, and knights: "I am dying. I commend you to God. I can no longer be with you. I cannot defend myself from death."

1237 MARSHALL, Peter (1902-1949) The Presbyterian minister, who served as pastor of the New York Avenue Presbyterian Church in Washington and as chaplain of the U.S. Senate, was stricken with a heart attack and told his wife to ask his friend Clarence Cranford to fill in for him: "You might ask Cranny to take the Senate prayer tomorrow."

1238 MARTIN of Tours (c.315–397) The Bishop of Tours, celebrated for his evangelization of Gaul, was pestered on his deathbed by an apparition of Satan. He cried: "What do you have to do with me, evil creature? You cannot do anything more to me, for already I see Abraham, who holds his arms outstretched to me!"

1239 MARTINDALE, Cyril Charlie (1879–1963) The English Roman Catholic Biblical scholar told a friend: "I'm pretty ill, and, in fact, one night they said the prayers for the dying for me. I find it hard to be brought back, but the Lord's will is the most lovable of all."

1240 MARTINEAU, Harriet (1802–1876) The English writer declared: "I have had an outstanding portion of life, and I do not ask for any other life. I see no reason why the existence of Harriet Martineau should be perpetuated."

1241 MARTO, Francisco (1908–1919) One of the three child visionaries at Fatima, Portugal, whose alleged encounter with the Virgin Mary attracted worldwide attention, he died in the epidemic of Spanish influenza—in accordance with a prophecy from his celestial visitor. The boy said to his mother: "Look, Mama, what a pretty light there, near the door! Now I don't see it any more. Mama, bless me and forgive me for all the trouble I have caused you in my life."

1242 MARTO, Jacinta (1910–1920) Francisco's sister was likewise told by the heavenly visitor that she would meet an early death. Dying in a hospital as a result of the same influenza epidemic that took away her brother (and millions of others worldwide), she told her nurse: "I have seen Our Lady. She told me that she was going to come for me very soon and take away my pains. I am going to die. I want the Sacrament." The nurse hurried to fetch the chaplain, but when she returned a few minutes later, Jacinta was dead.

1243 MARX, Julius (Groucho) (1890–1977) The comedian, during his last illness, usually could manage no more than, "How are you?" but several days before he died he exclaimed to a friend: "This is no way to live!"

1244 MARX, Leonard (Chico) (1887–1961) The oldest of the Marx Brothers comedy team told his daughter: "Remember, Honey, don't forget what I told you. Put in my coffin a deck of cards, a mashie niblick, and a pretty blonde."

1245 MARY, Queen of Scots (1542–1587) The last Roman Catholic ruler of Scotland was deposed in favor of her infant son (James VI) and fled to England, where she was held prisoner for 19 years before her condemnation for complicity in a plot to overthrow Elizabeth I. Just before she was beheaded at Fotheringay Castle, Mary told her attendants: "You ought to rejoice and not to weep, for that the end of all Mary Stuart's troubles is now come. Thou knowest that all this world is but vanity and full of trouble and sorrow."

After her eyes were bound with a cloth, Mary knelt down on the cushion provided for her in front of the block, praying: "Even as Thy arms, O Jesus, were spread upon the cross, so receive me into Thy arms of mercy and forgive me all my sins." She told her executioner: "I forgive you with all my heart, for now I hope you shall

make an end of all my troubles."
Three or four times she prayed: "In
Thee, Lord, I trust. Let me not be
confounded. Into Thy hands, O Lord,
I commend my spirit."

The executioner, missing the
queen's neck, crashed the axe into the
back of her skull. As he dug it out,
Mary, still conscious, groaned: "Sweet
Jesus!" The next blow severed her ver-
tebrae, and the executioner, using the
blade of his axe, sawed through the
sinews and tendons to remove the
head, which he held up before the witnesses. With the lips still moving, the
head separated from the auburn wig,
with which the queen had covered her
gray hair, and smashed to the floor,
leaving the executioner holding only
the hairpiece. The lips and mouth
continued to move for 15 minutes.

1246 MARY I, Queen of England
(1515–1558) Known as "Bloody Mary,"
the daughter of Henry VIII and
Catherine of Aragon is remembered
best for incinerating hundreds of Protestants who resisted her attempt to
restore Roman Catholicism as England's compulsory state religion. Dying after a long illness, Mary told
friends about her good dreams: "I see
many little children like angels playing before me, singing pleasing notes,
giving me more than earthly comfort."
She last spoke as Mass was celebrated
at her bedside. Before receiving Communion, she prayed responsively with
the priest: "Have mercy upon us. . . .
Have mercy upon us. . . . Grant us
peace." After receiving the Host, Mary
turned her head on her pillow, sighed
deeply, and, according to one witness,
"seemed only to go to sleep."

1247 MARY II, Queen of England
(1662–1694) Daughter of James II, who
was deposed in the Glorious Revolution, she and her husband, William
of Orange, were appointed by Parliament to reign as joint sovereigns. She

died of smallpox. She prayed: "When
the soul shall leave the body, may it be
presented without stain before Thee."
After receiving Communion, she
asked her friends and attendants to
pray for her: "Seeing that I am so little
able to pray for myself."

Refusing all further medical aid,
she declared: "I have but a little time
to live and I would spend it in a better
way." She motioned away her weeping husband, and, a few hours later,
according to her doctors, died "without such agonies as are usual."

1248 MARY Beatrice of Modena,
Queen Consort of James II of England
(1658–1718) The Italian princess who
became the second wife of the Duke of
York, afterwards James II, was mother
of James Edward Stuart, who was
barred from the English throne because
of his Roman Catholic affiliation. Dying of pneumonia, Queen Mary said
to Countess Molza: "Molza, I pray
you, when I am dead, send this crucifix to the king, my son."

1249 MARY Magdalene Dei Pazzi
(1566–1607) The Florentine Carmelite
nun devoted her life to prayer for the
reform of the Roman Catholic Church
and for the conversion of the world.
She was said to be able to read the
thoughts of others and predict the future. Dying, she told the nuns gathered around her: "I am about to leave
you, and the last thing I ask of you —
and I ask it in the name of our Lord
Jesus — is that you love Him alone, that
you trust implicitly in Him, and that
you encourage one another continually
to suffer for Him."

1250 MASSENET, Jules-Émile-
Frédéric (1842–1912) The French composer, author of more than two dozen
operas, spoke, on his deathbed of fel-
low-composer Camille Saint-Saëns:
"Saint-Saëns would wish a grand funeral, but I would be content with a
plain hearse and no fuss at all. I have

been embraced, right in the theatre, by the Prince of Monaco, but Saint-Säens has not."

1251 MASTERSON, William Barclay (Bat) (1853–1921) The renowned gunfighter and lawman of the Old West was working as a sportswriter for the *New York Morning Telegraph* when he died of a heart attack at his desk, after telling a colleague, who asked how he was: "All right."

He had just finished this column: Lew Tendler received a little more than $12,000 for his scrap with Rocky Kansas. Not so bad for a little job like that, and, by the way, Rocky got nearly $10,000 for the part he played in the show. No wonder these birds are flying high when they can get that sort of money for an hour's work. Just think of an honest, hardworking farmer laboring from daylight to dark for forty of the best years of his life and lucky if he finishes with as much as one of those birds gets in an hour. Yet there are those who argue that everything breaks even in this old dump of a world of ours. I suppose these ginks who argue that way hold that because the rich man gets ice in the summer and the poor man gets it in the winter, things are breaking even for both. Maybe so, but I can't see it that way.

1252 MATA HARI (1876–1917) The Dutch exotic dancer, born Margaret Gertrude Zelle, was executed by the French during World War I as a German spy. Preparing for her execution, she said to Sister Leonide, a nun assigned to her: "Don't be afraid, Sister. I'll know how to die." As she dressed in the presence of the prison doctor, the nun tried to shield her from the physician's gaze, prompting the response: "It doesn't matter, Sister. This is really not the time to be prudish." When the doctor offered her smelling salts, she refused: "Thank you, Doctor. You can see I don't need

them."

She confided to Sister Leonide: "Death is nothing, nor life either, for that matter. To die, to sleep, to pass into nothingness, what does it matter? Everything is an illusion." She spoke for the last time to the officer who conducted her to her place before the firing squad: "Thank you, sir."

1253 MATHER, Abigail Phillips (1670–1702) The first wife of the colonial American theologian and clergyman Cotton Mather died of cancer after a long illness, telling her weeping father: "Heaven, heaven will make amends for all."

1254 MATHER, Cotton (1663–1728) The Boston pastor, theologian, and historian, the author of over 400 works, said to his son the day before he died: "I am entirely above the love of life and the fear of death. I am going to eat the bread of life and drink freely the water of life. All tears will soon be wiped from my eyes. Everything looks smiling about me. It is impossible that I should be lost. I have a strong consolation."

To his assistant pastor Mather exclaimed: "And this is dying! This is all? Is that what I feared when I prayed against a hard death? Is it no more than this? Oh, I can bear this! I can bear it! I can bear it!" After that, Mather seemed to be in ecstasy. When the younger minister asked if he could see into the other world, Mather responded: "All glorious!"

As his wife Lydia wiped his eyes, he told her: "I am going where all tears shall be wiped from my eyes." When she asked why he was smiling while she was weeping, he replied: "Why should I not smile, when everything looks smiling upon me?" The following day, as his assistant offered the prayers for the dying, Mather whispered: "Now I have nothing more to do here. My will is now entirely resigned to the will of God." When someone in the room commented that God had answered his prayers for an easy death, Mather, just moments before breathing his last, uttered the word: "Grace!"

1255 MATHER, Increase (1639–1723) Father of Cotton, pastor of Boston's North Church and president of Harvard, he answered his son Cotton, who bent over and asked him if he believed the promise, "This day thou shalt be with me in paradise": "I do! I do! I do!"

1256 MATHER, Richard (1596–1669) The Puritan leader—father of Increase and grandfather of Cotton—he was asked how he felt and answered: "Far from well, but far better than my iniquities deserve."

1257 MATHEW, Theobald (1790–1856) The Irish Capuchin priest was famed as a temperance advocate who led thousands to "sign the pledge" against the use of alcoholic beverages. He was also renowned as a preacher and worker of miracles. On his deathbed, he asked his brother: "Promise me, oh promise me that you will remember me in your prayers during the Holy Sacrifice." When the brother, referring to deceased family members, asked, "Theobald, would you like to be buried with Frank and Tom," the dying priest shook his head. When asked, "In the cemetery?" he whispered: "Yes." Asked, "Under the cross," he again murmured: "Yes."

1258 MATHEWS, Charles (1776–1835) The English comedian declared: "I am ready."

1259 MATHEWSON, Christopher (1880–1925) The Hall of Fame pitcher for the New York Giants died of tuberculosis, the result of exposure to poison gas during World War I. He told his wife: "It's nearly over. I know it's nearly over. It's nearly over, Jane. We've got to face it. This is it. You want to go out and have a good cry, Jane. Go on. But don't make it a long one. This is something we can't help. Are you all right, Jane? Are you sure you're all right?"

1260 MAUGHAM, William Somerset (1874–1965) The English novelist and playwright said to his secretary: "Why, Alan! I want to say thank you—and goodbye."

1261 MAURICE, John Frederic Denison (1805–1872) The British church leader blessed his family: "The knowledge of the love of God, the blessing of God Almighty, the Father, the Son, and the Holy Ghost, be amongst you—be amongst us—and remain with us forever."

1262 MAURY, Matthew Fontaine (1806–1873) The American navigator and hydrographer, who studied ocean winds and currents, declared: "All is well."

1263 MAXIMILIAN (273–295) The son of a veteran in the Roman army, St. Maximilian refused induction into the service, telling the proconsul: "My army is the army of God and I cannot fight for this world." When the proconsul reminded him that other Christians were serving in the army, Maximilian declared: "That is their business. I am a Christian too, and I cannot serve." Warned that a refusal of induction was a capital offense, Maximilian declared: "I shall not die. When I leave this earth I shall live with Christ, my Lord." Condemned to death by decapitation, Maximilian told his father: "Take every measure to merit like a crown and thus obtain that you yourself may soon see God. Give the new uniform you intended for me to the soldier who strikes me."

1264 MAXIMILIAN I, Emperor of Mexico (1832–1867) The Hapsburg archduke, who briefly sat upon the Cactus Throne through the support of

French troops, was overthrown when the French, under American pressure, withdrew. Sentenced to the firing squad, the emperor declared: "I wish that my blood, which is to be shed, may be for the good of the country. Long live Mexico! Long live independence!"

1265 MAXIMINUS DAZA, Emperor of Rome (c.270–313) For many years a bitter persecutor of Christians, on his deathbed he had a vision. He cried: "I see God, with his servants arrayed in white robes, sitting in judgment on me. Christ, have mercy on me!"

1266 MAYHEW, Jonathan (1720–1766) The controversial pastor of the West Church in Boston, a leader in the early protests against British misrule, was visited by a colleague when he was dying of fever. When the other minister asked if he still subscribed to his point of view, Mayhew answered: "My integrity I hold fast and I will not let it go."

1267 MAZARIN, Jules Cardinal (1602–1661) The Italian-born churchman and politician, who served as chief minister of France during the early years of the reign of Louis XIV, dying after a long illness, prayed: "Ah, Holy Virgin, have pity on me and receive my spirit."

1268 MAZZINI, Giuseppe (1807–1872) The Italian revolutionary leader, who for many years had insisted that "God is a geometric solution," awoke briefly after three days in a coma, sat up in bed, and cried out, before falling back dead: "Yes, yes, I believe in God!"

1269 MEAD, Margaret (1901–1978) The American anthropologist told her nurse that she was going to die. When the nurse, trying to reassure her, said, "We all will, someday," Mead retorted: "But this is different!"

1270 MEADE, George Gordon (1815–1872) The Union general, who defeated Lee at Gettysburg, was serving as park commissioner of Philadelphia when he died of pneumonia. After the last rites were performed, he declared: "I am about crossing a beautiful wide river and the opposite shore is coming nearer and nearer."

1271 MEDICI, Lorenzo de' (1449–1492) The Florentine political and cultural leader, known as "Lorenzo the Magnificent," died of a "slow fever," which, in the words of a contemporary, "ate away his limbs, intestines, nerves, bones, and marrow." When he asked his sister about his prognosis, she told him, "Do you really want to know the truth? Know, then, there is no hope." Lorenzo calmly replied: "If it is God's will, nothing can be more pleasant to me than death." While a passage from the Scriptures was read to him, he moved his lips. When a silver crucifix was pressed to his lips, he kissed it and died.

1272 MEIR, Golda (1898–1978) The former Israeli prime minister said to her nurse: "See, even steel sometimes weakens." Later, when her son asked her what she was thinking about, she answered: "About the afterworld."

1273 MELANCHTHON, Philip (1497–1560) The German religious reformer who prepared the Augsburg Confession, which is a basic statement of Lutheran teaching, was asked if he wanted anything. He replied: "Nothing but heaven. And therefore do not ask me such questions any more."

1274 MELBA, Dame Nellie (1861–1931) The Australian operatic soprano (who took her stage name from her native city of Melbourne) complained to a friend: "John, why must I be subjected to a lingering death?" Later she tried to sing Gounod's "Ave Maria," but her voice failed after a few notes.

1275 MELCHIOR, Lauritz (1890–

1973) The Danish operatic tenor told his granddaughter: "Have a good life."

1276 MELVILLE, Herman (1819–1891) The American novelist, best known for *Moby Dick*, died in obscurity in New York of heart disease, murmuring the last words of Billy Budd, the hero of his latest work: "God bless Captain Vere!"

1277 MENCKEN, Henry Louis (1880–1956) The American literary critic, founder of the magazine *The American Mercury*, retired to bed ill, telling a friend: "Louis, this is the last time you'll see me." He was found dead in bed the next morning.

1278 MENDELEYEV, Dimitry Ivanovich (1834–1907) The Russian chemist, who developed the periodic classification of the elements, told the physician who was treating him for pneumonia: "Doctor, you have science. I have faith."

1279 MENDELSSOHN-BARTHOLDY, Felix (1809–1847) The German composer, after a series of strokes, replied to his wife, who asked him if he were tired: "Yes, I am tired. Terribly tired." Thereupon he had another stroke and fell into a coma from which he never emerged.

1280 MENELIK II, King of Ethiopia (1844–1913) The leader who created the modern nation of Ethiopia and kept it from European colonization through his victory in 1896 over Italy at Aduwa prayed: "God, help my people!"

1281 MERCIER, Désiré-Félicien-François-Joseph Cardinal (1851–1926) Archbishop of Malines in Belgium, he is remembered for his vigorous opposition to the German occupation of his country in World War I. Just before he was administered the last rites, he prayed: "I thirst to lead souls unto Thee, O Lord!" After the last rites, he declared: "Now there is nothing more to be done except wait."

1282 MEREDITH, George (1828–1909) The English poet, novelist, and critic, speaking of his doctor, commented: "I am afraid Sir Thomas thinks very badly of my case."

1283 MERGENTHALER, Ottmar (1854–1899) The German-born inventor of the linotype died in Baltimore, exhorting his loved ones: "Emma, my children, my friends, be kind to one another."

1284 MÉRIMÉE, Prosper (1803–1870) The French novelist and short-story writer said: "Goodnight now. I want to go to sleep."

1285 MERMAN, Ethel (1908–1984) The American singer and entertainer was told by a friend about a story that chorus people were telling about her, prompting her to respond: "Assholes!"

1286 MERRY Del Val, Rafael Cardinal (1865–1930) The papal secretary of state died of heart failure during surgery. Before going under the anesthesia, he looked at his doctor and commented: "I'm too heavy, doctor. Isn't it true? I know it."

1287 METASTASIO, Pietro (1698–1782) The Italian poet and operatic librettist, after a priest had administered the last rites, prayed: "I offer Thee, O Lord, Thine own son, who has already given me a pledge of love enclosed in this thin emblem. Turn on Him Thine eyes. Ah, behold Whom I offer Thee, and then desist, O Lord, if Thou canst desist from mercy!"

1288 METCHNIKOFF, Elie (1845–1916) The Russian bacteriologist, who, for more than 20 years preceding his death headed the Pasteur Institute in Paris, told his physician: "You remember your promise? You will do my postmortem and look at the intestines carefully, for I think there is something there now."

1289 METTERNICH, Klemens

Wenzel Nepomuk Lothar, Prince von (1773–1859) The Austrian foreign minister famous for his support of traditional monarchies and his opposition to democracy, reflecting on his long and influential career, observed to a friend a few days before his death, several years after reformers had forced him from office: "I was a rock of order!"

1290 MEW, Charlotte (1869–1928) The British poet died after drinking poison. To the doctors working to save her she protested: "Don't keep me. Let me go."

1291 MEYERBEER, Giacomo (1791–1864) The German composer of French grand opera died shortly after completing *L'Africaine*. Before retiring to bed for a sleep from which he never awoke, he told a friend: "I will see you in the morning. I bid you goodnight."

1292 MEYNELL, Alice Christiana Thompson (1847–1922) The English poet and essayist declared: "This is not tragic. I am happy."

1293 MICHELANGELO Buonarroti (1475–1564) The Italian sculptor, painter, architect, and poet dictated: "I commit my soul to the hands of God, my body to the earth, and my substance to my nearest relatives, enjoining upon these last, when their hour comes, to think upon the sufferings of Jesus Christ."

1294 MICHELET, Jules (1798–1874) The French historian, noted for his anticlerical views and for his 16-volume history of France, responded when his doctor ordered that his bed linen be changed: "Linen, doctor, you speak of linen? Do you know what linen is? . . . The linen of the peasant, of the worker . . . linen, a great thing . . . I want to make a book of it."

1295 MICHELSON, Albert Abraham (1852–1931) The American physicist, who first measured the speed of light, began dictating: "The following is a report on the measurement of the velocity of light made at the Irvine Ranch, near Santa Ana, California, during the period of September, 1929 to . . . ." Exhausted, he broke off there and fell asleep, never to awaken.

1296 MILL, John Stuart (1806–1873) The English philosopher whispered to his wife: "You know that I have done my work."

1297 MILLER, Cincinnatus Hiner (1839–1913) The American "Poet of the Sierras," who wrote under the penname Joaquin Miller, cried: "Take me away! Take me away!"

1298 MILLET, Jean-François (1814–1875) The French painter, famous for portraying scenes of ordinary life, was watching a deer, wounded by hunters, collapse outside his window. He observed: "It is an omen. The poor beast which comes to die beside me warns me that I too am about to die."

1299 MIRABEAU, Honoré-Gabriel-Victor Riqueti, Comte de (1749–1791) The French revolutionary leader died of natural causes while serving as president of the National Assembly. He complained to his physician: "Were you not my doctor and my friend? Did you not promise to spare me the agonies of such a death? Do you wish me to expire with the regret that I trusted you?"

1300 MIRANDE, Henri (1877–1955) The French painter looked at himself in the mirror and remarked: "Yes, I have the appearance of death!"

1301 MITCHELL, Martha Elizabeth Beall (1918–1976) The controversial wife of Nixon's attorney general during the Watergate years, she was divorced by her husband and died virtually alone. To her nurse, she spoke of her society friends, who had all abandoned her: "Those people sure let me down when I needed them most. I never did like them anyhow. I always felt more comfortable with plain, ordinary folks."

1302 MITCHELL, William (Billy) (1879–1936) The American army officer, who organized and commanded the American air force in Europe during World War I, spoke of his burial plans: "Although I should like to be with the pilots and my comrades at Arlington, I feel that it is better for me to go back to Wisconsin, the home of my family."

1303 MODIGLIANI, Amedeo (1884–1920) The Italian artist, dying of tubercular meningitis, en route to the hospital in an ambulance, commented: "I have only a fragment of brain left."

1304 MOHAMMED (570–632) The founder of Islam laid his head on his wife's lap and declared: "Rather, God on High and paradise."

MOHAMMED Reza Pahlavi *see* PAHLAVI, Mohammed Reza

1305 MOLIÈRE (1622–1673) The French playwright, whose real name was Jean-Baptiste Poquelin, suffering a lung hemorrhage, directed: "Go and ask my wife to come up to me."

1306 MONET, Oscar-Claude (1840–1926) Two weeks before he died, the French impressionist painter spoke to his friend, former premier Georges Clemenceau, about some seedlings planted in his garden: "You will see all that in the spring, but I won't be here anymore." Moments before the artist died, Clemenceau arrived for another visit and asked his friend if he were suffering. The painter answered: "No." A few minutes later he died.

1307 MONICA (c.330–387) The mother of Saint Augustine died in Italy shortly after his conversion to Christianity. She bade her three children: "Remember me at the altar of God." Asked if she were not unhappy

to die so far from her native Africa, she replied: "Nowhere is far from God."

1308 MONROE, James (1758–1831) The former president, dying in New York after a lingering illness, spoke to a mutual friend about James Madison: "I regret that I should leave this world without again beholding him."

1309 MONROE, Marilyn (1926–1962) The American actress and presidential favorite, just hours before she was discovered dead, spoke by telephone to Kennedy brother-in-law Peter Lawford: "Say goodbye to Pat, say goodbye to the president, and say goodbye to yourself, because you're a nice guy ... I'll see ... I'll see...."

1310 MONTAGU, Mary Wortley Pierrepont, Lady (1689–1762) The English author, ill with cancer, commented about her life: "It has all been very interesting."

1311 MONTCALM, Louis-Joseph, Marquis de (1712–1759) Mortally wounded in the Battle of Quebec, which resulted in the loss to Britain of France's North American colonial holdings, he died the next day, declaring: "Praise God that I live not to see the surrender of Quebec!"

1312 MONTESSORI, Maria (1870–1952) The Italian educator, told that she should not travel anymore, complained to her son, minutes before suffering a fatal stroke: "Am I no longer of any use, then?"

1313 MONTEZ, Lola (1818–1861) The dancer and actress, born Marie Dolores Gilbert in Ireland, was notorious as the mistress to King Ludwig I of Bavaria.

In later years she became a Christian and died of a stroke in New York, telling the Episcopal priest who was reading her a portion of Scripture: "Tell me more of my dear Savior." She then placed her hand on the Bible and died.

1314 MONTEZUMA II, Emperor of Mexico (c.1466-1520) The Aztec ruler, stoned by his people because of his friendliness to the Spanish conquistadores, told a priest who urged him to embrace Christianity: "I have but a few moments to live, and will not at this hour desert the faith of my fathers."

Entrusting his daughters to the care of Cortes, the Spanish leader, in hopes that Emperor Charles V would allow them at least part of their inheritance, Montezuma said: "They are the most precious jewels that I could leave you. Your lord will do this, if it were only for the friendly offices I have rendered the Spaniards and for the love I have shown them—though it has brought me to this condition. But for this I bear them no ill-will."

1315 MONTFORD, Simon de, Earl of Lancaster (1208-1265) The English political and military leader who ruled as virtual dictator up to the time of his death in battle at Evesham against the forces of the crown prince, was cut down as he made a desperate attempt to break through the enemy lines, crying: "God's grace!"

1316 MONTGOMERY, Bernard Law, Viscount of Alamein (1887-1976) The field marshal who commanded the British army during World War II relived the horror of the Battle of El Alamein in North Africa when he spoke his last coherent words several weeks before he died: "I couldn't sleep last night. I had great difficulty. I can't have very long to go now. I've got to meet God—and explain all those men I killed at Alamein." Shortly afterwards he fell into a coma.

1317 MONTGOMERY, James (1771-1854) The British poet and journalist, the afternoon before his death, laid his hand over his heart and

told a friend: "I feel considerable oppression here." Before retiring for the night, he told a servant: "Good-night." Next morning he was found unconscious on his bedroom floor, dying of a heart attack.

1318 MONTGOMERY, Anne, Duc de (1493-1567) The marshal of France was wounded mortally in battle. Misstating his age, the 74-year-old general declared: "Do you think a man who has known how to live honorably for eighty years does not know how to die for a quarter of an hour?"

1319 MOODY, Arthur Edson Blair (1902-1954) The columnist and longtime correspondent for the *Detroit News* was appointed senator by the governor of Michigan to complete an unexpired term in 1951. Defeated for re-election the next year, he later tried to regain his seat, but died of pneumonia during his primary campaign, after commenting: "I feel better."

1320 MOODY, Dwight Lyman Ryther (1837-1899) The American lay preacher and religious leader died of "fatty degeneration of the heart" at his Northfield, Massachusetts, home. According to accounts written by his two sons and by his son-in-law, the sick man awoke around 7 A.M. and said in a strong voice, almost shouting: "Earth is receding! Heaven is opening!" One of his sons thought that the invalid was dreaming and tried to rouse him from what he thought was sleep, only to have the dying man insist: "No, this is no dream, Will! It is beautiful! It is like a trance. If this is death, it is sweet! There is no valley here! God is calling me and I must go!"

As doctors and family members rushed into the room, the evangelist gave instructions. Speaking, in turn, to his sons, his son-in-law, and his nephew, Moody said: "Will, you will carry on Mount Hermon [school]. Paul will take up the seminary when he is older. Fitt will look after the [Moody Bible] Institute, and Ambert will help you with the business details." Gazing intently upwards, in ecstasy, smiling, he cried: "This is my triumph! This is my coronation day! I have been looking forward to this for years!" With his face illuminated with "inexpressible joy," he called the names of his young grandchildren, who had recently died: "Dwight! Irene! I see the children's faces!" Turning to his wife he told her: "Mama, you have been a good wife to me."

Moody then lost consciousness and seemed dead, but his doctors restarted his heart. Resuscitated, Moody, angry, demanded: "What are you doing here? I have been beyond the gates of death and to the very portals of heaven, and now here I am back again!" At this point his daughter began screaming, "Papa, Papa, don't leave us!" Gently, Moody told her: "Oh, I'm not going to throw my life away. I'll stay as long as I can, but if my time is come, I'm ready."

With great effort Moody struggled to his feet and was helped to a chair. After a few minutes he had to be returned to bed, where he lay silently for an hour.

Then he told his wife: "This is hard on you, Mother, and I'm sorry to distress you in this way. It is hard to be kept in such anxiety." Again he began to sink, and, turning to one of the doctors, he said: "Doctor, I don't know about this. Do you think it best? It is only keeping the family in anxiety." And so, in compliance with Moody's request, the physicians made no attempt to resuscitate him.

1321 MOORE, Sir John (1761–1809) The British general died of wounds received in his victory over Napoleon at La Coruna, telling a comrade: "I feel myself so strong. I fear I shall be along time in dying. It is a great uneasiness. It is a great pain. Everything François says is right. I have the greatest reliance on him. Remember me to your sister."

1322 MOORE, Thomas (1779–1852) The Irish romantic poet outlived all his children. To his wife, distraught upon being left alone, he said: "Lean upon God, Bessie, lean upon God."

1323 MOOREHOUSE, Henry (1840–1880) The English evangelist and Bible scholar, dying of a heart attack, said calmly: "All is well. God is love."

1324 MORE, Hannah (1745–1833) The English religious writer, known as "Holy Hannah," exclaimed: "Joy!"

1325 MORE, Sir Thomas (1478–1535) The English humanist, famous for his work *Utopia*, was serving as chancellor of England when he refused to sign the Act of Supremacy, which severed relations with the pope. Condemned to death by Henry VIII for high treason, More told his executioner: "I can manage to get down alone. Courage, my good man, don't be afraid. But, take care, for I have a short neck, and you have to look to your honor." Taking care to gather his beard away from the path of the axe, he commented: "It does not deserve to be cut off, since it betrayed nothing."

1326 MOREHEAD, John Alfred (1867–1936) Former president of Roanoke College, the Lutheran minister served as president of the Lutheran World Convention. Speaking of his recently deceased wife, he asked: "Will you do me a favor? Will you kindly ask my physician how long before I shall join my Nellie?"

1327 MORGAN, John Pierpont (1837–1913) The American financier and philanthropist died in Rome, babbling: "I've got to get up the hill."

1328 MORRIS, Gouverneur (1752–1816) The American statesman and diplomat, who helped to draw up the U.S. Constitution and later served as minister to France, U.S. senator from New York, and chairman of the Erie Canal Commission, quoted from Thomas Gray's "Elegy Written in a Country Churchyard": "A beautiful day, yes, but— 'Who, to dumb forget-fulness a prey,/ This pleasing, anxious being yet resigned,/ Left the warm precincts of cheerful day,/ Nor cast one longing, lingering look behind?' Sixty-four years ago it pleased the Almighty to call me into existence, here, on this spot, in this very room, and now shall I complain that He is pleased to call me hence?"

1329 MORRIS, William (1834–1896) The English poet, artist, and furniture designer said, enigmatically: "I want to get mumbo-jumbo out of the world."

1330 MORSE, Samuel Finley Breese (1791–1872) The American painter and inventor who devised the first successful electric telegraph was told by his doctor, who was tapping his chest, "This is the way we doctors telegraph." He replied: "Very good."

1331 MORTON, Oliver Hazard Perry (1823–1877) Governor of Indiana during the Civil War, he served as a U.S. senator the last ten years of his life, despite a stroke that left him partially paralyzed. After suffering another stroke that left him almost completely immobilized, he declared: "I am dying. I am worn out."

1332 MOSES (c.1200 B.C.) Ascending Mount Pisgah, the prophet who led the Israelites out of Egypt blessed the twelve tribes, saying: "Happy are you, O Israel! Who is like you, a people saved by the Lord, the shield of your help and the sword of your triumph! Your enemies shall come fawning to you and you shall tread upon their high places!" Remaining behind while his nation moved towards the Promised Land, he died at the age of 120.

1333 MOSES, Anna Mary Robertson (Grandma) (1860–1961) The American primitive painter, devastated at being in a nursing home, hid her doctor's stethoscope. When he insisted that she tell him where it was, she retorted: "That's what I won't tell you! I hid it. It's a forfeit. You take me back to Eagle Bridge [her home] and you'll get back your stethoscope." She died shortly afterwards—in the nursing home.

1334 MOSTEL, Samuel Joel (Zero) (1915–1977) The actor and painter collapsed after losing nearly 90 pounds on a diet. Hospitalized, he complained: "I feel dizzy—you better call a nurse."

1335 MOTT, Lucretia Coffin (1793–1880) The suffragette, abolitionist, and temperance leader died in her home near Phildelphia, crying: "Let me go! Do take me! Oh, let me die! Take me now, this little standard-bearer! The hour of my death!" Just before she became unconscious, she raised her hands to her head and cried in pain: "O my! my! my!"

1336 MOZART, Wolfgang Amadeus (1756–1791) According to his sister-in-law, the Austrian composer told her: "Ah, dear Sophie, how glad I am that you have come. You must stay here tonight and see me die." Sophie tried to persuade Mozart that he was not dying, but he answered: "Why, I am already tasting death. And if you do not stay, who will support my dearest Constanze [his wife] when I am gone?" Sophie replied, "Yes, yes, dear Mozart. But I must first go back to my mother and tell her that you would like me to stay with you tonight."

When Sophie Weber returned, she

found Mozart explaining to Franz Xavier Süssmayr, another composer, how to complete the *Requiem*, on which he had been at work. Then, referring to the undertaker, Mozart said to his wife: "Keep my death a secret until you have informed Albrechsberger." He did not speak again, but, until he lost consciousness, he seemed to "express with his mouth" the drum passages of the *Requiem*.

1337 MUHLENBERG, Henry Melchior (1711–1787) The German born clergyman who became known as the "Patriarch of the Lutheran Church in America" because of his work organizing congregations of his religious persuasion throughout the English colonies sang his favorite hymn just before he died. He sang in German, but the translation is: "Bring an end, O Lord, bring an end/ To all our sufferings./ Strengthen our feet and hands/ And let us, till death,/ At all times be devoted to Your providence,/ So that our paths will surely lead us to heaven."

1338 MUHLENBERG, William Augustus (1796–1877) The Episcopal priest and hymnist who founded St. Luke's Hospital in New York concluded his life with the simple greeting: "Good morning!"

1339 MUNI, Paul (1895–1967) The movie actor, looking at a picture of his father, exclaimed: "Papa, I'm hungry."

1340 MUNRO, Hector Hugh (1870–1916) The British humorist and satirist who wrote under the penname "Saki" was killed in action during World War I after shouting to one of his men: "Put that bloody cigarette out!"

1341 Münsterberg, Hugo (1863–1916) The German-American psychologist and philosopher, commented, with unfounded optimism, on the progress of World War I: "By spring we shall have peace!"

1342 MURAT, Joachim (1767–1815) An innkeeper's son who became marshal of France and, under Napoleon, King of Naples, was captured and executed when, after the fall of Bonaparte, he tried to recover his kingdom. He shouted to the firing squad: "Spare my face, aim at my heart! Fire!"

1343 MURGER, Louis-Henri (1822–1861) The French novelist, famous for his portrayal of Bohemian life, cried: "No more music! No more commotion! No more Bohemia!"

1344 MURPHY, Francis William (Frank) (1890–1949) The American statesman served as governor of Michigan, U.S. attorney general, and then, during the last nine years of his life, as an associate justice of the Supreme Court.

Dying of a heart attack, he asked: "Have I kept the faith?"

1345 MUSSET, Alfred de (1810–1857) The French poet, playwright, and short-story writer, ill with heart trouble, commented: "What a splendid thing peace is! People are certainly wrong to be afraid of death, which is no more than its highest expression." He sat up in bed with his hand on his heart. Asked if he were in pain, he lay back, shut his eyes, and said: "Sleep! At last I am going to sleep!"

1346 MUSSOLINI, Benito (1883–1945) The deposed Italian leader was seized by communist partisans as he tried to flee across the Swiss border. Pulling back his lapels, he invited his captors to: "Shoot me in the chest."

1347 MUSSORGSKY, Modest Petrovich (1839–1881) The Russian composer, best remembered for his opera *Boris Godunov*, lamented: "All is over! Woe is me!"

1348 NABOKOV, Vladimir Vladimirovich (1899–1977) The Russian-born American novelist and critic told his son, who was leaving the room: "A certain butterfly is already on the wing."

1349 NAPOLEON I, Emperor of the French (1769–1821) In exile on the island of St. Helena in the South Atlantic, the deposed French leader murmured: "France ... army ... head of the army ... Josephine...."

1350 NAPOLEON II, Duke of Reichstadt and King of Rome (1811–1832) The only legitimate son of Napoleon I spent most of his brief life at the court of his grandfather, Emperor Francis II of Austria. Dying of tuberculosis, he told his valet: "I am going under ... I am going under.... Call my mother ... my mother.... Take the table away ... I don't need anything anymore."

As the valet went out, the dying man grabbed his arm and gasped: "Packs! Blisters!" When a priest arrived a few minutes later and asked if he wanted to read the prayers for the dying, the duke shook his head. When the priest asked, "Do you want me to recite them?" the invalid nodded. Shortly afterwards he died.

1351 NAPOLEON III, Emperor of the French (1808–1873) Nephew of Napoleon I, he was declared emperor after serving a year as president of France. He was deposed after his defeat at the hands of the Germans at Sedan in 1871, after a rule of nearly 20 years. Dying in England, he relived the disaster: "Were you at Sedan?"

1352 NAPOLEON IV, Prince Imperial of the French (1856–1879) Son of Napoleon III, he lived in exile in England after his father's deposition and was killed fighting the Zulu in South Africa. Riding off to battle, he told a friend: "Lt. Carey will take good care of me."

1353 NARVÁEZ, Ramón María (1800–1868) The Spanish general and conservative political leader, who served as prime minister six times,

told the priest who asked him if he forgave his enemies: "I do not have to forgive my enemies, because I killed them all."

1354 NASSER, Gamal Abdel (1918–1970) The Egyptian president, just before dying of a heart attack, told his wife: "I don't think I could eat a thing."

1355 NAST, Thomas (1840–1902) The American political cartoonist commented: "I feel much better."

1356 NATION, Carry Amelia More (1846–1911) The radical temperance advocate, famous for smashing saloons with a hatchet, described herself as "just a bulldog at the feet of Jesus, barking and biting at what He don't like." Dying in a hospital after a long illness, she declared: "I did what I could."

1357 NEHRU, Jawaharlal (1889–1964) India's first prime minister, awakened by heart pains, told a servant: "I think the pain will pass, so you need not awaken the doctor."

1358 NEHRU, Motilal (1861–1931) One of the leaders of India's independence movement, and father of his country's first prime minister, he awoke from what appeared to be a coma and said to his friend, Mahatma Gandhi: "Bapu, if you and I happened to die at the same time, you, being a saintly man, would presumably go to heaven right off. But, with due deference, I think this is what would happen: you would come to our river of death; you would stand on the bank and then, most probably, you would walk across it, perhaps alone or maybe holding onto the tail of a cow. I would arrive much later. I'd get into a fast new motor boat, shoot past you, and get there ahead of you. Of course, being very worldly, I might not be allowed into heaven—if there is one."

1359 NELSON, George (Baby Face) (1908–1934) The bankrobber charged the FBI agents who were trying to arrest him. With blazing machine-gun, he roared: "Come on, you yellow-belly son of a bitch! Come and get it!" Struck by 17 bullets, he staggered into his car and told his wife: "You'll have to drive. I'm hit." His corpse was recovered the next day.

1360 NELSON, Horatio, Viscount (1758–1805) The English admiral died in the Battle of Trafalgar, in which his fleet inflicted a decisive defeat on Napoleon's navy. His spine severed by a sharpshooter's bullet, Nelson said to one of his officers: "Kiss me, Hardy. Now I am satisfied. Thank God I have done my duty. Who is that? God bless you, Hardy." Regretting that he had been moved from the deck to the infirmary, he said: "I wish I had not left the deck, for I shall soon be gone."

He told the surgeon: "Doctor, I have not been a *great* sinner." Referring to his illegitimate daughter and to his mistress, he said: "Remember that I leave Lady Hamilton and my daughter Horatia as a legacy to my country. Never forget Horatia. Thank God I have done my duty." As the surgeon massaged his chest, the admiral murmured until he lost consciousness: "Drink ... drink ... fan ... fan ... rub ... rub...."

1361 NERO, Emperor of Rome (37–68) The dissipated ruler who decreed the extermination of Christians was driven from power in a coup, and, overtaken in flight, took his life. As he prepared to cut his throat, he referred to his pretensions as an actor and poet: "What an artist is dying!" Then he added, sadly: "How vulgar my life has become!" Unable to summon the courage to kill himself, he muttered: "This is certainly no credit to Nero, no credit at all! One should be tough in such situations! Come, pull it together, man!"

Hearing riders approaching, he cried theatrically: "Hark, the sound I hear! It is the hooves of galloping steeds!" With the help of a servant, he managed to slit his throat. When the centurion dispatched to arrest the ex-emperor found him dying, he tried to stanch the flow of blood with his own cloak. Thinking the officer loyal after all, Nero rasped: "Too late! This is fidelity!"

1362 NEVIN, Ethelbert Woodbridge (1862–1901) The American composer and songwriter was a professor at Yale when he was stricken with a stroke. He told his wife: "Anne, I am dying and I do not wish to leave you."

1363 NEWMAN, Ernest (1868–1959) The British music critic answered his wife, who asked if he wanted anything: "Yes, I want my cup of tea."

1364 NEWMAN, John Henry Cardinal (1801–1890) Shortly before he died, the British church leader and theologian remarked: "I am not capable of doing anything more — I am not wanted — now mind what I say, it is not kind to me to wish to keep me longer from God." He spoke for the last time when, after telling his attendant, "I feel bad," he added, a few minutes later: "I hope to go to sleep." A few hours later he died.

1365 NEWTON, Sir Isaac (1642–1727) The English physicist who first described the Law of Gravity said to his nephew: "I do not know what I may appear to the world, but to myself I seem to have been only like a boy playing on the seashore and diverting myself in now and then finding a smoother pebble or a prettier shell than ordinary, while the great ocean of truth lay all undiscovered before me."

1366 NEWTON, John (1725–1807) The English slave-trader-turned Anglican priest is best remembered for his hymn, "Amazing Grace." To a friend who visited shortly before he died, Newton remarked: "My memory is almost gone, but two things I remember: that I am a great sinner and that Christ is a great Savior."

1367 NEY, Michel, Duke of Elchingen and Prince of Moskowa (1769–1815) The French general was shot as a traitor after supporting Napoleon in his unsuccessful attempt to regain power. Before the firing squad he said: "Don't you know, sir, that a soldier does not fear death? Frenchmen, I protest against my condemnation. My honor. . . ."

1368 NICHOLAS I, Emperor of Russia (1796–1855) Dying suddenly of pneumonia while his nation was being defeated by England and France in the Crimean War, he told his son and heir to inform the army: "I shall continue to pray for them in the next world." Then he dictated a dispatch to Moscow announcing his impending death and ordering all the Guards Regiments to the palace to swear allegiance to his son Alexander. Then he told his son: "If this is the beginning of the end, it is very painful. I wanted to take everything difficult, everything serious, upon my shoulders and leave you a peaceful, well-ordered, and happy realm. Providence decreed otherwise. Now I go to pray for Russia and for you all. After Russia, I loved you more than anything else in the world. Serve Russia."

1369 NICHOLAS II, Emperor of Russia (1868–1918) Forced to abdicate in March, 1917, the last tsar was imprisoned in Siberia by the communist government which seized power a few months after his overthrow. Murdered with most of his family by a Red death squad, he prayed the words of Christ on the cross: "Father, forgive them, for they know not what they do."

1370 NICOLL, Sir William Robertson (1851–1923) The British author and editor who wrote under the penname of Claudius Clear asserted: "I believe everything that I have written about immortality."

1371 NIEBUHR, Barthold Georg (1776–1831) The German historian and philologist asked about the medicine that he was being administered: "What essential substance is this? Am I so far gone?"

1372 NIETZSCHE, Friedrich (1844–1900) The German philosopher, incapacitated for many years by syphilis, whispered the name of his sister, who nursed him during his last years: "Elisabeth."

1373 NIJINKSY, VASLAV (1890–1950) The star of the Ballet Russe, he was incapacitated for more than 30 years by schizophrenia. Dying in England, he called for his mother: "*Mamasha!*"

1374 NIMITZ, Chester William (1885–1966) Commander-in-chief of the US Pacific Fleet during World War II, shortly before he lapsed into a coma, he told a visitor to his home who was sipping sherry: "Jack, you can have something stronger if you like."

1375 NIXON, Thelma Patricia Ryan (1912–1983) The wife of Richard Nixon, according to a tabloid, declared: "I've had a wonderful life!"

1376 NOBEL, Alfred Bernhard (1833–1896) The Swedish chemist, who invented and manufactured dynamite and established the annual Nobel Peace Prize through a bequest in his will, suffered a paralytic stroke. He tried to speak, but the only word that could be made out was: "Telegram."

1377 NODIER, Charles (1780–1844) The French romantic writer, known for his short stories, told his family: "It is very hard, my children. I no longer see you. Remember me. Love me always."

1378 NORDICA, Lillian (1859–1914) The American operatic soprano died on tour in Indonesia, speaking of her long-dead mother: "I am coming, Mother."

1379 NORTH, Frederick, Earl of Guilford (1732–1792) British prime minister during the American Revolution, he died after a long illness, during which he frequently declared: "While there is life, there is hope." Just before he died, in response to a question, he replied: "I feel no pain, nor have I suffered any."

1380 NOVALIS (1772–1801) The German Romantic poet, whose real name was Friedrich von Hardenburg, died of tuberculosis, bidding his brother: "Play to me a little on the harpsichord."

1381 OBERON, Merle (1911–1979) The actress told her husband: "Darling, I love you so much. Thank you for the happiest years of my life." Shortly afterwards she indicated that her face was paralyzed, and then fell unconscious.

1382 O'BRIEN, William Smith (1803–1864) The leader of the Young Ireland movement sat in Britain's House of Commons for 20 years, until exiled to Tasmania for fomenting a peasant revolt. Given a pardon eight years later, he died in Wales. He commented: "Well, the night is so long and dreary, I think I will wait up a little longer."

1383 O'CONNELL, Daniel (1775–1847) The Irish nationalist leader, for many years a member of the British House of Commons, died in Italy, praying: "Jesus! Jesus! Jesus!"

1384 O'CONNELL, William Henry Cardinal (1859–1944) The long-time archbishop of Boston told the priest who was reading to him: "You need not read any more. Run along. Jerry will be here soon. I would like to sit here and think." Shortly afterwards he suffered a stroke and spoke no more.

1385 OECOLAMPADIUS, John (1482–1531) The Swiss Protestant reformer declared: "I shall presently be with my Christ! Oh Christ, save me!"

1386 OEI TJIE SIEN (1835–1900) A Chinese emigrant who became a wealthy merchant and businessman in Java in the Dutch East Indies promised his wife, on her deathbed, that he would join her in death once their youngest child was grown. Shortly after the marriage of the youngest daughter, Oei took to his bed, insisting that it was time to die. When a ginseng root was placed in his mouth in an effort to prolong his life, he removed it and told his children: "This is no use. Your mother has come for me and I must go."

1387 OFFENBACH, Jacques (1819–1880) The composer of French comic operas died while working on *The Tales of Hoffmann*. A few hours before he died he said to his wife: "I well believe that this night will be the end. Let's drink."

1388 O'KANE, Tullius Clinton (1830–1912) The American composer of church music had finished family devotions, concluding the Our Father with the word: "Amen." He rose to go to his room and fell dead of a heart attack.

1389 O'KEEFFE, Georgia (1887–1986) The American artist, asked how she felt a few days before her death, responded: "It's time for me to go."

1390 OLD JOSEPH (Tuekakas) (1786–1871) Chief of the Nez Perce, he told his son and successor Young Joseph: "A few more years and the white men will be all around you. They have their eyes on this land. My son, never forget my words. This country holds your father's body. Never sell the bones of your father and mother."

1391 OLGA Alexandrovna, Grand Duchess (1882–1960) The last surviving daughter of Tsar Alexander III of Russia died in poverty in Canada. Shortly before she died she said that she saw her life as a sunset: "I can see every event in my life in the light of a setting sun." Just before she fell unconscious she whispered: "The sunset is over."

1392 OLGA Nicolayevna, Grand Duchess (1895–1918) Before being slaughtered by a communist death squad with her parents and other members of her family, the eldest daughter of Nicholas II wrote: "Send us, Lord, the patience/ In this year of stormy, gloom-filled days,/ To suffer popular oppression/ And the torturing hangman./ Give us strength, oh Lord of Justice,/ Our neighbor's evil to forgive/ And the cross so heavy and bloody/ With Your humility to meet./ And in upheaval restless,/ In days when enemies rob us,/ To bear shame and humiliation,/ Christ, our Savior, help us,/ Ruler of the world, God of the universe,/ Bless us with prayer/ And give our humble soul rest/ In this unbearable, dreadful hour./ At the threshold of the grave/ Breathe into the lips of Your slaves/ Inhuman strength—/ To pray meekly for our enemies."

1393 OLIPHANT, Laurence (1829–1888) The British author and mystic, who worked to establish a Jewish state in Palestine, called for: "More light."

1394 OLIPHANT, Margaret (1828–1897) The Scottish novelist and biographer exclaimed: "I seem to see nothing but God and Our Lord."

1395 OLIVIER, Sir Laurence (1907–1989) The British actor cursed a nurse who spilled juice in his face. Alluding to a character in *Hamlet* who was killed by poison administered through the ear, Olivier snapped: "My dear, we are not doing fucking *Hamlet!*"

1396 OMAR KHAYYÁM (c.1050–1131) The Persian astronomer, mathematician, and poet, famous for his poem, the Rubáiyát, prayed: "O God, verily I have sought to know Thee to the extent of my powers. Forgive me, therefore. My knowledge of Thee is my recommendation to Thee."

1397 ONASSIS, Jacqueline Bouvier Kennedy (1929–1994) According to the tabloids, the former first lady, speaking of her dead children, murmured: "My little angels—I'll be with you soon." Then she said to her two living children: "Don't cry for me. I'm going to be with your father now."

1398 O'NEILL, Eugene (1888–1953) The American playwright commented a few days before he died: "When I'm dying, don't let a priest or a Protestant minister or a Salvation Army captain near me. Let me die in dignity. Keep it as simple and brief as possible. No fuss, no man of God there. If there is a God, I'll see Him and we'll talk things over." A few minutes before he died, O'Neill raved: "I knew it! I knew it! Born in a goddamned hotel room, and dying in a hotel room!"

1399 O'NEILL, James (1847–1920) The actor famous for his interpretation of the role of the Counte of Monte Cristo whispered to his son Eugene: "Glad to go, boy ... a better sort of life ... another sort ... somewhere. This sort of life ... froth! rotten! ... all of it ... no good!"

1400 OPIE, Amelia Alderson (1769–1853) The British novelist, speaking of those who asked about her condition, responded: "Tell them I have suffered great pain, but I think on Him who suffered for me. Say that I am trusting in my Savior and ask them to pray for me."

1401 O'REILLY, John Boyle (1844–1890) The Irish-American poet and journalist, who edited the *Boston Pilot*, said to his wife: "Yes, Mamsie dear, I have taken some of your sleeping medicine. I feel tired now, and if you will let me lie down on that couch I will go to sleep right away.... Yes, my love! Yes, my love!"

1402 ORLÉANS, Louis-Philippe-Joseph, Duke of (1747–1793) A French royal who renounced his title to support the Revolution, he took the name "Philippe Egalité." Beheaded during the Reign of Terror, he told his executioner, who wanted him to remove his boots: "You can do that more easily to my dead body. Come, be quick."

1403 ORTEGA Y GASSET, José (1883–1955) The Spanish philosopher, writer, and statesman complained to his wife: "I have a great confusion in my head. I would like you to clear it up for me."

1404 OSCAR II, King of Sweden (1829–1907) The popular constitutional monarch whispered to his doctors as he died of a heart condition, brought on, many believed, by grief over the separation of Norway from Sweden a few years earlier: "Thank you."

1405 OSLER, William (1849–1919) The Canadian physician, whose book, *The Principles and Practices of Medicine*, remains (with frequent revisions) a standard text, said to his wife: "Nighty-night, a darling."

1406 OTHO, Emperor of Rome (32–69) The general who overthrew Galba, who had, in turn, overthrown Nero, was himself deposed in a coup led by another general, Vitellius. Just before he committed suicide, Otho told his followers: "If you love me in reality, let me die as I desire and do not compel me to live against my will, but make your way to the victor and gain his good graces."

1407 OUGHTRED, William (1574–1660) The English mathematician remarked, when he was told that the monarchy had been restored an that Charles II was now king: "And are ye sure he is restored? Then give me a glass of sack to drink to his Sacred Majesty's health!"

1408 OWEN, Wilfred (1893–1918) The British poet, killed in World War I, commended one of his soldiers: "You are doing very well, my boy!"

1409 OZANAM, Frédéric (1813–1853) The French historian who founded the Society of St. Vincent de Paul prayed: "My God, have mercy on me."

1410 PADEREWSKI, Ignace Jan (1860–1941) The Polish pianist who was elected premier of his country was offered a sip of champagne and responded: "Please."

1411 PAGANINI, Niccolò (1782–1840) The Italian violinist suffered from a throat ailment that deprived him of the ability to speak, but, just before he lost consciousness, he wrote down, in response to a question about laxatives: "I don't know the laxative *Red Roses*."

1412 PAHLAVI, Mohammed Reza, Shah of Iran (1919–1980) The Persian monarch, overthrown by the Ayatollah Khomeini, died in exile in Egypt. When his valet tried to reassure him, saying, "You will get better," the Shah answered: "No, you don't understand. I'm dying."

1413 PAHLAVI, Reza, Shah of Iran (1878–1944) The Persian soldier who rose to became a general, then premier, and then, in 1926, Shah (king) was deposed by the Allies during World War II, and died in exile in South Africa, conveying a message for his son: "Do not fear difficulties. Go forward to meet them. Never try to avoid them. One must confront difficulties face to face in order to remove them."

1414 PAINE, Thomas (1737–1809) The British philosopher and pamphleteer, whose writings were especially influential in the American Revolution, died in poverty in New Rochelle, New York. When two clergymen, a few days before he died, urged him to believe in Christ, he raised himself in his bed and cried: "Let me have none of your popish stuff! Get away with you! Good morning! Good morning!" Then he said to his nurse: "Don't let 'em come here again. They trouble me."

During the last few weeks, in great pain, he frequently moaned: "Oh, Lord, help me!" Just before he died, his physician, who was extremely fat, commented, "Your belly diminishes," which prompted the patient to respond: "And yours augments." When a friend asked, "Do you wish to believe that Jesus Christ is the Son of God?" Paine paused several minutes, then said deliberately: "I have no wish to believe on that subject!" A few hours before he died, he was asked if he was satisfied with the care he had received, and he told his nurse: "Oh, yes!"

1415 PALLOTTI, Vincent (1795–1850) The Roman priest who founded the Society of the Catholic Apostolate for religious and charitable work literally caught his death of pneumonia giving away his coat to a homeless person and then sitting for hours in a cold confessional box. Given Holy Communion, he stretched out his arms and prayed: "Jesus, bless the Congregation: a blessing of goodness, a blessing of wisdom."

1416 PALMER, Ray (1808–1887) The American Congregational minister, poet, and hymnist died quoting his own verse: "When death these mortal eyes shall seal,/ And still this throbbing heart,/ The rending veil shall Thee reveal,/ All glorious as Thou art!"

1417 PALMERSTON, Henry John (1784–1865) The British prime minister said to his physician: "Die, my dear doctor? That's the *last* thing I shall do!"

1418 PANZRAM, Carl (1891–1930) A serial murderer hanged at Leavenworth, Kansas, he declared, before his execution: "In my lifetime I have murdered twenty-one human beings. I have committed thousands of burglaries, robberies, larcenies, arsons, and, last but not least, I have committed sodomy on more than 1000 male human beings. For all these things I am not the least sorry. I have no conscience, and so that does not worry me. I don't believe in man, God, nor devil. I hate the whole human race, including myself."

As the rope was being prepared, Panzram roared: "Let's get going! What are we stalling around for?" When the hangman asked if there was anything he wanted to say, the killer retorted: "Yes! Hurry it up, you Hoosier bastard! I could hang a dozen men while you're fooling around!"

1419 PARNELL, Charles Stewart (1846–1891) The Irish nationalist leader in the British Parliament said to his wife: "Kiss me, sweet wife, and I will try to sleep a little."

1420 PASCAL, BLAISE (1623–1662) The French philosopher, mathematician, and scientist, dying after a long illness, prayed: "May God never abandon me."

1421 PASTERNAK, Boris Leonidovich (1890–1960) The Russian novelist and poet, best known for *Doctor Zhivago*, told his nurse: "I can't hear very well. And there's a mist in front of my eyes. But it will go away, won't it? Don't forget to open the window tomorrow."

1422 PASTEUR, Louis (1822–1895) The French bacteriologist, offered a glass of milk, declined, insisting: "I cannot."

1423 PATMORE, Coventry (1823–1896) The English poet embraced his wife and said to her: "I love you, dear, but the Lord is my life and my light."

1424 PATTISON, Dorothy Wyndlow (1832–1878) The British philanthropist, who became Sister Dora of the Sisterhood of the Good Samaritan, died of cancer, declaring: "I see Him standing there! The gates are open wide!" A little later she dismissed everyone from her room, arguing: "I have lived alone. Let me die alone. Let me die alone."

1425 PATTON, George Smith, Jr. (1885–1945) The American general died in Germany, several months after the conclusion of the Second World War, of injuries sustained in an automobile accident. He said: "It's too dark, I mean, too late."

1426 PAUL I, Emperor of Russia (1754–1801) After trying to reduce the privileges of the nobility, the tsar was murdered in his bedroom by irate courtiers. Pleading with his assassins, Paul begged: "Gentlemen, in heaven's name spare me! At least give me time to say my prayers!"

1427 PAUL I, King of the Hellenes (1901–1964) The Greek king, suffering from cancer, told his wife, Queen Frederica: "I had thought I had gone. I still feel far away. It takes a little time to get used to. I have been completely on the other side." Asked what it was like on the other side, the king replied: "Incredible! I had a vision of a long, dark road with a brilliant light shining at the end of it. It gives a marvelous feeling of peace and happiness. It is a great spiritual uplift, like coming close to heaven. *That* is Holy Communion. Yes, now I understand everything. It is the truth. This is the most wonderful time of our lives."

Next day, asked if he were in pain, Paul responded: "The body is nothing, compared with this heavenly feeling." The following day was the last of King Paul's life. He commented to the queen: "When you have known the road on the other side, you don't want to struggle along it on this side anymore. Come, let us go. We have finished here. Don't let's take the world with us. We shall always be together, you and I."

Rejecting narcotic injections and intravenous feeding, he insisted: "The injections will separate you and me, and the drip feedings will hold me back. I want to be quite conscious when I go." At the point of death the king cried: "I see the light! It is much larger now and the peace is getting stronger! Now we go!"

1428 PAUL III, Pope (1468–1549) Born Alessandro Farnese, he strengthened the power of the Inquisition and convened the Council of Trent to counteract the effects of the Protestant Reformation. Dying, he repeated in prayer the words of Psalm 19:13: "Keep back thy servant also from presumptuous sins; let them not have dominion over me! Then I shall be blameless, and innocent of great transgression."

1429 PAUL VI, Pope (1897–1978) Born Giovanni Battista Montini, he led the Church during the final years of the Second Vatican Council and the period of turmoil that followed. Asked what he wanted, the pontiff said: "Dear friend, a little patience." As the Nicene Creed was prayed, he murmured the phrase: "... apostolic church, apostolic church...." Then, after receiving Communion, he murmured faintly: "Our Father, who art in heaven...."

1430 PAUL of Tarsus (d. c.67) The Christian missionary, whose letters comprise a substantial portion of the New Testament, was beheaded during the persecution of Nero. With his last breath, according to one tradition, he cried: "Jesus!"

1431 PAUL, Maury Henry Biddle (1890–1942) The society editor of the Hearst newspapers who wrote under the name "Cholly Knickerbocker" commented to his mother: "Oh, Mother, how beautiful it is!"

1432 PAVLOVA, Anna (1880–1931) The Russian ballerina, ill with pleurisy, referred to one of her most famous roles, in which she represented a dying swan: "I'm dying. Give me something to ease my pain. Get my swan costume."

1433 PAYNE, John (1842–1916) The English poet and translator asked: "Did you get the pillow-cases?"

1434 PAYSON, Edward (1783–1827) The American Congregational minister was one of the most popular preachers of his day. He served for 20 years as pastor of Second Congregational Church in Portland, Maine. He studied twelve hours a day, prayed at least two hours, and spent one day each week in fasting and prayer. He died of tuberculosis after great suffering, exclaiming: "Faith and patience, hold out!" He had prepared a placard which was placed on his corpse when it lay in state: "Remember the words which I spoke unto you while I was yet present with you."

1435 PEABODY, George (1795–1869) The American merchant, banker, and philanthropist who founded, among other things, the Peabody Institute of Baltimore and the Natural History Museum at Yale, and in whose honor his hometown of South Danvers, Massachusetts, changed its name to Peabody, died in England, commenting: "It is a great mystery, but I shall know all soon."

1436 PEACOCK, Thomas Love (1785–1866) The British novelist and poet snapped at his minister, who urged him to leave his fire-damaged house:

"By the immortal gods, I will not move!"

1437 PEALE, Charles Wilson (1741–1827) The American painter, answering his daughter, who told him that she could not find his pulse, said: "I thought so. The law makes my will." Seconds later he was dead.

1438 PEEL, Sir Robert (1788–1850) The British statesman, who was prime minister in the 1840s, died of injuries sustained in a fall from a horse. He whispered to his family: "God bless you."

1439 PÉGUY, Charles (1873–1914) The French poet was killed while serving as an officer in World War I. When one of his men objected to exposing himself to enemy fire without a helmet, Péguy shouted: "I haven't one, either! Go on firing!" Seconds later he was shot through the head and killed.

1440 PELLICO, Silvio (1788–1854) The Italian poet, best remembered for *Francesca da Rimini* and *Laodamia*, placed his hands over his heart and declared: "Here my god is!"

1441 PENFIELD, Wilder (1891–1976) The eminent brain surgeon, as he was taken in an ambulance to a hospital, said of his cane: "I won't need this anymore, but maybe I'll keep it anyway, just for while I'm in the hospital." After his arrival, shortly before he lost consciousness, he scrawled in his diary: "Here I am."

1442 PENN, Guglielma Maria Springett (1644–1694) The wife of William Penn, founder of Pennsylvania, told a friend: "I have cast my care upon the Lord. My dear love to all my friends. May the Lord preserve and bless us."

1443 PENROSE, Boise (1860–1921) Republican senator for more than two decades from Pennsylvania, he served as chairman of the finance committee and was noted for his opposition to both prohibition and women's suffrage. Ill with a respiratory complaint, the day before he died he said to his valet: "See here, William. See here. I don't want any of your damned lies. How do I look? Am I getting any better? The truth now! ... All right, William. When you go to church tomorrow, pray for me, too." Next day Penrose suffered a pulmonary thrombosis and quietly died.

1444 PEPYS, Samuel (1633–1703) The British statesman, remembered for the diary he kept during the 1660s, joined the hands of his nephew and a Mrs. Skinner, saying: "Be good friends. I do desire it of you."

1445 PERCEVAL, Spencer (1762–1812) British prime minister, he was noted for his abrasive personality and his religious intolerance. Talking to a colleague in the lobby of the House of Commons, he was approached by a ruined businessman, who blamed his failures on Perceval's policies. The angry man shot the prime minister pointblank in the chest. Before falling dead, Perceval gasped: "I am murdered!"

1446 PERCY, Walker (1916–1990) The American novelist, suffering from prostate cancer, insisted: "Don't ask the Lord to keep me here. Ask Him to have mercy." When his nurse asked if she should awaken his wife, Percy replied: "No. She understands."

1447 PERICLES (490 B.C.–429 B.C.) The Athenian political and military leader during the "Golden Age" of his city-state died, according to Plutarch, of a "dull and lingering distemper." Responding to friends who, thinking him in a coma, sat by his bedside discussing his military accomplishments, Pericles commented: "I wonder that you should commend and take notice of things which owe as much to fortune as to anything else, and have happened to many other commanders, and, at the same time, not speak or mention the most excel-lent and greatest thing of all. For no Athenian, through my means, ever wore mourning."

1448 PERÓN, Juan Domingo (1895–1974) President of Argentina from 1946 to 1955, he died shortly after returning to power after many years in exile. He murmured: "I'm going."

1449 PERÓN, Maria Eva Duarte de (1919–1952) The Argentine political leader, ill for some time with cancer, told her maid, a few hours before she fell into a coma: "I have never felt happy in this life. That's why I left home. My mother would have married me to someone ordinary and I could never have stood it. Irma, a decent woman has to get on in the world."

1450 PERPETUA, Vibia (180–202) An aristocratic African lady, she was killed in an arena in Carthage, after refusing to renounce her Christian faith. Before being led out to be mangled by a vicious cow, she tied up her hair, since, in her culture, disheveled hair was considered a sign of mourning. She said: "It is not becoming for a martyr to suffer with disheveled hair, lest she appear to be mourning in her glory." After being mauled by the cow, she was carried back to her prison cell, where, in delirium, she mumbled: "When am I going to be taken out to the cow?" Shortly afterwards, she was beheaded.

1451 PERRY, Oliver Hazard (1785–1819) The U.S. naval officer, who was the hero of the Battle of Lake Erie in 1813 against Britain, after which he sent the famous message, "We have met the enemy and they are ours," died at sea in the West Indies of yellow fever. Perry, who was then a commodore, declared: "Few people have greater inducements to make them live than I, but I am perfectly ready to go if it pleases the Almighty to take me. The debt of nature must be paid."

Asked how he was, he said: "We have all been ill on this schooner." And then, when his secretary made preparations for him to make his will, Perry waved him away, saying: "But tomorrow will do." He died shortly afterwards.

1452 PERUGINO (1446–1523) The painter of the Italian Renaissance, whose real name was Pietro Vannucci, refused to see a priest and commented: "I am curious to see what happens in the next world to one who dies unshriven [that is, without making a confession]."

1453 PÉTAIN, Henri-Philippe (1856–1951) The French military hero of World War I was imprisoned for life after heading the hated Vichy Republic during World War II, as a puppet of the Germans. Dying, he told his wife: "Do not weep. Do not grieve."

1454 PETER I, Emperor of Russia (1672–1725) The tsar who tried to westernize his country and make it a great power prayed, after receiving the last rites of the Orthodox Church: "Lord, I believe. I hope God will forgive me my many sins because of the good I have tried to do for my people."

Then, calling for a writing tablet, he was able to scribble only the words: "Give all to. . . ." Finally, he called his daughter: "Anna!" By the time she arrived, Peter was unconscious. The next morning he died.

1455 PETER III, Emperor of Russia (1728–1762) Deposed by his German wife, who afterwards ruled as Catherine II, he was murdered shortly afterwards. He protested to his assassins: "It was not enough to deprive me of the crown of Russia, but I must be put to death as well!"

1456 PETER of Alcantara (1499–1562) The Spanish Franciscan mystic, author of *Treatise on Prayer and Meditation*, prayed the last verse of Psalm 122: "I rejoiced at the things

that they said unto me: let us go into the House of the Lord."

PETER, Saint *see* SIMON Peter

1457 PHILIP (c.3–c.90) According to tradition, the Apostle was martyred in Asia Minor by the governor of Hierapolis. Crucified, Philip prayed: "Clothe me in thy glorious robe and the seal of thy ever-shining light, until I have passed by all the rulers of the world and our adversary, the evil dragon."

1458 PHILIP I, King of France (1052–1108) Ruler for 48 years, he allegedly died of obesity. He declared: "I know the kings of France are buried in the Church of St. Denis, but I have been too great a sinner for my body to lie alongside so great a martyr. I fear indeed that my sins have been so great that I shall be delivered up to the devil . . . I have always revered St. Benedict. Dying, I call upon this father of these monks and I ask to be buried in his church by the Loire. He is filled with forgiveness and goodness. He welcomes sinners who wish to repent and be reconciled to God within his Rule."

1459 PHILIP II, King of Spain (1527–1598) The monarch who ruled over the Indies, southern Italy, and much of the New World died of a wasting disease, which, according to early biographers, caused his flesh to "consume away on his bones by incurable ulcers which sent forth swarms of worms, so that nobody could approach without fainting." To his 20-year-old son and successor, Philip declared: "I meant to save you this scene, but I wish you to see how the monarchies of the earth end. You see that God has denuded me of all the glory and majesty of a monarch in order to hand them to you. In a few hours I shall be covered only with a poor shroud and girded with a coarse rope. The king's crown is already falling from my brows and death will place it upon yours. Two things I especially commend to you: one is that you always keep faithful to the Holy Catholic Church, and the other is that you treat your subjects justly. The crown will one day fall from your head as it now falls from mine. You are young, as I once was. My days are numbered and draw to a close. The tale of yours God alone knows, but they, too, must end." Asking his confessor to administer extreme unction, Philip declared: "Father, give it to me now, for now is the time."

1460 PHILIP III, King of Spain (1578–1621) The son of Philip II died of a lingering illness, bargaining with God: "Oh, if it should please heaven to prolong my life, how different should be my future from my past conduct."

1461 PHILIP IV, King of Spain (1605–1665) Told that an illegitimate son had come to see him, the monarch answered: "Tell him to go back to Consuegra. It is now time for nothing but death."

1462 PHILIPPA of Hainault, Queen Consort of Edward III of England (1314–1369) The English queen told her husband: "My husband, we have enjoyed our long union in happiness, peace, and prosperity. I entreat, before I depart and we are forever separated in this world, that you will grant me three requests: the payment of my lawful debts, the fulfillment of the legacies of my will, and my wish that you be buried beside me in the cloisters of Westminster when your time comes."

1463 PHILLIPS, David Graham (1867–1911) The American novelist was shot six times in front of the Princeton Club in New York by an eccentric violin teacher named Fitzhugh C. Goldsborough. Dying in Bellevue Hospital the next day, Phillips commented: "It is of no use. I could have won against two bullets, but not against six."

1464 PHILLIPS, Philip (1834–1895) The American evangelist known as "The Singing Pilgrim" died after a lingering illness, telling a friend: "You see that I am still in the land of the dying. Why I linger so long is a problem. The gracious Savior is more to me now than I ever expected when I was well. Often during the night I have real visions. I walk on the banks of a beautiful river and get real glimpses of the bright beyond."

Then he burst into song: "We speak of the land of the blest,/ A country so bright and fair,/ And oft are its glories confessed,/ But what must it be to be there!" He exulted: "Blessed be God! I shall soon know! What a singing time we will have when we get there!"

1465 PHILLIPS, Ulrich Bonnell (1877–1934) The American historian, famed as an apologist for slavery and the antebellum South, was ill with cancer when, shortly before falling into a coma, he dictated a letter which concluded: "In body I'm down but not out; in mind, as lively as ever—a cricket!"

1466 PHILLIPS, Wendell (1811–1884) The American abolitionist and social reformer, stricken with a heart attack, spoke of his wife: "What will become of poor Ann?"

1467 PHOCION (c.402 B.C.–317 B.C.) The Athenian statesman and general, executed for treason, answered a friend who commiserated with him over the ingratitude of the city that he had served for so long: "Yes, but not surprising. This is what usually happens at Athens to her great men."

1468 PHOENIX, River (1970–1993) The popular movie actor collapsed from a drug overdose outside a Hollywood nightclub, announcing to the doorman (according to a tabloid): "I'm gonna die, Dude!"

1469 PIAF, Edith (1915–1963) The French singer told her sister: "I can die now. I've lived twice. Be careful, Momome. All the damned-fool things you do in life you pay for."

1470 PICASSO, Pablo (1881–1973) The Spanish painter who was a founder of the Cubist movement in art advised his doctor: "You are wrong not to marry. It's useful."

1471 PICCOLO, Louis Brian (1943–1970) A running-back for the Chicago Bears football team, his death from cancer at 26 inspired a movie and at least two books. Piccolo cried to his wife: "Can you believe it? I'm going to lick this! I'm going to get out of here! Can you believe it, Joy? Can you believe this shit?"

1472 PICKFORD, Mary (1892–1979) The Canadian-born movie actress and producer, known as "America's Sweetheart," pointed to pictures of her parents on the wall and to an icon of Christ, and murmured: "There's Mama and Papa. And there's Jesus."

1473 PIERCE, Franklin (1804–1869) The former president, dying in relative obscurity at the home of friends in Concord, New Hampshire, drifted in and out of a coma during his last weeks, responding only to answer various questions: "Yes" and "No."

1474 PIERCE, Jane Means Appleton (1806–1863) The melancholy wife of the fourteenth president, who was traumatized by the early death of all three of her children, the last of whom was decapitated before her eyes in a railroad accident, murmured the beginning of the second verse of Charles Wesley's hymn, "Jesus, Lover of My Soul": "Other refuge have I none. . . ."

1475 PIKE, Albert (1809–1891) The Arkansas journalist and poet was stricken with a throat ailment that gradually left him unable to speak or swallow. Just before his death he wrote on a sheet of paper the Hebrew word for peace: "Shalom. Shalom. Shalom."

1476 PIKE, James Albert (1913–1969) The American Episcopal bishop, controversial because of his unorthodox views, was overcome by heat and exhaustion while doing archaeological research on a desert in the Middle East. As his wife went to look for help, he told her: "Diane. . . . Tell them to bring lots of water—and yell 'help me' all the way along."

1477 PINZA, Ezio (1892–1957) The Italian basso who starred in opera, musicals, and in concert, was suffering from paralysis when he tried to speak to his wife: "I want . . . I want. . . ."

1478 PIO of Pietrelcina (1887–1968) Born Francesco Forgione, the Italian Capuchin priest was famed as a miracle-worker and for the stigmata—five wounds suggestive of the crucifixion of Christ—which were evident in his hands, feet, and side for 50 years. Collapsing into an armchair with a heart attack, evidently referring to the Virgin Mary and to his own mother, he murmured: "I see two mothers!" As doctors worked on him, Padre Pio whispered: "Jesus! Mary!" His head drooped to the left and his eyes closed. When one of the physicians cried, "Padre! Padre!" he opened his eyes, looked at him, and died.

1479 PIRANDELLO, Luigi (1867–1936) The Italian dramatist and novelist told his doctor: "No need to be so scared of words, doctor. This is called dying." A few hours before he died he spoke to his son about the delirious imaginings of the previous night: "I look forward to writing down, in a few days, all I imagined in those few hours."

1480 PISSARRO, Lucien (1863–1944) The French artist died in England, murmuring: "What's the use?"

1481 PITMAN, Sir Isaac (1813–1897) The English educator who invented phonetic shorthand declared: "To those who asked how Isaac Pitman passed away, say, 'Peacefully, and with no more concern than in passing from one room into another to take up some further employment.'"

1482 PITOËFF, Georges (1886–1939) The French actor, stage-director, and producer told his wife: "I am going to die in a half-hour. . . . Ludmilla, Ludmilla, you know that there are only 1500 francs left."

1483 PITT, William, Earl of Chatham (1708–1778) The British statesman who served twice as prime minister and was instrumental in building the British Empire told his son: "Go, my son, whither your country calls you. Let her engross all your attention. Spare not one moment in weeping over an old man who will soon be no more."

1484 PITT, William, the Younger (1759–1806) British prime minister for more than 20 years, the son of the Earl of Chatham exclaimed: "Oh, my country! How I love my country!"

1485 PIUS II, Pope (1404–1464) Born Enea Silvio Piccolomini, the learned Bishop of Siena took the name Pius on his elevation to the pontificate in reference to the hero of Vergil's *Aenead*, "Pious Aeneas." He died after organizing a crusade. He complained: "One of the miseries of princes is to have flatterers even around their deathbed."

1486 PIUS IV, Pope (1499–1565) Born Gianangelo de' Medici, he forbade Catholic laypersons to read the Scriptures without special permission. He declared: "God's will be done."

1487 PIUS V, Pope (1504–1572) Born Michele Ghislieri, the Dominican friar served as Grand Inquisitor before he was elected pope. He excommunicated Elizabeth I and supported Charles IX and Catherine de' Medici in their attempt to liquidate the Protestants of France. On his deathbed he prayed: "Lord, increase the suffering, but, if it please Thee, increase the patience also."

1488 PIUS VI, Pope (1717–1799) Born Gianangelo Braschi, he was captured by Napoleon when the French leader conquered the Papal States. Refusing to relinquish his temporal power, he died in prison in Valence, France, praying: "Lord, forgive them."

1489 PIUS VII, Pope (1742–1823) Born Gregorio Luigi Barnaba Chiaramonti, he resisted Napoleon and was imprisoned, first at Savona, then at Fontainebleau, before he was able to return to Rome after the fall of the French dictator. Dying of a broken hip, he relived the days of his imprisonment, murmuring: "Savona . . . Fontainbleau. . . ."

1490 PIUS IX, Pope (1792–1878) Born Giovanni Maria Mastai-Ferretti, he defined the doctrine of the Immaculate Conception and assembled the First Vatican Council, which proclaimed the doctrine of papal infallibility. Dying after a 32-year reign that saw all his political power and possessions stripped away by the modern Italian state, he told his physician: "Death wins this time, doctor." As the prayer was offered that begins, "Go forth, Christian soul," Pius murmured: "Yes, go forth. . . . Yes, go forth. . . ."

1491 PIUS X, Pope (1835–1914) Born Giuseppe Sarto, he was an unrelenting foe of "Modernism," which he believed to undermine traditional doctrine, and a proponent of frequent communion by Roman Catholic laypeople. His death from heart and lung problems was hastened by the outbreak of World War I. Just before extreme unction was administered, he announced: "I am dying for all the soldiers on the battlefield." After receiving the sacrament, he told Monsignor Zampini: "I give myself entirely to God's holy will." He died a few hours later, clinging with both hands to his crucifix.

1492 PIUS XI, Pope (1857–1939) Born Ambrosio Damiano Achille Ratti, he signed a concordat with the Italian state, which resulted in the creation of the independent nation of Vatican City. Dying of a heart condition, he declared: "My soul is in the hands of God."

1493 PIUS XII, Pope (1876–1958) Born Eugenio Pacelli, he was pope during World War II and later proclaimed the doctrine of the bodily assumption of Mary into heaven. In failing health for years, he dozed off, saying the rosary. When he awoke, he said: "We must finish the Rosary we began."

1494 PIZARRO, Francisco (1471–1540) The Spanish conqueror of the Incas was killed by the followers of a rival adventurer whom he had recently put to death. After the assassins cut his throat, Pizarro made the sign of the cross and gasped: "Jesus!"

1495 PLATT, Orville (1827–1905) Senator from Connecticut for more than a quarter century, he died of pneumonia after a brief illness, telling his physician: "You know what this means, doctor, and so do I."

1496 PLOTINUS (c.205–270) The Egyptian-born philosopher who taught in Rome for many years espoused a system of thought known as "Neoplatonism." On his deathbed he declared: "I am making my last effort to return that which is divine in me to that which is divine in the universe."

1497 POE, Edgar Allan (1809–1849) The alcoholic American poet, critic, and writer of short stories was found semiconscious in a Baltimore street. Dying shortly afterwards in a hospital, he cried: "God, help my poor soul!"

1498 POLK, James Knox (1795–1849) The former Democratic congressman from Tennessee, who served as speaker of the House and then as governor of his state, served a single term as president, during which he greatly expanded U.S. territory by acquiring Oregon and California. He died of an intestinal illness only three months after leaving office. Polk, who had never been baptized, sent for his wife's pastor, Dr. Edgar of the Presbyterian church in Nashville, and said to him: "Sir, if I had suspected twenty years ago that I should come to my deathbed unprepared, it would have made me a wretched man. Yet, I am about to die and have made no preparation. Tell me, sir, can there be any grounds for a man thus situated to hope?" The pastor prayed with him and baptized him the following day.

Afterwards Polk said of his mother, who was still en route to his home: "Tell her that should we not be permitted to meet on earth again, I have an abiding hope that, through divine mercy, we will meet again." Then he told his wife: "I love you, Sarah. For all eternity, I love you." Polk's mother arrived after her son had lost consciousness. Kneeling with the rest of the household around his bed as he breathed his last, she rendered, according to a newspaper account of the time, "a beautiful prayer committing the soul of her son into God's keeping."

1499 POLK, Sarah Childress (1803–1891) According to a Nashville paper, the widow of President Polk had been in excellent health until a few hours before her death, when she was stricken during a carriage ride. When Polk announced that she was going to get some sleep, her niece, Sallie Fall, prompted by the physicians, told her,

"This sleep will be eternal rest. The time has come now when we must part forever." The sick woman looked shocked and was silent for a few minutes. Then she said calmly: "Praise God from whom all blessings flow! I am ready and willing to go."

Calling all her relatives to her bedside, she spoke to them of her faith in Christ, repeating her favorite Bible verses and reciting portions of her favorite hymn, commencing: "I would not live alway, I ask not to stay,/ Where storm after storm rises dark o'er the way." She commented: "These words don't apply to me. I wouldn't object to living on. For my life has known but one sorrow, the death of my beloved husband." She then repeated another verse, which she explained did, in fact, apply to her: "There saints of all ages in harmony meet,/ Their Savior and brethren transported to greet,/ While anthems of rapture unceasingly roll,/ And the smile of the Lord is the feast of the soul."

The dying woman now placed her hands, in turn, on the heads of all ten persons in the room, declaring to each: "The Lord bless thee and keep thee and make His face shine upon thee and give thee happiness and love and everlasting peace!" Then, for a time, she said nothing. Sallie Fall began to weep, crying, "Aunt Sarah, do you love me? Tell me again if you love me!" Polk opened her eyes and reassured her: "I do! I do!" A few minutes later, Polk whispered: "Ice." When Fall tried to feed it to her with a spoon, the former first lady snatched the ice from the spoon and placed it in her mouth, protesting: "I am *not* a baby, my dear!" Two minutes later she gave "two gentle sighs" and died "with an expression of serenity and peace."

1500 POLYCARP (c.69–155) Bishop of Smyrna in Asia Minor, he was ordered to renounce his Christian faith or die under torture. He replied: "For eighty-six years I have been serving Him and He has done me no wrong. How can I now blaspheme my King, who saved me?"

After many tortures, during which the bishop emphatically insisted, "I am a Christian!" he was thrown onto a pile of logs with his hands tied behind his back. As the fire was kindled, he prayed: "Father of Thy beloved and blessed son, Jesus Christ, through whom we have received the knowledge of Thee, the God of angels and of powers and of the whole creation and of the entire race of the righteous who live in Thy presence, I bless Thee that Thou hast deemed me worthy of this day and hour, that I might receive a portion in the manner of the martyrs, in the cup of Christ, unto resurrection of eternal life, both of soul and body, in the immortality of the Holy Spirit. Among these may I be received before Thee this day, in a rich and acceptable sacrifice, as Thou, the faithful and true God, hast beforehand prepared and revealed, and hast fulfilled. Wherefore I praise Thee also for everything. I bless Thee. I glorify Thee through the eternal high priest, Jesus Christ, Thy beloved son, through whom, with Him, in the Holy Spirit, be glory unto Thee, both now and for the ages to come. Amen."

1501 POLYCRONIUS (d. 251) Bishop of Babylon, he was arrested, along with three presbyters and two deacons, and examined personally by the Roman Emperor Decius, who was determined to execute all Christians who refused to sacrifice to the Roman gods. Polycronius was beaten to death after declaring: "We offer ourselves in the Lord Jesus Christ and will not bow to idols made with hands."

1502 POMPADOUR, Jeanne-

Antoinette Poisson le Normant D'Étoiles, Marquise de (1721–1764) The mistress of Louis XV whom many considered the effective ruler of France died of pneumonia, telling a priest who was leaving her room: "One moment only, *Monsieur le Curé*, and we will take our departure together."

1503 POMPEY, Gnaeus (106 B.C.– 48 B.C.) The Roman political and military leader was the loser in a power-struggle with Julius Caesar. He was murdered in Egypt on the orders of the king there, who hoped to ingratiate himself with Caesar. To his assassin, Pompey said: "Surely I am not mistaken in believing you to have once been my fellow soldier?"

1504 POMPIDOU, Georges (1911– 1974) The French statesman, who succeeded DeGaulle as president, was tormented by bone cancer during much of his tenure in office. Shortly before he died he told a friend: "You cannot know what I am suffering."

1505 PONSELLE, Rosa (1897– 1981) The American operatic soprano, a few days before she died, pleaded with her nurse: "Why don't you just let me go?" A few hours before the end, she murmured the title of the Verdi opera which was one of her favorites: "*La Forza del Destino* . . . The Force of Destiny. It's ironic. It's as if my whole life has been the Force of Destiny."

1506 POPE, Alexander (1688–1744) The English poet commented: "There is nothing that is meritorious but virtue and friendship, and, indeed, friendship is part virtue."

1507 PORTER, Katherine Ann (1890–1980) The American novelist and short story writer told the nun who was nursing her: "Death is beautiful, I long to die, I love God, I know that He loves me." When her priest assured her that eternity would be better than this world, she responded: "Oh, yes, I know that."

1508 PORTER, Noah (1811–1892) The American educator said to his daughter: "Go, call your mother. Wake her up. I want to consult with her."

1509 PORTER, William Sydney (1862–1910) The American short story writer who used the penname O. Henry, ill with diabetes, said to his nurse, who had turned down the gas lights in his room: "Turn up the lights. I don't want to go home in the dark."

1510 POTAMIAENA (d. 203) A Christian African woman, she was arrested in Alexandria, Egypt, and sentenced to die for her faith. To the executioner who poured boiling pitch over her body, but who had prevented her from being gang-raped, she promised: "When I am in heaven I will ask the Lord to repay you for all that you have done for me."

1511 POTHINUS (c.85–177) The bishop of Lyon, in what is now France, was arrested, along with dozens of his flock, during the reign of Roman Emperor Marcus Aurelius, who attempted to exterminate Christians. Interrogated in the local forum by the governor, he was asked, "Who is the Christian's god?" He answered: "If you are worthy, you shall know." Enraged at his apparent impudence, his guards knocked him down and kicked him unconscious. Thrown into prison, the elderly bishop died a few days later, without speaking again.

1512 POTTER, Helen Beatrix (1866–1943) The English author and illustrator, famous for her Peter Rabbit stories, told the caretaker of her estate: "I'm dying. Stay on and manage the farm for Mr. Heelis when I am gone."

1513 POWELL, Adam Clayton, Jr. (1908–1972) The former congressman from Harlem and civil rights leader spoke to a female reporter who found her way into his Miami hospital room and requested an interview: "Sweetheart, I don't feel up to it now. Come back later."

1514 POWELL, Lewis Thornton (1844–1865) Sometimes known as Lewis Paine, he was executed for his part in the Lincoln death conspiracy. To the hangman who was adjusting the noose around his neck he said: "You know best."

1515 POWER, Tyrone (1914–1958) After collapsing during the filming of a motion picture in Spain, the actor tried to reassure a friend: "Don't worry. The same thing happened about a week ago."

1516 PRENTISS, Elizabeth Payson (1818–1878) The American poet, now remembered chiefly for her hymn, "More Love to Thee," died after a lingering, painful illness, crying out, in German: "Patience, my heart! Be still, my will!"

1517 PRESCOTT, William Hickling (1796–1859) The visually-impaired American historian was listening to his secretary read a book on Russia, which mentioned, but did not name, a certain diplomat. When neither man could call to mind the man's name, they asked the scholar's wife and sister. When the wife was able to name the diplomat, Prescott snapped his fingers and laughed: "How came *you* to remember?" Then he went into his room, suffered a massive stroke, and died three hours later, without regaining consciousness.

1518 PRESLEY, Elvis Aaron (1935–1977) The "King" of rock and roll told his female companion, several hours before he was discovered dead: "Precious, I'm going to go into the bathroom and read."

1519 PRIESTLEY, Joseph (1733–1804) The English chemist, who discovered oxygen, died in Pennsylvania, after having a dictation read back to him. When his secretary finished,

Priestley announced: "That is right. I have now done." Then he dropped dead.

1520 PRO JUÁREZ, Miguel (1891–1927) A Mexican priest, he was falsely accused of sedition and shot by his nation's anticlerical government. Before the firing squad, he quietly proclaimed: "Hail to Christ the King!"

1521 PUCCINI, Giacomo (1858–1924) The Italian composer died in Brussels, Belgium, where he developed heart failure while undergoing treatment for throat cancer. He whispered to his stepdaughter: "Remember that your mother is a remarkable woman."

1522 PULITZER, Joseph (1847–1911) The Hugarian-born owner and publisher of the New York *World* murmured in German: "Softly, quite softly."

1523 PULLIAM, Eugene (1889–1975) Publisher of the Indianapolis *Star* and *News* and the Phoenix *Republic* and *Gazette*, he commented in an ambulance, en route to hospital: "My God, it's taking a long time to get there!" Once in his hospital room, he scrawled on a tablet the name of his friend, the Arizona senator: "Goldwater."

1524 PUSEY, Edward Bouverie (1800–1882) The Anglican priest and Oxford professor spent his life as a leader of the "Oxford Movement" that tried to reconcile the Church of England with the Roman Catholic Church. Dying, he cried out: "My God!"

1525 PUSHKIN, Alexander Sergeyevich (1799–1837) The Russian poet was fatally wounded in a duel over his wife's honor, and died shortly afterwards. To a friend who was turning him in bed, the poet said: "Life is over." Misunderstanding, the friend replied, "Yes, it's over. We've finished turning you over." Pushkin insisted: "I said *life* is over. I can't breathe. Something is crushing me."

1526 PYLE, Ernest Taylor (1900–1945) The American journalist was killed while working as a war correspondent on the island of Ie Shima, off Okinawa, towards the end of World War II. Taking cover after the Japanese opened fire on the jeep in which he was riding, Pyle asked one of his companions, before taking a bullet through the head: "Are you all right?"

1527 QUARLES, Francis (1592–1644) The English poet prayed: "Oh, sweet Savior of the world, let Thy last words upon the cross be my last words in this world: "Into Thy hands, Lord, I commend my spirit. And what I cannot utter with my mouth, accept from my heart and soul."

1528 QUEZON, Manuel Luis (1878–1944) The first president of the Philippines died of tuberculosis in Washington, D.C., listening to a radio broadcast that conveyed the news that American forces had landed in New Guinea, where they would soon be poised to liberate his islands. He exclaimed: "Just six hundred miles!"

1529 QUIN, James (1693–1766) The day before he died, the English actor, ill with a "malignant fever," drank a bottle of claret and commented: "I could wish that the last tragic scene were over. I hope I shall be able to go through it with becoming dignity."

1530 QUINCY, Josiah (1772–1864) Long-time mayor of Boston and later president of Harvard, he died "quietly as an infant sinks to slumber," after telling his daughters: "I am sorry to leave you, but I wish to go. I have had a remarkably long, prosperous, and happy life, blessed in my children, grandchildren, and great-grandchildren. It is time that I should go. Weep not, mourn not for me."

1531 QUINCY, Josiah, Jr. (1744–1775) The Massachusetts lawyer and patriotic leader died of tuberculosis on a ship just off Gloucester, Massachusetts, returning from a diplomatic mission to England. Dictating a note to his family, he declared: "Had Providence been pleased that I should have reached America six days ago I should have been able to converse with my friends. I am persuaded that this voyage and passage are the instruments to put an end to my being. His Holy Will be done!"

1532 QUISLING, Vidkun (1887–1945) The Norwegian Nazi, who headed his country's puppet government under German occupation, was shot as a traitor after the war. He told the firing squad: "Do not allow your conscience to trouble you in later years, not on my account. You are acting under orders, and are only doing your duty as soldiers, like myself."

1533 QUITMAN, John Anthony (1798–1858) The former governor of Mississippi was serving as a congressman at the time of his death. He was an early advocate of secession. When his daughter urged him, "Father, put your trust in Jesus. He alone can help you now," the invalid answered: "I *do*, my child." A few hours later he died.

1534 RABELAIS, François (c.1494–1553) The French satirist allegedly said: "Draw the curtains. The farce is over."

1535 RACHEL (1820–1858) The French tragic actress, whose real name was Élisa Félix, died of tuberculosis, observing: "I am happy to die on a Sunday. It is sad to live on a Monday."

1536 RACHMANINOFF, Sergei Vasilyevich (1873–1943) The Russian pianist and composer died in Beverly Hills, California, hearing the strains of unearthly music. He asked his wife: "Who is it that keeps playing?" When told that there was no one playing, he responded: "A-ah! That means it's playing in my head."

1537 RACINE, Jean (1639–1699) The French dramatist, dying of a debilitating illness, expressed gratitude for the opportunity to suffer penance in this world rather than in purgatory: "I never had the strength to do penance. What a blessing for me that God has done me the mercy of sending me this penance." When his son repeated the assurance of his doctors that he was getting better, Racine chided him: "Let them have their say. We are not going to contradict them. But, my son, would you, too, deceive me? Are you, too, in the conspiracy? Believe me that God alone is master of the event. And I can assure you that, did He grant me the option — living or dying at choice — I should not know which to choose. But I have paid the price of death."

1538 RADCLIFFE, Ann Ward (1764–1823) The English Gothic novelist, commented as she was being fed: "There is some substance in that."

1539 RALEIGH, Sir Walter (1552–1618) The English soldier, author, explorer, and businessman was sentenced to die for disobeying orders on an expedition to South America. When he went to the scaffold, he noticed a bald man standing in the crowd and tossed his cap to him with the observation: "Thou hast more need of this than I." Of the axe that was to sever his head, Raleigh joked: "This is a sharp medicine to cure all my diseases." Finally, when the executioner seemed to hesitate, Raleigh called out: "What does thou fear? Strike, man, strike!"

1540 RAMAKRISHNA (Gadadhar Chatterji) (1836–1886) The Hindu philosopher, who taught the essential unity of all religions and held that sex and money hinder spiritual enlightenment, invoked the goddess of creation and destruction, whom he worshipped as the "supreme manifestation of God": "Kali! Kali! Kali!"

1541 RAMEAU, Jean (1683–1764) The French composer, after the last rites were administered, protested to his priest: "Why the devil do you have to *sing* to me, *Monsieur le Cure*? Your voice is out of tune!"

1542 RAMSEUR, Stephen Dodson (1837–1864) The youngest West Pointer ever to be commissioned a general (at 27), the Confederate officer was fatally wounded while serving as a divisional commander in the Shenandoah Valley. Dictating a letter to his wife, he said: "I have a firm hope in Christ, and I trust to meet you hereafter."

1543 RANDOLPH, John (1773–1833) The eccentric statesman who served first as representative and then as senator from Virginia, died in Philadelphia shortly after his return from a diplomatic mission to Russia. During his last days he was tormented by guilt over his ownership of slaves, whom he freed in his will. Holding the hand of his slave-valet John, he repeated the word "remorse" over and over, and directed his physician to write it down on a card and underline it. He exclaimed: "Remorse! You have no idea what it is. You can form no idea of it whatever. It has contributed to bring me to my present situation — but I have looked to the Lord Jesus Christ, and hope I have obtained pardon. Now let John take your pencil and draw a line under the word." When the slave had done as bidden, Randolph told the doctor to put the card in his pocket. "Take care of it — when I am dead, look at it."

Four witnesses arrived and arranged themselves in a semicircle around his bed. Randolph told them: "I confirm all the directions in my will respecting my slaves and direct them to be enforced, particularly in regard to a provision for their support." Then, placing his arm on the shoulder of his valet, he added: "Especially for this man." He asked the witnesses whether they understood him. When he was satisfied that they had, he said: "Yes. The young gentlemen will remain with me." Two hours later he died.

1544 RAPHAEL Santi (1483–1520) The Italian Renaissance painter and architect whispered: "Happy!"

1545 RASPUTIN, Grigori Efimovich (1871–1916) The illiterate and lecherous Siberian folk-healer, who became a favorite of the emperor and empress of Russia, was murdered by a group of noblemen who resented his influence. Shot and mutilated, he murmured: "May God forgive you.... What do they want of me? What do they want?"

1546 RATHBONE, Basil (1892–1967) The actor died of a heart attack, shortly after telling his wife, among other things: "You know, I'm not afraid to die, but I just wish it didn't have to be!"

1547 RAVEL, Maurice-Joseph (1875–1937) The French composer sighed: "I still had so much music to write."

1548 RAY, John (1627–1705) The English scientist directed: "When you happen to write to my singular friend, Dr. Hotton, I pray tell him I received his most obliging and affectionate letter, for which I return thanks, and acquaint that I am not able to answer it."

1549 READE, Charles (1814–1884) The British novelist and dramatist declared: "I have no hope but in God. God only can create and God only can re-create."

1550 RÉCAMIER, Jeanne-Françoise-Julie-Adélaïde Bernard (1777–1849) The French society leader whose salon, in Napoleonic times, attracted the most important political and literary figures of her country, died of cholera, declaring: "We shall meet again."

1551 RED JACKET (Sagoyewatha) (c.1750–1830) The chief of the Seneca, noted for his oratorical skills, told his family: "When I am dead, it will be noised abroad through all the world; they will hear about it across the great waters and say, Red Jacket, the great orator, is dead. And white men will come and ask you for my body. They will wish to bury me. But do not let them take me. Clothe me in the simplest dress, put on my leggings and my moccasins, and hang the cross I have worn so long around my neck and let it lie on my bosom. Then bury me among my people. Neither do I wish to be buried with pagan rites. I wish the ceremonies to be as you like, according to the customs of your new religion, if you choose. Your ministers say the dead will rise. Perhaps they will. If they do, I wish to rise with my old comrades. I do not wish to rise among pale faces. I wish to be surrounded by red men. Do not make a feast according to the custom of the Indians. Whenever my friends chose, they would come and feast with me when I was well, and I do not wish those who have never eaten with me in my cabin to surfeit at my funeral feast."

He asked to see the local missionary, declaring: "I do not hate him. He thinks I hate him, but I do not. I would not hurt him." Told that the missionary was away, the chief answered: "Very well, the Great Spirit will order it as He sees best, whether I speak with him or not." Still speaking of the missionary, he said: "He accused me of being a snake and trying to bite somebody. This was true and I wish to make satisfaction." With almost his last breath, he asked his wife, sons, and daughter: "Where is the missionary?"

1552 REED, John (1887–1920) The American journalist, founder of the Communist Labor Party, died in Moscow, telling his wife: "You know how it is, when you go to Venice. You ask people, 'Is this Venice?' just for the pleasure of hearing the reply."

1553 REED, Thomas Brackett (1839–1902) The congressman from Maine, who served as speaker of the House of Representatives in the 1890s, told his physician: "Doctor, you have no legal right to do that! It is the third time you have taken that liberty. I will have you to understand that the citizen is not obliged to submit to the dictation of the man with the hoe!"

1554 REED, Walter (1851–1902) The army medical researcher, whose work was instrumental in the control of yellow fever, died after surgery for a ruptured appendix. He lamented: "I leave so much!"

1555 REMINGTON, Frederic (1861–1909) The American painter and sculptor, about to undergo surgery for appendicitis, told his surgeon: "Cut her loose, Doc."

1556 RENAN, Joseph-Ernest (1823–1892) The French historian and philosopher who denied the supernatural and doubted the divinity of Christ, declared, the day before he died: "I die in the communion of mankind and the Church of the Future!" He told his wife: "Courage, little one, one must submit to the laws of nature, of which we are the manifestation. We all pass on. The heavens alone remain." After crying, several times, "Have mercy on me!' he began to mumble about architecture. Then he insisted: "Take away this sun from above the Acropolis!" When asked what he meant, he answered: "I know what I'm saying, but my words are dense."

1557 RENOIR, Pierre-Auguste (1841–1919) The French Impressionist painter observed: "Today I learned something!"

1558 RESPIGHI, Ottorino (1879–1936) The Italian composer, pianist, and conductor murmured: "Mamma."

1559 REVEL, Bernard (1885–1940) The Lithuanian-born rabbi, who was a leader in Orthodox Judaism in America and who founded Yeshiva College in New York, said to his wife as he died of the effects of a stroke: "I hope you have lived long enough with me not to resent the fact that I shall not live long. You don't measure life by the yardstick of years, but by accomplishments and achievements. It was my privilege to serve God, the Torah, and the children of the Torah."

1560 REYNOLDS, Sir Joshua (1723–1792) The English artist, who served as the first president of the Royal Academy and painter of over 2000 portraits, mused as he lay dying of cancer: "I have been fortunate in long good health and constant success, and I ought not complain. I know that all good things on earth must have an end, and I am come to mine."

1561 RHODES, Cecil John (1853–1902) The English businessman, who expanded the British Empire in South Africa, lamented as he died of heart disease: "So little done, so much to do!"

1562 RIBBENTROP, Joachim von (1893–1946) The German foreign minister during World War II, hanged as a war criminal, declared: "God save Germany! My last wish is that Germany rediscover her unity and that an alliance be made with East and West and that peace reign on earth."

1563 RICHARD I, King of England (1157–1199) The soldier king, known as "Lion Heart" because of his military exploits, spent only ten months of his ten year reign in England. Dying of an infected wound sustained in a minor feudal war in France, he told his mother, Eleanor of Aquitaine: "I place all my trust, after God, in thee, that thou wilt make provision for my soul's welfare with motherly care, to the utmost of thy power."

1564 RICHARD III, King of England (1452–1485) Immortalized by Shakespeare, the royal duke who attained the crown by his apparent murder of his nephew, Edward V, was killed in the Battle of Bosworth, which concluded the civil war known as the War of the Roses. Although his horse was killed, he did not shout, as in Shakespeare's play, "A horse! A horse! A kingdom for a horse!" Urged by his aides to withdraw, he stormed: "I will die King of England! I will not budge a foot!" He plunged on foot into the thick of the battle, swinging his axe, shouting: "Treason! Treason!" Finally, in the words of a chronicler, "pierced with numerous and deadly wounds, he fell in the field like a brave and valiant prince."

1565 RICHELIEU, Armand de Cardinal (1582–1642) Virtual dictator of France, the dying churchman was approached by his niece, who brought a religious relic, to which she attributed miraculous powers. The cardinal reproved her, saying: "Niece, there are no truths but those in the Gospels. One should believe in them alone."

1566 RICKEY, Branch (1881–1965) The baseball executive who, as general manager of the Brooklyn Dodgers, introduced the first acknowledged black players to major league baseball, collapsed while addressing a banquet: "Now I'm going to tell you a story from the Bible about spiritual courage.... I don't believe I'm going to be able to speak any longer."

1567 RIDLEY, Nicholas (1500–1555) Bishop of London, he was burnt at the stake under Mary I of England because of his Protestant faith. He was chained to the same stake as Hugh Latimer, Bishop of Worcester. Both men had bags of gunpowder placed around their necks that were supposed to explode upon first contact with the fire and so bring about instantaneous death. As the fire was kindled, Ridley prayed: "Into thy hands, O Lord, I commend my spirit! Lord, receive my spirit! Lord, Lord, receive my spirit!"

According to John Foxe's *Book of Martyrs*, the wood was too green and piled too high, causing the flames to burn the lower part of Ridley's body without reaching the gunpowder. In agony, the bishop screamed: "Let the fire come to me! I cannot burn! Lord, have mercy upon me!" He screamed for several minutes before bystanders, realizing what was happening, adjusted the fire. As it leapt up, Ridley leaned into it and ignited the gunpowder, which blew his body into two pieces, one of which fell at the feet of Latimer's already blackening corpse. Foxe recounts, "The dreadful sight filled almost every eye with tears, for some pitied their persons who thought their souls had no need thereof."

1568 RILEY, James Whitcomb (1849–1916) Indianapolis' beloved "Hoosier Poet," paralyzed by a stroke, was taken for an automobile ride by his brother-in-law. Concerned about the effect the July heat would have on the sick man, the brother-in-law suggested to Riley, "You should do the old-fashioned thing of wearing a cabbage leaf in your hat." The poet replied: "That reminds me of an old Greenfield man who used to wear a cabbage leaf in the seat of his pants to keep his brains cool!" After the ride, Riley was helped to his room. He requested: "Water." Then he fell asleep and never awakened.

1569 RILKE, Rainer Maria (1874–1925) The German poet, ill with leukemia, said: "I don't want the doctor's death. I want to have my freedom."

1570 RIMBAUD, Jean-Nicolas-Arthur (1854–1891) The day before he died, the French poet, who was suffering from cancer, dictated a letter to the manager of a passenger ship line: "I'm completely paralyzed, so I want to be on board in good time. Tell me what time I must be carried on board."

1571 RITA of Cascia (1381–1457) The Italian widow became an Augustinian nun and was renowned for her mystical gifts, which included spontaneous wounds on her head which suggested Christ's crown of thorns. She died gazing on the crucifix, after exhorting her nuns: "May God bless you and may you always remain in holy peace and love with your beloved spouse, Jesus Christ."

1572 RITTENHOUSE, David (1732–1796) The American astronomer and mathematician, who was a member of the Royal Society of London and president of the American Philosophical Society, remarked to his nephew: "You have made the way to God easier."

1573 RIVAROL, Antoine de (1753–1801) The French author supported the royalist cause during the Revolution and died in exile in Berlin, telling his friends: "My friends, the great darkness is now approaching. These roses will change into poppies. It is time to contemplate eternity."

1574 RIVERA, Diego (1886–1957) The Mexican painter, asked if he would like his hospital bed raised, replied: "On the contrary, lower it."

1575 RIZAL Y ALONSO, José (1861–1896) The Filipino nationalist, executed for sedition by the Spanish, told his confessor: "Oh, Father, how terrible it is to die! How one suffers! Father, I forgive everyone from the bottom of my heart. I have no resentment against anyone. Believe me, Your Reverence."

1576 RIZZO, Frank (1920–1991) The former mayor of Philadelphia was in the midst of a campaign to regain his old position. He walked into his office and gave his secretary a cheery greeting: "Hello there, Jodi!" Then he went into the bathroom and dropped dead.

1577 ROB ROY (Robert MacGregor) (1671–1734) The outlaw known as "The Scottish Robin Hood," immortalized by a novel written by Sir Walter Scott, was eventually sentenced to a penal colony on Barbados, but was pardoned and returned to Scotland, where he died, declaring: "Now all is over. Let the piper play, 'We Return No More.'"

1578 ROBERT I Bruce, King of Scots (1274–1329) The leader who defeated the British at the Battle of Bannockburn in 1314 and won his country's independence, desired to go to the Holy Land on crusade, but died before he could do so. He therefore directed Sir James Douglas: "I will that as soon as I shall be dead, you take my heart from my body, and have it well embalmed; you will also take as much money from my treasury as shall appear to you sufficient to perform your journey, as well as for those whom you may choose to take with you in your train; you will then deposit your charge at the Holy Sepulchre where Our Lord was buried. You will not be sparing of expense, but will provide yourself with such company and such things as may be suitable to your rank, and wherever you pass, you will let it be known that you bear the heart of King Robert of Scotland, which you are carrying beyond the seas by his command, since his body cannot go thither.... Gallant Knight, I thank you—you promise it, then? ... Thanks be to God! For I shall now die in peace, since I know that the most valiant and accomplished knight of my kingdom will perform that for me which I am unable to do for myself."

1579 ROBERTSON, Frederick William (1816–1853) The English minister, well-known as a preacher and for his published sermons, complained when his nurses tried to turn him in bed: "I cannot bear it. Let me rest. I must die. Let God do His work."

1580 ROBERTSON, Thomas William (1829–1871) The British playwright said to his son: "Goodbye, my son, and God bless you. Come and see me tomorrow. If I don't speak to you, don't be frightened, and don't forget to kiss your father."

1581 ROBESPIERRE, Maximilien-François-Marie-Isidore de (1758–1794) The French revolutionary dictator, who literally kept heads rolling during the Reign of Terror, was himself overthrown and guillotined. As he was untied to proceed to the guillotine, he told the executioner: "Thank you, sir."

1582 ROBINSON, Edwin Arlington (1869–1935) The American poet told a friend who came to see him in the hospital where he lay ill with cancer: "We'll have our cigarettes together."

1583 ROBINSON, John Arthur Thomas (1919–1983) The Anglican bishop of Woolwich was a noted theologian, best remembered for his book, *Honest to God*. When his wife asked if he would like a sip of water, he answered: "A little."

1584 ROCHAMBEAU, Jean-Baptiste-Donatien de Vimeur, Comte de (1725–1807) The French general who helped Washington defeat Cornwallis at Yorktown was talking to his wife about a party the previous night that he did not attend because of a bad cold: "You must agree that I would have cut a pretty figure at the wedding yesterday." She left him reading the papers and returned to find him dead.

1585 ROCHESTER, John Wilmot, Second Earl of (1647–1680) The English poet and satirist said of Gilbert Burnet: "Has my friend left me? Then I shall die shortly."

1586 ROCKEFELLER, John Davidson, Sr. (1839–1937) The billionaire oilman and philanthropist told his valet: "Raise me up a little bit."

1587 ROCKNE, Knute Kenneth (1888–1931) The coach of the Notre Dame football team, boarding a plane in Kansas to fly to California, remarked to a fellow passenger: "I suggest you buy some reading material. These plane engines make an awful racket and just about shut off most conversation." After the plane crashed, Rockne's body was found with a rosary clutched in the hands.

1588 ROCKWELL, George Lincoln (1918–1967) The leader of the American Nazi Party had just left a laundromat when he remarked to a passerby: "I forgot my bleach." As he started back, he was gunned down.

1589 RODGERS, James Charles (Jimmie) (1897–1933) The American blues singer, long suffering from tuberculosis, collapsed on a New York street, complaining of breathlessness: "Let me take a blow." He returned to his hotel room and died during the night.

1590 RODIN, Auguste (1840–1917) The French sculptor mused: "And people say that Puvis de Chavannes is not a fine artist!"

1591 RODNEY, George Brydges, First Baron (1718–1792) The British admiral, dying of gout, fainted with pain. When his doctor asked him if he felt better, he answered: "I am very ill indeed!"

1592 RODRÍGUEZ, Manuel Laureano (Manolete) (1917–1947) The celebrated Spanish matador, gored in the groin, told his doctor: "Don Luis, I can't feel anything in my right leg! Don Luis, I can't feel anything in my left leg! Doctor, are my eyes open? I can't see!"

1593 ROGERS, John (1773–1838) Commodore Rogers, a hero of the Barbary Wars and the War of 1812, asked his valet: "Butler, do you know the Lord's Prayer?" When the slave replied, "Yes, Master," the commodore told him: "Then repeat it for me." He died in the arms of his slave.

1594 ROLAND DE LA PLATIÈRE, Jeanne-Marie Philipon (1754–1793) The moderate French revolutionary was guillotined during the Reign of Terror. She cried on the scaffold: "Oh, liberty! Liberty! What crimes are commited in thy name!"

1595 ROMMEL, Erwin (1891–1944) Commander of Germany's Afrika Korps in World War II, the field marshal was accused of plotting against Hitler. He sent for his son and told him: "I have just had to tell your mother that I shall be dead in a quarter of an hour. To die by the hand of one's own people is hard. But the house is surrounded and Hitler is charging me with high treason. In view of my services in Africa, I am to have the chance of dying by poison. The two generals brought it with them. It's fatal in three seconds. If I accept, none of the usual steps will be taken against my family—that is, against you. They will also leave my staff alone."

1596 ROOSEVELT, Anna Eleanor (1884–1962) Widow of Franklin Roosevelt, she served as delegate to the United Nations General Assembly and helped to draft its Universal Declaration of Human Rights. Ill with tuberculosis, she told her nurse: "I wish to die." When the nurse argued that God would take her when the purpose for which she was put on earth was fulfilled, the former first lady scoffed: "Utter nonsense!"

1597 ROOSEVELT, Franklin Delano (1882–1945) Posing for a painter at his home in Warm Springs, Georgia, the president, three months into his fourth term, lifted his hand to the back of his head and complained: "I have a terrific pain in the back of my head!" Almost immediately he collapsed with a massive stroke.

1598 ROOSEVELT, Theodore, Sr. (1831–1878) The importer and philanthropist, succumbing to a long illness, called for his physician, his daughters, and his wife: "Call the doctor! Bamie! Corinne! Mother, come here—for God's sake—quick!"

1599 ROOSEVELT, Theodore (1858–1919) Having recently returned to his Long Island estate after a hospitalization, the former president spent all day in his bedroom, complaining of shortness of breath. After a physician came and gave him medication, he told his valet, James Amos: "James, will you please put out the light?" During the night he died of a blood clot in his lungs.

1600 ROOT, Elihu (1845–1937) The American lawyer and statesman, who served, at various times, as secretary of war, secretary of state, and as U.S. senator, he was asked, shortly before he died, if he believed in God, and replied: "I have devoted considerable thought to the question, with the result that, while as a lawyer I cannot prove a case for the existence of God, as an individual I firmly believe that there is a God and I have no fear of death."

1601 ROSA, Salvatore (1615–1673) The Italian painter and poet died after a long, painful illness. He answered a friend who asked how he was: "Bad! Bad! To judge by what I now endure, the hand of death grasps me sharply."

1602 ROSE of Lima (1586–1617) Born Isabel de Flores y del Oliva in Peru, she spent her brief life caring for the unfortunate. On her deathbed, she prayed: "Jesus, be with me."

1603 ROSSETTI, Christina Georgina (1830–1894) The English lyric poet declared: "I love everybody! If ever I had an enemy, I hope and trust to meet that enemy in heaven."

1604 ROSSETTI, Dante Gabriel (1828–1882) Brother of Christina, he was celebrated as both a painter and poet. When his brother proposed to read to him, from *Ecclesiastes*, one of his favorite Bible passages, the poet murmured: "Perhaps later."

1605 ROSSINI, Gioacchino (1792–1868) The Italian composer, suffering from a painful and debilitating illness, told his doctor: "Open the window and throw me into the garden. I'll do well there. I won't suffer anymore." Later that evening he cried: "Oh, Goodwife Death, oh, Goodwife Death, only come to me, then!" Then, brokenly, he muttered fragments of liturgical prayers; "Oh, cross, hail! . . . aflame . . . Holy Jesus . . . the glory of paradise. . . ."

Arguing with the Virgin Mary, he complained: "And just what are you doing, Virgin Mary? Here I am, suffering the torments of hell and I have been calling you since nightfall. You hear me. You hear me. If you want to, you can. That depends on you. Hurry up, then, get on with it now!" A few hours later, just before he breathed his last, he murmured the names of the Virgin, St. Anne, and his wife: "Santa Maria . . . Sant'Anna . . . Olympe. . . ."

1606 ROTHSCHILD, Meyer Amschel (1744–1812) The founder of the European banking house summoned his sons and exhorted them to be faithful to the law of Moses, to remain united, and to do nothing without consulting their mother. Then he said: "Observe these three points, and you will soon be rich among the richest, and the world will belong to you."

1607 ROTHSTEIN, Arnold (1882–1928) The gambler who reputedly fixed the 1919 World Series was shot and wounded by an assailant whom he refused to identify. He died two days later. He told his wife: "I want to go home. All I do is sleep here. I can sleep home . . . I feel fine. Besides, I've got to. Don't go away, I need you. I don't want to be alone. I can't stand being alone. I've got to get home."

1608 ROUSSEAU, Jean-Jacques (1712–1778) The French philosopher and political theorist, in "unbearable pain," unable even to lie in bed, was pacing the floor when suddenly he exclaimed: "Being of Beings, God! See how pure the sky is! There is not a single cloud! Do you see that its gates are open and that God awaits me?" With these words he fell to the floor, dying a few minutes later.

1609 ROYER-COLLARD, Pierre-Paul (1763–1845) The French statesman and philosopher insisted: "There is nothing substantial in the world but religious ideas. Never give them up, or, if you do, come back to them."

1610 RUBENS, Peter Paul (1577–1640) The Flemish painter commented sadly: "Death will soon close my eyes forever."

1611 RUBINSTEIN, Anton Grigoryevich (1829–1894) The Russian pianist and composer who founded the St. Petersburg Conservatory was stricken with a heart attack. He staggered to the doorway of his wife's room and gasped: "I am suffocating! A doctor! Quick! A doctor!"

1612 RUBINSTEIN, Arthur (1887–1982) The Polish-born pianist, two days before his death in Switzerland, was discussing other pianists with another musician. When asked what he thought of a certain pianist, he reminded his friend: "I've always said that if I'm ever going to miss a note, I'd commit suicide. Well, I wish to God he would miss one!"

1613 RUBINSTEIN, Helena (1871–1965) The founder of the cosmetics "empire" was asked, shortly before the end, if she were afraid of death, and she answered: "Not in the least now. But I've waited too long. It should be an interesting experience."

1614 RUBINSTEIN, Nicholas Grigoryevich (1835–1881) The Russian pianist — a brother of Anton — who founded the Moscow Conservatory, was suffering from tubercular enteritis. He awoke at ten in the morning feeling better, and demanded of the woman who was caring for him: "Oysters! Nothing, Helen Andreyevna, will do me so much good as a dozen cold oysters. And an ice afterwards." He sat up, began to eat, and immediately was seized with violent cramps and vomited. Then he lost consciousness and died a few hours later.

1615 RUFFIN, Edmund (1794–1865) The Virginia planter gained a reputation as one of America's foremost agricultural scientists before he became a spokesman for Southern secession, slavery, and the concept of Negro inferiority. He fired the first shot at Fort Sumter in the incident that opened the Civil War, and, at the age of 67, fought in the First Battle of Bull Run. When he learned that the war was lost, he wrote out a message that concluded: "And now, with my last writing and utterance and with that will be near to my last breath, I hereby repeat and would willingly proclaim — my unmitigated hatred to Yankee rule — to all political, social, and business connection with Yankees and to the perfidious, malignant, and vile Yankee race." After bidding "goodbye" to some house-guests, he retired to his room, seated himself with a rifle propped into his open mouth, and, just as his wife entered, activated the trigger with his foot.

1616 RUFFINI, Ernesto Cardinal (1888–1967) The respected and influential archbishop of Palermo, Sicily, declared: "I am dying, but I am tranquil. I am with the Madonna."

1617 RUPPERT, Jacob (1867–1939) The beer-brewer who owned the New York Yankees in the 1920s and 1930s held out his hand to Babe Ruth the evening before he died and gasped: "Babe!" Next morning, a few hours before his death, he whispered to his personal secretary, Albert Brennan: "Good morning."

1618 RUSH, Benjamin (1746–1813) The American physician and political leader who was a signer of the Declaration of Independence exhorted his son: "Be indulgent to the poor."

1619 RUSSELL, Charles, Baron (1832–1900) Lord chief justice of England, he prayed: "My God, have mercy on me."

1620 RUSSELL, Charles Marion (1864–1926) The American painter and sculptor, famous for portraying scenes and characters of the West, told his physician: "Doc, I guess I ain't going to make the grade for you this time."

1621 RUSSELL, George William (1867–1935) The Irish poet, painter, and philosopher, dying of cancer, told a friend: "Yes, I am not in pain. I have realized all my ambitions. I have had an astounding interest in life. I have great friends. What more can a man want?"

1622 RUTH, George Herman, Jr. (Babe) (1895–1948) The former baseball star, ill with throat cancer, struggled to his feet after he was blessed with a relic of St. Frances Cabrini. Asked by his nurse where he was going, the Bambino answered: "Not far. I'm just going over the valley." Helped back to bed, Ruth prayed aloud: "My Jesus, mercy.... My Jesus, mercy.... My Jesus...."

1623 RYAN, Cornelius John (1920–1974) The American journalist and author took his wife's hand and confided: "Katie, I'm so damned tired!"

1624 SACCO, Nicola (1891–1927) Convicted of the murder of a paymaster and guard at a shoe factory in Massachusetts in one of the most controversial trials of the century, the Italian-born radical, when asked, at his execution, if he had any last words, replied: "Long live anarchy! Farewell, my wife and child and friends! Good evening, gentlemen."

1625 SAINT-GAUDENS, Augustus Louis (1848–1907) The sculptor, ill with cancer, lay on a couch, a few days before his death, looking at the sun set on the mountains near his New Hampshire home. He commented: "It's beautiful, but I want to go farther away."

1626 SAINT-PIERRE, Charles-Irénée Castel, Abbé de (1658–1743) The French reformer who proposed an international organization to maintain peace told the priest who had just administered the last rites: "I am only to be reproached for this action. I do not believe a word of all this. It was a vile concession for the family and for the house, but I wanted to be the confessor of truth all my life."

1627 SAINT-SIMON, Claude-Henri de Rouvroy, Comte de (1760–1825) The French social scientist exhorted his disciples: "Remember, that to accomplish grand deeds you must be enthusiastic. All my life is comprised in this one thought — to guarantee to all men the freest development of their faculties. The future is ours!"

1628 SAKHAROV, Andrei Dimitriyevich (1921–1989) The Russian physicist died while serving in the Congress of People's Deputies. Retiring to his study to prepare for the next day's debate in Congress, he told his wife: "Tomorrow there will be a battle." Two hours later she found him dead of a heart attack.

1629 SALADIN (c.1137–1193) The Kurdish general, who became sultan of Egypt and extended his sway over Syria, Yemen, and Palestine, captured Jerusalem from the Crusaders. As he lay dying, Sheikh Abu S'afer recited the passage from the Koran which reads, "He is the God than whom there is no other God, who knows the unseen and the visible." Hearing those words, the sultan whispered: "It is true."

1630 SALOMON, Haym (1740–1785) The Polish Jewish emigrant to the American colonies became a prominent merchant and financier and a benefactor of the cause of independence. He is said to have lent more than half a million dollars to the Continental Congress. He died bankrupt, commending the care of his family to a friend: "Take care of them, McCrae. There will be very little, very little for them."

1631 SALTUS, Edgar Evertson (1855–1921) The American novelist whispered to his wife, calling her by her nickname: "Mowgy."

1632 SAMSON (12th century B.C.) The Israelite champion, blinded and imprisoned by the Philistines, prayed to his Lord for the strength to avenge himself upon his country's enemies, and, before pulling down the pillars supporting a crowded Philistine temple, cried: "Let me die with the Philistines!"

1633 SAN MARTÍN, José de (1778–1850) The Argentine liberator died in exile in France. Feeling ill, he asked to be taken back to his room: "This is the exhaustion of death! Mariano, back to my room!"

1634 SANCTUS (d. 177) A deacon in Lyon, in what is now France, he was arrested during the attempt by the

Roman emperor Marcus Aurelius to eradicate the Christian faith. As he was roasted alive in an iron chair, under which a fire was kindled, Sanctus cried out repeatedly, to affirm the faith for which he was dying a martyr: "I am a Christian! I am a Christian!"

1635 SAND, George (1804–1876) The French author, whose real name was Amandine-Lucie-Aurore Dupin, cried: "Death! My God, death!" After saying something unintelligible about leaving greenness or greenery ("*laissez verdure*"), she said goodbye to each of her grandchildren: "Farewell! Farewell! I'm going to die. Farewell, Lina. Farewell, Maurice. Farewell, Lolo. Farewell!"

1636 SANDBURG, Carl August (1878–1967) The American poet and biographer whispered his wife's name: "Paula."

1637 SANDERS, Harlan David (1890–1980) The restaurateur who founded Kentucky Fried Chicken told his doctor: "I just want to rest."

1638 SANGER, Margaret Higgins (1879–1966) The birth control advocate awoke in her nursing home to find that friends had brought some refreshments. Before falling back to sleep, she exclaimed: "A party! Let's have a party!"

1639 SANKEY, Ira David (1840–1908) The American evangelist and gospel-singer, blinded by glaucoma, died of Bright's disease at his home in Brooklyn, New York. Told, during his lingering illness, that the entire world was praying for him, he told his wife: "I wish to convey to all my friends the assurance of my love and that I hope to meet them by and by in the land where there is no more sorrow or pain and where God will wipe away all tears from our eyes. Tell them that God is love and that I have ordered those words cut on my tombstone in Greenwood [Cemetery], that future generations may know the faith in which I died."

As he lost consciousness, he sang: "Some day the silver cord will break,/ And I no more as now shall sing,/ But, oh, the joy when I shall wake/ Within the palace of the King!"

1640 SANTA ANNA, Antonio López de (1794–1876) The Mexican political and military leader, who lost Texas, California, and other territories to the United States in two wars, died in Mexico City, after a short illness. He told his wife: "Leave me alone, so I can get some rest." When she returned to his room, he was unconscious.

1641 SANTAYANA, George (1863–1952) The philosopher, essayist, and poet, who spent many years in America, died in Rome. Asked if he were suffering, he replied: "Yes, my friend. But my anguish is entirely physical. There are no more difficulties whatsoever."

1642 SAROYAN, William (1908–1981) Ill with cancer, the American author and playwright telephoned the Associated Press about a month before he died to dictate his "last words": "Everybody has got to die, but I have always believed an exception would be made in my case. Now what?" His actual last recorded words were: "It's the most beautiful time of my life — and death."

1643 SARSFIELD, Patrick, Earl of Lucan (d. 1693) The Irish general, who supported James II of England against William III, after Parliament deposed the former in favor of the latter, died fighting for France: "Would to God this were shed for Ireland!"

1644 SARTRE, Jean-Paul (1905–1980) The French existentialist philosopher told his companion, Simone de Beauvoir: "I love you very much, my dear Beaver."

1645 SAUCKEL, Fritz (1894–1946)

The Nazi director of slave labor was hanged as a war criminal and declared: "I pay my respects to American officers and American soldiers, but not to American justice!"

1646 SAUL, King of Israel (d. c.1000 B.C.) Wounded in battle against the Philistines, Israel's tragic first king, having witnessed the deaths of three of his sons, told his armor-bearer: "Draw your sword and thrust me through with it, lest these uncircumcised come and thrust me through and make sport of me." When the aide refused to kill him, Saul fell on his sword.

1647 SAVALAS, Aristotle (Telly) (1922–1994) The actor famed for his shaven head and his portrayal of the detective "Kojak," whispered (according to a tabloid) to his son, who sat sobbing beside his bedside: "I love you, son."

1648 SAVIO, Domenico (1842–1857) A student and aide of St. Giovanni Bosco (founder of the Salesian Order), the spiritually-precocious youth died of pneumonia, trying to comfort his weeping parents: "Surely you're not crying, Mom, at seeing me go to heaven? Look, Dad, look! Can't you see? The wonderful! The beautiful!"

1649 SAVONAROLA, Girolamo (1452–1498) The Dominican prior of St. Mark's in Florence vigorously denounced the moral laxity of his time and threatened the wrath of God. For a time he exerted great influence on the politics of his city-state, but he was finally excommunicated by Pope Alexander VI and hanged. As he was being led to the gallows, a bystander extended a word of sympathy, prompting the reply: "At the last hour, God alone can give mortals comfort." When a priest asked, "In what spirit do you bear this martyrdom?" Savonarola replied: "The Lord has suffered so much for me."

1650 SAXE, Maurice, Comte de (1696–1750) The marshal of France told his physician: "Doctor, life is but a dream. Mine has been beautiful, but it has been brief."

1651 SCARRON, Paul (1610–1660) The French poet and dramatist told his family: "Ah, my children, you cannot cry for me as much as I have made you laugh!"

1652 SCHILLER, Johann Christoph Friedrich (1759–1805) The German poet and playwright, whose favorite themes were freedom and liberation, lay dying of "catarrhal fever." His sister-in-law, observing a "beautiful serene expression illuminating his face," asked him how he felt. The author replied: "Calmer and calmer. Many things are growing clearer and clearer." He never spoke again.

Next day Schiller's wife tried to lift his head to arrange his pillows so that he could be more comfortable. The poet opened his eyes, smiled at her, then, after she kissed him, according to his doctor, "something like an electric shock vibrated through his frame; his head fell back; the most perfect peace reigned in his countenance."

1653 SCHIMMELPENNINCK, Mary Anne Galton (1778–1856) The English writer, dying after months of "bitter suffering," suddenly awoke from a coma and cried: "Rejoice with me! I am entering my Father's house! Oh, I hear such beautiful voices, and the children's are the loudest!" Then, in the words of a witness, "with scarcely a sigh," she expired.

1654 SCHLEIERMACHER, Friedrich Daniel Ernst (1768–1834) The German philosopher and theologian said to his wife: "My dear, I seem to be really in a state which hovers between consciousness and unconsciousness, but in my soul I experience the most delightful moments. I must ever be in deep speculations, but they are united with the deepest religious feelings."

1655 SCHNORR von Carolsfeld, Ludwig (1836–1865) The operatic tenor, a favorite of composer Richard Wagner, died suddenly of rheumatism. He spoke of the role that was being written for him: "Farewell, Siegfried! Console my Richard!"

1656 SCHOENBERG, Arnold (1874–1951) The Austrian-born composer of atonal music died in California, inquiring about his son, who was in a tennis match: "Has Ronny won?"

1657 SCHRÖDINGER, Erwin (1887–1961) The Austrian physicist, noted for his work in quantum mechanics, said to his wife: "Anny dear, stay with me—so that I don't crash."

1658 SCHUBERT, Franz Peter (1797–1828) The Viennese composer told a friend who was trying to reassure him: "No, no. This is the end."

1659 SCHULTZ, Dutch (1902–1933) The mobster, whose real name was Arthur Flegenheimer, delirious from gunshot wounds, cried out in words that were carefully noted by a police stenographer in his hospital room: "Look out, Mama! . . . Look out for her! . . . You can't beat him . . . Police! Mama! Helen! Mother! . . . Please take me out . . . I will settle the indictment. . . . Shut up, you got a big mouth! . . . Max, come over here. . . . French Canadian bean soup . . . I want to pay. . . . Let them leave me alone. . . ."

1660 SCHUMANN, Clara Wieck (1819–1896) The pianist and composer told her children that when she was dead: "You two must go to a beautiful place this summer."

1661 SCHUMANN, Robert Alexander (1810–1856) The German composer, died in a mental institution. He murmured to his wife: "My Clara . . .

I know. . . ."

1662 SCHUMANN-HEINK, Ernestine (1861–1936) The German-American contralto who starred in opera, concert, and, finally, in cinema, died of leukemia in Hollywood. She told her family: "I die without fear or regret." Told that a newsboy had sent his greetings, she said: "God bless him."

1663 SCHURZ, Carl (1829–1906) The Prussian-born American statesman and newspaper and magazine editor commented (in German): "It is so easy to die."

1664 SCHWEITZER, Albert (1875–1965) Before collapsing with a stroke in Lambaréné, Gabon, where he had operated a hospital for 40 years, the philosopher, theologian, musician, and medical missionary told his daughter: "I'm tired, very tired."

1665 SCHWIND, Moritz von (1804–1871) The German painter, asked how he felt, replied: "Excellent."

1666 SCOTT, Sir Walter (1771–1832) The Scottish poet and novelist, dying after a series of strokes, counseled his son-in-law: "My dear, be a good man. Be virtuous. Be religious. Be a good man. Nothing else will give you comfort when you come to lie here." When the son-in-law suggested that he call his wife and Scott's other daughter, the dying author said: "No, don't disturb them. Poor souls, I know they were up all night. God bless you all."

1667 SCOTT, Winfield (1786–1866) General-in-Chief of the U.S. Army for 20 years, he spoke to his valet about his horse: "Take good care of him, James."

1668 SCRIABIN, Alexander Nicolayevich (1871–1915) The Russian composer declared: "Suffering is necessary. It is good. I have a sense of well-being in suffering."

1669 SCRIPPS, Edward Wyllis (1854-1926) The journalist who started the first newspaper chain tried to make light of the symptoms of a heart attack: "Too many cigars this evening, I guess."

1670 SEDGWICK, John (1813-1864) The Union general during the Civil War was killed by enemy fire at Spotsylvania, seconds after he told his men: "Don't duck. They couldn't hit an elephant at that distance."

1671 SELWYN, George Augustus (1809-1878) British missionary to the South Sea islands, he eventually became the first Anglican bishop of New Zealand. Returning to his native country, he served as bishop of Litchfield during the last decade of his life. Just before he died he declared: "It is all light."

1672 SELZNICK, David Oliver (1902-1965) The American movie producer, best remembered for *Gone with the Wind*, suddenly stricken with a heart attack, asked: "Mind if I sit down?" Seconds later he was dead.

1673 SENECA, Lucius Annaeus (4 B.C.-A.D. 65) The Roman statesman and philosopher lost the favor of his former pupil Nero, who ordered him to commit suicide. Opening his veins, Seneca declared: "I offer this liquid a a libation to Jupiter the Liberator."

1674 SEPTIMIUS Severus, Emperor of Rome (145-211) The African general who ruled the Roman world for nearly two decades said dejectedly: "I have been all things and it has profited me nothing."

1675 SERAPHIM of Sarov (1759-1833) The Russian orthodox priest and monk, famed for his mystical gifts and for his skill as a counselor, was heard, one day in early January, singing in his cell an Easter chant: "O Passover, great and most Holy, O Christ, O Wisdom, Word, and Power of God! Grant that we may more perfectly partake of You in the day that knows no end, in Your kingdom." Next morning he was discovered dead, on his knees as if in prayer.

1676 SERLING, Rodman Edward (1924-1975) The television writer and producer, best known for his series, "The Twilight Zone," shortly before his death in surgery, kissed his wife and promised to see her soon. His last recorded words, spoken shortly before, were about death: "That's what I anticipate death will be: a totally unconscious void in which you float through eternity with no particular consciousness of anything."

1677 SERRA, Junípero (1713-1784) The Franciscan priest who founded missions for the Indians of California declared: "I promise, if the Lord in His infinite mercy grants me eternal happiness, which I do not deserve because of my sins and faults, that I shall pray for all and for the conversions of so many whom I leave unconverted."

1678 SERVETUS, Michael (Miguel Serveto) (1511-1553) The Spanish physician and philosopher, who described the circulation of the blood to and from the lungs, was burnt for heresy at Geneva, Switzerland, at the direction of Protestant reformer John Calvin, who was a virtual dictator there. Severtus prayed: "Jesus Christ, Thou son of the eternal God, have mercy upon me!"

1679 SETON, Anna Maria (1795-1812) One of the first American Sisters of Charity, "Annina" Seton died of tuberculosis of the bone at Emmitsburg, Maryland, telling her mother, Elizabeth Bayley Seton, the founder of the Order: "Can it be for me? Should you not rejoice? It will be but a moment — and — reunited for eternity! A happy eternity with my mother! What a thought! Laugh, Mother! Jesus!"

1680 SETON, Elizabeth Ann Bayley (1774–1821) The first native-born American to be made a saint in the Roman Catholic Church, she was the founder of the American Sisters of Charity. Dying of tuberculosis, she prayed: "May the most just, the most high, and the most amiable will of God be in all things fulfilled, praised, and exalted above all forevermore!" Later she prayed: "At the hour of death, call me and bid me come to Thee, that with Thy saints I may praise Thee, forever and ever!" A few minutes later she whispered: "Jesus." Seconds later she breathed her last.

1681 SETON, William Magee (1768–1803) A prominent New York merchant, he died of tuberculosis in Italy, telling his wife (later Mother Seton of the American Sisters of Charity): "I want to be in heaven. Pray for my soul. My wife and little ones ... my Christ Jesus, have mercy and receive me. My Christ Jesus." When his wife asked, "My love, do you feel that you are going to your Redeemer?" Seton whispered: "Yes."

1682 SEUME, Johann Gottfried (1763–1810) The German author, famous for his travel books, replied when a friend asked if he wanted anything: "Nothing, dear Weigel. I only wanted to tell you that you shouldn't be annoyed if I should say some things I wouldn't say in a different situation. I take a guilt with me. You I cannot repay. My eyes grow dim."

1683 SEWARD, William Henry (1801–1872) The American statesman, who served as governor of New York and later as senator, was secretary of state under Lincoln and Johnson. He told his sons: "Love one another."

1684 SHACKLETON, Sir Ernest Henry (1874–1922) The Irish explorer of the Antarctic died on shipboard during an expedition. When his doctor told him that he needed to make some changes in his lifestyle, Shackle-

ton retorted: "You're always wanting me to give up things—what is it I ought to give up?" The doctor replied, "Chiefly alcohol, boss."

1685 SHARBIL (d. 115) A Christian presbyter from Edessa in Asia Minor, he was ordered to sacrifice to the Roman gods, and was tortured to death after mocking the Roman deities: "One had intercourse with boys and another fell in love with a maiden who fled for refuge into a tree!"

1686 SHARP, Cecil James (1859–1924) The British composer, teacher, anthologist, and student of folk-song was given an injection and told that he would feel no more pain. He replied: "Never again."

1687 SHARP, William (1855–1905) The Scots poet and editor, who wrote under the penname Fiona Macleod, leaned forward in bed "with shining eyes" and "in a tone of joyous recognition" exclaimed: "Oh, the beautiful green life again!" Then he sank back into his wife's arms and declared: "Ah, all is well!"

1688 SHASTRI, Lal Bahadur (1904–1966) India's second prime minister, stricken with a heart attack, cried: "My Lord and my God!"

1689 SHAVE HEAD (d. 1890) A Sioux policeman mortally wounded in the attempt to arrest Sitting Bull (which resulted in the death of both men), he declared: "I will die in the faith of the white man and to which my five children already belong, and be with them. Send for my wife, that we may be married by the Black Gown before I die." His wife arrived minutes after Shave Head died in the arms of the priest.

1690 SHAW, George Bernard (1856–1950) The Irish playwright, novelist, and literary critic told his nurse, after breaking his hip: "Sister, you're trying to keep me alive as an old curiosity, but I'm done, I'm finished, I'm going to die."

1691 SHAW, Henry Wheeler (1818–1885) The American author and lecturer, who used the penname Josh Billings, was known for witticisms and epigrams in New England slang. Stricken with a heart attack in California, he told his doctor: "My doctors East ordered rest of brain, but you can see I do not have to work my brain for a simple lecture — it comes spontaneously." Seconds later he threw his hands over his head and fell back unconscious. He died three minutes later.

1692 SHAW, Irwin (1913–1984) The American author, asked how he was feeling, replied: "Not very good."

1693 SHEED, Francis Joseph (Frank) (1897–1981) The British publisher and theological writer, poking at a repulsive hospital meal, refused to eat, insisting: "I fancy I'll let it live."

1694 SHERIDAN, Philip Henry (1831–1888) The American military leader completed his memoirs just before he died. Commenting on the work, the proofs of which were sent off just a day before he died, he declared: "I hope that some of my old boys will find the book worth the purchase."

1695 SHERIDAN, Richard Brinsley (1751–1816) The British playwright sent a verbal message to his friend, Lady Bessborough: "Tell her that my eyes will look up to the coffin lid with the same brilliance as ever."

1696 SHERMAN, John (1823–1900) The American statesman who served for many years as a senator from Ohio, as well as secretary of the treasury under Hayes and secretary of state under McKinley, spoke to his daughter of the relatives and friends in their home: "You must show them hospitality."

1697 SHERMAN, William Tecumseh (1820–1891) The Civil War general who devastated part of the Confederacy in his "March to the Sea" was asked what words he wanted on his tombstone: "Faithful and honorable, faithful and honorable."

1698 SHERWOOD, Mary Martha Butt (1775–1851) The English author, best known for her works for children, told her family: "God is very good. Remember this, my children, that God is love. He that dwelleth in love dwelleth in God and God in him."

1699 SHORE, Dinah (1917–1994) The singer and entertainer, according to a tabloid, whispered to her family: "You all have brought such joy to my life. I love every one of you."

1700 SIBELIUS, Jan (1865–1957) The Finnish composer, two days before his death, told his wife: "I think that the cranes have taken leave of me. I was on my usual walk. The cranes were flying low over Ainola — I have never seen them fly that low before. Straight above Ainola one of them parted with a sad cry and banked in a steep curve around the hill, almost as if it meant to say goodbye."

1701 SICKINGEN, Franz von (1481–1523) The leader of the German Knights and a supporter of Luther in the Reformation, he was mortally wounded in battle. When a Roman Catholic priest attempted to administer the last rites and offered to hear his confession, the knight replied: "I have confessed God in my heart. He is the one to give absolution and administer the Sacrament."

1702 SIDNEY, Sir Philip (1554–1586) The English poet, statesman, and soldier was mortally wounded fighting the Spanish while serving as governor of Flushing, in Holland. Dying several days later, he dictated instructions for his family: "Love my memory, cherish my friends. Their faith to me may assure you that they are honest. But, above all, govern your will, not your affections, by the will and word of your Creator, in me beholding the end of this world with all her vanities."

1703 SIGOURNEY, Lydia Howard (1791–1865) The American poet commented repeatedly to her daughter in her final days: "I am so tired . . . so tired." Several hours before the end, after being given a few sips of wine, she whispered: "Thank you."

1704 SIMON of Sudbury (d. 1381) The Archbishop of Canterbury was lynched by a mob during what became known as Wat Tyler's Rebellion. He warned: "Take heed, my beloved brethren in the Lord, what ye now do. For what offense is it that ye doom to death your pastor, your prelate? Oh, take heed, lest for the act of this day all England be laid under the curse of the interdict [a closure of all churches and suspension of all sacramental activity]."

After the archbishop laid his head on an improvised block, an amateur executioner tried to sever his head. After the first blow, Simon cried: "Ah! Ah! It is the hand of the Lord!" When he raised his hand to the wound in his neck, the peasant axeman struck again, severing his fingers. It took six more strokes to sever the churchman's head.

1705 SIMON PETER (c.4 B.C.–A.D. 67) The apostle, awaiting crucifixion in Rome, comforted his wife, who was being led away to a similar fate: "Perpetua, my dear, remember the Lord."

1706 SITTING BULL (c.1831–1890) The Hunkpapa Sioux leader, arrested by Indian police as a troublemaker, cried: "I am not going. Do with me what you like, but I am not going." Calling for help, he shouted: "Come on! Come on! Take action! Let's go!" During the ensuing struggle, Sitting Bull was shot dead.

1707 SITWELL, Dame Edith

(1887–1964) The English author apologized: "I'm afraid I'm being an awful nuisance."

1708 SIXTUS II, Pope (d. 258) Put to death during the persecution of the Roman emperor Valerian, which targeted the clergy, he told one of his deacons: "My son, don't think that I'm abandoning you, but greater battles still await you in behalf of the faith of Christ. In three days you will follow me, as the Levite follows the priest. While you are waiting, take the treasures of the Church and distribute them to whom you think best."

1709 SMITH, Abigail Amelia Adams (1765–1813) The only daughter of former president John Adams, she died of breast cancer after a long and painful illness, singing her favorite hymn: "O, could I soar to worlds above,/ That blessed state of peace and love!/ How gladly would I mount and fly/ On angels' wings to joys on high!"

1710 SMITH, Adam (1723–1790) The Scottish economist, famous for his book, *The Wealth of Nations*, was forced to leave a gathering of friends because of illness. He told them: "I believe we must adjourn this meeting, gentlemen, to some other place."

1711 SMITH, Alfred Emmanuel (1873–1944) The four-time governor of New York who ran unsuccessfully in 1928 for president on the Democratic ticket told his priest: "Start the Act of Contrition."

1712 SMITH, Bessie (1894–1937) The blues singer, fatally injured in a car crash, murmured: "I'm going, but I'm going in the name of the Lord."

1713 SMITH, Donald Alexander, Baron of Strathcona and Mount Royal (1820–1914) The Canadian businessman and political leader murmured: "O God of Bethel, by whose hand Thy people still are fed . . . ."

1714 SMITH, Erastus (Deaf)

(1787–1837) Scout and spy in the Texas War for Independence, he directed: "When I die, bury me standing on my head, because I came into this world feet first and I've had bad luck ever since."

1715 SMITH, Frederick Edwin, First Earl of Birkenhead (1872–1930) The British statesman held out his hand to his clerk and said: "I'm afraid, Peteil!"

1716 SMITH, Joseph (1805–1844) The founder of the Mormon religion was shot while trying to escape an Illinois lynch mob. He cried: "Oh, Lord! My God!"

1717 SMITH, SYDNEY (1771–1845) The English humorist joked with his nurse. Looking for his medicine bottle, she found a half-filled bottle of ink where she thought his medication should have been. When she remarked in jest, "You probably took a dose of ink by mistake," Smith replied: "Then bring me all the blotting paper there is in the house!"

1718 SMITH, William (1727–1803) The Scottish-born American clergyman and educator, who served as a delegate to the First Continental Congress and was a founder of the University of Pennsylvania, complained to his doctor: "By the Lord God, if you don't stay longer with me I will send for another doctor!"

1719 SMOLLET, Tobias George (1721–1771) The Scots novelist died in Leghorn, Italy, shortly after writing a friend: "With respect to myself I have nothing to say but that, if I can prevail upon my wife to execute my last will, you shall receive my poor carcase in a box after I am dead to be placed among your rarities. I am already so dry and emaciated, that I may pass for an Egyptian mummy, without any other preparation than some pitch and painted linen."

1720 SNOW, Edgar Parks (1905–1972) The American journalist famous for his books on China died in that country. As two friends entered his sickroom, Snow exclaimed: "Well, we three old bandits!" He then slipped into a coma from which he never emerged.

1721 SOCRATES (469 B.C.–399 B.C.) The Athenian philosopher, condemned to drink hemlock, referred to Asclepius, the god of healing, whom he wished to thank for curing him of life: "Crito, I owe a cock to Asclepius. Will you remember to pay the debt?"

1722 SOUBIROUS, Bernadette (1844–1879) At the age of 14 she experienced a series of apparitions of the Virgin Mary that made her hometown of Lourdes, France, one of the world's most popular religious shrines. She spent her later life as a Sister of Charity in the town of Nevers, where she slowly died of tuberculosis. Her fellow-religious meticulously noted everything she said during the last days of her life.

Two days before she died, she said to Sister Leontine: "Haven't you got anything to strengthen my heart and help me to breathe? I am ground up like a grain of wheat. I should never have thought that one had to suffer so much to die!" During much of that day she was silent, but, towards evening, she said to Sister Bernarde: "Farewell, Bernarde. This time it is the end." Throughout the night, Bernadette kept crying: "Go away, Satan! Go away, Satan!"

The following day she said little, but moaned from time to time. In the afternoon she declared: "I will do everything for heaven. There I will find my mother in all the brightness of her glory." Seeing that her pain was atrocious, Mother Eleonore told the dying woman, "My dear sister, this moment you are on the cross." Bernadette responded by extending her arms and exclaiming: "My Jesus, oh, how I love Him!"

On the last day of her life, Bernadette, unable to breathe, was moved from her bed to an armchair. When Mother Eleonore said, "I will ask our Immaculate Mother to give you some consolation," Bernadette shook her head and whispered: "No. No consolation, but strength and patience. All this can be used for heaven. I saw her! I saw her! Oh, how beautiful she was and how I long to see her again!"

After this reference to her visions of some 20 years earlier, she fell silent. After several hours, according to Sister Chanoine, Bernadette "raised her left hand to her brow. With glowing eyes she looked upwards and her gaze was fixed immoveably on a certain point. Her face was calm, serene, tinged with melancholy. And then, with an expression not of fear, but of surprise, on an ever-increasing emphatic note, she uttered the triple exclamation: 'Oh! Oh!! Oh!!!'" Then, wracked with terrific internal pains, Bernadette whispered: "My God, I love Thee with all my heart and with all my soul and with all my strength!" Then she kissed the crucifix and said to Mother Natalie: "My dear sister, forgive me. Pray for me! Pray for me!"

In agony, Bernadette cried: "Oh, my God!" Two nuns held her hands and she gasped: "Mother of God, pray for me, poor sinner! Mother of God, pray for me, poor sinner!" She stretched out her arms, looking imploringly at Mother Natalie, who asked, "What do you want me to do for you?" Bernadette gasped: "I want you to help me." A few minutes later the dying woman whispered: "Poor sinner." Then, clutching the crucifix to her heart, she breathed her last, her eyes filled with tears, as the nuns about her prayed aloud, "Jesus, Mary, and Joseph, have pity on her and protect her."

1723 SOUSA, John Philip (1854–1932) America's "March King" died of a heart attack while on tour in Reading, Pennsylvania. Seized with chest pains in his hotel room, he made light of his condition: "Oh, I don't need a doctor."

1724 SOUTHEY, Robert (1774–1843) The English poet and biographer, who was poet laureate for 30 years, lost his mental faculties in his sixties. During his last days he sat in a rocking chair, muttering: "Memory, memory, where art thou gone?"

1725 SPAFFORD, Horatio Gates (1828–1888) The American businessman founded an American colony in Jerusalem. Dying of malaria, he told his wife: "Annie, I have experienced a great joy! I have seen wonderful things!"

1726 SPEAKER, Tristram (Tris) (1888–1958) The Hall of Fame baseball outfielder, celebrated for both batting and fielding, was on a fishing trip in Texas with a friend when he slumped forward on the tongue of the trailer, stricken with a heart attack. As his friend and another fisherman lifted him into the back seat of the car to take him to a hospital, Speaker whispered: "My name is Tris Speaker." He died seconds later.

1727 SPELLMAN, Francis Cardinal (1889–1967) Taken away on a stretcher suffering from a heart atatck, the long-time archbishop of New York tried to reassure his physician: "Now don't you worry about anything."

1728 SPENCER, Herbert (1820–1903) The English philosopher who taught Social Darwinism declared: "Now I take this step for the benefit of my executors: my intention being that my body be conveyed by sea to Portsmouth."

1729 SPINOZA, Baruch (1632–

1677) The Dutch philosopher, dying of tuberculosis, told friends who were on their way to church: "God willing, we shall resume our conversation after the sermon."

1730 SPRUANCE, Richard Ames (1886–1969) The American admiral, who was responsible for several important naval victories in World War II and who served as commander-in-chief of the Pacific Fleet for a year following the war, said to his nurse: "I want to say goodnight to my wife."

1731 SPURGEON, Charles Haddon (1834–1892) The English clergyman who was one of the greatest preachers of his time emerged from a coma and told his wife: "Oh, Wifie, I have had such a blessed time with my Lord!" He lapsed into unconsciousness again and died several days later.

1732 SQUANTO (d. 1622) The Pawtuxet Indian who befriended the English settlers at Plymouth, serving as guide and interpreter, died near Chatham, saying: "I desire the governor pray for me, that I might go to the Englishmen's God in heaven."

1733 STAHL, Charles (Chick) (1873–1907) Player-manager of the Boston Red Sox, after complaining to friends about the strain of his job, he drank hydrochloric acid and then told his horrified players: "Boys, it drove me to it!"

1734 STALLINGS, George Tweedy (1867–1929) Manager of the Boston Braves baseball team, he was famous for his insistence that his pitchers avoid walking batters. On his deathbed, he groaned: "Oh, those bases on balls!"

1735 STANISLAVSKY, Konstantin (1863–1938) The Russian actor, producer, and director, who founded the Moscow Art Theatre, was asked by his nurse if he had a message for his sister: "I've lots to say to her, not just something. But not now. I'm

sure to get it all mixed up."

1736 STANISLAW I Leszcynski, King of Poland (1677–1766) King of Poland for five years, he was deposed in his early thirties. Father of the wife of Louis XV of France, he spent his last years in France as Duke of Lorraine, renowned as a patron of the arts. He died in his palace of burns suffered when his robe caught on fire. He commented: "You gave it to me to warm me, but it has kept me too hot!"

1737 STANLEY, Sir Henry Morton (1841–1904) The Welsh journalist and explorer of Africa murmured: "Oh, I want to be free! I want to go into the woods and be free!" Hearing a clock strike, he remarked: "So strange.... So that is time."

1738 STANTON, Edwin McMasters (1814–1869) Secretary of war under Lincoln and Andrew Jackson, he died shortly after his appointment to the Supreme Court. Stricken with a heart attack, he asked for the rector of Washington's Episcopal Church of the Epiphany: "Send for Dr. Starkey."

1739 STANTON, Elizabeth Cady (1815–1902) The American women's rights leader, the day before her death, told her doctor: "Now, if you can't cure this difficulty of breathing, and if I am not to feel brighter and more like work again, I want you to give me something to send me packing-horse straight to heaven." Next day, when her maid arranged her hair, Stanton announced: "Now I'll be dressed." Helped by her doctor and nurse, she got up and drew herself very straight and stood several moments, as though addresing an audience. Then she sat down, fell asleep, and never awoke.

1740 STARKWEATHER, Charles (1940–1959) The serial murderer of 11, just before he went to the electric chair of the Nebraska State Penitentiary, was asked if he wished to donate his eyes to an organ bank. He roared: "Hell no! No one ever did anything for me! Why the hell should I do anything for anyone else?"

1741 STEIN, Edith (1891–1942) The German philosopher, a convert from Judaism, became a Carmelite nun. Along with other Jewish Catholics from Holland, she was sent to Auschwitz and killed. Her train halted at Breslau, her birthplace, beside another train carrying German soldiers. She told a soldier: "This is my home. I'll never see it again." When the soldier said that he did not know what she meant, she said: "We are going to our death." When the soldier asked if the other prisoners were aware of this, Stein said: "It's better for them not to know." Offered something to eat, she declined, "No, thank you. We won't take anything."

1742 STEIN, Gertrude (1874–1946) The American writer died in France, where she had spent most of her adult life. Before undergoing surgery, she demanded of her friend, Alice Toklas: "What is the answer?" When Toklas said nothing, Stein asked: "In that case, what is the question?"

1743 STEINBECK, John Ernst (1902–1968) The American author, referring to a friend named Shirley Fisher, answered his wife, who leaned over him and asked, "What is it?": "I seem to hear the sound of distant drums.... Maybe it's just Shirley playing the bagpipes."

1744 STEINBERG, Milton (1903–1950) The influential conservative Jewish rabbi, who headed the Park Avenue Synagogue in New York, commented to his wife and sons: "Crazy Steinbergs—here I am dying, and we are making jokes and waving to each other at a time like this." Later he said to his nurse: "I have to apologize to my wife and children for leaving them in such a spot."

1745 STEINER, Rudolf (1861– 1925) The Austrian philosopher and educator, called the "Scientist of the Invisible," founded the Anthroposophical Society. On his deathbed he asked a friend: "Why do modern poets feel such a fear of supersensible wisdom?" When the friend answered, "Because they are no poets," Steiner answered: "Yes, but it must be a poet who says that."

1746 STEINMETZ, Charles Proteus (1865–1923) The German-born electrical engineer who, as a member for 30 years of the staff of General Electric in Schenectady, New York, was credited with more than 100 electrical inventions, was urged to stay in bed and replied: "All right, I will lie down." A few minutes later he died.

1747 STENGEL, Charles Dillon (Casey) (1890–1975) Former manager of the New York Yankees and the New York Mets, he was watching a game on television when he struggled to his feet, placed his hand over his heart when the National Anthem was played, and declared: "I might as well do this one last time." He never spoke again.

1748 STEPHEN (d. c.35) Considered the first Christian martyr, the Jerusalem deacon was stoned to death after preaching to a crowd of hostile Jews. Looking heavenward, Stephen cried: "Behold, I see the heavens opened and the Son of Man standing at the right hand of God! ... Lord, lay not this sin to their charge."

1749 STEPHENS, Alexander Hamilton (1812–1883) The Georgia attorney and politician who served as vice-president of the Confederacy, died while serving as his state's governor. After reliving his long career in delirium, he murmured: "Get ready. We are nearly home."

1750 STERNE, Laurence (1713– 1768) The English novelist, famous for *Tristram Shandy*, commented: "Now it has come." He held up his arm as if to ward off a blow, and, a minute later, died.

1751 STEVENS, Thaddeus (1792–1868) The Pennsylvania congressman who led the "Radical Republicans" and championed the rights of blacks was asked if he would like to see a black minister, and replied, either: "Certainly! Certainly!" or "Oh, yes!" Afterwards he was baptized by two black Sisters of Charity. Told that he was dying, he nodded silently. Then when his housekeeper, Lydia Smith, asked him if he wanted anything, he told her: "Nothing more in this world."

1752 STEVENSON, Adlai Ewing II (1900–1965) Governor of Illinois, he ran twice unsuccessfully for president on the Democratic ticket. Serving as ambassador to the United Nations, he dropped dead on a London street after telling a companion: "I feel faint!"

1753 STEVENSON, Robert Louis Balfour (1850–1894) The Scottish author died suddenly at his home in Samoa. Putting his hand to his head, he asked his wife, who was making salad: "What's that? Do I look strange?" Immediately he collapsed with a massive brain hemorrhage.

1754 STILLWELL, Joseph Warren (1883–1946) The commander of American forces in East Asia during World War II asked: "Say, isn't this Sunday?"

1755 STOLBERG-STOLBERG, Friedrich Leopold, Count von (1750–1819) The German romantic lyric poet said to his doctor: "Tell me, will it truly be all over tomorrow or the next day?" When told that it would, he cried: "Praise God! Thanks! Thanks! I thank you with all my heart! Jesus Christ be praised!"

1756 STOLYPIN, Peter Arcadeyevich (1863–1911) The Russian premier died a few days after being shot

in the Municipal Theatre in Kiev. In delirium he cried: "Give me the letter. Take it away. Give me a red pencil. Lift me. Light up."

1757 STONE, Harlan Fiske (1872–1946) The American jurist was made an associate justice of the Supreme Court in 1924, and chief justice five years before his sudden death, which came just as he was about to deliver a decision. He said in a low voice: "The case should be stayed; we decided to send this case back to conference for reconsideration." Stricken with a cerebral hemorrhage, he was helped from the bench to a washroom, where he lost consciousness.

1758 STONE, Lucy (1818–1893) The women's rights leader told her daughter: "Make the world better."

1759 STONE, Samuel (1610–1663) The Puritan clergyman and theologian, speaking of two deceased colleagues, commented: "Heaven is the more desirable since men like Hooker and Shepherd have taken up their abode there."

1760 STORY, Joseph (1779–1845) Associate justice of the Supreme Court for more than three decades, the American jurist murmured: "God."

1761 STOWE, Calvin Ellis (1801–1886) The American biblical scholar and college and seminary professor is best known as the husband of novelist Harriet Beecher Stowe. On his deathbed he shouted: "Peace with God! Peace with God!"

1762 STOWE, Harriet Beecher (1811–1896) The American novelist, whose *Uncle Tom's Cabin* raised the consciousness of many northerners about the evils of slavery, was physically and mentally incapacitated for some time, but just before she died she looked at her nurse and professed: "I love you."

1763 STRACHEY, Giles Lytton (1880–1932) The English biographer and literary critic declared: "Well, if this is dying, then I don't think much of it."

1764 STRAFFORD, Thomas Wentworth, Earl of (1593–1641) The English statesman, hated for his harsh administration as Lord Deputy of Ireland, was beheaded on charges of treason. Rejecting a blindfold, the Earl said: "Nay, for I will see it done."

STRATHCONA and Mount Royal, Donald Alexander Smith, Baron of *see* SMITH, Donald Alexander

1765 STRAUS, Oskar (1870–1954) The Viennese composer of operettas, the best known of which is *The Chocolate Soldier*, was asked, "Maestro, how are you?" and answered: "Well, good."

1766 STRAUSS, Johann, Jr. (1825–1899) The Viennese "Waltz King," ill with pneumonia, replied to his wife, who urged him to sleep: "I will, whatever happens."

1767 STRAUSS, Richard (1864–1949) The German composer commented to his daughter-in-law: "Funny thing, Alice, dying is just the way I composed it in *Death and Transfiguration*."

1768 STRAVINSKY, Igor Feodorovitch (1882–1971) Wheeled around his new apartment, the Russian-born composer commented to his nurse: "How lovely! This belongs to me. It is my home." That night he died.

1769 STREICHER, Julius (1885–1946) The Nazi journalist and political leader, condemned at the Nuremberg trials, shouted, before he was hanged: "Heil Hitler!"

1770 STRESEMANN, Gustav (1878–1929) The German chancellor died suddenly. He insisted: "I'm all right, perfectly all right."

1771 STRINDBERG, August (1849–1912) The Swedish novelist and playwright said to his nurse, who had gotten up to adjust his pillow: "No, lie where you were before. Don't bother about me. I no longer exist."

1772 STRITCH, Samuel Alphonsus Cardinal (1887–1958) The archbishop of Chicago was appointed head of the Congregation for the Propagation of the Faith, the first American ever to head a congregation in the Vatican. He died in Rome shortly after he took up his duties. After celebrating Mass for the first time after the amputation of an arm, he commented: "Well, I feel like a priest again." Then he suffered a stroke and never spoke again, except, a few days later, when asked if he were all right, he answered: "Yes."

1773 STUART, James Ewell Brown (1833–1864) The Confederate cavalry general, wounded at Yellow Tavern, died in Richmond of his wounds. Speaking of his dead daughter, he commented: "I will soon be in heaven with my little Flora." After singing, "Rock of Ages, Cleft for Me," he remarked: "I am sinking fast now. God's will be done."

1774 STUART, Jesse Hilton (1907–1984) The American author, after saying a prayer with his wife and a friend, said: "Amen." He then suffered a stroke and never spoke again.

1775 SUÁREZ, Francisco (1548–1617) The Spanish Jesuit author, who insisted on the right of popes to depose kings, commented: "I would never have believed it so sweet to die."

1776 SULEIMAN I the Magnificent, Sultan of Turkey (1494–1566) The ruler under whom the Ottoman Empire reached its height of power conquered Hungary and part of Persia. He died of a stroke while his troops were in battle. He lamented: "The drums of victory have not yet sounded."

1777 SULLIVAN, Sir Arthur

(1842–1900) The British composer collapsed, gasping: "My heart! My heart!"

1778 SULLIVAN, John Lawrence (1858–1918) The retired bare-knuckle boxing champion, stricken with a heart attack, told a friend: "I'll be all right in a little while."

1779 SUMNER, Charles (1811–1874) The Massachusetts senator was concerned about the future of the civil rights bill he was attempting to push towards passage. He pleaded with his friend, Judge Hoar, who sat by his bedside: "You must take care of the civil rights bill—my bill—the civil rights bill. Don't let it fail!" To his friend, Frederick Douglass, he said: "Don't let the bill fail!" After begging the nurse for another injection of morphine and being refused, he spoke to Hoar of his friend, writer Ralph Waldo Emerson: "Judge, tell Emerson how much I love and revere him." In violent pain, Sumner went into convulsions, vomited, threw himself backward in bed, gasped for air, and died.

1780 SUN YAT-SEN (1866–1925) The Chinese revolutionary leader who became president of the unenduring Chinese Republic in 1912 and founded the National People's Party grasped the hand of his brother-in-law and said: "You are a Christian. I, too, am a Christian. I am a messenger of God to help China obtain equality and freedom." He begged a communist supporter: "Don't make trouble for Christians." As he drifted into a coma, he murmured: "Peace ... struggle ... save China...."

1781 SUNDAY, William Ashley (1862–1935) The Presbyterian minister, celebrated for his colorful evangelistic meetings, died of a heart attack at the home of relatives in Chicago. A physician, who came to the house when Sunday complained of chest pain, took his pulse and found it nor-

mal. Insisting that nothing was wrong, he left. As he went out, Sunday said: "Don't forget me, Doc." Minutes later he leaned forward and away from his pillow and then fell back dead, after telling his wife: "I'm getting dizzy, Ma."

1782 SURRATT, Mary Eugenia Jenkins (1820–1865) An innkeeper hanged for complicity in the Lincoln assassination, she told her priest just before her execution: "Holy Father, may I tell you something? ... That I am innocent."

1783 SUSANN, Jacqueline (1918–1974) The American author, dying after a long illness with cancer, bade a friend: "Goodbye, my darling."

1784 SUTTER, John August (1803–1880) A founder of Sacramento, California, at whose mill gold was discovered in 1848, reacted in disappointment when told that the U.S. House of Representatives had not acted on a long-standing land claim: "Next year ... they will surely...." He never spoke again.

1785 SWEDENBORG, Emmanuel (1688–1772) The Swedish scientist and philosopher, whose teachings led to the foundation of the Church of the New Jerusalem, died in England. Having been told the time, he commented: "That be good."

1786 SWETCHINE, Anne Sophie Soymonov (1782–1857) The Russian-born author died in Paris. She commented: "It will soon be time for Mass. They must raise me."

1787 SWIFT, Ann Higgins (1843–1922) The widow of meat-packer Gustavus Swift, she responded to her doctor when he told her to take some sherry to stimulate her heart: "Well, doctor, I'm your patient and it's my duty to cooperate with you and I will—even to the extent of drinking sherry."

1788 SWIFT, Gustavus Franklin (1839–1903) The American industrialist who founded Swift & Co., one of the largest meat-packing companies in the world, died suddenly while recuperating from surgery. He told his wife: "I like to hear you read." While she read to him, he died.

1789 SWIFT, Jonathan (1667–1745) The Irish writer, best remembered for *Gulliver's Travels*, was incapacitated physically and mentally in his last years. Shortly before the end, his nurse found him holding a knife, and took it away from him. Swift shrugged and said vacantly: "I am that I am that I am . . . ."

1790 SYDNEY, Algernon (1622–1683) An English politician condemned for high treason, he answered the executioner, who asked him if he was going to keep changing his position on the block. When the executioner, exasperated, demanded, "Will you rise again?" Sydney answered: "Not till the general resurrection. Strike on!"

1791 SYLVESTER I, Pope (c.270–335) Bishop of Rome during the reign of Constantine I (the emperor who legalized and promoted the Christian faith), he exhorted his clergy: "Love one another, govern your churches diligently, and protect your flocks from the teeth of wolves."

1792 SYNGE, John Millington (1871–1909) The Irish playwright, suffering from cancer, declared: "It is no use fighting death any longer."

1793 TAFT, Robert Alphonso (1889–1953) The Ohio senator known as "Mr. Republican," ill with cancer, greeted his paralyzed wife as she was wheeled into his hospital room. He whispered: "Well, Martha. . . . You're looking well today. . . ."

1794 TAFT, William Howard (1857–1930) The former president died shortly after resigning his position as chief justice of the Supreme Court. Suffering from a stroke, he greeted the two doctors who entered his room in his Washington home: "Good morning."

1795 TAGORE, Sir Rabindranath (1861–1941) The Bengali poet, in a Calcutta hospital, just before undergoing surgery from which he never regained consciousness, dictated: "Your creation's path you have covered/ With a varied net of wiles,/ Thou guileful one./ False belief's snare you have/ Laid with skillful hands/ In simple lives./ With this deceit you have left a mark/ On greatness;/ For him kept no secret night. . ./ He who has easefully borne your wile/ Gets from your hands/ The unwasting right to peace."

1796 TALLEYRAND-PERIGORD, Charles-Maurice de (1754–1838) The French statesman, visited by the king, replied in great pain: "Sire, you have come to assist at the last moments of a man who is dying. Those who truly care for him can have but one wish: to see them come to an end." He told Princess Adelaide: "Madame, I love you very much." Concluding the last rites, a priest gave Talleyrand the final anointing. When he tried to anoint the palms, the sick man said: "No, no, *Monsieur l'Abbe.* You forget that I am a bishop." And so the priest anointed the tops of Talleyrand's hands.

1797 TALMA, François-Joseph (1763–1826) The French actor, dying after a long illness, murmured: "Voltaire . . . like Voltaire . . . always like Voltaire. . . ." Then he added: "The hardest thing of all is not to see."

1798 TAMERLANE (1336–1405) Timur the Lame, the Central Asian leader who built an empire that extended from Asia Minor to India, was noted for his cruelty, but the dying words attributed to him give no indication of that side of his personality. He exhorted his sons and grandsons: "Do not forget the precepts I gave you for the good of the people. Keep yourselves informed about the condition of the common people, sustain the weak, and, above all, restrain the avarice and ambition of the powerful. May justice and kindness constantly direct your conduct. Know how to wield your sword with wisdom and valor, if you want to enjoy a long reign and a strong empire. Beware of discord among yourselves, for your courtiers and your enemies will never cease to exploit your reverses of fortune. Faithfully observe the rules of government I left you in my political testament. Finally, always remember the last words of a dying father."

1799 TANEY, Roger Brooke (1777–1864) The chief justice of the U.S. Supreme Court for nearly three decades, he is remembered chiefly for writing the notorious Dred Scott Decision, which ruled that Congress has no right to limit slavery. A devout Catholic, dying after a long and painful illness, he prayed: "Lord Jesus, receive my spirit."

1800 TANNER, Henry Ossawa (1859–1937) The American artist who lived much of his adult life in France, spoke his last recorded words to a friend a week before his death: "How beautiful spring-time is in Paris!"

1801 TARBELL, Ida Minerva (1857–1944) The American journalist, best known for her *History of the Standard Oil Company*, was visited by carolers as she lay in her hospital bed. Asked what carol she wanted them to sing, she answered: "'Hark, the Herald Angels Sing.'" Shortly afterwards she lost consciousness. She died several days later.

1802 TASSO, Torquato (1544–1595) The Italian poet died in Rome, shortly before he was to have been crowned by the pope as poet laureate. He commented: "This is the crown with which I hoped to be crowned: not

as a poet in the capital, but with the glory of the blessed in heaven. Into Thy hands, O Lord, I commend my spirit."

1803 TATUM, Art (1909–1956) The jazz pianist died a few minutes after telephoning his sister and asking her to come to his sickbed. He ended the call saying: "I'll be looking for you."

1804 TAYLOR, Bayard (1825–1878) The American poet died while serving as ambassador to Germany. He remarked to his wife and doctor: "I want — oh, you know what I mean! — the *stuff* of life."

1805 TAYLOR, Jeremy (1613–1667) The English theologian who served as Bishop of Down and Connor in Ireland requested: "Bury me at Dromore."

1806 TAYLOR, Robert (1911–1969) The actor, ill with lung cancer, spoke to a friend of his wife: "I only have one request right now. Tell Ursula, be happy."

1807 TAYLOR, Zachary (1784–1850) The American general, who won several important battles in the Mexican War, died in the White House, after serving 16 months as president. His last "intelligible" words were "I am not afraid to die. I have done my duty. My only regret is in leaving those who are dear to me."

1808 TCHAIKOVSKY, Pyotr Ilich (1840–1893) The Russian composer, dying of cholera, murmured in delirium: "Hope ... accursed...." After he was given a drink, he whispered: "That's enough."

1809 TECUMSEH (1768–1813) The Shawnee leader allied himself with the British in the War of 1812. Serving as a brigadier general, he was killed fighting American forces at the Battle of the Thames, in Canada. Just before he fell, he was heard exhorting his men: "Be brave! Be strong! Be brave!"

1810 TEILHARD DE CHARDIN, Pierre (1881–1955) The French theologian and palaeontologist, stricken with a heart attack, declared: "I go to meet Him who comes!" Revived, he asked: "What happened?" Told that he had suffered a heart attack, he commented: "I can't remember anything. This time I feel it's terrible."

1811 TEKAKWITHA, Kateri (1656–1680) A Christian Algonquin woman who made a vow of chastity and was renowned for her goodness and piety, she was eventually beatified by the Roman Catholic Church. At the point of death she cried: "Jesus! Mary! I love you!"

1812 TEN BOOM, Cornelia (Corrie) (1892–1983) A few days before she died, the Dutch religious writer and lecturer, incapacitated by strokes, whispered to her secretary: "Happy." When asked, "Are you happy, Tante Corrie?" the dying woman answered: "Yes." Then she sang in Dutch: "Praise God with waves of joy,/ You, my soul, have such cause to be thankful,/ For as long as I live I will dedicate my psalms to His praise!/ As long as I see light I will extol God in my song!"

1813 TEN BOOM, Elisabeth (1885–1944) A Dutch watchmaker arrested for hiding Jews in her house in Nazi-occupied Holland, she died in a concentration camp in Germany, whispering: "So much work to do. . . ."

1814 TEN BOOM, Willem (1887–1946) A Dutch reformed minister and theologian, he was imprisoned by the Germans for his efforts to assist the escape of Dutch Jews. His health broken by his imprisonment, he was distressed in his last days by anxiety about one of his sons, about whom he had received no word since the boy's arrest two years before by the Nazis. Just before he died Ten Boom opened his eyes and told his wife: "It is well—it is very well—with Kik." (Years later it was established that the son had died in prison.)

1815 TENNYSON, Alfred Lord (1809–1892) The English poet, ill with heart trouble, insisted: "I want the blinds up. I want to see the sky and the light." Later, he spoke of "a most beautiful vision of blue and other colors." He then asked his son: "Have I not been walking with Gladstone in the garden and showing him my trees?" Told that he had not, the poet asked: "Are you sure?" Then he called his son's name, "Hallam," and lay quietly. When his doctor came in, Tennyson commented: "What a shadow this life is and how men cling to what is, after all, but a small part of the world's great life!" Then he looked up at his physician and asked: "Death?" When the doctor nodded, the poet replied: "That's well."

Fumbling with a volume of Shakespeare, the poet said: "I have opened it." Then, to his wife and son, he mumbled a last blessing. They thought he said: "God bless you, my joy!" After that Tennyson lay silently, holding the hand of his daughter-in-law. His doctor describes his last hours: Nothing could have been more striking than the scene during the last few hours. On the bed a figure of breathing marble, flooded and bathed in the light of the full moon streaming through the oriel window; his hand clasping the Shakespeare he had asked for only recently, and which he kept by him to the end; the moonlight, the majestic figure as he lay there, "drawing thicker breath," irresistibly brought to our minds his own "Passing of Arthur." As he breathed his last, his family, as he requested, prayed, "God, accept him. Christ, receive him."

1816 TERESA of Avila (1515–1582) Born Teresa de Cepeda y Ahumada, the Spanish mystic and theologian prayed: "How I have longed for Thee! Oh, welcome the hour, the end of exile! My Lord, with a great joy it is time to set out. May the journey be a propitious one and may Thy will be done!" Then she quoted from Psalm 51: "A sacrifice to God is an afflicted spirit. A broken and contrite heart, O God, Thou wilt not despise." According to her biographer, Teresa died a few minutes later and "the wrinkles caused by age and sickness disappeared, and her face, transfigured, was so calm and radiant that it seemed like the moon at full."

1817 TERHUNE, Albert Payson (1872–1942) The American journalist and author, best known for his dog stories, told his wife: "I shall come back. I shall be here at Sunnybank with you always. I promise you that when you walk in the rose garden I shall be with you. When you wander about the place, when you sit by the pool, when you sit on the veranda and watch our 'Light at Eventide,' I shall be with you. I shall surely be here. You must believe me."

1818 TERRY, Ellen Alice (1847–1928) The British actress murmured: "Up to the skies . . . down to the. . . ."

1819 TEYTE, Maggie (1888–1976) The English soprano who starred in opera and recitals remarked shortly before she died: "I have not lived like a Catholic, but I hope I shall die like one."

1820 THACKERAY, William Makepeace (1811–1863) The British novelist, who was suffering from a debilitating illness, told his daugther, who found him in pain: "It can't be helped, darling. I didn't take enough medicine last night. I have taken some more. I shall be better presently." He died the next day.

1821 THALBERG, Irving (1899–1936) The production manager of MGM known as "The Boy Wonder of Hollywood," quoted, to a friend who tried to reassure him that he would recover, the title of what was then a popular funeral hymn: "Nearer, my God, to Thee." Then he begged his wife: "Don't let the children forget me."

1822 THAYER, William Sidney (1864–1932) The American cardiologist declared: "This is the end, and I am not sorry."

1823 THEODOSIA (288–304) A Christian girl arrested in Caesarea in Palestine during the persecutions of the Roman Emperor Diocletian, she was raked with iron claws when she refused to offer incense to the Roman gods. Before she was sealed in a bag and thrown into the sea, she declared: "Don't you see that I am experiencing what I have prayed for—to be found worthy of joining the company of the martyrs of God!"

1824 THEOPHRASTUS (372 B.C.–287 B.C.) The Greek philosopher and scientist, noted for his writings on botany, exhorted his disciples: "Farewell, and may you be happy. Either drop my doctrine, which involves a world of labor, or stand forth its worthy champion, for you will win great glory. Life holds more disappointment than advantage. But, as I can no longer discuss what we ought to do, do you go on with the inquiry into right conduct."

1825 THERAMENES (d. 404 B.C.) An Athenian statesman, he was forced to drink poison, and, as he did, he said of his accuser: "This is to the health of the lovely Critias!"

1826 THÉRÈSE of Lisieux (1873–1897) The French Carmelite nun, author of A Story of a Soul, is one of the most popular Roman Catholic saints. One of four biological sisters in a convent, her last days were meticulously documented by her siblings. Suffering from tuberculosis, she told the prioress: "Oh, Mother, present me quickly to the Blessed Virgin. I'm a baby who can't stand any more. Prepare me for death." Told that she was already prepared because she had always understood humility, Thérèse responded: "Yes, it seems to me I never sought anything but the truth. Yes, I have understood humility of heart. It seems to me I'm humble."

Thérèse, who had always prayed for the opportunity to join in the sufferings of Christ, affirmed: "All I wrote about my desires for suffering, oh, it's true just the same! And I am not sorry for delivering myself up to love. Oh, no, I'm not sorry. On the contrary." A little later she added: "Never would I have believed it was possible to suffer so much, never, never! I cannot explain this except by the ardent desire I have had to save souls."

At five that evening, all the community assembled in her room. Holding a crucifix, Thérèse smiled sweetly at the sisters. In terrible pain, she lay moaning for two hours, without speaking. Convinced that the sick woman was not going to expire that evening after all, the prioress dismissed the community after two hours. When the sisters had left, Thérèse asked the prioress: "Mother, isn't this the agony? Am I not going to die?" when the prioress suggested that she might linger several more hours, Thérèse answered: "Well, all right. All right. Oh, I would not want to suffer for a shorter time." Then, gazing at the crucifix in her hands, she suddenly cried: "Oh, I love Him! My God, I love You!"

After this exclamation, Thérèse slumped to the right. Once more the prioress summoned the other sisters. Mother Agnes, one of Thérèse's biological sisters, noted that Thérèse's face "had regained the lily-white complexion it always had in full health. . . . Her eyes were fixed above, brilliant with peace and joy. She made certain beautiful movements with her head, as though someone had divinely wounded her with an arrow of love, then had withdrawn the arrow to wound her again. . . . Sister Marie of the Eucharist approached with a candle to get a closer view of the sublime look. In the light of the candle, there didn't appear any movement of the eyelids. This ecstasy lasted almost the space of a Credo, and then she gave her last breath. After her death, she had a heavenly smile. She was ravishingly beautiful."

1827 THOMAS the Twin (d. c.72) The apostle, according to an ancient tradition, organized the Christian community near Mylapore, India, where he was attacked and stabbed by Brahmins as he knelt in prayer in a cave. Dragging himself to a hut where some of his disciples lived, Thomas prayed: "Lord, I thank Thee for all Thy mercies. Into Thy hands I commend my spirit."

1828 THOMAS, Dylan (1914–1953) The Welsh poet, an alcoholic, declared: "I've had eighteen straight whiskies. I think that's the record." Told that his delirium tremens would pass, he said: "Yes, I believe you." He fell into a coma, never to awake.

1829 THOMAS, George Henry (1816–1870) The Union general known as the "Rock of Chickamauga" died of a sudden heart attack. He gasped: "I want air!"

1830 THOMPSON, Francis (1859–1907) The British poet, best known for "The Hound of Heaven," kept repeating a phrase from a poem: "My withered dreams . . . my withered dreams. . . ."

1831 THOMPSON, Sir John Sparrow David (1844–1894) Prime minister of Canada, he died suddenly in office, telling the doctor who was ministering to him: "I have a pain in my chest."

1832 THOMPSON, William Hale (1867–1944) "Big Bill" Thompson, Chicago mayor in the 1920s, responded to a friend who assured him that his affairs were in order: "That's right. That's right."

1833 THOREAU, Henry David (1817–1862) A few days before he died, the philosopher, suffering from tuberculosis, told a Unitarian minister: "It is better that some things should end." To his friend, Bronson Alcott, he said: "I shall leave the world without regret." And to Edmund Hosmer, another friend, who described a spring robin, Thoreau said: "Yes, this is a beautiful world, but I shall see a fairer." Speaking of the kindness of the people of his hometown of Concord, Massachusetts, the author said: "I should be ashamed to stay in this world after so much had been done for me, for I could never repay my friends."

Refusing painkillers, he insisted: "I prefer to endure with a clear mind the worst penalties of suffering rather than be plunged into a turbid dream of narcotics." To another friend he related: "When I was a little boy I learned that I must die, and I set that down, so, of course I am not disappointed now. Death is as near to you as it is to me." Asked how he stood towards Christ, Thoreau replied: "A snowstorm is more to me than Christ." When his aunt asked him if he had made his peace with God, the dying man replied: "I did not know we had ever quarreled." To someone who said, "I almost wonder how the opposite shore may appear to you," Thoreau replied: "One world at a time!"

On the last day of his life, Thoreau told Alcott: "It took nature a long time to do her work, but I am almost out of the world." Given a bouquet of hya-

cinths, he remarked: "I like them. Raise me." An hour before he died, Thoreau tried to say something, possibly about a book that he was writing about the Maine woods, but the only words that could be understood were: "Moose ... Indian...." Gradually, his breathing grew fainter and fainter, and, according to witnesses, he died "without the slightest struggle."

1834 THORNDIKE, Edward Lee (1874–1949) The psychologist and educator who taught educational psychology at Columbia University for many years remarked to a friend: "Poff, you're looking at a tired old man!"

1835 THRALE, Hester Lynch Piozzi (1741–1821) The English author remarked, when two of her children arrived: "Now I shall die in state." When her doctor came in, she traced the outline of a coffin with her fingers in the air.

1836 THURBER, James Grover (1894–1961) The American humorist and illustrator murmured: "God bless ... God damn...."

1837 THURLOW, Edward, Baron (1731–1806) The English lawyer and statesman, Tory leader in the House of Lords and a bitter foe of American independence, commented: "I'm shot if I don't think I am dying."

1838 TIBBLES, Susette la Flesche (1854–1903) The American writer, artist, and spokeswoman for Indian rights, realizing that she had spoken to a friend in her native Omaha language, apologized: "Sorry, dear. Forgot you don't know our language."

1839 TIBERIUS, Emperor of Rome (43 B.C.–A.D. 37) The hated ruler, who left a reputation for cruelty and perversion, said angrily to aides who were leaving the sickroom: "You know when to abandon the setting and hasten to the rising sun!" He was found dead in his room later.

1840 TILLICH, Paul (1886–1965) The German theologian stopped eating. He told a doctor in the hospital where he was being treated that, after working with the dietary nurse, he was cancelling all his meals: "All my hard work. All my work in vain. I am eating nothing at all ... absolute asceticism."

1841 TILLMAN, Benjamin Ryan (Pitchfork Ben) (1847–1918) The populist governor of South Carolina later served as senator. He was notorious for his racial bigotry. Obsessed with the idea that angry blacks were praying for his death, he told a friend: "Don't ever let these niggers pray for you!"

1842 TIMROD, Henry (1829–1867) The American poet, dying of tuberculosis, commented: "I shall soon drink of the river of eternal life."

1843 TITUS, Emperor of Rome (39–81) When the popular ruler died after a brief reign he was evidently sorry that he failed to liquidate his brother Domitian, who succeeded him. He mused: "I have made but one error."

1844 TOJO, Hideki (1884–1946) Japanese prime minister during World War II, he was hanged as a war criminal. He declared: "My execution is some consolation, although it certainly cannot compensate for my responsibility to the nation. But, internationally, I declare myself innocent. I gave in only to superior force. I now walk to the gallows, happy to shoulder my responsibility."

1845 TOKLAS, Alice Babette (1877–1967) The American author, best known as the companion of Gertrude Stein, replied, when her maid asked her if she wanted to eat: "No." Asked if she wanted to drink, Toklas said: "No." Asked if she wanted to die, she answered: "Yes!"

1846 TOLAND, John (1670–1722) The British writer and proponent of deism is best remembered for his *Christianity Not Mysterious*. He declared: "I want nothing but death."

1847 TOLKIEN, John Ronald Reuel (1892–1973) The British author, five days before his death from pneumonia, told a friend: "I feel on top of the world."

1848 TOLSTOY, Leo Nicolayevich (1828–1910) The Russian author, dying of pneumonia in a railroad station, told the doctors who were ministering to him: "This is all foolishness! What's the point in taking medicine?" He whispered brokenly to his son: "The truth ... I care a great deal.... How they...."

1849 TONE, Theobald Wolfe (1763–1798) The Irish revolutionary leader, dying in prison, told a friend: "Come and take charge!"

1850 TONKS, Henry (1862–1936) The English painter told his housekeeper, who found him unconscious the next morning: "You may as well say goodbye, as I shall not be here in the morning."

1851 TOOMBS, Robert Augustus (1810–1885) The Georgia political leader, a supporter of the Confederacy and an enemy of Reconstruction, was informed that prohibitionists were holding a rally and commented: "Prohibitionists are men of small pints."

1852 TOPLADY, Augustus Montague (1740–1778) The Anglican clergyman and writer, best remembered for writing the words to "Rock of Ages, Cleft for Me," died of tuberculosis, exclaiming: "Come, Lord Jesus, come quickly! No mortal can live after the glories which God has manifested to my soul!"

1853 TORRES-ACOSTA, Maria Soledad (1826–1887) A Spanish social worker, who founded the Handmaidens of Mary Serving the Sick, was asked by her religious for a blessing. She responded: "Children, live together in peace and unity."

1854 TOSCANINI, Arturo (1867–1957) The orchestral conductor, dying after a series of strokes, a few days before the end imagined that he was conducting a rehearsal: "No, not like that, more smoothly, please, more smoothly. Let's repeat. More smoothly. That's it, good, now it's right."

1855 TOUHY, Roger (1898–1959) The reputed mobster and bootlegger was gunned down in Chicago shortly after his release from prison. Waiting for the ambulance to arrive, he murmured: "I've been expecting it. The bastards never forget!"

1856 TOULOUSE-LAUTREC, Henri (1864–1901) The French painter told the priest who came to see him: "I am happier to see you now than I shall be in a few days, when you come with your little bell."

1857 TOUSSAINT, Pierre (1766–1853) The Haitian-born American philanthropist died in New York, telling a friend: "God is with me." When she asked if he wanted anything, he replied: "Nothing on earth."

1858 TRAUBEL, Horace (1858–1919) The American author, best remembered as the editor of the works of his friend Walt Whitman, complained: "I am tired, damned tired."

1859 TREE, Sir Herbert Beerbohm (1853–1917) The British actor and director commented on a part in a play that he was about to produce: "I shall not need to study the part at all. I know it already."

1860 TREXLER, Samuel (1877–1949) The American clergyman who was a leading figure in the Lutheran church and a promoter of the unity of Lutherans in the United States, died suddenly after a short illness, telling a friend: "I'm feeling fine. Let me see the papers."

1861 TRISTAN, Flora (1803–1844)

The French feminist, socialist, and author died of a stroke in Bordeaux. She declared: "If I should die, tell everyone who has loved me that I too love them—immensely, religiously." Later, somewhat confused, she murmured: "The sea, isn't it beautiful, so shining . . . but am I not in Bordeaux?"

1862 TROLLOPE, Anthony (1815–1882) The English novelist suffered a debilitating stroke after which the only word he could utter was: "No."

1863 TROLLOPE, Frances Milton (1780–1863) The English novelist, best remembered for her writings about her travels in America, spoke of her daughter: "Poor Cecelia!"

1864 TROMP, Maarten Harpertzoon (1597–1653) The Dutch admiral was a hero of the Thirty Years' War against Spain and her allies. Five years after the conclusion of that devastating conflict, he was killed in battle with the English, and exhorted his men: "Take courage, children! Act so that my end will be glorious, as my life has been."

1865 TROTSKY, Leon (1879–1940) The Russian revolutionary leader was murdered in exile in Mexico by an agent of his archenemy Joseph Stalin. Stabbed in the head with an ice-pick, Trotsky told a body guard who was trying to assure him that the wound was superficial: "No, this time they succeeded." Speaking of his wife, he said: "Take care of Natalia. She has been with me many, many years."

1866 TRUMAN, Harry S (1884–1972) Dying after a lingering illness in a Kansas City hospital, the thirty-third president commented: "I feel all right." Asked if he were in pain, he replied: "No."

1867 TRUTH, Sojourner (c.1797–1883) The abolitionist and reformer,

who was born Isabella Baumfree, exclaimed ecstatically: "Stepping out
into the light, oh, won't that be glorious? Oh, I'm not going to die! I'm just
going home like a shooting star!"

1868 TUBMAN, Harriet Ara-
minta Ross (c.1820–1913) A slave from
Maryland who escaped to become a
"conductor" of the Underground Railroad and lead more than 300 bonds-
men to freedom, she died in Auburn,
New York. Summoning her friends,
she proposed: "Now, a song." Then
she sang: "Swing low, sweet chariot,/
Coming for to carry me home...."

1869 TUCKER, Richard (1913–
1975) The operatic tenor died suddenly of a heart attack in his hotel
room in Kalamazoo, Michigan, after
telling his wife, in a telephone conversation: "Anyway, how about you?
What are you up to today? Tell me so
I can call you after Bob [Merrill] and
I get done rehearsing."

1870 TURENNE, Henri de la
Tour d'Auvergne, Vicomte de (1611–
1675) The marshal of France, who
had distinguished himself during the
Thirty Years' War, was killed years
later, fighting the Holy Roman Empire. When his officers urged him to
take cover, he replied, just seconds before he was killed: "Then I will gladly
come, for I particularly wish not to be
killed just now."

1871 TURGENEV, Ivan Sergeyevich (1818–1883) The Russian novelist died in Paris. He told his family: "Come nearer ... near. Let me
feel you all near me. The moment of
parting has come. Goodbye, my darlings."

1872 TURGOT, Anne-Robert-
Jacques (1727–1781) The French minister of finance was chided for ruining
his health through overwork, and
answered: "You blame me for attempting too much, but you know that in
my family we die of gout at fifty."

1873 TURNER, Frederick Jackson (1861–1931) The American historian, stricken with a heart attack, told
his wife: "I know this is the end. I
know this is the end. Tell Max I am
sorry that I haven't finished my book."

1874 TURNER, Joseph Mallord
William (1775–1851) The English
landscape painter remarked: "The sun
is God."

1875 TUSSAUD, Anne Marie
Grosholtz (1761–1850) The French
artist who first attracted attention by
modeling in wax the heads of the victims of the French Revolution set up
her famous wax museum in London
in 1802. On her deathbed she enjoined
her sons: "Do not quarrel."

TWAIN, Mark *see* CLEM-
ENS, Samuel Langhorne

1876 TWEED, William Marcy
(1823–1878) The New York political
boss was jailed for graft. Dying of diabetes in prison, he spoke of the men
responsible for his conviction: "Tilden
and Fairchild — they will be satisfied."

1877 TYLER, John (1790–1862)
The first vice-president to succeed to
the presidency on the death of his pre-
decessor, he was serving in the Confederate Congress when he suffered a
stroke in Richmond. When his baby
daughter (he had 15 children by two
wives) began crying, he told his wife:
"Poor little thing! How I disturb her!"
When a doctor prescribed brandy and
mustard plasters, Tyler refused to cooperate, insisting: "Doctor, I think
you are mistaken." When another
doctor appeared, Tyler announced:
"Doctor, I am going." When the
physician replied, "I hope not," Tyler
gently suggested: "Perhaps it is best."
Then, turning to his wife, he smiled
and died "as if falling asleep."

1878 TYLER, Julia Gardiner
(1820–1889) Second wife of President
Tyler, she died in Richmond of a
stroke. Responding to a nurse who

asked her what she would like to drink: "Tea."

1879 TYNAN, Kenneth Peacock (1927–1980) The British drama critic begged his wife: "Please come back soon."

1880 TYNDALE, William (1492–1536) The English Bible translator, strangled and burnt near Brussels for criticizing Henry VIII, prayed: "Lord, open the King of England's eyes."

1881 TYNDALL, John (1820–1893) The English physicist who proved why the sky is blue died when his wife accidentally gave him the wrong medication. Getting out of bed, he said: "Yes, my poor darling, you have killed your John. Let us do all we can. Tickle my throat! Get a stomach pump!" He became unconscious, but awoke a few hours later. When his wife asked him if he knew that the doctors were working to save him, he answered: "Yes, I know you are all trying to rouse me."

1882 TYNG, Dudley Atkins (1825–1855) The dying words of the abolitionist inspired the hymn, "Stand Up, Stand Up for Jesus!" He was an Episcopal priest who was fatally injured when, blessing some equipment on a Pennsylvania farm, he got the sleeve of his cassock caught in a machine, which ripped his arm off. Dying in agony, he urged his father: "Father, stand up for Jesus! Tell them, 'Let us all stand up for Jesus!' I know Jesus. I have a steadfast trust in Jesus, a calm and steadfast trust." Asked, "Are you happy?," Tyng replied: "Perfectly."

1883 TZU-HSI (1835–1908) Dowager empress of China, she ruled her country as a virtual dictator for three decades, but on her deathbed she declared: "Never again allow a woman to hold supreme power in the state. It is against the house law of our dynasty and should be forbidden. Be careful not to allow eunuchs to meddle in government matters. The Ming Dynasty was brought to ruin by eunuchs and its fate should be a warning to my people."

UMBERTO I, King of Italy
see HUMBERT I
UMBERTO II, King of Italy
see HUMBERT II

1884 URBAN V, Pope (1310–1370) Born William of Grimoard, he died at the papal palace at Avignon, France, instructing his aides: "Leave the doors open, so that everyone may enter and see how a pope dies."

1885 USSHER, James (1581–1656) The English clergyman and scholar, who served as Anglican bishop of Armagh in Ireland, is best remembered for dating the creation of the world at 4004 B.C. On his deathbed he prayed: "But Lord, in special, forgive my sins of omission."

1886 VALDES, Gabriel de la Conception (1809–1844) A Cuban poet, executed by the Spanish for sedition, cried out after surviving the first volley of the firing squad: "There is no mercy for me.... Fire here...."

1887 VALENTINO, Rudolph (1895–1926) The silent film star, suffering from a perforated ulcer, mumbled in delirium disjointed phrases which were dutifully recorded by his nurses: "Mama mia, I didn't mean it ... Maria, your turn ... George, last night, remember, we were lost in the woods.... Je t'aime, Freckle Nose ... Indian Chief Black Feather ... I took all the bugs out of the rose bushes.... Babykins.... On the other hand, the other hand—I love you—you!" Then, lucidly, he said: "Please raise the shade. I want to see the sunlight."

1888 VALLÉE, Rudy (1901–1986) The singer and entertainer was watching a telecast of the ceremonies commemorating the centennial of the Statue of Liberty. Turning to his wife, he remarked: "I wish we could be there. You know how I love a party." Then, according to his wife, he "took a big breath and died."

1889 VAN BUREN, Martin (1782–1862) The statesman who served as U.S. senator, governor of New York, secretary of state, and, then, for one term, as president, died at Lindenwald, his estate in New York. He told his sons: "There is but one reliance."

1890 VANDERBILT, Alfred (1877–1915) The millionaire horse breeder and racer died when the *Lusitania* was torpedoed by a German U-boat. According to a survivor, Vanderbilt was "absolutely unperturbed" and stood on deck like "a gentleman waiting for a train," as he helped women and children into lifeboats. He was last heard urging his valet: "Find all the kiddies you can, boy."

1891 VANDERBILT, Cornelius (1794–1877) The railroad and shipping magnate, who owned the New York Central Railroad, exhorted his son: "Keep the money together, hey! Keep the Central our road. That's my boy Bill!"

1892 VANDERBILT, Cornelius II (1843–1899) Stricken with a cerebral hemorrhage, the chairman of the board of the New York Central Railroad called his wife: "Alice, Alice, I think I am dying."

1893 VANDERBILT, George Washington (1862–1914) The businessman, philanthropist, and art collector, who constructed the Biltmore mansion in Asheville, North Carolina, and gave away sizeable sums to education and to the arts, died suddenly of "clogged arteries" in his Washington home, after eating breakfast with his wife and daughter. Waving a doctor away, he held out his arms to his wife and whispered, just minutes before expiring in her arms: "Edith."

1894 VANE, Sir Henry (1613–1662?)

The English statesman, who served for a time as colonial governor of Massachusetts and was a member of the council of state during the protectorate of Oliver Cromwell, was executed for treason when the Stuart monarchy was restored. On the scaffold he prayed: "Father, glorify Thy servant in the sight of men, that he may glorify Thee in the discharge of his duty to Thee and to his country."

1895 VAN GOGH, Vincent (1853–1890) The eccentric Dutch painter, dying of a self-inflicted gunshot wound, told his brother, who cradled his head in his arm: "I wish I could pass away like this."

1896 VANZETTI, Bartolomeo (1888–1927) An Italian-born fish peddler, he was executed along with Nicola Sacco, after a long and controversial trial, for the murder of a paymaster and guard at a factory. Protesting his innocence, Vanzetti declared at his execution: "I wish to tell you that I am innocent and never committed any crime, but sometimes some sin. I am innocent of all crime, not only of this one, but all. I am an innocent man. I wish to forgive some people for what they are doing to me."

1897 VAUGHAN, Sarah (1924–1990) The jazz vocalist, ill with lung cancer, asked to be taken home from the hospital: "I want to go home! Take me home!" She was taken home and died shortly afterwards.

1898 VEGA, Lope de (1562–1635) The Spanish poet and playwright declared: "True glory is in virtue. Ah, I would willingly give all the applause I have received to have performed one good action more."

1899 VERDI, Giuseppe (1813–1901) When his housekeeper noticed that the composer was fastening the buttons of his vest to the wrong buttonholes, she tried to help him. He remarked: "One button more, or one button less." Seconds later he suffered a massive stroke and fell backward, unconscious, dying several days later without emerging from his coma.

1900 VERLAINE, Paul (1844–1896) When the French poet overheard someone in the room remark, "He's dying," he responded: "Don't sole the dead man's shoes yet!" He died shortly afterwards, murmuring the names of two of his friends: "Lepelletier . . . Coppée. . . ."

1901 VERNE, Jules (1828–1905) The French author said to his family: "Good, you're all there. Now I can die." After a priest administered the last rites, he told him: "You have done me good. I feel regenerated."

1902 VESPASIAN, Emperor of Rome (9–79) Making fun of the Roman practice of declaring emperors gods after their death, he exclaimed: "I think I'm turning into a god!" Struggling to his feet, he insisted: "An emperor ought to die standing!" He expired in the arms of his aides.

1903 VEYGOUX, Louis Desaix de (1768–1800) A French general, killed in Napoleon's victory at Marengo, gasped: "Death!"

1904 VIANNEY, Jean-Marie-Baptiste (1786–1859) The pastor of the village of Ars-en-Dombes in France was renowned for his holiness, his skill as a confessor, and for the miracles that accompanied his ministry. Asked where he wanted to be buried, he replied: "At Ars, but my body is not much."

1905 VICTOR EMMANUEL II, King of Italy (1820–1878) The first king of a united Italy bade his son and successor: "I entreat you to be strong, to love your country, and to love freedom."

1906 VICTOR EMMANUEL III, King of Italy (1869–1947) The third king of Italy lost his throne after World War II and died in Egypt, asking his doctor about his heart attack: "How long will it last? I have some important things to attend to." Seconds later he died.

1907 VICTORIA, Empress Frederick of Germany (1840–1901) Daughter of Britain's Victoria and widow of Frederick III, she suffered for two years with bone cancer. She told a church official who showed her plans for renovating a bell tower, which she realized that she would never see completed: "I feel like Moses on Pisgah, looking at the promised land which I must not enter." The day before she lost consciousness, as she was brought into her room from the garden, she told her attendants: "Stop, so that I can take a last look at the garden I made in memory of a great and undying love."

1908 VICTORIA, Queen of Great Britain (1819–1901) After a reign of nearly 64 years, Britain's longest-reigning sovereign died at Osborne House, her home on the Isle of Wight. She told her daughter Louise: "I don't want to die yet. There are several things I want to arrange." A few hours later she held out her arms to her olest son, Albert Edward, calling: "Bertie!" Six hours later she died.

1909 VICTORIA KAIULANI, Crown Princess of Hawaii (1875–1899) The beloved princess died several years after the abolition of her country's monarchy, whispering: "Mama."

1910 VIDOCQ, François-Eugene (1775–1857) The founder of a private detective agency in France, he told his priest: "You . . . my only physician. . . ."

1911 VIGNY, Alfred-Victor de (1797–1863) The French romantic poet and novelist, dying of cancer, urged those around his bed: "Pray for me. Pray to God for me."

1912 VILLARS, Claude-Louis-Hector, Duke of (1653–1734) As marshal of France, he commanded his nation's forces during the War of the Spanish Succession. Dying a natural death in old age, he remarked, when told of an English commander who had recently lost his life in battle: "I had always contended that that man was born luckier than I."

1913 VITELLIUS, Emperor of Rome (15–69) The general who overthrew Otho was himself overthrown and murdered by another general, Vespasian. He argued with his assassins: "Yet I was your emperor."

1914 VOLTAIRE (1694–1778) The French author, whose real name was François-Marie Arouet, angered when a priest was called in, snapped: "Jesus Christ! Jesus Christ! Never speak to me again about that man! Let me die in peace!"

1915 WADDELL, George Edward (Rube) (1876–1914) The colorful, eccentric, but brilliant left-handed pitcher for the Philadelphia Athletics and several other baseball clubs died of tuberculosis in a Texas hospital. He joked about his emaciated condition with some former teammates who had come to visit him: "I'll be over tomorrow to show you guys how to run. I've got my weight down now."

1916 WADE, Benjamin Franklin (1800–1878) The Ohio senator, a leader of the Radical Republicans during the Reconstruction era, told his wife: "I cannot speak at all."

1917 WAGNER, Cosima Liszt (1837–1930) Daughter of composer Franz Liszt and wife of composer Richard Wagner, she whispered: "Glorious ... sorrow...."

1918 WAGNER, Wilhelm Richard (1813–1883) The German composer, stricken with a heart attack in Venice, was alarmed when his watch dropped from his pocket as his wife helped him to a sofa, and cried: "My watch!"

1919 WAIBLINGER, Wilhelm (1804–1830) The German poet died in Rome, bidding farewell to his loved ones in Italian: "Farewell."

1920 WALKER, James Alexander (1832–1901) The Confederate general who later served as Republican congressman from Virginia told his daughter: "The sun is setting, daughter. I can't wait. Once more I want to stand up by the window and watch the sun set. Help me to get up, Will. I want to stand on my feet again and die like a man and a soldier." His daughter tried to lift him on his pillow, but he lost consciousness immediately and died.

1921 WALKER, James John (Jimmy) (1881–1946) The former mayor of New York City protested when his nurse ordered him to return to bed: "Am I not the master of my own house?" When she protested, "Yes, Mr. Walker, but..." the sick man interrupted: "Oh, you must be a good Democrat!" When the nurse answered that she was, Walker said: "In that case I shall abide by the wishes of a fair constituent." He went to bed and died.

1922 WALKER, Sarah Breedlove (1867–1919) The African American businesswoman who became a millionaire marketing "Madam C.J. Walker's Hair Grower" and other beauty products, died at her villa in Irvington, New York, telling her nurse: "I want to live to help my race."

1923 WALLACE, Lewis (1827–1905) The American lawyer, soldier, diplomat, and writer, best known for his novel *Ben Hur*, told his wife: "We meet in heaven."

1924 WALLER, Thomas Wright (Fats) (1904–1943) The jazz performer and composer fell suddenly ill with pneumonia in his private room on a train attempting to make its way through a blizzard towards Kansas

City. He compared the wind to the playing of a saxophonist friend: "Hawkins is still blowing out there tonight!" When a friend complained about his cold room, Waller said: "You'll be okay when you get into bed." When the train finally pulled into the station an hour and a half later, Waller was dead.

1925 WALTHER, Carl Ferdinand Wilhelm (1811–1887) The German-American Lutheran pastor, who helped to found the Lutheran Church-Missouri Synod and who served as its first president, was asked, on the point of death, if he was willing to die cheerfully in the grace of Christ. He whispered: "Yes."

1926 WALTON, William (1902–1983) The British composer died in his wife's arms, pleading: "Don't leave me, please don't leave me."

1927 WARD, Mary Josephine (Maisie) (1889–1975) The British biographer and publisher remarked a few days before her death: "I still have enthusiasm. But what use is enthusiasm without energy?"

1928 WARHAM, William (1450–1532) The archbishop of Canterbury who married Henry VIII and Catherine of Aragon responded to a servant who told him that he had only 30 pounds left: "That will suffice till my arrival in heaven."

1929 WARREN, Earl (1891–1974) The lawyer and statesman who served as governor of California and then as chief justice of the U.S. Supreme Court, died in retirement. Hospitalized with a heart condition, he told Justice William Brennan, who had told him of the Court's decision to force President Nixon to hand the Watergate tapes over to a district court: "Thank God! If you don't do it this way, Bill, it's the end of the country as we have known it!" Moments later he suffered a heart attack and died.

1930 WASHINGTON, Booker Taliaferro (1856–1915) The African American leader, while hospitalized in New York, insisted on returning home to Tuskegee, Alabama, to die: "I was born in the South. I have lived and labored in the South. And I wish to die and be buried in the South." Taken by train to Cheehaw, Alabama, he was being driven to his mansion, The Oaks, when, with dimming consciousness, he asked his son about his infant grandson: "How is Booker?" Four hours after reaching home, Washington died.

1931 WASHINGTON, George (1732–1799) After the former president was diagnosed as suffering from "a violent inflammation of the membranes of the throat," Dr. Elisha Dick, one of three physicians in attendance, argued against further bleeding the patient and urged a trachaeotomy, but was overruled by his colleagues and by the general himself. Washington, despite the frantic pleas of his wife, urged the doctors to draw more blood. At 4:30 in the afternoon, the general asked his wife to take two wills from his desk and burn the one he indicated.

He told his secretary, Colonel Tobias Lear, who sat holding his hand: "I find I am going. My breath cannot continue long. I believed from the first attack it would be fatal. Do you arrange and settle my books, and you know more about them than anyone else, and let Mr. Rawlins finish recording my other letters, which he has begun." When Lear told him that he would comply with his wishes, Washington asked: "Do you recollect anything which is essential for me to do, as I have but a short time to continue with you?"

Experiencing increased difficulty in breathing, the general sat in a chair for a while, then returned to bed. Lear lay down beside him and tried to make him comfortable by raising and turning him. When Washington protested that he was going to too much trouble and Lear denied it, he conceded: "Well, it is a debt we must pay to each other, and I hope, when you want aid of this kind, you will find it."

To Dr. Craik, a lifelong friend, Washington said: "Doctor, I die hard, but I am not afraid to go. My breath cannot last long." The physician pressed the general's hand, but could not speak and had to leave the room. Washington dismissed the other two physicians with the words: "Let me die without further interruption. I feel myself going. I thank you for your attention. You had better not take any more trouble about me, but let me go off quietly. I cannot last long."

There are two versions of what Washington said next to Lear. In his diary, the colonel wrote that the general said: "I am just going. Have me decently buried, and do not let my body be put into the vault in less than three days after I am dead." In a letter written to his mother, Lear quoted Washington as saying: "My dear friend, I am just about to change my scene. My breath cannot continue for but a few moments. You will have me decently interred, and do not let my body be put in the tomb in less than two days after my death." Both accounts agree that Washington then said to Lear: "Do you understand me?" "Yes, sir!" answered the aide. "'T is well."

Lear was sitting beside Washington, holding his hand. Nearby stood Dr. Craik and Washington's black valet Christopher. "Rigid as stone," Lady Washington sat at the foot of the bed. Towards midnight, Washington withdrew his hand from Lear's to feel for his own pulse. Seconds later, the hand fell from the wrist. In a voice described as "calm and controlled," Lady Washington asked, "Is he gone?" Lear, unable to speak, held up his hand. Echoing her husband's last words, the widow murmured, "'T is well," and walked out of the bedroom, to which she never returned.

1932 WASHINGTON, Martha Dandridge Custis (1731–1802) The widow of George Washington died of a "prolonged severe fever," which she bore with "composure and resignation." She told her grandchildren: "I am now undergoing my final trial, but I have been prepared for a long time." After the last rites were administered and she received communion, she blessed her family and her slaves and then asked for the dress in which she wanted to be buried: "Bring me my white gown, the one I have laid by as my last dress."

1933 WATERS, Ethel (1896–1977) The singer and actress, just moments before her death after years of ill health, murmured: "Merciful Father! Precious Jesus!"

1934 WATSON, Thomas Edward (1856–1922) The Georgia senator, noted for his support for the populist movement and of agricultural interests, and for his hatred of Jews and blacks, died of asthma, gasping: "It's my finish. I am not afraid of death. I am not afraid of death."

1935 WATTEAU, Antoine (1684–1721) The French painter said to the priest who came to administer the last rites: "Take this crucifix away from me! How could an artist portray so poorly the features of a God?"

1936 WATTS, George Frederic (1817–1904) The English artist, known as "The Poet Painter" because of the allegorical nature of his work, died proclaiming: "Now I see that great book! Now I see that great light!"

1937 WATTS, Isaac (1674–1748) The English clergyman and poet, whose *Psalms of David, Imitated* was one of the first Protestant hymnals in the English language, told a friend, as he lay dying from a lingering, painful illness: "I bless God that I can lie down with comfort at night, not being solicitous of whether I wake in this world or another." In severe pain, Watts commented: "The business of a Christian is to bear the will of God as well as to do it. If I were in health, I ought to be doing it. And now it is my duty to bear it. The best thing in obedience is a regard to the will of God, and the way to that is to have our inclinations and aversions as much mortified as we can." When a friend quoted Hebrews 13:5 and asked, "Do you experience the comfort of the words, 'I will never leave thee nor forsake thee?,' Watts, with his last breath, affirmed: "Yes."

1938 WATTS, James (1736–1819) The Scots engineer and inventor, who built the first efficient steam engine, told friends: "I am very sensible of the attachment you show me, and I hasten to thank you for it, as I feel that I am now come to my last illness."

1939 WAYNE, Anthony (1745–1796) The Revolutinary war general spent his last years fighting Indians in what is now the American Midwest. Dying, he told his men: "This is the end . . . I am dying . . . I can't bear up much longer. . . . Bury me here on the hill—by the flagpole."

1940 WAYNE, John (1907–1979) When his companion asked him if he knew her, the actor replied: "Of course I know who you are. You're my girl. I love you."

1941 WEBB, Mary Gladys Meredith (1881–1927) The English novelist, told that tea was being prepared for her, replied: "That will be nice."

1942 WEBER, Carl Maria, Baron von (1786–1826) The German composer died in London, where he was supervising the production of his opera *Oberon*. Retiring for the night, he told his servant: "Now let me sleep." Next morning he was discovered dead in bed.

1943 WEBSTER, DANIEL (1782–1852) The Massachusetts senator demanded of his doctor: "Give me life! Give me life!" Once or twice, during his last day, the statesman inquired: "Am I alive or am I dead?" When his pastor read the verse, "Yea, though I walk through the valley of the shadow of death, I will fear no evil, for thou art with me, thy rod and thy staff, they comfort me," the senator interrupted: "Yes, thy rod, thy staff, but the *fact*, the *fact* I want!"

Webster asked his doctor for painkillers, but the physician told him that he would provide them at the appropriate time. Webster replied: "When you give it to me, I shall know that I may drop off at once. I will then put myself in the position to obtain a little repose." A few hours later he awoke and whispered: "I still live." He tried to say something, but the only word his son could make out was: "Poetry." He then read to his father Gray's "Elegy Written in a Country Churchyard." Hearing his favorite poem, the senator smiled. Two hours later he died.

1944 WEBSTER, Noah (1758–1843) The American educator and lexicographer declared: "I'm ready to go. My work is all done. I know in whom I have believed. I have struggled with many difficulties. Some I have been able to overcome, and by some I have been overcome. I have made many mistakes, but I love my country and have labored for the youth of my country, and I trust no precept of mine has taught any dear youth to err."

1945 WEED, Thurlow (1792–1882) The American journalist and politician, a founder of the Whig Party, seemed to imagine that he was leaving a meeting with Lincoln and Seward (both of whom were long since dead) and hailing a carriage. He insisted: "I want to go home."

1946 WEIL, Simone (1909–1943) The French social philosopher, working with the French Resistance (to German occupation) in Britain, died of an illness which was aggravated by her refusal to eat. Urged to eat by her doctor, she replied: "When I think of my fellow citizens who are dying of hunger in France, I cannot eat."

1947 WEIZMAN, Chaim (1874–1952) The Zionist leader who served as Israel's first president told his nurse: "I am going on a very, very long journey. Prepare everything."

1948 WELD, Angelina Emily Grimké (1805–1879) The abolitionist and women's rights advocate murmured: "Death! Death! Life eternal! Eternal life!" Then, quoting James 5:4, she said brokenly: "The hire of the laborers kept back by fraud cried, and the cries are in the ear of the Lord."

1949 WELLES, George Orson (1915–1985) The actor and director spoke his last recorded words at the close of an interview, when, asked how he felt, he replied: "Oh, sure. All those old people that walk along, saying they feel just the way they did when they were kids ... liars, every one of them!" After the interview, he had dinner and went home and died.

1950 WELLINGTON, Arthur Wellesley, Duke of (1769–1852) The general who defeated Napoleon at Waterloo and later served as Britain's prime minister, upon feeling ill, sent for an apothecary, who said, "I am sorry that Your Grace is an invalid. What do you complain of?" The duke, pointing to his heart, said: "I think some derangement." After the apothecary left, a servant asked the sick man if he wanted tea. Wellington replied:

"Yes, if you please."

1951 WELLS, Herbert George (1866–1946) The British author stared at his son and said: "I just don't understand you."

1952 WENCESLAS, King of Bohemia (907–929) The subject of the Christmas carol tried to promote the Christian faith, but was murdered by his pagan brother Boleslas. Good King Wenceslas breathed his last with the words: "May God forgive you, brother."

1953 WESLEY, Charles (1707–1788) The English clergyman and poet, author of more than 6500 hymns, dictated to his wife: "In age and feebleness extreme,/ Who shall a sinful worm redeem?/ Jesus, my only hope Thou art,/ Strength of my failing flesh and heart!/ Oh, could I but catch a smile from Thee/ And drop into eternity!" When his wife asked him to press her hand if she still knew her, Wesley said: "My Lord, my heart, my God!"

1954 WESLEY, John (1703–1791) The Anglican priest who founded what became the Methodist Church told his housekeeper that he wished to write, but when she brought him pen and paper, was unable to do so. When she asked what he wanted to say, Wesley answered: "Nothing, but that God is with us." He then repeated the words of a hymn: "I'll praise my maker while I've breath,/ And when my voice is lost in death,/ Praise shall employ my nobler powers;/ My days of praise shall ne'er be past,/ While life and thought and being last,/ Or immortality endures!"

When his sister-in-law kissed him, Wesley said: "He giveth His beloved rest." When she moistened his lips, he prayed: "We thank Thee, O Lord, for this and all Thy mercies. Bless the Church and king and grant us peace and truth through Jesus Christ, Our

Lord." Later he said distinctly: "The best of all is, God with us." Throughout the night he kept repeating, 20 or more times: "I'll praise! I'll praise!" At ten the next morning, he opened his eyes, and, looking at the people gathered in his room, said: "Farewell." Moments later he died.

1955 WESLEY, Martha (1706–1791) The Methodist leader, a sister of John and Charles, was asked by her niece if she were in pain, and replied: "No, but a new feeling. I have the assurance which I have long prayed for. Shout!"

1956 WESLEY, Samuel, Sr. (1662–1735) The Anglican priest, father of John, Charles, and Martha Wesley, told Charles: "Now let me hear you talk about heaven." When asked if he were worse, he answered: "Oh, my Charles, I feel a great deal. God chastens me with strong pain, but I praise Him for it; I thank Him for it; I love Him for it." When John asked, "Aren't you near heaven," Samuel replied: "Yes, I am." After John offered the prayers for the dying, the father declared: "Now you have done all."

1957 WESLEY, Samuel Sebastian (1810–1876) The English organist and composer of church music, dying of Bright's disease, said to his sister: "Let me see the sky." She later wrote, "His death was calm and peaceful, it was only ceasing to breathe."

1958 WESLEY, Susanna Annesley (1664–1742) The mother of the 19 Wesley children enjoined her family: "Children, as soon as I am released, sing a psalm of praise to God."

1959 WHATELEY, Richard (1787–1863) The English educator and social reformer, who served as Anglican archbishop of Dublin, objected when the pastor administering the last rites read a translation of Philippians 3:21 which contained the phrase "change our vile body." The clergy-

man, noting the bishop's displeasure, substituted the alternative translation, "this body of our humiliation." Whateley, satisfied, said: "That's right. Not 'vile.' Nothing that He has made is vile."

1960 WHISTLER, James Abbot McNeill (1834–1903) The last recorded words of the American painter were spoken two days before he died in London, when chicken broth was brought to him. He rejected it, saying: "Take the damned thing away!" Then, when a friend rose to leave, he said: "Why do you go so soon?"

1961 WHITE, Joseph Blanco (1775–1841) The Spanish-born British romantic poet said tersely: "Now I die."

1962 WHITE, Walter Francis (1893–1955) The civil rights leader, for many years the head of the NAACP, fell to the floor with a heart attack, taking a table with him. When his wife rushed to his assistance, he complained: "I knew that darned table was going to tip!"

1963 WHITEFIELD, George (1714–1770) The British evangelist died of a heart attack in Rhode Island. He observed: "I am almost suffocated. I can scarce breathe. My asthma chokes me. I am dying."

1964 WHITGIFT, John (1530–1604) Archbishop of Canterbury under Queen Elizabeth I, he murmured: "In behalf of the Church of God."

1965 WHITMAN, Walt (1819–1892) The American poet, put on a waterbed to ease his pain, declared: "Oh, I feel so good!"

1966 WHITNEY, William Collins (1841–1904) The American financier, politician, and sportsman who served as secretary of the navy under Cleveland, told his nurse, after she informed his children that he was too sick to see them: "Don't get angry, nurse. I love my son and daughter. It does me good to chat with them."

1967 WHITTIER, John Greenleaf (1807–1892) The American Quaker poet dismissed his doctors: "You have done all that love and human skill can do. I thank you. It is of no use. I am worn out." Then, to no one in particular, he exclaimed: "Love, love to all the world!" When his niece began to pull down the blinds, Whittier protested: "No! No!" When she asked him if he recognized her, the poet replied, in the style of the Quakers of the time: "I have known thee all the time." As a group of relatives and friends gathered around his bed and read from his poems, he quietly drifted away.

1968 WHITTLE, Daniel Webster (1840–1901) The American soldier, watchmaker, and evangelist, dying after a long and agonizing illness, responded to a friend distressed at his intense sufferings: "It is all right. The Lord knows best and all will result in my good. All sorrow will fade away and all pain depart as dew before the morning sun."

1969 WIELAND, Christoph Martin (1733–1813) The German poet and novelist muttered a quotation from *Hamlet*: "To be or not to be. . . ."

1970 WILBERFORCE, William (1759–1833) The English statesman who fought successfully for the abolition of slavery in the British Empire told his family: "I can leave you without regret, not because I love you less, but because I love God more."

1971 WILDE, Oscar (1854–1900) The English writer, dying in France, told a friend: "You ought to be a doctor, as you always want people to do what they don't want to." Later, speaking of a play which he was writing, he commented, in reference to a French coin worth a hundredth of a franc: "It's worth fifty centimes."

WILHELM I, Kaiser of Germany *see* WILLIAM I, Emperor of Germany

WILHELM II, Kaiser of Germany *see* WILLIAM II, Emperor of Germany

1972 WILKES, John (1725–1797) The British statesman, who took the side of the colonies in Parliament during the Revolution, toasted his daughter, lifting up the glass of water she had just brought him: "To my beloved and excellent daughter!"

1973 WILLARD, Frances Elizabeth Caroline (1839–1898) President of the World Women's Temperance Union, she told her doctor, who informed her that she was dying: "It is well, for I am very weary." As she breathed her last, she whispered: "How beautiful to be with God!"

1974 WILLIAM I, Emperor of Germany (1797–1888) The first monarch of a united Germany told his chancellor, Otto von Bismarck: "I've always been pleased with you. You've done everything well."

1975 WILLIAM I, King of England (1027–1088) William the Conqueror, the Norman duke who successfully invaded England in 1066, retained extensive territories in France. Angry about jokes concerning his great weight, he burned down the town of Mantes, where the citizens were making fun of him. While inspecting the devastation, his horse shied at a corpse and threw him against the pommel of the saddle, causing internal injuries. Dying a few days later, William prayed: "I commend myself to Mary, the Holy Mother of God, my heavenly lady, that by her intercession I may be reconciled with her son, Our Lord Jesus Christ."

1976 WILLIAM II, Emperor of Germany (1859–1941) The third kaiser of Germany's Second Reich was deposed at the end of World War I and died in Doorn, Holland, where he had lived for two decades in exile. While he lay dying, Germany was conducting bombing raids on England and there was an expectation that Hitler would attempt an invasion of the island. The former kaiser said to his daughter: "Are we still going to attack England? Should that really happen— and should we win— we must immediately stretch out our hand to England and go together. Without England we cannot endure."

1977 WILLIAM II, King of England (1056–1100) Known as "Rufus" or "The Red King," the sovereign characterized by chroniclers as "tyrannical, cruel, and blasphemous" was on a hunting expedition. After shooting at a stag and missing it, he called to a member of his party named Walter Tirel: "Shoot, you devil! Shoot, in the devil's name! Shoot, or it will be the worse for you!" The arrow ricocheted and hit the king in the heart.

1978 WILLIAM III, King of England (1650–1702) Injured in an accident caused when his horse stumbled on a molehill, the king asked his doctor how long he would live, receiving the blunt response, "An hour, an hour and a half, though you may be snatched away in a twinkling of an eye." When the doctor took the king's pulse, William grabbed his hand and pleaded: "I do not die yet. Hold me fast." When his friend, the Earl of Portland, arrived, William took his hand and pressed it to his heart, then his head fell back on his shoulder. He closed his eyes, took two or three soft gasps, and was gone.

1979 WILLIAM IV, King of England (1765–1837) Known as the "Sailor King" because of his long career in the British Navy, and "Silly Billy" because of his intellectual aptitude, he noted the anniversary of the British victory over Napoleon at Waterloo. Asking to hold the tricolored banner, he said: "Unfurl it and let me feel it.... Glorious day...."

1980 WILLIAMS, Alice Johnson (1861–1925) The wife of Daniel Hale Williams, who performed the first successful heart operation, died at her estate, Oakmere, in Michigan. Like her husband, she was an unbeliever, and when someone suggested that prayer be offered, she responded: "A little late, don't you think?"

1981 WILLIAMS, Charles Walter Stansby (1886–1945) The English writer, a few days before he died, asked his friend, Gervase Matthew, an Anglican priest: "Will you say a Mass for anyone I have ever loved in any way?"

1982 WILLIAMS, Daniel Hale (1856–1931) The American surgeon, who performed the first successful heart operation, died after a series of incapacitating strokes. Staying with a niece in Chicago, he spoke his last recorded words about his estate Oakmere, in the town of Idlewild: "Take me to Idlewild to die." Returned to his home, he died a few weeks later.

1983 WILLIAMS, Edward Bennett (1920–1988) The Washington attorney who owned the Baltimore Orioles baseball team, after years of illness, spoke his last recorded words to his physician: "Have I put up a good fight? Have I tried? Do I have to keep fighting? Can I quit?"

1984 WILLIAMS, Egbert (Bert) (1874–1922) The comedian, ill with pneumonia, commented: "I feel eighty percent better."

1985 WILLIAMS, Hiram (Hank) (1923–1953) The bibulous country singer, composer, and lyricist, known as "The Hillbilly Shakespeare," died in Oak Hill, West Virginia, in the back seat of his Cadillac, en route to an engagement in Ohio. Before getting into the car, where he promptly fell into an alcoholic stupor, he told his wife: "Billie, I think I see God comin' down the road ... I just wanted to look at you one more time."

1986 WILLIAMS, John Sharp (1854–1932) The Mississippi senator declared: "I've done things that seemed at the time worth doing. I think that if a man can get to my age and, looking back, believe a majority of things he did were worth the effort, he has nothing to regret."

1987 WILLKIE, Wendell Lewis (1892–1944) The Republican political leader, who failed to thwart Franklin Roosevelt's bid for a third term in 1940, died of a heart attack while being hospitalized with a throat infection. When the nurse who was swabbing his throat asked him how he felt, Willkie replied: "How can I talk with my mouth full of that stuff?" Asked if he would like scotch and water, he answered: "Okay, if you make it warm." Minutes later he died.

1988 WILLS, James Robert (Bob) (1905–1975) The American bandleader and composer of country music asked his wife to turn him in bed: "Roll me down." He then suffered a stroke and fell into a coma, dying 18 months later, without regaining consciousness.

1989 WILSON, Ellen Louise Axson (1860–1914) The first wife of President Woodrow Wilson died in the White House, telling her physician: "Doctor, if I go away, promise me that you will take good care of my husband." She died "with a divine smile playing over her face."

1990 WILSON, Thomas Woodrow (1856–1924) Two days before he died, when his regular physician announced that two specialists were coming to examine him, the World War I president, disabled by strokes, remarked: "Too many cooks spoil the broth!" The following evening Wilson's doctor told him that he was dying. The former president responded by saying: "I am a broken piece of machinery. When the machinery is broken ... I am ready." Next day, when his wife turned to leave the room, he called her back: "Edith!" Moments later he died.

1991 WINDSOR, Wallis Warfield, Duchess of (1896–1986) The American divorcée, for whom King Edward VIII of Great Britain renounced his throne to marry, died in France, in a state of senility. The last time anyone recalled her saying anything was several years before her death, when, speaking of her dead husband, she declared to a friend: "Look at the way the sun is lighting the trees! You can see so many colors! Tell David to come in. He wouldn't want to miss this!"

1992 WINTHROP, John (1588–1649) The Puritan leader, who was the first governor of the Massachusetts Bay Colony, was pressed by an aide to sign an order banishing a religious heretic from the colony. Winthrop refused, insisting: "I have done too much of that work already."

1993 WISE, Isaac Mayer (1819–1900) The Bohemian-born rabbi, who founded Hebrew Union College in Cincinnati and was also a founder of the Reform Jewish movement in America, wished those around his bedside: "A good Sabbath!"

1994 WISE, Stephen Samuel (1874–1949) The Hungarian-born Reformed rabbi, founder of the Free Synagogue in New York City and a leader of the Zionist movement in America, told his children: "Take my hand, darlings. I am entering the Valley."

1995 WISHART, George (1513–1546) When his executioner said, "Sir, I pray you forgive me, for I am not guilty of your death," the Scots Presbyterian reformer, sentenced to be burned to death, answered: "Come hither to me." Then he kissed the executioner on the cheek. As the flames were kindled, Wishart said to himself: "My heart, do thine office."

1996 WITTGENSTEIN, Ludwig (1890–1915) The German philosopher died in England, declaring: "I have had a wonderful life!"

1997 WOLCOT, John (1738–1819) The British satirist, who wrote under the penname Peter Pindar, joked when asked if there was anything that could be done for him: "Bring me back my youth!"

1998 WOLF, Hugo (1860–1903) The Austrian composer succumbed to the ravages of syphilis. Before he lost the power of speech, more than a year before he died, Wolf expressed revulsion towards his life's work: "Loathesome music!"

1999 WOLFE, Charles (1791–1823) The British poet, remembered for one poem, "The Burial of Sir John Moore," directed: "Close this eye. The other is closed already. And now, farewell."

2000 WOLFE, James (1727–1759) Commander of the victorious British army at the Battle of Quebec, which resulted in British control of Canada, he was wounded three times. As he lay dying, he was told that the French were in retreat and their commander mortally wounded. Wolfe said: "Who run? Then, God be praised, I die happy! Lay me down. I am suffocating."

2001 WOLFE, Thomas (1900–1938) The American novelist, suffering from tuberculosis of the brain, told his brother: "Fred, I've had a dream. We were riding in a big car, a big shining car, out in the country. And we had a lot of good things to eat and drink in the car. You were all dressed up, Fred. You looked pretty good. And I looked pretty good, too." Just before he died he whispered the word: "Scotch."

2002 WOLLSTONECRAFT, Mary (1759–1797) The English writer and feminist, dying after childbirth, responded when her husband, not wishing to mention the possibility of her death, asked how she wanted her daughter reared in her illness: "I know what you are thinking of."

2003 WOLSEY, Thomas Cardinal (c.1475–1530) The English churchman, once virtual dictator of England, fell out of favor because of his opposition to Henry VIII in his plans to divorce Catherine of Aragon. En route to London to stand trial for treason, Wolsey fell ill of the "bloody flux" and died in a monastery, declaring: "If I had served God as diligently as I have done the king, he would not have given me over in my grey hairs."

2004 WOOD, Grant (1891–1942) The American painter, ill with cancer, spoke the name of his sister (who had been the model for the farmer's wife in his best known painting, "American Gothic"): "Nan."

2005 WOOD, Sir Henry Joseph (1869–1944) The British conductor and composer declared: "I am not afraid to die."

2006 WOOLLCOTT, Alexander Humphreys (1887–1943) The American journalist, critic, and radio personality was part of a panel, discussing a book on Germany on a radio broadcast. After remarking, "Germany was the cause of Hitler," he was gripped with heart pains and left the broadcast. Before losing consciousness he gasped: "I am dying! Where are my tablets? Get my glycerin tablets!"

2007 WOOLMAN, John (1720–1772) The American Quaker leader, best remembered for the journal he kept for 30 years, died of smallpox in

York, England, praying: "O Lord, my God, the amazing horrors of darkness were gathered around me and covered me all over, and I saw no way to go forth. I felt the depth and the extent of the misery of my fellow-creatures separated from the divine harmony, and it was heavier than I could bear, and I was crushed down under it. In the depths of misery, O Lord, I remembered that Thou art omnipotent, that I had called Thee Father, and I felt that I loved Thee and was quiet in my will." Next morning, unable to speak, he scribbled: "I believe my being here is in the wisdom of Christ. I know not as to life or death."

2008 WOOLSTON, Thomas (1670-1733) The English religious writer, who advocated the theory of deism, denying divine intervention in the world, said of his death agony: "This is a struggle which all men must go through and which I bear not only patiently, but with willingness."

2009 WORDSWORTH, William (1770-1850) The English romantic poet was told by his wife, who spoke of their recently-deceased daughter, "You are going to Dora."

He showed no sign of comprehension, but, the next day, as a niece was arranging the blinds, the old man asked: "Is that Dora?"

2010 WRIGHT, Joseph (1855-1930) The English philologist who edited several grammar books and dictionaries murmured: "Dictionary."

2011 WRIGHT, Orville (1871-1948) Co-builder with his brother Wilbur of the first successful airplane, he was hospitalized after a heart attack, when he told his nurse to defer to his long-time housekeeper: "You had better let Carrie do that, Miss. She knows all my cranky little ways."

2012 WYCHERLEY, William (1640-1716) The English dramatist told his much-younger wife to promise him something. When she asked what it was, he replied: "It is only this, that you will never marry an old man again."

2013 WYLIE, Elinor Hoyt (1885-1928) The American poet was proofreading her latest volume of verse when she asked her husband for a glass of water. When he brought it, she asked: "Is that all it is?" Then, overtaken with a stroke, she fell dead.

2014 WYTHE, George (1726-1806) The Virginia lawyer and statesman, who signed both the Declaration of Independence and the Constitution, was poisoned by a nephew. Shortly before his death, he insisted: "I am murdered!" Later, he added: "I want to die righteous."

2015 XIMÉNES de Cisneros, Francisco Cardinal (1437-1517) The Spanish Grand Inquisitor, praying from the *Te Deum*, murmured: "In Thee, Lord, have I trusted...."

2016 YANCEY, Robert Davis (1855-1931) The prominent Virginia attorney, for more than 30 years Commonwealth's attorney for Lynchburg, told his daughter: "I will just lie here for a few minutes. I will stay here a little while, just to please you. Don't leave me, little lady. I love to watch your bright young face. Two things in this world I have always loved—a bright young face and walking in the sunshine."

2017 YANCEY, William Lowndes (1814-1863) The Alabama political leader, who fought for secession and ultimately served in the Confederate Senate, declared to his wife: "I am dying.... All is well.... It is God's will.... Sarah."

2018 YOUNG, Brigham (1801-1877) Dying of appendicitis, the Mormon leader spoke the name of the long-dead founder of his church, Joseph Smith: "Joseph! Joseph! Joseph!"

2019 YOUNG, Francis Brett (1884–1954) The English novelist, succumbing to a long, agonizing illness, told his wife: "Let me go now, darling. I can't go on suffering like this."

2020 YOUNG, Whitney Moore (1921–1971) The civil rights leader who directed the Urban League died in Lagos, Nigeria, in the ocean surf. He shouted to his companions, before suddenly sinking below the waves: "This is great!"

2021 YSAŸE, Eugene (1858–1931) The Belgian violinist, hearing another musician play his Fourth Sonata, commented: "Splendid! The finale is just a little too fast!"

2022 ZAHARIAS, Mildred Didriksen (Babe) (1911–1956) The American sportswoman, who starred in track and in golf, died of cancer, after a long illness, telling her husband: "Bye, bye, honey. I'm going to go now. I love you and thank you for everything."

2023 ZANGARA, Giuseppe (1901–1933) In his attempt to kill president-elect Franklin Roosevelt in Miami, he fatally wounded Chicago mayor Anton Cermak. Just before his electrocution, Zangara raved: "I go contented because I go for my idea. I salute the poor of the world. I want no minister. There is no God. It's all below. I'll go myself. I no scared of electric chair. See, I no scared of electric chair. No cameramen? No movie to take picture of Zangara? Lousy capitalists! Lousy bunch of crooks! Goodbye! Adios to the world. Go ahead, push the button."

2024 ZECHARIAH (d. c.796 B.C.) The Israelite priest was stoned to death in the Temple courtyard, on the orders of King Joash, because he denounced the people for forsaking God. Dying, he cried: "May the Lord see and avenge!"

2025 ZEISBERGER, David (1721–1808) The Moravian missionary to the Delaware and Iroquois tribes for more than 60 years died in Goshen, Ohio, exclaiming: "The Savior is near. Perhaps He will soon call and take me home."

2026 ZENO of Citium (c.336 B.C.–264 B.C.) The founder of the Greek school of philosophy known as Stoicism declared: "Earth, dost thou demand me? I am ready."

2027 ZEPPELIN, Ferdinand Adolph August Heinrich, Count von (1838–1917) The German builder of dirigible airships, dying after surgery, told his daughter: "I have perfect faith."

2028 ZHOU ENLAI (1898–1976) The Chinese statesman remarked to his wife: "Little Chao, there are so many things, so many things that I have not told you, and now it is too late."

2029 ZIMMERMANN, Johann Georg von (1728–1795) The Swiss philosopher insisted: "Leave me alone. I am dying."

2030 ZINZENDORF, Nicolaus Ludwig, Count von (1700–1760) The founder of the reorganized Moravian Church told his son-in-law: "Now, my dear, son, I am going to the Savior. I am ready. I am quite resigned to the will of my Lord. If He is no longer willing to make use of me here, I am quite ready to go to Him, for there is nothing more in my way."

2031 ŽIŽKA, Jan, Count (c.1360–1424) The Czech nationalist leader instructed his troops: "Make my skin into drum-heads for the Bohemian cause."

2032 ZOLA, Émile (1840–1902) The French novelist, not realizing that the bedroom was filling with carbon monoxide from a blocked chimney, complained of feeling ill and remarked to his wife (who was revived): "I feel sick.... My head is splitting.... No, don't you see the dog is sick, too...."

We are both ill. It must have been something we have eaten. . . . It will pass away. . . . Let us not bother them . . . ."

2033 ZWINGLI, Ulrich (1484–1531) The Swiss religious reformer was killed while serving as chaplain to the Protestant army which was defeated by Roman Catholic forces at the Battle of Kappel. Zwingli declared: "What does it matter? They can kill the body, but not the soul!"

Sources

Citations are indicated for those quotations which appear in only *one* published source. There will be no citation for quotations which are found in two or more sources. The letter (I) indicates that the words in the text are reconstructed from an indirect quotation.

Adams, Abigail Smith: Paul G. Nagel, *Adams Women*. (NY: Oxford University Press, 1987), p. 157 (I).

Addams, Jane: Marshall Fishwick, *Jane Addams*. (Morristown, NJ: Silver Burdett, 1968), p. 88.

Adenauer, Konrad: Terrence Prittie, *Konrad Adenauer*. (Chicago: Cowles Book Co., 1971), p. 310 (I).

Albert, Prince Consort of Victoria: Daphne Bennett, *King Without a Crown*. (Philadelphia: Lippincott, 1977), p. 373.

Albert Victor: Michael Harrison, *A Biography of HRH The Duke of Clarence*. (New York: Drake, 1972), pp. 236–237.

Albertoni, Louisa: Herbert Thurston and Donald Attwater, *Butler's Lives of the Saints*, Vol. 1. (Westminster, MD: Newman Press, 1956), p. 447.

Alexander I of Russia: Henri Troyat, *Alexander of Russia*. (NY: E.P. Dutton, 1982), p. 291.

Alexander II of Russia: Charles Lowe, *Alexander III of Russia*. (New York: Macmillan, 1895), p. 46.

Alexander III of Russia: Lowe, *op. cit.* pp. 287–288; Ian Vorres, *The Last Grand Duchess*. (New York: Scribner, 1964), p. 52.

Alexander VI, Pope: Rafael Sabatini, *The Life of Cesare Borgia*. (London: 1912), p. 404.

Alexis I of Russia: Joseph Fuhrmann, *Tsar Alexis*. (Gulf Breeze, FL: Academic International Press, 1981), p. 219.

Alfonso XII of Spain: Theo Aronson, *Royal Vendetta*. (London: Oldboure, 1967), pp. 141–142.

Alfonso, Count Covadongo: *Miami Herald*, September 7, 1938; description comes from John D. Bergamini, *The Spanish Bourbons*. (NY: G.P. Putnam's Sons, 1974), p. 363.

Alfred the Great: Thomas Hughes, *Alfred the Great*. (NY: Macmillan, 1869), pp. 309–310.

Alger, Horatio: Ralph Gardner, *Horatio Alger*. (Mendota, IL: Wayside Press, 1964), p. 303.

Allen, Ethan: Stewart H. Holbrook, *Ethan Allen*. (Portland, OR: Bindfords & Mort, 1958), p. 251.

Allen, Gracie: George Burns, *Gracie: A Love Story*. (NY: Putnam's, 1988), p. 318.

Allingham, William: Geoffrey Grigson, ed., *William Allingham's Diary*. (Fontwell, England: Centaur P., 1967), pp. 387–388.

Ambrose of Milan: F. Homes Dudden, *The Life and Times of St. Ambrose*, Vol. II. (Oxford: The Clarenden Press, 1935), p. 490.

Anderson, Sherwood: James Schevill, *Sherwood Anderson*. (Denver: University of Denver Press, 1951), p. 339.

Andrews, Roy Chapman: *Washington Post*, March 12, 1960.

Anne, Queen of England: Justin McCarthy, *The Reign of Queen Anne*, Vol II. (London: Harper & Brothers, 1902), p. 377.

Anne Hyde: Henri and Barbara Van Der Zee, *William and Mary*. (NY: Alfred A. Knopf, 1973), p. 60.

Anthony, Susan Brownell: Kathleen Barry, *Susan B. Anthony: A Biography of a Singular Feminist*. (NY: New York University Press, 1988), pp. 355–356.

Armistead, Lewis Addison: David M. Jordan, *Winfield Scott Hancock*. (Bloomington, IN: Indiana University Press, 1988), p. 99.

Armour, Philip Danforth: Harper Leach and John Charles Carroll, *Philip Danforth Armour*. (NY: Appleton-Century Company, 1938), p. 345.

Arnould, Sophie: Claude Aveline, *Les Mots de la Fin*. (Paris: Hachette, 1957), p. 253.

Arthur, Chester Alan: The New York *World*, November 19, 1886.

Atahuallpa: William H. Prescott, *History of the Conquest of Mexico and History of the Conquest of Peru*. (New York: Modern Library, 1936), p. 476.

Attlee, Clement: Kenneth Harris, *Attlee*. (NY: Weidenfeld & Nicolson, 1982), p. 563.

Audubon, John James: Donald Culross Peattie, *Singing in the Wilderness*. (New York: G.P. Putnam's Sons, 1935), p. 238.

Augustine: Claude Aveline, *op. cit.* p. 188.

Babar: Harold Lamb, *Babur, the Tiger*. (Karachi: Pak Britain Pub., 1989), p. 231.

Baer, Max, Sr.: Barnaby Conrad, *Famous Last Words*. (Garden City, NY: Doubleday, 1961), p. 36.

Baker, Josephine: Jean-Claude Baker and Chris Chase, *Josephine*. (Boston: Adams Pub., 1995), p. 483.

Baldwin, James: W.J. Weatherly, *James Baldwin: Artist on Fire*. (NY: D.Z. Fine, 1989), p. 372.

Baldwin, Stanley: Robert Keith Middlemas and John Barnes, *Baldwin*. (NY: Macmillan, 1970), p. 1071.

Ball, Lucille: Coyne Steven Sanders and Tom Gilbert, *Desilu*. (NY: Morrow, 1993), p. 359.

Barbirolli, John: Michael Kennedy, *Barbirolli*. (London: MacGibbon & Kee, 1971), p. 326.

Barnum, Phineas Taylor: Irving Wallace, *The Fabulous Showman*. (NY: Knopf, 1959), p. 257.

Barth, Karth: Eberhard Busch, *Karl Barth*. (London: S.C.M. Press, 1975), p. 497.

Bartok, Bela: Agatha Fassett, *The Naked Face of Genius*. (Boston: Houghton Mifflin, 1958), p. 357.

Baum, Lyman Frank: Frank Joslyn Baum and Russell P. MacFall, *To Please a Child*. (Chicago: Reilly & Lee Co., 1961), pp. 274–275.

Beard, James: Robert Clark, *James Beard: A Biography*. (NY: HarperCollins, 1993), p. 326.

Beaverbrook, William Maxwell Aitken: Anne Chisholm and Michael Davie, *Lord Beaverbrook*. (NY: Knopf, 1993), p. 523.

Bede the Venerable: G.F. Browne, *The Venerable Bede*. (Philadelphia: R. West, 1978), pp. 14–15.

Beethoven, Ludwig van: Martin Cooper, *Beethoven, The Last Decade*. (London: Oxford University Press, 1970), pp. 83–84.

Behan, Brendan: Ulick O'Conner, *Brendan*. (Englewood Cliffs, NJ: Prentice-Hall, 1970), p. 317.

Bellarmine, Robert: James Brodrick, *Robert Bellarmine*. (Westminster, MD: Newman Press, 1961), p. 418.

Bellini, Vincenzo: William A.C. Lloyd, *Vincenzo Bellini*. (London: Sisley's, Ltd., 1908), p. 189.

Belmont, Alva E.S.V.: Arthur T. Vanderbilt II, *Fortune's Children: The Fall of the House of Vanderbilt*. (NY: Morrow, 1989), p. 293.

Benedict: Mary Fabyan Windeatt, *St. Benedict*. (NY: Sheed & Ward, 1943), p. 179.

Benedict XIV, Pope: Friedrich Gontard, *The Chair of Peter*. (NY: Holt, Rinehart and Winston, 1964), p. 470.

Berg, Alban: Karen Monson, *Alban Berg*. (Boston: Houghton Mifflin, 1979), p. 333.

Berg, Morris: Louis Kaufman, et. al., *Moe Berg*. (Boston: Little, Brown, 1974), p. 264.

Bergman, Ingrid: Laurence Leamer, *As Time Goes By: The Life of Ingrid Bergman*. (NY: Harper & Row, 1986), p. 359.

Berlioz, Hector: D. Kern Holomon, *Berlioz*, (Cambridge, MA: Harvard University Press, 1989), p. 592.

Bernhardt, Sarah: Cornelia Otis Skinner, *Madame Sarah*. (Boston: Houghton Mifflin, 1966), p. 332.

Bernstein, Leonard: *Newsweek*, October 29, 1990, p. 80.

Bessette, Andre: C. Bernard Ruffin, *The Life of Brother Andre*. (Huntington, IN: Our Sunday Visitor, 1988), p. 194.

Bevan, Aneurin: Michael Foot, *Aneurin Bevan: A Biography*, Vol. II. (New York: Atheneum, 1974), p. 656 (I).

Bishop, Bernice Pauahi: Cobey Black and Kathleen Mellen, *Princess Pauahi Bishop and Her Legacy*. (Honolulu: Kamehameha Schools Press, 1965), p. 88.

Bixby, Bill: *National Enquirer*, December 7, 1993.

Black, Hugo Lafayette: Hugo L. Black and Elizabeth Black, *Mr. Justice and Mrs. Black*. (NY: Random House, 1986), p. 278.

Black Elk, Nicholas: Michael F. Steltenkamp, *Black Elk: Holy Man of the Oglalas*. (Norman, OK: University of Oklahoma Press, 1993), pp. 128–129.

Bloch, Marc: Claude Aveline, *op. cit.*, p. 151.

Blum, Leon: Jean Lacouture, *Leon Blum*. (NY: Holmes & Meier, 1982), p. 513.

Bogart, Humphrey DeForest: Lauren Bacall, *By Myself*. (NY: Knopf, 1979), p. 255.

Bolivar, Simon: Gerhard Masur, *Simon Bolivar*. (Albuquerque, NM: University of New Mexico Press, 1948), p. 691.

Bonhoeffer, Dietrich: Eberhard Bethge, *Dietrich Bonhoeffer*. (NY: Harper & Row, 1970), pp. 830–831.

Boone, Daniel: John Mack Faragher, *Daniel Boone*. (NY: Holt, 1992), pp. 318–319 (I).

Booth, Catherine Mumford: F. de L. Booth-Tucker, *The Life of Catherine Booth*, Vol. II. (NY: Fleming H. Revell Co., 1892), p. 641.

Booth, William: St. John Ervine, *God's Soldier*. (London: W. Heinemann, Ltd., 1934), pp. 809–810.

Boothby, Robert John Graham: Robert Rhodes James, *Robert Boothby: A Portrait of Churchill's Ally*. (NY: Viking, 1991), p. 453.

Borah, William Edgar: *Washington Post*, January 20, 1940.

Boulanger, Lili: Leonie Rosenstiel, *Nadia Boulanger*. (NY: W.W. Norton, 1982), p. 135.

Boulanger, Nadia: Leonie Rosenstiel, *op. cit.* p. 412.

Bradbury, William Batchelder: Fanny Crosby, *Memories of Eighty Years*. (Boston: James H. Earle, 1906), p. 118.

Britten, Benjamin: Humphrey Carpenter, *Benjamin Britten*. (NY: C. Scribner's Sons, 1992), p. 581.

Brownson, Orestes Augustus: Thomas R. Ryan, *Orestes A. Brownson*. (Huntington, IN: Our Sunday Visitor, 1976), p. 721.

Bruch, Max: Christopher Fifield, *Max Bruch* (NY: G. Braziller, 1988), p. 324.

Bruno, Giordano: William Boulting, *Giordano Bruno*. (London: K. Paul, Trench, Trubner & Co., Ltd., 1916), p. 303 (I).

Bryan, William Jennings: Charles Morrow Wilson, *The Commoner: William Jennings Bryan*. (Garden City, NY: Doubleday, 1970), p. 437.

Brynner, Yul: Rock Brynner, *Yul*. (NY: Simon and Schuster, 1989), p. 257; Jhan Robbins, *Yul Brynner*. (NY: Dodd, Mead, 1987), p. 149.

Buber, Martin: Maurice Friedman, *Martin Buber's Life and Work, The Later Years . . . .* (NY: Dutton, 1983), p. 420.

Buck, Pearl Sydenstricker: Nora Stirling, *Pearl Buck: A Woman in Conflict*. (Piscataway, NJ: New Century Publishers, 1983), p. 332.

Bunche, Ralph Johnson: Peggy Mann, *Ralph Bunche*. (NY: Coward, McCann & Geoghegan, 1975), p. 359.

Burdett-Coutts, Angela: Edna Healy, *Lady Unknown*. (NY: Sidgwick & Jackson, 1978), p. 224.

Burghley, William Cecil: David Cecil, *The Cecils of Hatfield House*. (London: Constable, 1973), p. 89.

Burke, Edmund: James Prior, *Memoir of the Life and Character of Edmund Burke*. (Boston: Ticknor, Leed, and Fields, 1854), p. 364.

Burr, Raymond: *National Enquirer*, September 28, 1993.

Butler, Samuel: Peter Raby, *Samuel Butler*. (Iowa City: University of Iowa Press, 1991), p. 292.

Byng, Julian Hedworth George: Jeffrey Williams, *Byng of Vimy*. (London: L. Cooper, 1983), p. 364.

Cajetan: Herbert Thurston and Donald Attwater, *op. cit.*, Vol. III, p. 273.

Candy, John: *National Enquirer*, March 22, 1994.

Cardozo, Benjamin: George S. Hellman, *Benjamin N. Cardozo, American Judge* (NY: Whittlesey House, 1940), p. 311.

Carnot, Marie-Francois-Sadi: *New York Times*, June 26, 1894.

Carroll, Charles: Kate Mason Rowland, *The Life of Charles Carroll of Carrollton*. (NY: G.P. Putnam's Sons, 1898), pp. 368–370.

Casals, Pablo: Robert Baldock, *Pablo Casals*. (Boston: Northeastern University Press, 1992), p. 256.

Catherine de'Medici: Irene Mahoney, *Madame Catherine*. (NY: Coward, McCann & Geoghegon, 1975), p. 334.

Cayce, Edgar: Mary Ellen Carter, *My Years with Edgar Cayce*. (NY: Harper & Row, 1972), p. 129.

Cerretti, Bonaventura: Giusseppe de Luca, *Il Cardinale Bonaventura Cerretti*. (Rome: Istituto grafico timerino, 1939), pp. 413–414.

Chaliapin, Feodor Ivanovich: Victor Borovsky, *Chaliapin: A Critical Biography*. (NY: Knopf, 1988), p. 532.

Chanel, Gabrielle: Marcel Heedrich, *Coco Chanel*. (Boston: Little, Brown, & Co., 1971), p. 261.

Charlemagne: Claude Aveline, *op. cit.*, p. 105.

Charles I of England: Bowle, John: *Charles the First*. (Boston: Little, Brown, & Co., 1975), pp. 334–335.

Charles III of Spain: John D. Bergamini, *op. cit.*, p. 101.

Charles V of France: Claude Aveline, *op. cit.*, p. 195.

Charles VI of France: *Ibid.* p. 197.

Charles VIII of France: *Ibid.* p. 199.

Charles X of France: *Ibid.* p. 266.

Chase, Salmon Portland: The Washington *Evening Star*, May 8, 1873.

Chenier, André: Francis Scarfe, *André Chenier*. (Oxford: Clarendon Press, 1965), p. 364.

Chevalier, Maurice: Edward Behr, *Thank Heaven for Little Girls*. (NY: Villard Press, 1993), p. 398.

Chopin, Frederic François: James Huneker, *Chopin: The Man and His Music*. (NY: Scribner, 1899), p. 49.

Christian IX of Denmark: Hans Roger Madol, *Christian IX*. (London: Collins Publishers, 1930), pp. 290–291.

Christian X of Denmark: *New York Times*, April 21, 1947.

Church, Frank: F. Forester Church, *Father and Son*. (NY: Harper & Row, 1985), p. 172.

Churchill, Jennie Jerome: Ralph G. Martin, *Jennie: The Life of Lady Randolph Churchill*, Vol. II. (Englewood Cliffs, NJ: Prentice-Hall, 1971), p. 398.

Churchill, Randolph Frederick Edward Spencer: Brian Roberts, *Randolph: A Study of Churchill's Son*. (London, H. Hamilton, 1984), p. 363.

Clare of Assisi: Ernest Gilliat-Smith, *Saint Clare of Assisi*. (London, 1914), p. 98.

Clemenceau, Georges: *New York Times*, November 24, 1929.

Clemens, Oliva Langdon: These words were conveyed to the author by a clergy-man in New Haven, Connecticut, in 1971, who, in turn, learned them from an older minister who claimed to have known the Clemens family. One of the early biographies of Mark Twain attributes a similar statement to his wife, but does not associate it with her deathbed.

Clement XI, Pope: Ludwig Pastor, *A History of the Popes*, Vol. 33. (St. Louis: B. Herder, 1941), p. 533.

Clement XII, Pope: Alexis François Artaud de Montor, *The Lives of the Roman Pontiffs*, Vol. II. (NY: The Catholic Publication Society of America, 1897), p. 264.

Clement XIV, Pope: Artaud de Montor, *op. cit.*, p. 376.

Cleveland, Stephen Grover: Robert McElroy, *Grover Cleveland*, Vol. II. (NY: Harper & Row, 1923), p. 385.

Cochise: Dee Brown, *Bury My Heart at Wounded Knee.* (NY: Holt, Rinehart, & Winston, 1970), pp. 216–217.

Cody, William F.: Henry Blackman Sell, *Buffalo Bill and the Wild West.* (NY: Oxford University Press, 1955), p. 256.

Coffin, Robert Peter Tristram: *Portland Press Herald*, January 21, 1955.

Cole, Nathaniel Adams: A.S. Young, *The Incomparable Nat King Cole.* (Fort Worth, 1965), p. 16.

Coleridge-Taylor, Samuel: W.C. Berwick Sayer, *Samuel Coleridge-Taylor, Musician.* (Chicago: Afro-Am Press, 1969), p. 308.

Connelly, Cornelia: anonymous, *Life of Cornelia Connelly.* (London: Longmons, Green, & Co., 1922), p. 469.

Consalvi, Ercole: Friedrich Gontard, *op. cit.,* p. 498.

Constantine XI, Byzantine Emperor: Claude Aveline, *op. cit.*, p. 197.

Cooke, Terence: Benedict J. Groeschel and Terrence L. Weber, *Thy Will Be Done*.... (NY: Alba House, 1990), p. 209.

Cooper, Gary: A radio broadcast heard by the author in a barber's chair in Washington, DC on the day of the actor's death.

Cowles, Anna Roosevelt: Lilian Rixey, *Bamie: Theodore Roosevelt's Remarkable Sister.* (NY: D. McKay Co., 1963), p. 290.

Crane, Hart: John Unterecker, *Voyager: A Life of Hart Crane.* (NY: Farrar, Straus & Giroux, 1969), p. 757.

Crazy Horse: Edward Kadlacek and Mabell Kadlecek, *To Kill an Eagle: Indian Views on the Death of Crazy Horse.* (Boulder, CO: Johnson Books, 1981), p. 53, 100.

Cristina, Queen Consort of Spain: Theo Aronson, *Royal Vendetta*, p. 125.

Cromwell, Oliver: Antonia Fraser, *Cromwell: The Lord Protector.* (NY: Knopf, 1973), p. 676.

Curley, James Michael: Jack Beatty, *The Rascal King.* (Reading, Mass.: Addison-Wesley, 1992), p. 523.

Cushman, Charlotte: Joseph Leach, *Bright Particular Star.* (New Haven: Yale University Press, 1970), p. 395.

Czolgosz, Leon: Robert J. Donovan, *The Assassins.* (NY: Popular Library, 1964), p. 106.

Damrosch, Walter Johannes: George Martin, *The Damrosch Dynasty.* (Boston: Houghton Mifflin, 1983), p. 405.

Dante Alighieri: Claude Aveline, *op. cit.*, pp. 193–194.

Davis, Bette: *National Enquirer*, October 16, 1989.

Davis, Varina Anne Banks Howell: Ishbel Ross, *First Lady of the South.* (NY: Harper, 1958), p. 416.

Day, Dorothy: James Forest, *Love Is the Measure.* (NY: Paulist Press, 1986), p. 199.

Dayan, Moshe: Robert Slater, *Warrior Statesman.* (NY: St. Martin's Press, 1991), p. 437.

Delane, John Thadeus: Arthur Irwin Dasant, *John Thadeus Delane.* Vol. II. (NY: W. Holt & Co., 1908), p. 344.

DeMille, Cecil B.: Charles Higham, *Cecil B. DeMille.* (NY: Scribner, 1973), p. 312.

DePorres, Martin: Giuliana Cavallini, *St. Martin de Porres.* (St. Louis: B. Herder, 1963), pp. 191–192.

DeReszke, Jean: Clara Leiser, *Jean DeReszke*. (Freeport, NY: Books for Libraries Press, 1970), p. 298.

DeSmet, Pierre-Jean: Helene Magaret, *Father DeSmet*. (NY: Bruce Pub. Co., 1940), pp. 364–365.

Dickinson, Emily: Martha Dickinson Bianchi, *The Life and Letters of Emily Dickinson*. (NY: Biblo and Tan, 1924), p. 100.

Dietrich, Marlene: The word "Maria" comes from *People* magazine. The longer quotation: Steven Bach, *Marlene Dietrich, Life and Legend*. (NY: Morrow, 1992), pp. 476–477.

Disney, Walter Elias: Marc Eliot, *Walt Disney: Hollywood's Dark Prince*. (Seacaucus, NJ: Carol Pub. Group, 1993), p. 265 (I).

Disraeli, Benjamin: Robert Blake, *Disraeli*. (NY: Oxford University Press, 1966), pp. 747–749.

Dix, Dorothea Lynde: Dorothy Clarke Wilson, *Stranger and Traveler*. (Boston: Little, Brown, 1975), p. 341.

Dorsey, Thomas Francis: *New York Times*, November 27, 1956 (I) and *New York World Telegram and Sun*, November 27, 1956.

Dostoevsky, Feodor Mikhailovich: Anna Dostoevsky, *Reminiscences*. (NY, 1975), p. 348.

Douglas, Alfred Bruce: H. Montgomery Hyde, *Lord Alfred Douglas*. (NY: Dodd, Mead, 1985), pp. 337–338.

Douglas, Sir James: Thomas Costain, *The Three Edwards*. (Garden City, NY: Doubleday, 1962), p. 254.

Douglas, Stephen Arnold: Carl Sandburg, *Abraham Lincoln, The War Years*, Vol. I. (NY: Scribners, 1939), pp. 268–269.

Drake, Sir Francis: John Sugden, *Sir Francis Drake*. (NY: Simon & Schuster, 1990), p. 314 (I).

DuBois, William Edward Burghardt: Shirley Graham DuBois, *His Day Is Marching On*. (Philadelphia: Lippincott, 1971), p. 367.

Duke, James Buchanan: John Wilber Jenkins, *James B. Duke: Master Builder*. (NY: George H. Doren, 1927), pp. 259–260.

Dulles, John Foster: Eleanor Lansing Dulles, *John Foster Dulles, The Last Year*. (NY: Harcourt, Brace & World, 1963), p. 230.

Duse, Eleonora: Giovanni Pontiero, *Eleonora Duse*. (NY: V.P. Lang, 1986), p. 363. According to another version, Duse said: "We must move! We must leave! Do something! Do something! Cover me!"

Early, Jubal Anderson: *Richmond Times*, March 3, 1894.

Earp, Baxter Warren: Frank Waters, *The Earp Brothers of Tombstone*. (Lincoln, NE: University of Nebraska Press, 1960), p. 229.

Earp, Celia Ann Blaylock: Glenn Boyer, *Suppressed Murder of Wyatt Earp*. (San Antonio: Naylor Co., 1967), p. 94 (I).

Earp, Morgan S.: Stuart N. Lake, *Wyatt Earp*. (Boston: Houghton Mifflin, 1931), p. 323; Josephine Sarah Marcus Earp, *I Married Wyatt Earp*. (Tucson: University of Arizona Press, 1976), p. 103; and Roger S. Peterson, "Wyatt Earp: Man Versus Myth." *American History*. Aug., 1994, p. 68.

Earp, Wyatt Berry Stapp: Josephine Sarah Marcus Earp, *op. cit.* p. 240.

Edward III of England: James MacKinnon, *The History of Edward III*. (Totowa, NJ: Rowman & Littlefield, 1974), p. 604.

Edward VIII of Great Britain: Elizabeth Longford, ed., *The Oxford Book of Royal*

Anecdotes. (Oxford: Oxford University Press, 1989), p. 468. According to Michael Thornton, *The Royal Feud* (NY: Simon and Schuster, 1985), p. 319, the former king's last words, to his wife, who wanted to stay up with him, were: "No, Darling, I shall soon be asleep. Get some more rest, please."

Einstein, Albert: Abraham Pais, *Subtle Is the Lord: The Science and the Life of Albert Einstein*. (Oxford: Oxford University Press, 1982), p. 477; Peter Michelmore, *Einstein: Profile of the Man*. (NY: Dodd, Mead, 1962), p. 261.

Eisenhower, Dwight David: John S.D. Eisenhower, *Strictly Personal*. (Garden City, NY: Doubleday, 1974), p. 336.

Elisabeth, Queen Consort of Romania. Elizabeth Burgoyne, *Carmen Sylva: Queen and Woman*. (London: Eyre & Spottiswoode, 1941), p. 293.

Elisabeth Kaahumanu, Queen Consort of Hawaii: Hiram Bingham, *A Residence of Twenty-One Years in the Sandwich Islands*. (Hartford, CT, 1847), p. 433.

Elizabeth I of England: Mary M. Luke, *Gloriana*. (NY: Coward, McCann & Geoghegan, 1973), p. 692.

Elizabeth of the Trinity: Conrad DeMeester, *Light, Love, Life*. (Washington: ICS Publications, 1987), p. 137, 139.

Emerson, Ralph Waldo: John McAleer, *Ralph Waldo Emerson*. (Boston: Little, Brown, 1984), p. 661.

Erasmus, Desiderius: Roland Bainton, *Erasmus of Christendom*. (NY: Scribner, 1969).

Ernst August: H.R.H. Viktoria Luise, *The Kaiser's Daughter*. (Englewood Cliffs, NJ: Prentice-Hall, 1977), p. 237.

Eugene IV, Pope: Joseph Gill, *Eugenius IV*. (Westminster, MD: Newman Press, 1961), p. 166.

Ewell, Richard Stoddert: *Knoxville Daily Chronicle*, January 28, 1872.

Fanon, Frantz: Peter Geismer, *Fanon*. (NY: Dial Press, 1971), p. 186.

Farley, John: *New York Times*, September 18, 1918.

Ferdinand I of Rumania: Hannah Pakula, *The Last Romantic*. (NY: Simon & Schuster, 1984), pp. 364–365.

Ferrier, Kathleen Mary: Winifred Ferrier, *The Life of Kathleen Ferrier*. (London: H. Hamilton, 1955), p. 180.

Field, Cyrus West: *New York Tribune*, July 13, 1892.

Fields, William Claude: Carlotta Monti, *W.C. Fields and Me*. (Englewood Cliffs, NJ: Prentice-Hall, 1971), p. 218.

Fillmore, Millard: *The Buffalo Commercial Advertiser*, March 9, 1874, which reported that the dying statesman commented that "the food tasted good." This was apparently translated in a 1915 biography into the more pompous "The nourishment is palatable," which is sometimes given as his last words.

Flagstad, Kirsten: Howard Vogt, *Flagstad*. (London: Secker and Warburg, 1987), p. 273.

Fleming, Sir Alexander: Gwyn MacFarlane, *Alexander Fleming: The Man and the Myth*. (Cambridge, MA: Harvard University Press, 1984), p. 242.

Ford, Arthur: Allen Spragget, *Arthur Ford: The Man Who Talked with the Dead*. (NY: New American Library, 1973), pp. 282–283.

Forrest, Nathan Bedford: Jack Hurst, *Nathan Bedford Forrest*. (NY: A.A. Knopf, 1994), pp. 378–379.

Fosdick, Harry Emerson: Robert Moats Miller, *Harry Emerson Fosdick*. (NY: Oxford University Press, 1985), p. 570.

Foster, Stephen Collins: John Tasker Howard, *Stephen Foster*. (New York: Crowell, 1934), p. 342.

Frances of Rome: Herbert Thurston and Donald Attwater, *op. cit.* Vol. I, p. 532.

Francis of Assisi: Marion A. Habig, ed., *St. Francis of Assisi: Writings and Early Biographies*. (Chicago: Franciscan Herald Press, 1973), pp. 536, 826–828.

Francis Solano: Herbert Thurston and Donald Attwater, *op. cit.* Vol. III, p. 95.

Franco, Francisco: J.P. Fusi, *Franco*. (NY: Harper & Row, 1985), p. 169.

Frankfurt, Felix: Leonard Baker, *Brandeis and Frankfurter*. (NY: Harper & Row, 1984), p. 491.

Franz, Robert: David Ewen, *Composers of Yesterday*. (NY: H.W. Wilson, 1937), p. 157.

Frederick III of Germany: Daphne Bennett, *Vicky: Princess Royal of England and German Empress*. (NY: St. Martin's Press, 1971), p. 351.

Frederick VIII of Denmark: The London *Daily Telegraph*, May 16, 1912.

Fremont, John Charles: Ferol Egan, Fremont. (Garden City, NY: Doubleday, 1977), p. 524.

Frost, Robert Lee: Lawrence Thompson and R.H. Winnick, *Robert Frost, The Later Years.* ... (NY: Holt, Rinehart, & Winston, 1976), p. 345.

Gaitskell, Hugh Todd Naylor: *Florida Times-Union*, January 19, 1963.

Galli-Curci, Amelita: C.E. LeMassena, *Galli-Curci's Life of Song*. (Beverly Hills, CA: Monitor Book Co., 1972), p. 245.

Garner, John Nance: *Portland Press Herald*, November 8, 1967.

Gehrig, Henry Louis: *New York Post*, June 3, 1941.

George II of the Hellenes: Queen Frederica, *A Measure of Understanding*. (NY: St. Martin's Press, 1971), p. 94 (I).

George III of Great Britain: Carrolly Erickson, *Our Tempestuous Day*. (NY: Morrow, 1986), p. 272.

George V of Great Britain: *History Today*, Vol. 36, December, 1986, pp. 21–30.

George VI of Great Britain: Michael Thornton, *Royal Feud*. (NY: Simon & Schuster, 1985), p. 253.

Geronimo: *Lawton Constitutional Democrat*, February 25, 1909 (I).

Gershwin, George: David Ewen, *George Gershwin*. (Englewood Cliffs, NJ: Prentice-Hall, 1970), p. 281.

Giacometti, Giovanni Alberto: James Lord, *Giacometti*. (NY: Farrar, Straus, Giroux, 1983), pp. 512–515.

Gladstone, William Ewart: Joyce Marlow, *The Oak and the Ivy*. (Garden City, NY: Doubleday, 1977), p. 289.

Glinka, Mikhail Ivanovich: Alexandra Orlova, *Glinka's Life in Music*. (Ann Arbor: University of Michigan Press, 1988), p. 749 (I).

Goebbels, Joseph: Ralf Georg Reuth, *Goebbels*. (NY: Harcourt, Brace, 1990), p. 362.

Goering, Hermann Wilhelm: David Irving, *Göring*. (NY: Morrow, 1989), pp. 509–510.

Gogol, Nikolai Vasilyevich: Henri Troyat, *Divided Soul: The Life of Gogol*. (Garden City, NY: Doubleday, 1973), p. 433.

Goretti, Maria: Marie Cecelia Buehrle, *St. Maria Goretti*. (Milwaukee: Bruce Publishing Co., 1950), pp. 124–128.

Goudonov, Boris: Stephen Graham. *Boris Godunof*. (New Haven, CT: Yale University Press, 1933), p. 244.

Gould, Glenn: Friedrich Otto, *Glenn Gould.* (NY: Vintage Books, 1989), p. 325.

Gould, Jay: John Stuart Ogilvie, *Life and Death of Jay Gould.* (NY: J.S. Ogilvie, 1981), p. 5 (I).

Gounod, Charles François: James Harding, *Gounod.* (London: Allen & Unwin, 1973), pp. 222–223.

Grable, Ruth Elizabeth: Doug Warren, *Betty Grable.* (NY: St. Martin's Press, 1974), p. 209.

Grainger, Percy Aldridge: John Bird, *Percy Grainger.* (London: Faber & Faber, 1976), p. 249.

Grant, Cary: Warren G. Harris, *Cary Grant: A Touch of Elegance.* (Garden City: Doubleday, 1987), p. 3.

Gregory I, Pope: Friedrich Gontard, *op. cit.* p. 169.

Gregory XV, Pope: Artaud de Montor, *op. cit.,* Vol. II, p. 21.

Gregory XVI, Artaud de Montor, *op. cit.,* Vol. II, p. 847.

Grey, Katherine: Richard Davey, *The Sisters of Lady Jane Grey.* (New York: E.P. Dutton, 1912), pp. 234–235.

Grimaldi, Joseph: Richard Findlater, *Grimaldi.* (London: Macgibbon & Kee, 1955), p. 209.

Grisi, Giulia: Elizabeth Forbes, *Mario and Grisi.* (London: V. Gollancz, 1985), p. 199.

Guevara de la Serna, Ernesto: Daniel James, *Che Guevara* (New York: Stein & Day, 1960), p. 15.

Guiteau, Charles Julius: Robert J. Donovan, *op. cit.,* p. 72.

Guizot, F.P.G.: Henriette Guizot Witt, *Monsieur Guizot in Private Life.* (Boston: Estes and Lauriat, 1880), pp. 355–356.

Gustav III: Robert Nisbet Bain, *Gustavus III*, Vol. II. (London: K. Paul, Trench, Trübner & Co., 1894), p. 213.

Haakon VII of Norway: Tim Greve, *Haakon VII of Norway.* (London: Hurst, 1983), p. 186.

Hadley, Samuel Hopkins: *New York Times,* February 13, 1906.

Halevy, Jacques: David Ewen, *Composers of Yesterday.* (NY: H.W. Wilson, 1937), p. 199.

Hamer, Fannie Lou Townsend: Kay Mills, *This Little Light of Mine.* (NY: Dutton, 1993), p. 308 (I).

Hamilton, Alexander: Robert A. Hendrickson, *Hamilton.* Vol. II. (NY: Mason/Charter, 1976), p. 643.

Hamilton, Edith: Doris Reid, *Edith Hamilton.* (NY: W.W. Norton, 1967), p. 142.

Hammerstein, Oscar II: Hugh Fordin, *Getting to Know Him: A Biography of Oscar Hammerstein II.* (NY: Ungar Publishing Co., 1977), pp. 357–359.

Hampton, Wade: (Columbia, SC) *The State,* April 12, 1902.

Hancock, Winfield Scott: David M. Jordan, *op. cit.,* p. 314.

Harding, Florence Kling De Wolfe: *Washington Times,* November 24, 1924.

Hardy, Oliver Norvell: Fred Lawrence Guiles, *Stan: The Life of Stan Laurel.* (NY: Stein and Day, 1980), p. 220.

Hardy, Thomas: Robert Gittings, *Thomas Hardy's Later Years* (Boston: Little, Brown, 1978), p. 211.

Harlan, John Marshall (1833–1911): *New York Tribune,* October 15, 1911.

Harlan, John Marshall (1899–1971): Tinsley E. Yarbrough, *John Marshall Harlan* (NY: Oxford University Press, 1992), p. 334.

Harlow, Jean: David Stenn, *Bombshell: The Life and Death of Jean Harlow*. (NY: Doubleday, 1993), p. 235.

Harrison, Benjamin: *The Indianapolis Sentinel*, March 14, 1901.

Harrison, Caroline Lavinia Scott: The Washington *Evening Star*, October 24, 1892.

Harrison, Carter Henry: *New York Tribune*, October 29, 1893.

Hart, Lorenz Milton: Samuel Marx and Jan Clayton, *Rodgers and Hart*. (NY: Putnam, 1976), p. 266.

Havergal, Frances Ridley: Maria V.G. Havergal, *Memorials of Frances Ridley Havergal*. (New York: A.D.F. Randolph, 1880), pp. 303–308.

Hawthorne, Nathaniel: Arlin Turner, *Nathaniel Hawthorne*. (NY: Oxford University Press, 1980), p. 390.

Hayes, Patrick: *New York Times*, September 5, 1938.

Hayward, Susan: Beverly Linet, *Susan Hayward: Portrait of a Survivor*. (NY: Arbor House, 1980), p. 307.

Hayworth, Rita: Barbara Leaming, *If This Was Happiness*. (NY: Viking, 1989), p. 361.

Healy, James Augustine: Albert S. Foley, *Bishop Healy: Beloved Outcaste*. (NY: Farrar, Straus and Young, 1954), p. 237.

Henie, Sonja: Raymond Strait and Leif Henie, *Queen of Ice, Queen of Shadows*. (Chelsea, MA: Scarborough House, 1985), p. 313.

Henry VII of England: Francis Hackett, *Henry the Eighth*. (NY: Liveright, 1945), p. 29.

Henry VIII of England: Mary M. Luke, *A Crown for Elizabeth*. (NY: Coward, McCann & Geoghegan, 1970), p. 160; Alison Weir, *The Six Wives of Henry VIII*. (NY: Grove Weidenfeld, 1991), p. 529.

Henry Frederick, Prince of Wales: John Bowle, *Charles the First*. (Boston, 1975), p. 32.

Henry, Patrick: Moses Coit Tyler, *Patrick Henry*. (Boston: Houghton Mifflin, 1887), p. 377 (I).

Hepburn, Audrey: *National Enquirer*, February 9, 1993.

Hill, Daniel Harvey: Leonard Hal Bridges, *Lee's Maverick General*. (NY: McGraw-Hill, 1961), p. 279.

Hill, Joe: Gibbs M. Smith, *Labor Martyr, Joe Hill*. (NY: Grosset & Dunlap, 1969), p. 177.

Hilton, Conrad Nicholson: Karl S. Guthke, *Last Words*. (Princeton, NJ: Princeton University Press, 1992), p. 6.

Himmler, Heinrich: Peter Padfield, *Himmler Reichsführer-SS*. (NY: Holt, 1990), p. 611.

Hitchcock, Alfred Joseph: Donald Spoto, *The Dark Side of Genius*. (Boston: Little, Brown, 1983), pp. 554–555.

Holmes, John: Thomas D. Bedell, "The Tongues of Dying Men," *Reader's Digest*, July 1979, p. 122.

Hoover, Herbert Clark: Richard Norton Smith, *An Uncommon Man: The Triumph of Herbert Hoover*. (NY: Simon and Schuster, 1984), p. 429.

Hope, John: Ridgely Torrence, *The Story of John Hope*. (NY: Macmillan, 1948), p. 374.

Hopkins, Harry Lloyd: George McJimsey, *Harry Hopkins*. (Cambridge, MA: Harvard University Press, 1987), p. 397.

Hopkins, Johns: Helen Hopkins Thom, *Johns Hopkins*. (Baltimore: Johns Hopkins Press, 1929), pp. 69–70.

Horney, Karen Danielson: Jack L. Rubins, *Karen Horney: Gentle Rebel of Psychoanalysis*. (NY: Dial Press, 1978), p. 338.

Houston, Samuel: "Texas ... Texas ... Margaret" is given in nearly every biography. The earlier words come from the *Albany Journal* (Albany, NY), July 28, 1863, which quotes the Rev. C.H. Clark, who claimed to be at Houston's bedside.

How, William Walsham: Frederic Douglas How, *Bishop Walsham How*. (London: Ibister & Co., 1899), p. 368.

Howard, Moses: Joe Besser, *Once a Stooge, Always a Stooge*. (Santa Monica, CA: Roundtable Pub., 1988), p. 218.

Howard, Oliver Otis: John A. Carpenter, *Sword and Olive Branch: Oliver Otis Howard*. (Pittsburgh: University of Pittsburgh Press, 1964), p. 299. (The context of the quotation does not make it clear how long the words were spoken before the General's death — minutes, hours, or even days or weeks.)

Hudson, Rock: Tom Clark, *Rock Hudson: Friend of Mine*. (NY: Pharos Books, 1989), p. 262.

Hughes, Charles Evans: Merlo J. Pusey, *Charles Evans Hughes*, Vol. 2. (NY: Macmillan, 1951), pp. 803–804.

Humphrey, Hubert Horatio: Edgar Berman, *Hubert: The Triumph and Tragedy of the Humphrey I Knew*. (NY: Putnam, 1979), p. 284.

Husserl, Edmund: Waltraud Herbstrith, *Edith Stein: A Biography*. (San Francisco: Harper & Row, 1985), p. 78.

Huxley, Aldous Leonard: Sybille Bedford, *Aldous Huxley*. (NY: Knopf, 1974), p. 740.

Innocent X, Pope: Artaud de Montor, *op. cit.*, Vol. II, p. 93.

Innocent XI, Pope: Artaud de Montor, *op. cit.*, Vol. II, p. 164.

Iqbal, Muhammed: Rajmohan Gandhi, *Eight Lives*. (Albany, NY: State University of New York, 1986), p. 78.

Isabella II of Spain: Theo Aronson, *Royal Vendetta*. p. 177.

Jackson, Andrew: Robert V. Remini, *Andrew Jackson and the Course of American Democracy (1833–1845)*. (NY: Harper & Row, 1984), pp. 521–524.

Jackson, Joseph Jefferson: *Sporting News*, February 8, 1961.

James I, King of England: Bowle, John, *Charles the First*. (Boston: Little, Brown, 1975), pp. 84–85.

James II, King of England: Peter Earle, *The Life and Times of James II*. (London: Weidenfeld and Nicolson, 1972), p. 216.

James, Henry: Leon Edel, *Henry James, The Master, 1901–1916*. (Philadelphia: Lippincott, 1972), p. 560.

James, Henry, Sr.: R.W.B. Lewis, *The Jameses: A Family Narrative*. (NY: Farrar, Straus, & Giroux, 1991), p. 349.

James, Jesse Woodson: Carl W. Breihan, *The Day Jesse James Was Killed*. (NY: Fell, 1961), p. 154.

James, William: Gay Wilson Allen, *William James*. (NY: Viking Press, 1967), pp. 490–491.

Janacek, Leos: Jaroslav Vogel, *Leos Janacek*. (NY: Orbis Pub., 1981), p. 378.

Jinnah, Mahomed Ali: Stanley Wolpert, *Jinnah of Pakistan*. (NY: Oxford University Press, 1984), p. 370.

John of Kronstadt: Semenoff-Tian-Chansky, *Father John of Kronstadt*. (Crestwood, NY: St. Vladimir's Seminary Press, 1979), p. 192.

Johnson, Andrew: most of the information is from the Memphis *Avalanche* of August 1, 1875 and the *Nashville Union and American* of August 1, 4, and 5, 1875.

Johnson, John Albert: Winifred Helmes, *John A. Johnson*. (Minneapolis: University of Minnesota Press, 1949), p. 305.

Johnson, Walter Perry: The Washington *Evening Star*, December 11, 1946.

Jolson, Al: Herbert G. Goldman, *Jolson*. (NY: Oxford University Press, 1988), pp. 298–299.

Jones, Robert Reynolds Davis: R.K. Johnson, *Builder of Bridges: The Biography of Dr. Bob Jones*. (Murfreesboro, TN: Sword of the Lord, 1969), p. 351.

Jones, Robert Tyre: Dick Miller, *Triumphant Journey: The Saga of Bobby Jones and the Grand Slam of Golf*. (NY: Holt, Rinehart, and Winston, 1980), p. 239.

Kalakaua of Hawaii: *San Francisco Chronicle*, January 21, 1891.

Kaufman, George Simon: Scott Meredith, *George S. Kaufman and His Friends*. (Garden City, NY: Doubleday, 1974), p. 648.

Keeler, William Henry: *New York Times*, January 2, 1923.

Kelly, Michael Joseph: Connie Mack, *My Sixty-Six Years in the Big Leagues*. (Philadelphia: Universal House, 1950), p. 73.

Kenny, Elisabeth: Victor Cohn, *Sister Kenny*. (Minneapolis: University of Minnesota Press, 1975), p. 237.

Kerr, Michael Crawford: *New York Times*, August 19, 1876 and Washington *Evening Star*, August 20, 1876.

Kierkegaard, Soren Aaby: Johannes Hohlenberg, *Soren Kierkegaard*. (NY: Pantheon Books, 1954), p. 269; Josiah Thompson, *Kierkegaard*, (NY: Knopf, 1973), p. 234.

Kipling, Rudyard: Frederick Birkenhead, *Rudyard Kipling*. (NY: Random House, 1978), p. 357.

Kirkpatrick, William Joseph: George Coles Stebbins, *Reminiscences*. (NY: George H. Doran, 1924), p. 293.

Krauth, Charles Porterfield: Adolph Spaeth, *Charles Porterfield Krauth*, Vol. II. (NY: The Christian Literature Co., 1898), p. 397 (I).

Kuhlman, Kathryn: Helen Kooiman Hosier, *Kathryn Kuhlman*. (Old Tappan, NJ: Fleming H. Revell, 1976), p. 156.

Lamy, Jean-Baptiste: Paul Horgan, *Lamy of Santa Fe*. (NY: Farrar, Straus, and Giroux, 1975), p. 437.

Landon, Michael: Cheryl Landon Wilson, *I Promised My Dad*. (NY: Simon & Schuster, 1992), p. 211.

Lansky, Meyer: Robert Lacey, *The Little Man: Meyer Lansky and the Gangster Life*. (Boston: Little, Brown, 1991), p. 421.

Lanza, Mario: Raymond Strait and Terry Robinson, *Lanza: His Tragic Life*. (Englewood Cliffs, NJ: Prentice-Hall, 1980), p. 166.

Laski, Harold Joseph: Isaac Kramnick and Barry Sheerman, *Harold Laski: A Life on the Left*. (NY: Allen Lane, 1993), p. 577.

Laughton, Charles: Simon Callow, *Charles Laughton: A Difficult Actor*. (London: Methuen, 1987), p. 285.

Laurel, Stanley: Fred Lawrence Guiles, *Stan: The Life of Stan Laurel*. (NY: Stein & Day, 1980), p. 226.

Laurencin, Marie: Claude Aveline, *op. cit.*, p. 301.

Lawrence, Ernest Orlando: Herbert Child, *An American Genius: The Life of Ernest Orlando Lawrence*. (NY: Dutton, 1968), p. 533.

Ledbetter, Huddie: Charles Wolfe and Kip Lornell, *The Life and Legend of Leadbelly*. (NY: HarperCollins, 1992), p. 255.

Lee, Gypsy Rose: Erik Lee Preminger, *Gypsy and Me*. (Boston: Little, Brown, 1984), p. 265.

Lekeu, Guillaume: David Ewen, *Composers of Yesterday*. (NY: H.W. Wilson, 1937), p. 247.

Lenin, Vladimir Ilich: Ronald Clark, *Lenin: The Man Behind the Mask*. (London: Faber & Faber, 1988), p. 482.

Leo X: Charles L. Mee, Jr. *White Robe, Black Robe*. (NY: Putnam, 1972), p. 288.

Leo XI: Artaud de Montor, *op. cit.*, Vol. I, p. 931.

Leo XIII; Bernard O'Reilly, *Life of Leo XIII*. (London: S. Low, Marston, & Co., 1903), p. 750; William J. Kiefer, *Leo XIII: A Light from Heaven*. (Milwaukee: Bruce Pub. Co., 1961), p. 208.

Leonardo da Vinci: Maurice Rowdon, *Leonardo da Vinci*. (Chicago: Follett Pub. Co., 1975), p. 217. There is some evidence that King Francis was nowhere near Leonardo when the artist died.

Leopold I of Belgium: Louis, Comte de Lichtervelde, *Leopold First*. (NY: The Century Co., 1930), p. 322.

Leopold II of Belgium: The New York *World*, December 17, 1909.

Lewis, George: Tom Bethell, *George Lewis*. (Berkeley, CA: University of California Press, 1977), p. 275.

Liberace, Walter Valentino: Bob Thomas, *Liberace: The True Story*. (NY: St. Martin's Press, 1987), p. 269.

Liguori, Alphonsus: Antonio Maria Tamoja, *The Life of St. Alphonsus Liguori*. (Baltimore, 1855), p. 558.

Liliuokalani of Hawaii: *Hawaiian Gazette*, November 12, 1917.

Lincoln, Abraham: The source of the quotation, which appears in several biographies is a letter from Anson G. Henry to his wife, dated April 19, 1865, which is in the Illinois State Historical Society.

Lincoln, Mary Todd: Homer Croy, *The Trial of Mrs. Abraham Lincoln*. (NY: Duell, Sloan, and Pearce, 1962), p. 137. In his preface, the author concedes that he has invented some dialogue, but it not indicated *which* dialogue.

Lincoln, Nancy Hanks: Philip Kunhardt, et. al. *Lincoln*. (NY: Knopf, 1992), p. 38 (I).

Lind, Jenny: Gladys Denny Schultz, *Jenny Lind*. (Philadelphia, Lippincott, 1962), p. 334. Lind's daughter, in her memoirs, mentions "The Sunshine Song," but not the prayer.

Lloyd George, David: Peter Rowland, *David Lloyd George*. (NY: Macmillan, 1975), p. 803.

Loewe, Frederick: Gene Lees, *Inventing Champagne: The Worlds of Lerner and Loewe*. (NY: St. Martin's Press, 1990), p. 316.

Logan, John Alexander. *Washington Post*, December 27, 1886.

Lombardi, Vincent Thomas: Michael O'Brien, *Vince: A Personal Biography of Vince Lombardi*. (NY: Morrow, 1987), pp. 373–374.

Longfellow, Mary Storer Potter: Andrew Hilan, ed., *The Letters of Henry Wadsworth Longfellow, Vol. I*. (Cambridge, MA: Harvard University Press, 1966), p. 527.

Longfellow, Samuel: Joseph May, *Samuel Longfellow*. (Boston: Houghton Mifflin, 1894), p. 305.

Longstreet, James: William Garrett Piston, *Lee's Tarnished Lieutenant*. (Athens, GA: University of Georgia Press, 1987), p. 169.

Louis VI of France: Claude Aveline, *op. cit.*, p. 190.

Louis VIII of France: Joy Law, *Fleur de Lys*. (NY: McGraw-Hill, 1976), pp. 35–36.

Louis XII of France: Claude Aveline, *op. cit.*, p. 124.

Louis XIV of France: mostly from Olivier Bernier, *Louis XIV*. (NY: Paragon House, 1987), pp. 346–348.

Louis XV of France: Olivier Bernier, *Louis the Beloved*. (Garden City, NY: Doubleday, 1984), pp. 248–249.

Louis XVIII: Rene de la Croix, Duc de Castries, *Louis XVIII, Portrait d'un roi*. (Paris: Hachette, 1969), pp. 384–385.

Louis Philippe I of France: Claude Aveline, *op. cit.*, p. 272.

Louis, Joe: Joe Louis Barrow, Jr., *Joe Louis: 50 Years an American Hero*. (NY: McGraw-Hill, 1988), p. 232. It is not clear how long before death the words were spoken.

Louise of Savoy: Claude Aveline, *op. cit.*, p. 70.

Louise, Princess, Marchioness of Lorne: Jehanne Wake, *Princess Louise: Queen Victoria's Unconventional Daughter*. (London: Collins, 1988), p. 411.

Lully, Jean-Baptiste: David Ewen, *Composers of Yesterday*. (NY: H.W. Wilson, 1937), p. 266.

Lunalilo of Hawaii: *Hawaiian Gazette*, February 11, 1874.

Luther, Katharina von Bora: Roland Bainton, *Women of the Reformation in Germany and Italy*. (Minneapolis: Augsburg, 1971), p. 42.

MacArthur, Douglas: *Washington Post*, March 25, 1964 and April 5, 1964.

Macaulay, Thomas Babington: G. Otto Trevelyan, *The Life and Letters of Lord Macaulay*, Vol. II. (NY: Harper & Row, 1876), p. 405.

McCloskey, John: John Farley, *The Life of John Cardinal McCloskey*. (NY: Longmans, Green, & Co., 1918), p. 366.

McCormack, John Francis: Lily Foley McCormack, *I Hear You Calling Me*. (Milwaukee: Bruce Pub. Co., 1949), p. 189.

McDaniel, Hattie: Carlton Jackson, *Hattie: The Life of Hattie McDaniel*. (Landham, MD: Madison Books, 1990), p. 160.

Macdonald, George: William Raeper, *George Macdonald*. (Herts, England: Tring, 1987), p. 390.

MacDonald, Jeanette Anna: James Robert Parish, *The Jeannette MacDonald Story*. (NY: Mason/Charter, 1976), p. 174.

Macdonough, Thomas: Rodney Macdonough, *Life of Commodore Thomas Macdonough*. (Boston: Fort Hill Press, 1909), p. 251 (I).

McKinley, Ida Sexton: The Columbus *Ohio State Journal*, May 27, 1907.

McLaury, Thomas Clark: Frank Waters, *op. cit.*, p. 169.

Macmillan, Harold: Alistair Horne, *Harold Macmillan, Vol. II*. (NY: Viking, 1989), p. 630.

McQueen, Terrence Steven: Terrill Marshall, *Steve McQueen: Portrait of an American Rebel*. (NY: D.I. Fine, 1993), p. 400.

Malibran, Maria: Edward B. Marks, *They All Had Glamour*. (NY: J. Messner, 1944), p. 102.

Manet, Edouard: Henri Perruchot, *Manet*. (Cleveland: World Pub. Co., 1962), p. 252.

Manning, Henry Edward: Robert Gray, *Cardinal Manning*. (NY: St. Martin's Press, 1985), p. 320.

Manzoni, Alessandro: Archibald Colquhoun, *Manzoni and His Times*. (London: Dent, 1954), p. 258.

Mao Zedong: Ross Terill, *Mao: A Biography*. (NY: Harper & Row, 1980), p. 420.

Maria Theresa of Austria: Edward Crankshaw, *Maria Theresa*. (NY: Viking Press, 1969), p. 338.

Mariam of Jesus Crucified: Ann Ball, *Modern Saints: Their Lives and Faces*, Vol. II. (Rockford, IL: Tan Books and Publishers, 1990), p. 146.

Marie Leczinska, Queen Consort of France: Claude Aveline, *op. cit.*, p. 237.

Marie-Therese of Austria, Queen Consort of France: Bruno Cortequise, *Madame Louis XIV*. (Paris: Perrin, 1992), p. 156.

Marie-Therese-Charlotte, Duchess of Angouleme: Claude Aveline, *op. cit.*, p. 272.

Maris, Roger Eugene: Maury Allen, *Roger Maris*. (NY: Donald I. Fine, Inc., 1986), p. 239 (I).

Marshal, William: Sidney Painter, *William Marshal*. (Baltimore: Johns Hopkins Press, 1933), p. 288.

Martineau, Harriet: Claude Aveline, *op. cit.*, p. 279.

Marx, Julius (Groucho): Hector Arce, *Groucho*. (NY: Putnam, 1979), p. 509.

Marx, Leonard (Chico): Maxine Marx, *Growing Up with Chico*. (Englewood Cliffs, NJ: Prentice-Hall, 1980), p. 175.

Mary, Queen of Scots: Antonia Fraser, *Mary, Queen of Scots*. (NY: Delacorte Press, 1969), p. 539.

Mary II of England: Henri and Barbara Van Der Zee, *William and Mary*. (NY: Alfred A. Knopf, 1973), pp. 384–386.

Mary Beatrice, Queen Consort of England: Marie Halle, *Queen Mary of Modena*. (NY: Dutton, 1905), p. 504.

Mary Magdalene dei Pazzi: Herbert Thurston and Donald Attwater, *op. cit.*, Vol. II, p. 418.

Massenet, Jules-Emile-Frederic: Demor Irvine, *Massenet: A Chronicle of His Life and Times*. (Seattle: University of Washington Press, 1974), p. 343.

Mather, Abigail Phillips: Cotton Mather, *Diary, Vol. I*. (NY: Frederick Ungar, 1911), p. 449.

Mather, Cotton: Kenneth Silverman, *The Life and Times of Cotton Mather*. (NY: Harper & Row, 1984), pp. 421–422.

Mayhew, Jonathan: Alden Bradford, *Memoir of the Life and Writings of Rev. Jonathan Mayhew*. (Boston: C.C. Little, 1838), p. 431.

Mazarin, Jules: Claude Aveline, *op. cit.*, p. 222.

Mead, Margaret: Jane Howard, *Margaret Mead*. (NY: Simon & Schuster, 1984), p. 424.

Meir, Golda: Menachem Meir, *My Mother, Golda Meir*. (NY: Arbor House, 1983), p. 210.

Melchior, Lauritz: Shirlee Emmons, *Tristanissimo*. (NY: Schirmer Books, 1990), p. 323.

Mencken, Henry Louis: Fred Hobson, *Mencken: A Life*. (NY: Random House, 1994), p. 532.

Merman, Ethel: Bob Thomas, *I've Got Rhythm: The Ethel Merman Story*. (NY: Putnam's, 1985), p. 218.

Merry Del Val, Rafael: Marie Cecelia Buehrle, *Rafael Cardinal Merry del Val*. (Milwaukee: Bruce Publishing Co., 1957), p. 304.

Michelson, Albert Abraham: Dorothy Michelson Livingston, *The Master of Light*. (NY: Scribner, 1973), p. 338.

Mitchell, William: Isaac Don Levine, *Mitchell: Pioneer of Air Power*. (NY: Arno Press, 1972), pp. 399–400.

Mohammed: Muhammed Husayn Haykal, *The Life of Muhammed*. (Philadelphia: American Trust Publications, 1976), p. 503.

Monroe, James: George Morgan, *The Life of James Monroe*. (Boston: Small, Maynard and Company, 1921), p. 452.

Monroe, Marilyn: Donald Spoto, *Marilyn Monroe*. (NY: HarperCollins, 1993), p. 571.

Montez, Lola: Helen Holdredge, *The Woman in Black*. (NY: Putnam, 1955), p. 296.

Montezuma II of Mexico: William H. Prescott, *op. cit.*, p. 435.

Montgomery, Bernard Law: Nigel Hamilton, *Monty, The Final Years*. (NY: McGraw-Hill, 1987), p. 941.

Moore, Sir John: Carola Oman, *Sir John Moore*. (London: Hodder and Houghton, 1953), p. 600.

Moses, Anna Mary Robertson: Tom Biracree, *Grandma Moses*. (NY: Chelsea House, 1989), p. 186.

Mostel, Samuel Joel: Jared Brown, *Zero Mostel*. (NY: Atheneum, 1989), p. 307.

Mott, Lucretia Coffin: Anna Davis Hallowell, *James and Lucretia Mott*. (Boston: Houghton, Mifflin, 1884), p. 465.

Mozart, Wolfgang Amadeus: Francis Carr, *Mozart and Constanze*. (London: J. Murray, 1983), p. 126.

Nabokov, Vladimir Vladimirovich: Brian Boyd, *Vladimir Nabokov, The American Years*. (Princeton, NJ: Princeton University Press, 1991), p. 661.

Nehru, Motilal: M.J. Akbar, *Nehru: The Making of India*. (London: Viking, 1988), p. 229.

Newman, Ernest: Vera Newman, *Ernest Newman*. (London: Putnam, 1963), p. 270.

Newman, John Henry: Meriol Trevor, *Newman, Light in Winter*. (Garden City, NY: Doubleday, 1963), p. 642, 645 (I).

Nicholas I of Russia: W. Bruce Lincoln, *Nicholas I*. (Bloomington, IN: Indiana University Press, 1978), p. 350.

Nicholas II of Russia: Edvard Radzinsky, *The Last Tsar*. (NY: Doubleday, 1992), pp. 387–388.

Nimitz, Chester William: E.B. Potter, *Nimitz*. (Annapolis: Naval Institute Press, 1976), p. 471.

Nixon, Thelma Patricia Ryan: The *Star*, a supermarket tabloid, spring of 1993.

Nobel, Alfred Bernhard: Kenne Fant, *Alfred Nobel*. (NY: Arcade, 1991), p. 313.

Nordica, Lillian: Ira Glackens, *Yankee Diva*. (NY: Coleridge Press, 1963), p. 271.

North, Frederick: Reginald Lucas, *Lord North*, Vol. II. (London: A.L. Humphreys, 1913), p. 326.

Oberon, Merle: Charles Higham and Roy Moseley, *Princess Merle*. (NY: Coward-McCann, 1983), p. 298.

O'Connell, William Henry: Dorothy G. Wayman, *Cardinal O'Connell*. (NY: Farrar, Strauss and Young, 1955), p. 273.

Oei Tjie Sien: Yoshihara Kunio, ed., *Oei Tjiong Ham Concern*. (Kyoto, 1989), p. 32.

O'Kane, Tullius Clinton: Jacob H. Hall, *Biography of Gospel Song and Hymn Writers*. (Chicago: Fleming H. Revell, 1914), p. 63.

O'Keeffe, Georgia: Roxana Robinson, *Georgia O'Keeffe*. (NY: Harper & Row, 1989), p. 550 (I).

Old Joseph: David Lavender, *Let Me Be Free*. (NY: Harper Collins, 1992), p. 6.

Olga Alexandrovna: Ian Vorres, *The Last Grand Duchess*. (NY: Scribner, 1964), p. 227.

Olga Nicolayevna: Edvard Radzinsky, *op. cit.*, pp. 358–359.

Olivier, Sir Laurence: Donald Spoto, *Laurence Olivier* (NY: HarperCollins, 1992), p. 411.

Omar Khayyam: J.K.M. Shirazi, *Life of Omar Al-Khayyami*. (Edinburgh: T. Foulis, 1905), pp. 93–95.

Onassis, Jacqueline Kennedy: *The Globe* and the *National Enquirer*, June 7, 1994.

Ortega y Gasset, José: Claude Aveline, *op. cit.*, p. 301.

Oscar II of Sweden: *New York Times*, December 8, 1907 (I).

Pahlavi, Mohammed Reza: William Shawcross, *The Shah's Last Ride*. (NY: Simon and Schuster, 1988), p. 404.

Pahlavi, Reza: Donald N. Wilber, *Riza Shah Pahlavi*. (Hicksville, NY: Exposition Press, 1975), p. 222.

Paine, Thomas: David Freeman Hawke, *Paine*. (NY: Harper and Row, 1974), pp. 396–397.

Pallotti, Vincent: Herbert Thurston and Donald Attwater, *op. cit.*, Vol. III, p. 149.

Pasternak, Boris Leonidovich: Olga Ivinskaya, *A Captive of Time*. (Garden City, NY: Doubleday, 1978), p. 323.

Paul I of the Hellenes: Queen Frederica, *A Measure of Understanding*. (NY: St. Martin's Press, 1971), pp. 257–259.

Paul III, Pope: Artaud de Montor, *op. cit.*, Vol. I, p. 732.

Paul VI, Pope: Peter Hebblethwaite, *Paul VI: The First Modern Pope*. (NY: Paulist Press, 1993), p. 710.

Peabody, George: Franklin Parker, *George Peabody*. (Nashville, TN: Vanderbilt University Press, 1971), p. 181.

Peel, Sir Robert: Tresham Lever, *The Life and Times of Sir Robert Peel*. (London: G. Allen & Unwin, Ltd., 1942), p. 301.

Péguy, Charles: Marjorie Villiers, *Charles Péguy*. NY: Harper & Row, 1965), p. 382.

Penfield, Wilder: Jefferson Lewis, *Something Hidden*. (Garden City, NY: Doubleday, 1981), p. 304.

Pepys, Samuel: John Drinkwater, *Pepys*. (London: Heineman, 1934), p. 349.

Percy, Walker: Jay Tolson, *Pilgrim in the Ruins*. (NY: Simon and Schuster, 1992), p. 187.

Peron, Eva Duarte: Nicholas Fraser and Marysa Navarro, *Eva Peron*. (NY: W.W. Norton, 1980), pp. 162–163.

Perry, Oliver Hazard: Charles S. Dutton, *Olivar Hazard Perry*. (NY: Longmans, Green and Co., 1935), pp. 283–284.

Perugino: Thomas Bedell, *op. cit.*, p. 123.

Peter I of Russia: Robert K. Massie, *Peter the Great*. (NY: Alfred A. Knopf, 1980), p. 845.

Philip II of France: Joy Law, *op. cit.*, p. 36.

Phillips, Ulrich Bonnell: Merton L. Dillon, *Ulrich Bonnell Phillips*. (Baton Rouge, LA: LaState University Press, 1985), p. 163.

Phoenix, River: *National Enquirer*, November 16, 1993.

Piaf, Edith: Simon Berteaut, *Piaf*. (NY: Harper & Row, 1972), p. 475.

Pickford, Mary: Scott Eyman, *Mary Pickford*. (New York: D.I. Fine, 1990), p. 306.

Pike, James Albert: Diane Kennedy Pike, *Search*. (Garden City, NY: Doubleday, 1970), pp. 30–31.

Pinza, Ezio: Robert Magidoff, ed., *Ezio Pinza, An Autobiography*. (NY: Rinehart, 1958), p. 282.

Pirandello, Luigi: Gaspare Giudice, *Pirandello*. (London: Oxford University Press, 1975), p. 206.

Pissarro, Lucien: W.J. Meadmore, *Lucien Pisarro* (NY: Knopf, 1963), p. 235.

Pius II, Pope: Artaud de Montor, *op. cit.*, Vol. I, p. 612.

Pius V, Pope: Artaud de Montor, *op. cit.*, Vol. I, p. 804.

Pius VI: Ludwig von Pastor, *op. cit.*, Vol. 40, p. 388.

Pius VII: Artaud de Montor, *op. cit.*, Vol. II, p. 715.

Pius XI: *New York Times*, February 10, 1939.

Pius XII: Philip S. Land, "How Pius XII Died," *America*. November 8, 1958, p. 163.

Polk, Sarah Childress: *Nashville Daily American*, August 14, 1891; Anson and Fanny Nelson, *Memorials of Sarah Childress Polk*. (NY: A.D.F. Randolph, 1892), pp. 274–275.

Pompidou, Georges: *Newsweek*, April 15, 1974, p. 48.

Ponselle, Rosa: Rosa Ponselle and James A. Drake, *Ponselle, A Singer's Life*. (Garden City, NY: Doubleday, 1982), p. 246.

Porter, Katherine Ann: Joan Givner, *Katherine Ann Porter*. (NY: Simon and Schuster, 1982), p. 508.

Powell, Adam Clayton, Jr.: Will Haygood, *King of the Cats*. (Boston: Houghton Mifflin, 1993), p. 409.

Power, Tyrone: Fred Lawrence Guiles, *Tyrone Power*. (Garden City, NY: Doubleday, 1979), p. 305.

Pulliam, Eugene: Russell Pulliam, *Gene Pulliam: Last of the Newspaper Titans*. (Ottawa, IL: Jameson Books, 1984), p. 304.

Pyle, Ernest Taylor: Lee G. Miller, *The Story of Ernie Pyle*. (Westwood, CT: Greenwood Press, 1970), p. 425.

Quincy, Josiah: Edmund Quincy, *Life of Josiah Quincy*. (Boston: Ticknor and Fields, 1867), pp. 544–545.

Quincy, Josiah, Jr.: Josiah Quincy, *Memoir of the Life of Josiah Quincy, Junior*. (Boston: Cummings, Hilliard, & Company, 1825), p. 348.

Quitman, John Anthony: Robert E. May, *John A. Quitman*. (Baton Rouge, LA: Louisiana State University Press, 1985), p. 349.

Rachel: Claude Aveline, *op. cit.*, p. 274.

Ramseur, Stephen Dodson: Gary W. Gallagher, *Stephen Dodson Ramseur*. (Chapel Hill, NC: University of North Carolina Press, 1985), p. 165.

Randolph, John: Hugh A. Garland, *The Life of John Randolph of Roanoke* (Philadelphia: D. Appleton, 1850), pp. 373–375.

Rasputin, Gregory Efimovich: Maria Rasputin and Patte Barham, *Rasputin*. (Englewood Cliffs, NJ: Prentice-Hall, 1977), pp. 234–235.

Red Jacket: J. Niles Hubbard, *An Account of Sa-Go-Ya-Wat-Ha*. (NY: B. Franklin, 1971), pp. 348–350.

Reed, John: Richard O'Connor and Dale L. Walker, *The Lost Revolutionary*. (NY: Harcourt, Brace, & World, 1967), p. 300.

Reed, Thomas Brackett: Samuel W. McCall, *The Life of Thomas Brackett Reed*. (Boston: Houghton Mifflin, 1914), pp. 276–277.

Revel, Bernard: Aaron Rakeffet-Rothkoff, *Bernard Revel*. (Philadelphia: Jewish Publication Society of America, 1972), p. 221.

Richard I of England: Kate Norgate, *Richard the Lion Heart*. (London: Macmillan, 1924), p. 328.

Richelieu, Armand de: D.P. O'Connell, *Richelieu*. (Cleveland: World Publishing Co., 1968), p. 433.

Rickey, Wesley Branch: *Portland Press Herald*, December 10, 1965.

Rilke, Rainer Maria: Wolfgang Leppman, *Rilke: A Life*. (NY: Fomm International Publishing Corp., 1984), p. 386.

Rimbaud, Jean-Nicolas-Arthur: Pierre Petitfils, *Rimbaud*. (Charlottesville, VA: University of Virginia Press, 1987), p. 329.

Rita of Cascia: Jose Sicardo, *Life of St. Rita of Cascia*. (Chicago: D.B. Hanson & Sons, 1916), p. 130.

Rivarol, Antoine de: Claude Aveline, *op. cit.*, p. 253.

Rizzo, Frank: S.A. Paolantonio, *Frank Rizzo*. (Philadelphia: Camino Books, 1993), p. 364.

Robinson, John Arthur Thomas: Eric James, *A Life of Bishop John A.T. Robinson*. (Grand Rapids, MI: Eerdmans, 1987), p. 312.

Rockefeller, John Davison, Sr.: William Manchester, "The Founding Grand-father," *American History*, Vol. II. (Guilford, CT: Duskin Publishing Group, 1987), p. 73.

Rockne, Knute: Jerry Brondfield, *Rockne*. (NY: Random House, 1976), p. 14.

Roosevelt, Anna Eleanor: Joseph P. Lash, *Eleanor: The Years Alone*. (NY: Norton, 1972), p. 327.

Roosevelt, Theodore, Sr.: David McCullough, *Mornings on Horseback*. (NY: Simon and Schuster, 1981), p. 184.

Root, Elihu: Philip Jessup, *Elihu Root*, Vol. II. (NY: Dodd, Mead & Co., 1938), p. 505 (I).

Rossetti, Dante Gabriel: William Michael Rossetti, *Dante Gabriel Rossetti*, Vol. I, (Boston, 1895), p. 398.

Rothstein, Arnold: Leo Katcher, *The Life and Times of Arnold Rothstein*. (NY: Harper, 1958), p. 333.

Rubinstein, Arthur: Radio interview with violinist Shlomo Mintz, aired on WETA Radio, Washington, DC, February 13, 1994.

Rubinstein, Helena: Patrick O'Higgins, *Madame*. (NY: Viking Press, 1971), p. 284.

Ruffini, Ernesto: Emanuele Gambino, *Il Pastore Sulla Breccia*. (Palermo: Ancora, 1967), p. 246.

Ruppert, Jacob: *New York Times*, January 14, 1939.

Russell, George William: Henry Summerfield, *That Myriad-Minded Man: A Biography of George William Russell*. (Totowa, NJ: Rowman & Littlefield, 1975), p. 284.

Ruth, George Herman, Jr.: Mac Davis, *One Hundred Greatest Sports Heroes.* (NY: Grosset & Dunlap, 1954), p. 111; The *New York World-Telegram*, August 19, 1948.

Ryan, Cornelius John: Cornelius Ryan and Kathryn Ryan, *A Private Battle.* (NY: Simon and Schuster, 1979), p. 442.

Salomon, Haym: Howard Fast, *Haym Salomon: Son of Liberty.* (NY: J. Messner, 1941), p. 241.

Saltus, Edgar Evertson: Marie Saltus, *Edgar Saltus.* (Chicago: P. Covici, 1925), p. 324.

Sanger, Margaret Higgins: Madeline Gray, *Margaret Sanger.* (NY: R. Marek, 1979), p. 442.

Sankey, Ira David: "Some day..." is from *New York Times*, August 16, 1908.

Santa Anna, Antonio Lopez de: Oakah L. Jones, *Santa Anna.* (NY: Twayne Publishers, 1968), p. 150 (I).

Santayana, George: Daniel Cory, *Santayana.* (NY: Braziller, 1963), p. 325.

Savalas, Aristotle: *National Enquirer*, February 8, 1994.

Savio, Domenico: Peter Lappin, *The Life of Dominic Savio.* (New Rochelle, NY: Don Bosco Publications, 1954), p. 124.

Schnorr von Carolsfeld, Ludwig: Wilfrid Blunt, *The Dream King.* (Hammondsworth, England: Penguin Books, 1973), p. 54.

Schoenberg, Arnold: H.H. Stuckenschmidt, *Schoenberg.* (London: Calder, 1977), p. 521.

Schrödinger, Erwin: Walter Moore, *Schrödinger.* (Cambridge, England: Cambridge University Press, 1989), p. 482.

Schumann, Robert Alexander: Claude Aveline, *op. cit.*, p. 128.

Selznick, David Oliver: David Thompson, *Showman, The Life of David O. Selznick.* (NY: Knopf, 1972), p. 691.

Seraphim of Sarov: Valentine Zander, *St. Seraphim of Sarov.* (London: SPCK, 1975), p. 113.

Serling, Rodman Edward: Joe Engel, *Rod Serling.* (Chicago: Contemporary Books, 1989), p. 341.

Shave Head: Robert M. Utley, *The Lance and the Shield.* (NY: Henry Holt, 1993), p. 305.

Sheed, Francis Joseph: Sheed, Wilfred, *Frank and Maisie: A Memoir with Parents.* (NY: Simon and Schuster, 1985), p. 286.

Sherman, John: Theodore E. Burton, *John Sherman.* (Boston: Houghton Mifflin, 1906), p. 417.

Sherman, William Tecumseh: John F. Marszalek, *Sherman: A Soldier's Passion for Order.* (NY: The Free Press, 1993), p. 492.

Shore, Dinah: *National Enquirer*, March 15, 1994.

Sibelius, Jean: Harold E. Johnson, *Sibelius.* (London: Faber & Faber, 1960), pp. 215–216.

Simon Peter: Philip Schaff, *History of the Christian Church, Vol. I, Apostolic Christianity, A.D. 1–100.* (NY: Scribners, 1887), p. 255.

Sitting Bull: Stanley Vestal, *Sitting Bull.* (Norman, OK: University of Oklahoma Press, 1932), p. 300.

Smith, Bessie: Carman Moore, *Somebody's Angel Child.* (NY: T.Y. Crowell, 1969), p. 109.

Smith, Erastus: Cleburne Huston, *Deaf Smith.* (Waco, TX: Texion Press, 1973), p. 120.

Smith, Frederick Edwin: John Campbell, *F.E. Smith: First Earl of Birkenhead*. (London: J. Cape, 1983), p. 834.

Smith, Joseph: Carl Carmer, "The Death of the Prophet," *American Heritage*, December, 1962, p. 89.

Smith, William: Thomas Firth Jones, *A Pair of Lawn Sleeves*. (Philadelphia: Chilton Book Co., 1972), p. 195.

Smollett, Tobias George: David Hanney, *Tobias George Smollett*. (London: W. Scott, 1887), p. 158.

Snow, Edgar Parks: John Maxwell Hamilton, *Edgar Snow*. (Bloomington, IN, 1988), p. 282.

Soubirous, Bernadette: Margaret Trouncer, *Saint Bernadette: The Child and the Nun*. (NY: Sheed & Ward, 1958), pp. 238–240.

Spafford, Horatio Gates: Bertha Spafford Vester, *Our Jerusalem*. (Garden City: Doubleday, 1950), p. 154.

Speaker, Tristram: *Washington Post*, December 9, 1958.

Spellman, Francis: John Cooney, *The American Pope*. (NY: Dell, 1984), p. 325.

Spruance, Richard Ames: Thomas B. Buell, *The Quiet Warrior*. (Boston: Little, Brown, 1974), p. 428.

Spurgeon, Charles Haddon: Ernest Bacon, *Spurgeon: Heir of the Puritans*. (London: Allen & Unwin, 1967), p. 167.

Stanton, Elizabeth Cady: Elisabeth Griffith, *In Her Own Right*. (NY: Oxford University Press, 1984), p. 217.

Stein, Edith: Waltraud Herbstrith, *Edith Stein: A Biography*. (San Francisco: Harper & Row, 1971), p. 112.

Steinbeck, John Ernst: Jackson J. Benson, *The True Adventures of John Steinbeck, Writer*. (NY: Viking, 1984), p. 1036.

Steinberg, Milton: Simon Noveck, *Milton Steinberg*. (NY: Ktav Publishing House, 1978), p. 245.

Stephens, Alexander Hamilton: E. Ramsay Richardson, *Little Alec: A Life of Alexander H. Stephens*. (Indianapolis, IN: Bobbs-Merrill, 1932): p. 340.

Stevens, Thaddeus: Elsie Singmaster, *I Speak for Thaddeus Stevens*. (Boston: Houghton Mifflin, 1947), p. 445.

Stolypin, Peter Arcadeyevich: The *New York Tribune*, September 19, 1911.

Stone, Harlan F.: Alpheus T. Mason, *Harlan Fisk Stone*. (Hamden, CT: Archon Books, 1968), p. 806.

Strauss, Richard: Norman Del Mar, *Richard Strauss*, Vol. III (Philadelphia: Chilton Book Co., 1962), p. 471.

Stritch, Samuel Alphonsus: Marie Cecelia Buehrle, *The Cardinal Stritch Story*. (Milwaukee: Bruce Publishing Co., 1959), p. 187, 189.

Stuart, Jesse Hilton: H. Edward Richardson, *Jesse: The Biography of An American Writer*. (NY: McGraw-Hill, 1984), p. 458.

Suleiman I of Turkey: Barnaby Conrad, *op. cit.*, p. 190.

Sumner, Charles: David Donald, *Charles Sumner and The Rights of Man*. (NY: Knopf, 1970), pp. 586–587.

Susann, Jacqueline: Barbara Seaman, *Lonely Me: The Life of Jacqueline Susanna*. (NY: Morrow, 1987), p. 456.

Swift, Gustavus Franklin: Helen Swift, *My Father and My Mother*. (Chicago: Lakeside Press, 1937), p. 146.

Sylvester I, Pope: Claude Aveline, *op. cit.*, p. 187.

Taft, William Howard: The *Washington Herald*, March 9, 1930.

Tagore, Sir Rabindranath: Krishna Kripalani, *Rabindranath Tagore*. (NY: Oxford University Press, 1962), pp. 396–397.

Talleyrand-Perigord, Charles-Maurice: Jack F. Bernard, *Talleyrand*. (NY: Putnam, 1973), p. 619.

Tamerlane: Claude Aveline, *op. cit.*, p. 196.

Tanner, Henry Ossawa: Marcia M. Matthews, *Henry Ossawa Tanner*. (Chicago: University of Chicago Press, 1969), p. 248.

Tarbell, Ida M.: Kathleen Brady, *Ida Tarbell*. (NY: Seaview/Putnam, 1984), p. 255.

Tatum, Art: James Lester, *Too Marvelous for Words*. (NY: Oxford University Press, 1994), p. 218.

Taylor, Robert: Jayne Ellen Wayne, *The Life of Robert Taylor*. (NY: Warner Paperback Library, 1973), p. 275.

Taylor, Zachary: *The National Intelligencer*, July 10, 1850.

Tecumseh: Allan W. Eckert, *A Sorrow in Our Heart: The Life of Tecumseh*. (NY: Bantam, 1992), p. 676.

Teilhard de Chardin, Pierre: Claude Cuenot, *Teilhard de Chardin*. (Baltimore: Helican, 1965), p. 387.

Tekakwitha, Kateri: Daughters of Saint Paul, *Blessed Kateri Tekakwitha*. (Boston: Daughters of St. Paul, 1980), p. 85.

Ten Boom, Cornelia: Pamela Rosewell, *The Five Silent Years of Corrie Ten Boom*. (Grand Rapids, MI: Zondervan, 1986), pp. 183–184.

Ten Boom, Elisabeth: Corrie Ten Boom, *The Hiding Place*. (NY: Bantam Books, 1971), p. 218.

Ten Boom, Willem: Corrie Ten Boom, *The Hiding Place*. (NY: Bantam Books, 1971), p. 240.

Tennyson, Alfred: Hallam Tennyson, *Alfred Lord Tennyson, A Memoir*, Vol. II. (London: Macmillan, 1897), pp. 427–428; Robert Bernard Martin, *Tennyson, The Unquiet Heart*. (NY: Clarendon Press, 1980), p. 581.

Teresa of Avila: Marcelle Auclair, *Teresa of Avila*. (NY: Pantheon, 1953), p. 429.

Terhune, Alfred Payson: Irving Litvag, *The Master of Sunnybank*. (NY: Harper & Row, 1977), p. 238.

Teyte, Maggie: Garry O'Connor, *The Pursuit of Perfection: A Life of Maggie Teyte*. (NY: Atheneum, 1979), p. 262. It is not clear how long before her death she made this remark.

Thackeray, William Makepeace: Anne Monsarrat, *An Uneasy Victorian*. (NY: Dodd, Mead, 1980), p. 423.

Thalberg, Irving: Bob Thomas, *Thalberg Life & Legend*. (Garden City, NY: Doubleday, 1962), p. 317.

Thompson, Francis: Brigid M. Boardman, *Between Heaven and Charing Cross: The Life of Francis Thompson*. (New Haven, CT: Yale University Press, 1988), p. 350.

Thoreau, Henry David: Walter Harding, "This is a Beautiful World, but I Shall See a Fairer," *American Heritage*, Vol. XIV, no. 1, December 1962, pp. 106–111.

Thrale, Hester Lynch Piozzi: James L. Clifford, *Hester Lynch Piozzi (Mrs. Thrale)*. (Oxford: Clarendon Press, 1952), pp. 455–456.

Tillich, Paul: Hannah Tillich, *From Time to Time*. (NY: Stein and Day, 1973), p. 223.

Tillman, Benjamin Ryan: Rosina Corrothers-Tucker (1881–1987), interview, 1974. According to Mrs. Tucker, the words were overheard by a servant, who relayed them to her. She herself was not certain how long before his death they were spoken.

Toklas, Alice Babette: Linda Simon, *The Biography of Alice B. Toklas.* (Garden City, NY: Doubleday, 1977), p. 253.

Tolkien, John Ronald Reuel: Daniel Grotta, *The Biography of J.R.R. Tolkien.* (Philadelphia: Running Press, 1976), p. 155.

Tone, Theobald Wolfe: Marianne Elliott, *Wolfe Tone.* (New Haven, CT: Yale University Press, 1989), p. 399.

Tonks, Henry: Joseph Hone, *The Life of Henry Tonks.* (London: W. Heinemann Ltd., 1939), p. 317.

Toombs, Robert Augustus: William Y. Thompson, *Robert Toombs of Georgia.* (Baton Rouge, LA: Louisiana State University Press, 1966), p. 257.

Toplady, Augustus Montague: Osman C. Baker, *The Last Witness.* (NY: Carlton and Lanahan, c.1870), p. 44.

Toussaint, Pierre: Arthur and Elizabeth Odell Sheehan, *Pierre Toussaint.* (NY: P.J. Kennedy, 1955), p. 229.

Trexler, Samuel: Edmund Devol, *Sword of the Spirit: A Biography of Samuel Trexler.* (NY: Dodd, Mead, 1954), p. 280.

Tristan, Flora: Joyce Ann Schneider, *Flora Tristan.* (NY: Morrow, 1980), p. 244.

Tucker, Richard: James A. Drake, *Richard Tucker.* (NY: Dutton, 1984), p. 260.

Turner, Frederick Jackson: Ray Allen Billington, *Frederick Jackson Turner.* (NY: Oxford University Press, 1973), p. 415.

Tyler, John: Robert Seager, *And Tyler, Too: A Biography of John and Julie Gardiner Tyler.* (NY: McGraw-Hill, 1963), p. 471.

Tynan, Kenneth Peacock: Kathleen Tynan, *The Life of Kenneth Tynan.* (NY: Wm. Morrow Co., 1987), p. 517.

Valentino, Rudolph: Robert Oberfirst, *Rudolph Valentino.* (NY: Citadel Press, 1962), p. 314.

Van Buren, Martin: Joseph Nathan Kane, *Facts About the Presidents.* (NY: Ace Books, 1959), p. 426.

Vanderbilt, Alfred: Arthur T. Vanderbilt II, *Fortune's Children: The Fall of the House of Vanderbilt.* (NY: Morrow, 1989), p. 456.

Vanderbilt, George Washington: The *Washington Herald*, March 7, 1914.

Vaughan, Sarah: Leslie Gourse, *Sassy: The Life of Sarah Vaughan.* (NY: C. Scribner's Sons, 1993), p. 233.

Victor Emmanuel III of Italy: Robert Katz, *The Fall of the House of Savoy.* (NY: Macmillan, 1971), p. 381.

Victoria, Empress Frederick of Germany: Daphne Bennett, *Vicky.* (NY: St. Martin's Press, 1971), pp. 446–447.

Waddell, George Edward: Connie Mack, *My Sixty-Six Years in the Big Leagues.* (Philadelphia: Universal House, 1950), p. 96.

Walker, James Alexander: Willie Walker Caldwell, *Stonewall Jim.* (Elliston, VA: Northcross House, 1990), p. 259.

Walker, Sarah Breedlove: A'Lelia Perry Bundles, *Madam C.J. Walker.* (NY: Chelsea House Publishers, 1991), p. 208.

Waller, Thomas Wright: Maurice Waller and Anthony Calabrese, *Fats Waller.* (NY: Schirmer Books, 1977), p. 176.

Walther, Carl Ferdinand Wilhelm: D.H. Steffens, *Doctor Carl Ferdinand Wilhelm Walther.* (Philadelphia: The Lutheran Publication Society, 1917), p. 365.

Walton, William: Susana Walton, *William Walton: Behind the Facade.* (Oxford: Oxford University Press, 1988), p. 231.

Ward, Mary Josephine: Wilfred Sheed, *Fred and Maisie: A Memoir with Parents.* (NY: Simon and Schuster, 1985), p. 262.

Warren, Earl: Bernard Schwartz, *Super Chief.* (NY: New York University Press, 1983), p. 772.

Washington, George: James Thomas Flexner, *George Washington, Anguish and Farewell.* (Boston: Little, Brown, 1969), pp. 458–462.

Washington, Martha Dandridge Custis: *Alexandria Gazette*, May 25, 1802 (I).

Waters, Ethel: Juliann DeKorte, *Finally Home.* (Old Tappan, NJ: Fleming H. Revell, 1978), p. 120.

Watson, Thomas: C. Van Woodword, *Tom Watson* (Savannah: Beehive Press, 1938), p. 420.

Watteau, Antoine: Claude Aveline, *op. cit.* p. 231.

Wayne, John: Pat Stacy, *Duke: A Love Story.* (NY: Atheneum, 1983), p. 220.

Weed, Thurlow: Glyndon Van Deusen, *Thurlow Weed.* (Boston: Little, Brown, & Co., 1947), p. 346.

Weil, Simone: Gabriella Fiori, *Simone Weil: An Intellectual Biography.* (Athens, GA: University of Georgia Press, 1989), p. 1.

Weizmann, Chaim: Norman Rose, *Chaim Weizmann.* (NY: Viking, 1986), p. 459.

Weld, Angelina Emily Grimke: Catherine H. Birney, *The Grimke Sisters.* (Boston: Lee and Shepard, 1885), p. 312.

Welles, George Orson: Frank Brady, *Citizen Welles.* (NY: Scribner, 1989), p. 591.

Wesley, Martha: Franklin Wilder, *Martha Wesley.* (Hicksville, NY: Exposition Press, 1976), p. 127.

Wesley, Samuel: Adam Clarke, *Memoirs of the Wesley Family.* (NY: Bangs and Mason, 1824), p. 181.

Wesley, Samuel Sebastian: Paul Chappel, *Dr. S.S. Wesley: Portrait of a Victorian Musician.* (Great Wakering, England: Mayhew-McCrimmon, 1977), p. 145.

Wesley, Susanna Annesley: J.B. Wakeley, *Anecdotes of the Wesleys.* (NY: Darlton and Lonahan, 1869), p. 55.

Whistler, James Abbot McNeill: E.R. and J. Pennell, *The Life of James McNeill Whistler.* (Philadelphia: Lippincott, 1908), p. 434.

White, Walter Francis: Poppy Cannon, *A Gentle Knight.* (NY: Rinehart, 1956), p. 275.

Whitney, William Collins: Mark D. Hirsch, *William C. Whitney.* (NY: Dodd, Mead, 1948), p. 595.

Whittle, Daniel Webster: Fanny J. Crosby, *op. cit.* p. 137.

Wilkes, John: Owen Aubrey Sherrard, *A Life of John Wilkes.* (London. G. Allen & Unwin Ltd., 1930), p. 309.

William I of Germany: Theo Aronson, *The Kaisers.* (Indianapolis, IN: Bobbs-Merrill, 1971), p. 169.

William II of England: Edward A. Freeman, *The Reign of William Rufus,* Vol. 2. (Oxford: Clarendon Press, 1882), p. 333.

William II of Germany: H.R.H. Viktoria Luise, *The Kaiser's Daughter.* (Englewood Cliffs, NJ: Prentice-Hall, 1977), p. 208.

William III of England: Henri and Barbara Van Der Zee, *William and Mary.* (NY: Alfred A. Knopf, 1973), p. 475.

William IV of Great Britain: Elizabeth Longford, *Queen Victoria*. (NY: Harper & Row, 1964), p. 60.

Williams, Alice Johnson: Helen Buckler, *Doctor Dan*. (Boston: Little, Brown, 1954), p. 271.

Williams, Charles Walter Stansby: Alice Mary Hadfield, *Charles Williams*. (NY: Oxford University Press, 1983), p. 235.

Williams, Daniel Hale: Helen Buckler, *Doctor Dan*. (Boston: Little, Brown, 1954), p. 359 (I).

Williams, Edward Bennett: Evan Thomas, *The Man to See: Edward Bennett Williams*. (NY: Simon and Schuster, 1991), p. 494.

Williams, Hiram (Hank): Jay Caress, *Hank Williams: Country Music's Tragic King*. (NY: Stein & Day, 1979), pp. 206–207.

Willkie, Wendell Lewis: Ellsworth Barnard, *Wendell Willkie*. (Marquette, MI: Northern Michigan University Press, 1966), p-. 498.

Wills, James Robert: Charles R. Townsend, *San Antonio Rose*. (Utica, IL: University of Illinois Press, 1976), p. 319.

Wilson, Ellen Louise Axson: Frances Wright Saunders, *Ellen Axson Wilson: First Lady Between Two Worlds*. (Chapel Hill, NC: University of North Carolina Press, 1985), p. 276.

Wilson, Thomas Woodrow: Gene Smith, *When the Cheering Stopped*. (NY: Morrow, 1964), pp. 237–241.

Windsor, Wallis Warfield: Charles Higham, *The Duchess of Windsor*. (NY: McGraw-Hill, 1988), p. 432.

Winthrop, John: Robert C. Winthrop, *Life and Letters of John Winthrop*, Vol. II. (NY: Da Capo Press, 1971), p. 393.

Wise, Stephen Samuel: Carl Hermann Voss, *Rabbi and Minister*. (Cleveland, 1964), p. 349.

Wolf, Hugo: Frank Walker, *Hugo Wolf*. (London: Dent, 1951), p. 445.

Wolfe, Thomas: Mabel Wolfe Wheaton, *Thomas Wolfe and His Family*. (Garden City, NY: Doubleday, 1961), p. 304; David Herbert Donald, *Look Homeward: A Life of Thomas Wolfe*. (Boston: Little, Brown, 1987), p. 463.

Wood, Sir Henry Joseph: Reginald Pound, *Sir Henry Wood*. (London: Cassell, 1967), p. 322.

Woollcott, Alexander Humphreys: Howard Teichmann, *Smart Alec: The Wit, World, and Life of Alexander Woollcott*. (NY: Morrow, 1976), p. 313.

Young, Francis Brett: Jessica Brett Young, *Francis Brett Young*. (London: Heinemann, 1962), p. 345.

Zangara, Giuseppe: Robert J. Donovan, *op. cit.* pp. 152–153.

Zhou Enlai: Han Suyin, *Eldest Son: Zhou Enlai and the Making of Modern China*. (NY: Kodansha International, 1994), p. 410.

Key Word Index

where G. calls me 1158; G. causes it to
appear 1162; G. and Father and our
Lord Jesus Christ 1171; G. of all consolation 1171; without G. 1171; G. so
loved the world 1171; a G. of salvation
1171; G. of truth 1171; G. will take care
of it 1172; G. has been good to me
1180; please G., if it be Thy will 1192;
It is G. way 1193; nearer, my G., to
Thee 1193, 1821; to G. 1196; G. is just
1204; G. is love 1215, 1323, 1639, 1698;
G., I ask pardon for my sins 1229;
Thank G., I can lay my hand on my
heart 1231; commend you to G. 1236;
knowledge of love of G. 1261; army of
G. 1263; may soon see G. 1263; I see
G. 1265; I believe in G. 1268; G. bless
Captain Vere 1276; G., help my people 1280; the hands of G. 1293; G. on
High and Paradise 1304; the altar of
G. 1307; nowhere is far from G. 1307;
praise G. 1311, 1499, 1812; G. grace
1315; meet G. 1316; G. is calling 1320;
lean upon G. 1322; thank G. I have
done my duty 1360; keep me longer
from G. 1364; G. of the universe 1392;
see nothing but G. 1394; o G., verily
I have sought 1396; no man of G.
there 1398; if there is a G. 1398; born
in a G. damned hotel room 1398; my
G., have mercy on me 1409, 1619; believe in man, G., nor devil 1418; may
G. never abandon me 1420; here my
G. is 1440; G. will forgive me 1454;
reconciled to G. 1458; G. has denuded
me 1459; G. alone knows 1459; blessed
be G. 1464; G. holy will 1491; in the
hands of G. 1492; G., help my poor
soul 1497; the G. of angels 1500; faithful and true G. 1500; I love G. 1507,
1970; my G., it's taking a long time
1523; my G. 1524; G. has done me
the mercy 1537; G. alone is master of
the event 1537; G. forgive you 1545,
1952; no hope but in G. 1548; G. only
can (re-)create 1548; my privilege to
serve G. 1559; G. save Germany 1562;
all my trust, after G., in thee 1563;
may G. bless you 1571; the way to G.
easier 1572; let G. do His work 1579;
for G. sake 1598; the existence of G.

1600; believe that there is a G. 1600;
Being of Beings, G! 1608; G. awaits
me! 1608; I wish to G. 1612; my G.,
have mercy on me 1619; death, my G.,
death 1635; G. will wipe away all tears
1639; would to G. 1643; G. alone can
give mortals comfort 1649; G. bless
him 1662; G. bless you all 1666; Wisdom, Word, and Power of G. 1675;
Son of the eternal G. 1678; my Lord
and my G. 1688; G. is very good 1698;
dwelleth in G. and G. in him 1698;
confessed G. in my heart 1701; G. of
Bethel 1713; oh, Lord, my G! 1716; by
the Lord G. 1718; my G., I love thee
1722; oh, my G! 1722; G. willing 1729;
G. in heaven 1732; right hand of G.
1748; peace with G! 1761; a messenger
of G. 1780; extol G. in my song 1812;
sacrifice to G. 1816; o G., Thou wilt
not despise 1816; martyrs of G. 1823;
my G., I love you 1826; G. bless 1836;
G. damn 1836; glories which G. has
manifested 1852; G. is with me 1857;
the sun is G. 1874; turning into a g.
1902; pray to G. 1911; features of a G.
1935; I bless G. 1937; the will of G.
1937; my heart, my G. 1953; G. is
with us 1954; G. chastens me 1956;
psalm of praise to G. 1958; the Church
of G. 1964; beautiful to be with G.
1973; I see G. comin' down the road
1985; if I had served G. as diligently
2003; o Lord, my G. 2007; no G.
2023

gods: g. that you worship 347; sacrifice
to the g. 740; by the immortal g. 1436

good: g. 817; in g. form 18; g. little wife
19; take g. care of the queen 26; how
g. 29; a g. Lord 45; old, but g. 45; g.
Christian people 55, 975; g., gentle,
and sovereign Lord 55; times were g.
75; a g. thing 110; the love of g. 155;
thou art g. and merciful 168; how g.
God is 169, 384; a g. old age 207; the
g. things 324; a g. cause 360; g. and
kind to me 442; g. right to be curious
450; the g. (working) people 484; how
g. life can be 501; how much g. have I
spread 510; the g. people 536, 975;
you are so g. to me 537; g. and exalted

592; it tastes g. 646; g. enough 653; for my g. 686; you're very g. to me 695; it does me g. 731, 1966; a g. day 743; a g. and silver light 752; every g. officer 806; a g. time 814; a g. life 814; want to die on G. Friday 818; rejoining my g. God 818; that's g. 822; God only can do me g. 839; too g. to be true 842; a g. one 921; God is g. 941; g. of the Church 949; g. people, I come hither to die 975; g. people, I pray you assist me 975; a g. fight 997; the greatest g. 1026; except my g. name 1046; it is g. 1067; my g. friends 1097; the g. they have . . . done me 1097; be so g. 1103; be g. and kind 1127; be g. 1173; been g. to me 1180; be g. enough now to take me home 1180; all the g. 1213; the g. of the country 1264; have a g. life 1275; my g. man 1325; very g. 1330; take g. care of me 1352; no g! 1399; be g. friends 1444; the g. I have tried to do 1454; fortunate in long g. health 1560; all g. things . . . come to an end 1560; in g. time 1570; so much g. 1614; be a g. man 1666; not very g. 1692; God is very g. 1698; well, g. 1765; that be g. 1785; the g. of the people 1798; g., now it's right 1854; performed one g. action 1898; done me g. 1901; a g. Democrat 1921; I feel so g. 1965; result in my g. 1968; take g. care of my husband 1989; a g. Sabbath 1993; g. things to eat and drink 2001; looked pretty g. 2001

good morning: g. m. 1338, 1617, 1794; g. m. Robert 444; g. m.! g. m.! 1414

goodbye: g. 80, 459, 825, 890, 896; g. gentlemen 83; once more, g. 127; g. kid 197; g. all that is charming 350; g. wit and gaiety 350; g. merry friends 350; g. dear 403; g. my dear sons 483; bid your mother g. for me 483; all my friends, who are here or far away, g. 483; I want to tell you g. 577; tell Ma and Pa g. 580; g. boys 890; g. all 1193; g. Gibb 1235; thank you and g. 1260; g. my darling 1783; you may as well say g. 1850

goodnight: g. 76, 644, 847, 923, 1008,

1317; g. my dear 5; g. Mike 244; a general g. 353; g. Lushington 448; g. my kitten 860; now, g. 995; I bid you all g. 1212; g. now 1284; I bid you g. 1291; want to say g. 1730

grace: g. 1254; with overflowing g. 173; in g. and peace and love 296; the g. of pardon 594; Mother of G. 614; peace and g. be with you 991; by God's g. 1085; God grant you g. 1148; God's g. 1315

grieve: do not g. for me 46; it is wrong to g. about it 10; don't g. 146; do not g. 207, 1453; g. not for my death 592; why should you g., daughter 899

happiness: I attain this h. 68; that's h. 155; h. is not money 177; a world of h. 207; a pledge of h. 231; more h. into the world 288; always in joy and h 592; share this h. with anyone 1050; your h. will depend 1152; the h. of the French people 1154; of peace and h. 1427; in h., peace, and prosperity 1462; h., and love, and everlasting peace 1499; eternal h. 1677

happy: h. 428, 447, 852, 1194, 1544, 1812; you should be h. 62; is everyone h. 114; I know I'm h. 114; we have been so h. 125, 247; if you want to be h. 145; all the world to be h. 155; I am h. 185, 384, 915, 988, 1119, 1292; for everlastingly h. 283; I die h. 300, 2000; h. day 440; supremely h. 447; I am h. to see you 523; were they h. 534; I shall die h. 669; make me very h. 749; I shall be h. after I leave here 782; a h. childhood 814; led a h. life 851; so h! 852, 1001; how h. I could have been 867; am going to be h. 964; how h. this had made Mary 1007; so few h. and so many ungrateful 1011; a h. life 1015; I'm very h. 1050; want to make you all h. 1107; made me h. 1117; enjoyed a h. life 1134; h. anniversary 1137; very h. Christmas 1174; not known a single h. day 1230; h. are you 1332; never felt h. in this life 1449; long, prosperous, and h. life 1530; h. to die on a Sunday 1535; a h. eternity